Transnational Crime

Philip Jessup coined the term 'transnational law' in his Storrs Lecture on Jurisprudence delivered in 1956 to describe law that regulates activities or actions that transcend national borders. The term redefined the development and practice of the law, and became a distinct field of study. In 2001, Neil Boister applied Jessup's concept to the field of criminal law and identified the emergence of transnational criminal law in a formative article published in the *European Journal of International Law*. Inspired by Boister's work, the editors of the journal *Transnational Legal Theory* sought contributions from leading academics and practitioners for a symposium issue on transnational criminal law. In their papers, the authors built upon and developed novel approaches to legal issues arising in an increasingly globalised world, where both crimes and the regulation of crimes transcend borders. The publication of this book marks the sixtieth anniversary of Jessup's seminal lecture and exemplifies the significant impact that Jessup, and later Boister, have had on legal scholarship and practice in the area of criminal law. We are honoured to publish the symposium as a monograph and to contribute to this rapidly evolving field.

This book was previously published as a special issue of *Transnational Legal Theory*.

Jessica Simone Roher graduated from Osgoode Hall Law School, where she was a Senior Editor of the journal *Transnational Legal Theory*. Prior to law school, she completed a master's degree in Conflict Studies at the London School of Economics and worked on a range of immigration issues in Canada, Ghana and Geneva. She articled at Lenczner Slaght LLP, a leading litigation firm in Toronto, and was called to the Bar of Ontario in 2016.

Nicola Dalla Guarda graduated from Osgoode Hall Law School in 2014 and is currently completing a Master of Public Policy degree at the University of Toronto. He focuses his research on the influence of technology on new forms of governance.

Maryam Khalid graduated from Osgoode Hall Law School in 2015, where she served as the Managing Editor of the journal, *Transnational Legal Theory*, for two years. She is now Counsel for the Ministry of the Attorney General in Toronto, Canada.

Transnational Crime

Law, theory and practice at the crossroads

Edited by

Jessica Simone Roher, Nicola Dalla Guarda and Maryam Khalid

Routledge
Taylor & Francis Group
LONDON AND NEW YORK

First published 2017 by Routledge

2 Park Square, Milton Park, Abingdon, Oxfordshire OX14 4RN
711 Third Avenue, New York, NY 10017

Routledge is an imprint of the Taylor & Francis Group, an informa business

First issued in paperback 2018

British Library Cataloguing in Publication Data
A catalogue record for this book is available from the British Library

ISBN 13: 978-1-138-20981-7 (hbk)
ISBN 13: 978-0-367-02985-2 (pbk)

Typeset in Times New Roman
by RefineCatch Limited, Bungay, Suffolk

Publisher's Note
The publisher accepts responsibility for any inconsistencies that may have arisen during the conversion of this book from journal articles to book chapters, namely the possible inclusion of journal terminology.

Contents

Citation Information

The chapters in this book were originally published in *Transnational Legal Theory*, volume 6, issue 1 (June 2015). When citing this material, please use the original page numbering for each article, as follows:

Introduction
Jessica Roher, Nicola Dalla Guarda and Maryam Khalid
Transnational Legal Theory, volume 6, issue 1 (June 2015), pp. 1–8

Chapter 1
Further reflections on the concept of transnational criminal law
Neil Boister
Transnational Legal Theory, volume 6, issue 1 (June 2015), pp. 9–30

Chapter 2
Transnational counter-terrorism law: law, power and legitimacy in the 'wars on terror'
Cian C. Murphy
Transnational Legal Theory, volume 6, issue 1 (June 2015), pp. 31–54

Chapter 3
Rethinking the 'international law of crime': provocations from transnational legal studies
Prabha Kotiswaran and Nicola Palmer
Transnational Legal Theory, volume 6, issue 1 (June 2015), pp. 55–88

Chapter 4
The 'elephant in the room' in debates about universal jurisdiction: diasporas, duties of hospitality, and the constitution of the political
Frédéric Mégret
Transnational Legal Theory, volume 6, issue 1 (June 2015), pp. 89–116

Chapter 5
Bird's-eye view and worm's-eye view: towards a defendant-based approach in transnational criminal law
Sabine Gless
Transnational Legal Theory, volume 6, issue 1 (June 2015), pp. 117–140

Chapter 6
Global policing and transnational rule with law
Ben Bowling and James Sheptycki
Transnational Legal Theory, volume 6, issue 1 (June 2015), pp. 141–173

Chapter 7
International criminal law's incongruity in Colombia: why core crime prosecution in national jurisdictions should be included in analyses of transnational criminal law
Michael Reed-Hurtado
Transnational Legal Theory, volume 6, issue 1 (June 2015), pp. 174–210

Chapter 8
Governing the ungovernable: international relations, transnational cybercrime law, and the post-Westphalian regulatory state
Nicola Dalla Guarda
Transnational Legal Theory, volume 6, issue 1 (June 2015), pp. 211–249

Notes on Contributors

Neil Boister is Professor in the Te Piringa Faculty of Law, University of Waikato, New Zealand. His current research interests include the International Military Tribunal for the Far East, international tobacco control, global simplification of extradition and the area of transnational crime. He is co-editor of *The Routledge Handbook of Transnational Criminal Law* (2015).

Ben Bowling is Professor of Criminology and Criminal Justice, and Acting Dean at The Dickson Poon School of Law, King's College, London, UK. He is also co-editor of the recently published, *Global Policing and Transnational Law Enforcement* (2015). His research focuses on issues of transnational crime and policing.

Sabine Gless is Professor of Criminal Law and Criminal Procedure in the Faculty of Law, Basel University, Switzerland. Her research looks at various areas of transnational criminal law as well as comparative criminal law.

Nicola Dalla Guarda graduated from Osgoode Hall Law School in 2014 and is currently completing a Master of Public Policy degree at the University of Toronto. He focuses his research on the influence of technology on new forms of governance.

Maryam Khalid graduated from Osgoode Hall Law School in 2015, where she served as the Managing Editor of the journal, *Transnational Legal Theory*, for two years. She is now Counsel for the Ministry of the Attorney General in Toronto, Canada.

Prabha Kotiswaran is Reader in Law and Social Justice at The Dickson Poon School of Law, King's College London, UK. Her main areas of research include transnational criminal law, postcolonial theory and feminist legal theory. Her recent publications appear in journals such as *Criminology and Criminal Justice*, the *Journal of Law and Society* and *Transnational Legal Theory*.

Frédéric Mégret is Associate Professor in the Faculty of Law, and William Dawson Scholar at McGill University, Canada. His research interests include international criminal law, international protection of human rights, the laws of war and international relations. He is co-editor of the forthcoming second edition of *The United Nations and Human Rights: A Critical Appraisal.*

Cian C. Murphy is Academic Co-Director at the Center for Transnational Legal Studies, London, UK, and Senior Lecturer in Law at The Dickson Poon School of Law, King's College London, UK. His work focuses on the relationship between collective power and individual rights. He is co-editor of *EU Security and Justice Law* (2014).

Nicola Palmer is Senior Lecturer in Criminal Law at The Dickson Poon School of Law, King's College London, UK. She is the author of the recently published monograph, *Courts in Conflict: Interpreting the Layers of Justice in Post-Genocide Rwanda* (2015). Dr Palmer's work examines international criminal law, transitional justice and the compatibility of plural responses to violence.

Michael Reed-Hurtado is Senior Lecturer in Latin American Studies at Yale University, New Haven, USA. He previously worked as a Consultant for the Office of the UN High Commissioner for Human Rights. His research interests include state crime and control, and conceptual and practical limits of transitional justice.

Jessica Simone Roher graduated from Osgoode Hall Law School, where she was a Senior Editor of the journal *Transnational Legal Theory*. Prior to law school, she completed a master's degree in Conflict Studies at the London School of Economics and worked on a range of immigration issues in Canada, Ghana and Geneva. She articled at Lenczner Slaght LLP, a leading litigation firm in Toronto, and was called to the Bar of Ontario in 2016.

James Sheptycki is Professor of Criminology in the Faculty of Liberal Arts and Professional Studies, York University, Toronto, Canada. His current project looks at guns, crime and social order in the context of transnational crime and policing. Professor Sheptycki is the author of several books, including *Crafting Transnational Policing* (2007) and *In Search of Transnational Policing* (2003).

Introduction

Jessica Roher[a], Nicola Dalla Guarda[b] and Maryam Khalid[c]

[a]*JD 2015, Osgoode Hall Law School, York University, Toronto, Canada;* [b]*JD 2014, Osgoode Hall Law School, York University, Toronto, Canada;* [c]*JD 2015, Osgoode Hall Law School, York University, Toronto, Canada and Managing Editor, Transnational Legal Theory*

Since the seventeenth century, Western legal theory has confined the law to a particular jurisdiction or nation state. There is a presumption that the law's creation, adjudication and enforcement reflect the politics, values and culture of the society that inhabits a particular territory. This is especially true of criminal law, which emerges from a society's history and norms, and then becomes embedded within it. The balance of crime control with due process, theories of punishment, and laws themselves varies from jurisdiction to jurisdiction. The state bears the authority to prosecute and punish, and the state has the power to criminalise, except where individuals are penalised for specified international crimes.

Globalisation, however, changes the nature of law within and between states. In a world where both criminal activities and the normative foundations of the law transcend borders, domestic legal responses to crime are increasingly shaped by transnational forces. The field of transnational criminal law (TCL) examines the phenomenon of transnational crime and the transnational nature of criminal law, and was brought to the fore of legal scholarship by Neil Boister in his paper '"Transnational Criminal Law"?', published in the *European Journal of International Law* in 2003.[1] This symposium issue of *Transnational Legal Theory* addresses the content of TCL and its potential as an evolving and still largely under-explored area of legal theory and practice that sits at the intersection of domestic and international criminal law.

The contributors to this symposium grapple with the definition, nature and substance of TCL; attempt to identify the actors, norms and processes engaged in and impacted by TCL's development; and analyse the theoretical frameworks that support or are challenged by the evolution of criminal law in a globalised

[1]Neil Boister, '"Transnational Criminal Law"?' (2003) 14(5) *European Journal of International Law* 953.

world. In addressing this contemporary issue, this symposium challenges traditional ideas of state sovereignty, crime, law enforcement, regulatory politics and societal values. Inspired by Boister's formative work on the subject, the symposium endeavours to chart the uncharted territory of TCL, and begins with an essay from Boister himself.

Neil Boister

Neil Boister first popularised the term 'transnational criminal law' in the early 2000s. The term referred to domestic criminal law enacted to fulfil obligations arising from multilateral crime suppression agreements formed in response to crimes of international concern. Boister observed that while international criminal law (ICL) imposes individual criminal responsibility directly through international mechanisms, TCL imposes individual criminal responsibility indirectly through domestic law. The purpose of ICL, on the one hand, is to protect international order and security, and to further the basic common values of an international society. The purpose of TCL, on the other hand, is to develop substantive criminal law and procedures to effectively suppress transnational criminal conduct and certain transnational crimes, thereby advancing the basic common interest in security that is shared by states.

Over a decade later – in this symposium issue and elsewhere – Boister continues to explore the nature of TCL by identifying its components, functions and sources. He has broadened his definition of TCL to cover criminal law that suppresses 'criminal activities that have actual or potential trans-boundary effects or trans-boundary moral impacts'.[2] Boister argues that TCL is not just a legal order or system through which states commit to suppression treaties and to criminalising certain conduct within their jurisdiction, but is instead a 'non-hierarchical normative' legal field.[3]

In his contribution to the symposium, Boister argues that the transnational nature of criminal law arises not only because of the transnationalisation of crime but also because of the transplantation of norms derived from transnational efforts, actions and ideas. Boister suggests that the normative cross-pollination of criminal law occurs in two ways: first, through the integration of substantive law and procedure in multilateral or bilateral crime suppression treaties into the domestic laws of states parties to those treaties; and second, through the domestic criminalisation of transnational criminal conduct and the enforcement of TCL.

While Boister maintains that the state is the ultimate mediator and arbitrator of TCL, he challenges the assumption that the state has a normative monopoly over the transnationalisation of criminal law and argues that the normative actions and

---

[2]Neil Boister, 'Further reflections on the concept of transnational criminal law', this volume.
[3]*Ibid.*

ideas of non-traditional law-making authorities (e.g. non-state actors) influence the transplantation of criminal law norms in the absence of suppression treaties. For Boister, TCL serves as a lens that reveals the relationships between national criminal laws and transnational legal institutions in a globalised society. This is a theme that runs through the symposium issue. Each of the authors use TCL as a theoretical tool for understanding the evolution of criminal law at international, regional, national and local levels, as well as its impact on both victims and perpetrators.

Cian Murphy

Cian Murphy challenges Boister's analysis of TCL by highlighting the benefits that a less formalistic approach can bring to the field. Using transnational counter-terrorism law as an illustration, Murphy points to how 'quasi-criminal' measures (e.g. civil or administrative) are implemented in states worldwide but are overlooked by or left out of Boister's approach to TCL. Murphy calls for greater clarity to Boister's approach, claiming that Boister may be shifting from a categorical to a more contextual approach to TCL in his current contribution, but that this shift is not organic.

Murphy suggests that some transnational criminal legal issues are broader than the definition of TCL, as delineated by Boister, currently accounts for. TCL must not only focus on criminal law at a transnational level civil and administrative law must be incorporated in the TCL framework, especially in the case of transnational counter-terrorism law. Using United Nations Resolution 2178[4] as an example, Murphy demonstrates how a focus on only the juridical aspects of TCL ignores the influence and significance of related disciplinary powers that are employed transnationally to counter terrorism. While the forces of denationalisation and globalisation were certainly in play before 9/11, Murphy suggests that the aftermath of those attacks have prompted a shift wherein the responsibility of countering terrorism has fallen on the executive branches of various individual states. The outcome is an increasing absence of legitimacy or control over the norms that result. Furthermore, a by-product is a shift in governance from the national to the international, which has resulted in a new form of social and political control 'beyond the state', as Murphy puts it. However, since states remain the sites of power and rule enforcement, Murphy proposes that we contemplate the effect of the transnationalisation of counter-terrorism law and the decategorisation of TCL with these new forms of regulation in mind.

Prabha Kotiswaran and Nicola Palmer

In their piece, Prabha Kotiswaran and Nicola Palmer argue that embracing the contradictions and complexities of transnational law provides new opportunities to

[4]UN Security Council Resolution 2178 (24 September 2014) UN Doc S/RES/2178.

conceptualise and understand the nature of both international and domestic criminal law in a globalised world.

First, they challenge Boister's division of ICL and TCL, arguing that ICL faces the same challenges that plague TCL (e.g. regarding criminalisation, democracy deficits, fragmentation and hegemony), but suggest that TCL may offer a solution for these challenges by opening a discursive space for lawyers to develop a better understanding of the nature of criminal law. They do not dismiss Boister, but rather they highlight the benefits of engaging with the various dimensions of the 'international law of crime' through the legal pluralist lens of TCL, particularly in responding to transnational social problems. Second, the authors suggest that as a field, TCL must be open to a broadening or reconfiguration of what constitutes 'transnational crime', as well as to a wider range of 'technologies of governance', observing these through comparative, post-colonial, legal pluralist and legal realist lenses, amongst others.

Readers will benefit from the authors' insights as researchers and educators in the field of transnational law and legal theory, the experiences of which clearly informed their enquiries into both the theoretical bases of Boister's propositions and the practical challenges it poses for lawyers, as well as the future practice of criminal law in the context of neo-liberal globalisation.

Frédéric Mégret

Frédéric Mégret's contribution shifts our focus to those affected by TCL. By examining victim and perpetrator diasporas, Mégret demonstrates that universal jurisdiction is a transnational strategy of justice. He argues that the three traditional models that provide the theoretical basis for a state invoking universal jurisdiction to prosecute perpetrators of international crimes – the cosmopolitan model, the interstate realist model and the global civil society model – fail to capture the use of and potential for universal jurisdiction. TCL as a normative system can bridge the gap and account for the shortcomings of prior theories of universal jurisdiction. Mégret suggests that a theory of universal jurisdiction should be rooted in the transnational communities of victims and perpetrators who are exposed to and confronted with each other in the diaspora.

Mégret applies the philosophical concept of hospitality, arguing that hospitality demands that states apply universal jurisdiction in order to seek accountability for atrocities that occur abroad. By refusing to invoke universal jurisdiction in order to prosecute perpetrators, the state demonstrates its sincere *in*hospitality; indeed, 'the denial of such justice might be considered to be a form of revictimisation, or at least a trivialisation of "their" suffering'.[5] Further, when victims transition from immigrants to citizens, hospitality demands an even greater respect

[5] F Mégret, 'The "elephant in the room" of debates about universal jurisdiction: diasporas, duties of hospitality, and the constitutional of the political', this volume.

for their rights, which gives rise to heightened pressure on states to invoke universal jurisdiction in order to prosecute perpetrators. This is because the decision to become a citizen of a particular country is a normative and political choice that integrates the victim into the host society and confirms the victim's faith in the juridical system. The 'hospitable state' must therefore affirm the rights of victims by trying those who have committed crimes. Mégret argues that universal jurisdiction affirms a transnational right to effective remedies, which demands that states exercise their criminal law in upholding the rights of victims.

Sabine Gless

Sabine Gless also asks us to shift our approach to TCL from a focus on national and inter-state criminal regulation towards an examination of the effect TCL has on individuals – namely the accused and the victim. Gless calls the former approach a 'bird's-eye view', focused on rule making and enforcement in the global criminal legal landscape, and the impact this has on inter-state criminal regulation. She argues that if we examine TCL from this perspective, it seems that a legal order exists to punish transnational crimes that are agreed upon. However, if we examine TCL from the perspective of affected individuals especially defendants – from a 'worm's-eye view' – TCL seems more like a patchwork of laws. An examination of TCL from the defendant's perspective elucidates problems, such as the existence of conflicting criminal laws between jurisdictions, where individuals become defendants subject to unfamiliar legal procedures (and other accompanying challenges) in a foreign state.

For Gless, therefore, the central challenge for TCL is how to import the defendants' interests into the 'bird's-eye view'. Since criminal prosecution carries harsh consequences for individual defendants, rules that safeguard their rights should be consistent and coordinated from state to state so as to protect the rights of defendants. She suggests that in order to do this, states must identify a shared set of aspirational *general principles* that ought to be applied in transnational criminal cases to protect the rights of defendants while prosecuting them for transnational crimes, and to develop a legal structure accordingly. Such principles would be deducted through, first, an empirical, comparative-inductive method to identify convergences of rules in different areas of TCL, and, secondly, an individual and objective-based approach to TCL to identify 'aspirational' principles (e.g. the presumption of innocence). States should strive to develop a coordinated transnational criminal system that upholds both the procedural and the substantive rights of victims and defendants, thus actualising a modified bird's-eye view.

Benjamin Bowling and James Sheptycki

Benjamin Bowling and James Sheptycki explore the connection between transnational law and policing from a socio-legal approach, illustrating how legal instruments are used as tools by police to counter transnational crime and how police contribute to the development of these legal instruments. In exploring the way in which police use and develop the law to investigate crimes, maintain order, undertake intrusive surveillance and arrest or restrain suspects, Bowling and Sheptycki demonstrate that the global system of policing is better described as *rule with law* rather than *rule of law.* They argue that police maintain particular institutional, corporate and state interests, and deploy the law to advance these interests. The authors share Boister's concern that TCL is used instrumentally in that TCL broadens the scope of transnational crime control and policing, which then operate at the expense of human rights and the rule of law.

The authors argue that while Boister assumes that the rule of law doctrine forms part of the conceptual framework of TCL, in the transnational sphere of crime control, rule of law cannot be assumed; law enforcement agencies, instead, rule *with* law by being actively involved in creating the law that govern enforcement, police practices and the regulation of transnational criminal acts. The police have great discretion as to when they invoke the law. The culture of policing and the subculture of transnational policing shape the decisions that agencies make, and therefore the law itself, particularly since transnational crime often takes place in an extraterritorial legal space. Bowling and Sheptycki use four examples to illustrate how legal instruments shape state-based and private institutions around particular policing mandates in a transnational context: the global monetary system, transnational mobility, intellectual property, and high policing.

By examining the law as it is applied rather than the law as it is written, the authors provide us with another distinctive lens through which we can examine transnational criminal regulation and frameworks.

Michael Reed-Hurtado

In his invaluable contribution grounded in practical insight, Michael Reed-Hurtado uses the example of Colombian involvement with ICL to demonstrate why the national prosecution of 'core crimes' should be seen through the lens of TCL, contrary to what Boister may submit. The goals and direct enforcement of ICL are found on the ground, according to Reed-Hurtado, leaving their operation open to influence from the national criminal justice systems in question, as well as local social and political histories, varying layers of international and regional human rights obligations, and international political pressures.

Reed-Hurtado paints a picture of how Colombia has developed and interacted with ICL – historically, politically, socially and judicially. This example illustrates how national authorities and societies integrate ICL into their domestic laws in order to address atrocities, which in turn influences local regimes. Although Colombian laws have retained their primacy, they are conditioned by ICL and other forms of international law, such as international humanitarian law.

By viewing ICL through the lens of TCL, as Reed-Hurtado suggests, we are exposed to the restrictions of a monolithic global governance structure of criminal law (e.g. the International Criminal Court model), as well as to the influence of local legal pluralism in states on the application and development of ICL. In so doing, a more critical approach can be taken to ICL and its domestic implementation, in the case of Colombia and elsewhere. Reed-Hurtado provides tangible examples to illustrate how domestic prosecutors use ICL for efficiency gains and political ends. As such, TCL gives us new perspectives not only on the realities of ICL, but also on forging new paths forward. This, however, can only come once TCL is used as a tool to turn attention to the ways local law can and does influence the application of ICL.

Nicola Dalla Guarda

The closing contribution turns to what can be learned from the evolving subfield of transnational cybercrime law. Nicola Dalla Guarda begins by conducting a comparative analysis of six of the world's leading regional cybercrime agreements. He canvasses insights from international relations theories and the practical consequences of attempting to implement such norms. The regimes are thereby shown to be inherently state-based systems of regulation, not only in their origin but also in their implementation.

A global tapestry of transnational cybercrime law is emerging. The different characteristics of each regime are attributable to the legal and political differences between signatories. Dalla Guarda suggests that this is part of a broader trend: modern nation states are now also performing their traditionally domestic roles and responsibilities as 'security providers' or 'sovereignty generators' in the transnational realm, and are creating the necessary legal and institutional frameworks in the process – for better or worse. He then asks whether the same issues of enforcement or accountability that are currently present can be avoided or minimised in the future, given the path that the modern nation state is taking in order to deal with issues of transnational crime and security. The author closes with a call for a new approach to transnational cybercrime law, however unlikely it may seem at the moment.

Conclusion

We live in a world in which the law is at once individual, local, national, transnational and international. TCL has continued to evolve since its inception nearly 15 years ago to capture the dynamic nature of criminal law in a globalised world. The contributors to this symposium help us to better understand the complexities of the creation, enforcement and adjudication of criminal law across and within borders. More than anything, these papers anticipate and call for a much-needed discussion and debate on the issue of TCL. We at *Transnational Legal Theory* are privileged to have received, and now publish, outstanding essays that engage with theoretical issues on the transnationalisation of law that will no doubt continue to evolve as criminal law has for centuries.

Acknowledgements

We would like to thank the contributors to this symposium issue for their invaluable insights, the anonymous peer reviewers for their time and feedback, the student editors of *Transnational Legal Theory* for their tireless efforts, and Peer Zumbansen for his guidance and encouragement.

Further reflections on the concept of transnational criminal law

Neil Boister*

Te Piringa Faculty of Law, University of Waikato, New Zealand

In an attempt to clarify the concept of transnational criminal law, this piece examines its basic elements, analysing questions about what its essential components are and whether purely national crimes and laws for criminal cooperation are part of transnational criminal law. It then turns to the difficult question of whether transnational criminal law can accurately be termed a legal system, examining whether – and if so, how – apparently unrelated national criminal laws dealing with transnational crime are in a systemic relation. The piece then shifts its attention to whether it is possible to expand the transnational legal space to include rules that are made autonomously from state or international authority. After discussing whether transnational criminal law is a pluralist legal order, it concludes by examining who benefits from transnational criminal law, focusing on whether – and if so, how – transnational criminal law can escape the taint of Western hegemony.

Introduction

In 2001, I proposed consideration of use of the term 'transnational criminal law' as a suitable label for the category of domestic crimes established through treaty obligations in multilateral crime suppression conventions such as the 1988 Vienna Convention[1] – the so-called 'treaty

---

*Versions of this paper were presented at the WG Hart Legal Workshop 2012, Criminalisation, Criminal Law and Criminal Justice, Institute of Advanced Legal Studies, School of Advanced Study, University of London, 26–28 June 2012; 'International Law in the Next Two Decades', 20th Annual Conference of the Australia New Zealand Society of International Law, 4–7 July 2012, Victoria University, Wellington, New Zealand; and at the Faculty of Law, University of Hamburg, 15 November 2012. An altered version appears as ch 1 of the Routledge Handbook of Transnational Criminal Law (2014). All websites accessed April 2015.

[1]United Nations Convention against Illicit Traffic in Narcotic Drugs and Psychotropic Substances (adopted 20 December 1988, entered into force 11 November 1990) 1582 UNTS 95.

crimes'[2] or 'crimes of international concern'.[3] I argued that transnational criminal law provided a suitable doctrinal match for the criminological term 'transnational crime', while making it possible to distinguish this category of criminal law from international criminal law in a strict sense, i.e. the criminal law applicable in international criminal tribunals where individual criminal responsibility was directly applied under international law. My motivation was to focus attention on this relatively neglected area because of concerns about the process of criminalisation of transnational conduct, legitimacy in the development of the system, doctrinal weaknesses, human rights considerations, legitimacy in governance, and implementation problems unique to transnational criminal law. With the claim that crimes with a transnational element fell within international criminal law in an undifferentiated sense[4] firmly in my sights, in 2001 I looked for distinguishing features of what I additionally, albeit rather tentatively, claimed was a 'system' of transnational criminal law. I argued that the distinction could be made on four grounds: the indirect nature of transnational criminal law as opposed to the direct nature of international criminal law; the application only of limited forms of extraterritorial jurisdiction to transnational crimes as opposed to the application of absolute universality to truly international crimes; the protection only of limited transnational values and interests by transnational criminal law as opposed to the international values and interests intrinsic to international criminal law; and the differently constituted international societies that project these penal norms.

The latter distinction involved what was really my central contention: that the identity of the community that international criminal law was constructed to serve was different from that of transnational criminal law. While the former was claimed to be an instrument of a Grotian society of states where communitarian values dominated and laws of cooperation were the result, I suggested that the latter was at most a creature of a loosely aligned pluralist Vattelian society of states where sovereignty and self-interest were the dominant values and laws of coordination the result.[5] The degree of coordination varies from crime to crime, depending on the threat of harm or actual harm perceived to be offered by the particular harmful conduct concerned, balanced against complex factors like vested

[2]See Neil Boister, '"Transnational Criminal Law"?' (2003) 14(5) *European Journal of International Law* 953.
[3]See M Cherif Bassiouni, 'An Appraisal of the Growth and Developing Trends of International Criminal Law' in John Dugard and Christine van den Wyngaert (eds), *International Criminal Law and Procedure* (Dartmouth, 1996) 85.
[4]See M Cherif Bassiouni, 'The Sources and Content of International Criminal Law: A Theoretical Framework' in M Cherif Bassiouni (ed), *International Criminal Law: Crimes* (Transnational, 2nd edn 1999) 13. 'Transnational criminal law' was used in a much broader sense in Albin Eser and Otto Lagodny (eds), *Principles and Procedures for a New Transnational Criminal Law* (Max Planck Institute, 1992) to include all forms of criminal law with an international dimension, including international criminal law in the strict sense.
[5]Boister (n 2) 967–74.

societal interests in carrying out that conduct, the spatial impact of the conduct, and so forth. This analysis was focused on differentiating transnational criminal law from international criminal law in a strict or narrow sense, rather than thinking about the unique features of transnational criminal law.

In 2012 I attempted a crisper answer to the question of what is transnational criminal law.[6] In that piece I again claimed that it is a system and that it has two distinct functions: (i) to suppress transnational crime; and (ii) to transnationalise criminal law by diffusing criminal offences that originate in one or more states through the agency of international law into the law of other states. The instruments of agency were the crime suppression conventions through which states parties embrace tortious or delictual treaty obligations to criminalise the activities specified in those conventions and to adopt procedural provisions that enable them to cooperate with other states which seek to take and exercise jurisdiction over the criminals concerned.

The label 'transnational criminal law' is now fairly well used.[7] My interest in this piece is to provide greater conceptual clarity about transnational criminal law by trying to identify more carefully the sources and the boundaries of transnational criminal law. Section I of this piece re-examines the basic elements of the concept. Section II examines whether transnational criminal law can accurately be termed a legal system. Section III asks whether it is possible to expand the transnational legal space. Section IV considers whether transnational criminal law is a pluralist legal order. Section V asks who benefits from transnational criminal law. In this five-part examination, I also try to answer the following nagging questions about the concept: (i) Is a transnational element a necessary element of a transnational crime? (ii) Is a treaty element necessary? (iii) Are purely national crimes and the national laws for criminal cooperation in their regard part of transnational criminal law? (iv) Does transnational criminal law include rules that are made autonomously from state or international authority? (v) How are the apparently unrelated national criminal laws in a systemic relation to each other? (vi) How can transnational criminal law escape the taint of Western hegemony?

I. The basic elements of the concept of transnational criminal law revisited

The perception that certain forms of criminality have become increasingly globalised drives the globalisation of the legal response to these actions. The starting

---

[6]Neil Boister, *An Introduction to Transnational Criminal Law* (Oxford University Press, 2012) 13–23.

[7]See Robert Cryer, 'The Doctrinal Foundations of International Criminalization' in M Cherif Bassiouni (ed), *International Criminal Law: Sources, Subjects and Contents* (Martinus Nijhoff, 3rd edn 2008) 108; Robert Cryer, Hakan Friman, Darryl Robinson and Elizabeth Wilmshurst, *An Introduction to International Criminal Law and Procedure* (Cambridge University Press, 2nd edn 2010) 5; Robert J Currie, *International and Transnational Criminal Law* (Irwin Law, 2010) 19; Claus Kress, 'International Criminal Law' in Rüdiger Wolfrum (ed), *Max Planck Encyclopedia of Public International Law: Online edition* (March 2009), www.mpepil.com, para 6.

point is the notion of transnational crime, a term coined by the UN Crime Prevention and Criminal Justice Branch to 'identify certain criminal phenomena transcending international borders, transgressing the laws of several states or having an impact on another country'.[8] This idea has received explicit expression in the 'Scope of Application' of the United Nations Convention against Transnational Organized Crime (UNTOC). According to Article 3, the Convention applies to a range of offences that are 'transnational in nature', including any offence that is

> committed in more than one State; (b) ... committed in one State but a substantial part of its preparation, planning, direction or control takes place in another State; (c) ... committed in one State but involves an organised criminal group that engages in criminal activities in more than one State; or (d) ... committed in one State but has substantial effects in another State.[9]

Evidence of a transnational element provides what Nadelmann terms a 'transnational hook'[10], the hook used to convince states that they should participate in the construction of a suppression convention in which they promise to criminalise that behaviour. The suppression conventions on a particular crime and resultant domestic law and practice together create a 'global prohibition regime' on drugs, money laundering, corruption and so forth. The first question of some importance to the concept of transnational criminal law is whether there must be a cross-border element in the definition of the transnational crimes in these conventions. Somewhat paradoxically, the answer is no. The suppression conventions include within their scope behaviour that (i) actually crosses borders or (ii) has substantial effects in other states. Nadelmann's critical insight is that the practice of states as reflected in the suppression conventions (iii) also includes local crime that has only the most tenuous potential extraterritorial impact but which is of transboundary moral concern sufficient to include this behaviour within the scope of treaty obligations obliging its criminalisation.[11] As Scott points out, transnational issues also include

> phenomena not involving physical acts or events across borders that are nonetheless understood by relevant participants and/or observers as 'transnational' situations because of how the issue has come to be constructed by interacting normative (legal, policy, and moral) discourses as transcending ... national frontiers.[12]

[8]Gerhard Mueller, 'Transnational Crime: Definitions and Concepts' in Phil Williams and Dimitri Vlassis (eds), *Combating Transnational Crime* (Frank Cass, 2001) 13.
[9]United Nations Convention against Transnational Organised Crime (adopted 15 November 2000, entered into force 29 September 2003) 2225 UNTS 209 (UNTOC), Art 3.
[10]Ethan Nadelmann, 'Global Prohibition Regimes: The Evolution of Norms in International Society' (1990) 44 *International Organisation* 479, 482.
[11]*Ibid*, 525.
[12]Craig Scott, '"Transnational Law" as Proto-Concept: Three Conceptions' (2009) 10 *German Law Journal* 859, 864.

The concept of transnational criminal law broadly matches this view of what constitutes transnational crime. When Philip Jessup coined the term 'transnational law' he was concerned with a legal space that included actions and events that transcended boundaries.[13] 'Transnational criminal law' conjoins the criminological term 'transnational crime' with Jessup's term 'transnational law'. It is concerned with governance of transnational criminal actions. It involves the indirect suppression by international law through domestic penal law of criminal activities that have (i) actual or (ii) potential transboundary effects or (iii) transboundary moral impacts. Thus, in addition to criminalisation of those events, people and goods that actually cross borders, transnational criminal law includes within its scope purely domestic situations where the actors offer substantial threats to other states, as well as situations where although their actions offer at most only tenuous transnational effects, they are constructed as transnational situations out of moral concern. Article 3(2) of the 1988 Vienna Convention's obligation on states parties to criminalise the possession of drugs for non-medical and scientific purposes is the quintessential example of such a cosmopolitan moral concern, generating a legal norm.[14] In other words, the actions and ideas of those who clarify, normativise and apply the norms transcend territorial boundaries. The actions of the lawmakers are as transnational as the actions of the lawbreakers.

II. Transnational criminal law as a system

A. *Legal order or legal field?*

As defined above, transnational criminal law is part of what Scott has termed 'transnational legalized traditionalism', an approach that takes Jessup's 'all law which regulates actions or events that transcend national frontiers' and includes within it those legal rules and juridical acts located within public international law (mainly the rules in the multilateral suppression conventions placing obligations on states to enact criminal laws and procedures against transnational crime) and domestic law (the national criminal laws that implement those treaty obligations), considered both independently and in combination.[15] Describing transnational criminal law as a system suggests a legal order of reference with

[13]Philip C Jessup, *Transnational Law* (Yale University Press, 1956) 2.
[14]While use of drugs in drug 'consumer' states is a key element of drug supply chains, use in supply states is of relatively little impact in consumer states yet historically it has been a major issue in international drug control. See, for example, Western response to Japanese drug policy in Asia in Kathryn Meyer, 'Japan and the World Narcotics Trade' in Jordan Goodman, Paul E Lovejoy and Andrew Sherratt (eds), *Consuming Habits: Drugs in History and Anthropology* (Routledge, 1995), 186; William O Walker III, *Opium and Foreign Policy: The Anglo American Search for Order in Asia 1912–1954* (University of North Carolina Press, 1991).
[15]See Scott (n 12) 868–72.

an identifiable legislative source in a hierarchical system of legal norms. Yet, as defined above, it consists of an autonomous set of international treaty norms and many autonomous sets of domestic criminal norms with quite distinctive points of authority. Is it more apt to describe transnational criminal law simply as a non-hierarchical normative area, or a fixed system of norms of similar content, type and purpose?[16] The answer to this question requires a closer look at the horizontal international and vertical national components of transnational criminal law.

B. *The international component*

The horizontal component is found within international law and more specifically within the international treaties directed at suppressing crime. There is no general customary international law duty to cooperate against crime but there is no reason in principle why a custom could not serve as the basis for such a normative transplantation or cross-pollination so long as the customary obligation is to enact an offence in national law and does not apply direct penal responsibility to the offence itself.[17] In practice, however, it is crime suppression treaties – bilateral, regional or the large UN backed multilateral suppression conventions – that permit action to be taken against different harmful activities at different paces by different states parties. The consensus of the signatories is managed on an ongoing basis through regular meeting of the parties. In theory, this permits amendment, but this is rare in practice and incremental normative development generally occurs within the various prohibition regimes by periodic negotiation of new treaties. In this process of development, new treaties frequently borrow agreed substantive and procedural innovations already adopted in older treaties concerned with different crimes. For example, the obligation to criminalise money laundering pioneered in Article 3(1)(b) and (c) of the 1988 Vienna Convention was included in Article 6 of UNTOC some 12 years later in 2000 and is now a stock feature of new suppression conventions.[18] This transfer is rationalised on the basis that the transferrable provisions deal with a common problem – transnational crime – which manifests itself in different forms. The increase in the number and complexity of these provisions and their transmutation into domestic laws increases the integration of national criminal laws into the prohibition regime. But the relationship is not simple, as international norms do not always determine national norms in a linear fashion. National, regional, quasi-global and global norms interact in a complex and dynamic fashion.

[16] *Ibid.*
[17] In this regard, *US v Arjona*, 120 US 479 (1887) appears to establish a customary obligation to punish the counterfeiting. See Roger S Clark, 'Reflections on International Criminal Law and Jurisdiction' (2011) 22 *Criminal Law Forum* 519, 520 fn 2.
[18] UNTOC, Art 6.

The second challenge facing the concept of transnational criminal law is whether it should include the horizontal diffusion of criminal law norms from state to state without the agency of a suppression convention.[19] The trans-state provenance of these norms suggests that they should be included within transnational criminal law. It is reasonable to object to their inclusion if they are simply the unilateral borrowings by states of norms to address purely national issues rather than issues of transnational conduct, effect or concern, because in that case they are absolutely parochial in nature and do not involve two or more states coordinating their repressive responses. But things are more difficult if these norms have been developed to address an issue of transnational conduct, effect or concern. Their inclusion within transnational criminal law would imply that the existence of the horizontal international component is not a necessary condition of transnational criminal law. In other words, it is the transnational transfer of the norm and the shared purpose of the states involved which distinguishes transnational criminal law. The actual mode of transfer can be a formal legal obligation – a treaty – or some more informal agreement to do so. But it is arguable that a horizontal treaty element is a necessary element of transnational criminal law because it is indicative of a formal inter-sovereign relationship, a set of formal promises among sovereigns, which distinguishes transnational criminal law from mere international relations. To put it another way, without the international treaty component there is no legal framework to these sovereign relations.

Just because there is an international component to transnational criminal law, however, does not mean that we are really talking about international criminal law, except perhaps in the very broad sense of criminal law in which there is an international law dimension. The most obvious distinctions from international criminal law in a strict sense[20] are as follows: (i) the right to criminalise remains with the state and, unlike international criminal law,[21] there is no individual penal responsibility under international law; (ii) the right to adjudicate remains with the state and there is no international jurisdiction. We might lazily talk of crimes in the drug trafficking conventions but they are not crimes, only obligations to enact crimes usually couched in broad terms and highly conditioned on compatibility with the general structure and basic principles of domestic laws. Nor is there delegation of jurisdiction over transnational crimes to an international criminal court of any kind.[22] State participants exercise only their own criminal jurisdiction over transnational crimes. While international criminal law suggests a hierarchical order established by an international community that came into being in the twentieth century in order to suppress actions subject to universal opprobrium or

[19]This is quite common. See William Twining, *General Jurisprudence* (Cambridge University Press, 2009) 250–1.
[20]Cryer (n 7) 108.
[21]Rome Statute of the International Criminal Court (adopted 17 July 1998, entered into force 1 July 2002) 2187 UNTS 90 (Rome Statute), Art 25(2).
[22]See, for example, Rome Statute, Art 1.

threatening the security of the international community,[23] transnational criminal law is the product of an orthodox nineteenth-century non-hierarchical order of formally equal centres of legal authority based on reciprocity, equality and sovereign consent.[24]

International criminal law may be a staging post on the way to a true world legal order, in that it may be trying to detach itself from its roots in national law and become autonomously supranational in both substance and process. But transnational criminal law lags behind, a burden too great for the international community to hoist. The *aut dedere aut judicare* (extradite or prosecute) provisions usually contained in suppression conventions might be considered to transform the crimes in these conventions into true international crimes. However, these extradite or prosecute obligations are of two types: (i) those that require a party to establish and exercise jurisdiction only when the person in question is subject to an extradition request from another state party to the particular convention; and (ii) those more rare treaties that follow the example of Article 4(2) of the 1970 Hague Convention for the Suppression of Unlawful Seizure of Aircraft[25] and oblige a state party to establish its jurisdiction even if no extradition request is received, simply on the basis that it does not extradite that person. Kress points out that while the former type of provision suggests a system based on self-interested sovereigns coordinating their positions, the latter type suggests something that serves a broader international community interest. He concedes that it is not decisive of the view that hijacking (or other 'crimes' which follow suit) is an international crime because of the absence of state practice accepting this.[26]

States claim in preambular mantra in the suppression conventions that these conventions are directed at matters of concern to the international community. Yet to argue that the suppression conventions are products of the international community and serve its interests is to ignore the roots of these crimes in state-interest policies in controlling the crimes of private individuals committed for private gain. The distinction between criminal law emanating from an international community and one in which international law serves as an instrument for coordinating sovereign positions is reflected in the German distinction between *Völkerstrafrecht* and *Internationales Strafrecht*, in the French distinction between *droit international pénal* and *droit pénal international*, and in the Spanish distinction between *derecho internacional penal* and *derecho penal*

[23]See principle 3 in UNWCC, 'Report of the UNWCC summarising the elements of Crimes against Humanity in Eight Principles' in *History of the United Nations War Crimes Commission and the Development of the Laws of War* (HMSO, 1948).

[24]Richard A Falk, 'International Jurisdiction: Horizontal and Vertical Conceptions of Legal Order' (1959) 32 *Temple Law Quarterly* 295.

[25]Hague Convention for the Suppression of Unlawful Seizure of Aircraft (adopted 16 December 1970, entered into force 14 October 1971) 860 UNTS 105 (Hague Hijacking Convention), Art 4(2).

[26]Kress (n 7) para 8.

internacional.[27] However, I am not sure that 'criminal international law' is really fit for this purpose. Like the term 'crimes of international concern', it does not express the heavy sovereign interest immanent in transnational legal relations around crime.

In my view, the two main purposes of the suppression conventions are (i) substantive criminalisation and (ii) procedural cooperation.

(i) *Substance*

The development of a suppression convention is considered by its authors to be a virtuous exercise that has a clear deontological purpose – the suppression through criminal law of certain harmful activities of transnational nature, effect or concern. Consider, for example, preambular paragraph 3 of the 2001 Council of Europe Convention on Cybercrime: 'Convinced of the need to pursue, as a matter of priority, a common criminal policy aimed at the protection of society against cybercrime, *inter alia*, by adopting appropriate legislation … '[28]

Preambular paragraphs of this kind seldom mention criminalisation specifically, choosing rather to use verbs like 'combating' crime. Yet obligations to criminalise within suppression conventions have become a common transnational legislative tool across a range of different sectors, with roots back into the nineteenth century. They usually entail the setting out of a number of material elements coupled with subjective mental elements. In some offences, transnational conduct is required, but in the main it is excluded so as to enable the laying down of criminal offences that apply to intra- as well as inter-state conduct. When it is used, such as in Article 3(1) of the 1997 Convention on Combating Bribery of Foreign Public Officials in International Business Transactions, which provides that 'bribery of a foreign public official shall be a punishable offence',[29] the transnational element in the definition of a crime is both substantive in nature and also jurisdictional in nature, because it implies the necessity of a state party establishing jurisdiction over activities that will usually occur extraterritorially. The scope of these offences has been quite broad, including obligations to suppress repugnant conduct heavily invasive of human rights, such as trading in slaves,[30] but also directed at actions *mala prohibitum*, such as manufacturing of tobacco without

[27] Cryer *et al* (n 7) 6.

[28] Council of Europe Convention on Cybercrime (adopted 23 November 2001, entered into force 1 July 2004) ETS No 185 (Convention on Cybercrime).

[29] OECD Convention on Combating Bribery of Foreign Public Officials in International Business Transactions (adopted 18 December 1997, entered into force 15 February 1999) 37 ILM 1 (OECD Anti-Bribery Convention).

[30] See Convention to Suppress the Slave Trade and Slavery (adopted in force 9 March 1927, entered into force 9 March 1927) 60 LNTS 253 (1926 Slavery Convention), Art 1(1) and (6).

a licence.[31] There may arguably be a thicker cosmopolitan consensus to criminalise the former than the latter, but this does not explain why criminalisation of certain highly repugnant forms of behaviour such as weapons trafficking is much narrower in scope than more innocuous forms of behaviour such as money laundering. Differences of this kind can only be understood on the basis of a fully contextual analysis of the political, social and economic forces that have shaped criminalisation of the particular form of conduct. With regard to subjective elements of culpability, older provisions such as Article 3 of the 1929 International Convention for the Suppression of Counterfeiting Currency seldom mention *mens rea*.[32] The only mention is 'intentional' participation in paragraph 4, but more recent provisions such as Article 3(1) of the 1988 Vienna Convention expressly require intention.

(ii) *Procedure*

The other key purpose of the suppression conventions is to make provision for effective procedural cooperation among the states parties with regard to the various transnational crimes in the suppression conventions. These allied procedural regimes are devoted to the tasks of either obliging or permitting states parties to establish both territorial and extraterritorial jurisdiction over the particular crimes, and then to take steps to enforce that jurisdiction through policing and adjudication. Five points are worth making about the nature of these regimes. First, some of the procedural provisions usually found in a suppression convention are directed at increasing the efficiency of domestic prosecution of these transnational crimes rather than having anything to do directly with international cooperation (on the thesis that the more efficient domestic suppression becomes, the more useful it will be to other states when called upon). Second, the procedures directed towards international cooperation rely heavily on the existing and much larger system for criminal law cooperation between states, which was built to make cooperation possible in addressing a whole range of criminal activities, not all of transnational concern. Third, the base value of procedural cooperation is the sovereignty that criminal law expresses, and thus cooperation is not a conflict of laws situation where choice of law or recognition of foreign judgments are the principal questions.[33] The chief question here is which state shall get the opportunity to apply its criminal laws first.[34] These provisions make it possible

[31]See Protocol to Eliminate Illicit Trade in Tobacco Products (opened for signature 10 January 2013) UNTS (Protocol), Art 14(1)(a).
[32]International Convention for the Suppression of Counterfeiting Currency (adopted 20 April 1929, entered into force 22 February 1931) 112 LNTS 371.
[33]Marcus D Dubber, 'Criminal Law in Comparative Context' (2006) 56 *Journal of Legal Education* 433, 434.
[34]*Ze'ev Rosenstein v Israel* Appeal judgment, Crim A 4596/05, para 43; ILDC 159 (IL 2005), 30 November 2005.

for states parties to apply their laws to help other states, not to apply the laws of other states. Fourth, the question of the extent of the enforcement power granted in a suppression convention will depend on the particular subject matter of that treaty, and, as Clark points out after reviewing the extensive powers for extraterritorial enforcement jurisdiction at sea in the 1884 Convention for the Protection of Submarine Cables[35] (compared to the absence of such powers with regard to national crimes *malum in se* like murder),

> [d]o not underestimate the randomness in all of this: one might think that killing someone is worse than damaging a piece of wire (albeit an expensive one) and others probably ought to be able to board and investigate homicides, but the treaty dealt with cables, not dead people.[36]

C. *The national component*

The vertical component in transnational criminal law involves domestic criminalisation of the specified conduct of individuals and the enactment of allied procedures and provisions for cooperation with regard to those individuals by the states parties to the particular suppression convention. These national laws constitute the legal normative goal of the system because they enable suppression of criminal activities domestically, and transnational cooperation in the suppression of criminal activity that occurs in that state, but which concerns other states, by ensuring double criminality. In a way, it is an example of subsidiarity: the state is left the task of criminalisation and enforcement because it is the most effective unit to take these steps, with the distinction that there is no supranational unit available to do so, only other states. Many states will make the necessary domestic changes before actually ratifying the treaty in question. Some states take legislative action independently of the international treaty obligation. The US's Trafficking Victims Protection Act 2000, for example, was adopted in the same year as the Protocol to Prevent, Suppress and Punish Trafficking in Persons, Especially Women and Children, supplementing the United Nations Convention against Transnational Organized Crime,[37] but was adopted out of domestic concerns in the US about human trafficking.[38] Methods of implementation vary widely;

---

[35]Convention for the Protection of Submarine Cables (adopted 14 March 1884, entered into force 1 May 1888) TS 380.

[36]See Roger S Clark, 'Reflections on International Criminal Law and on Jurisdiction' (2012), http://camlaw.rutgers.edu/sites/camlaw/files/International%20Criminal%20Law%20%20Reflections_0.pdf (accessed 18 January 2015).

[37]Protocol to Prevent, Suppress and Punish Trafficking in Persons, Especially Women, and Supplementing the United Nations Convention against Transnational Organized Crime (adopted 15 November 2000, entered into force 29 September 2003) A/55/383.

[38]Sally Engle Merry, 'Sex Trafficking and Global Governance in the Context of Pacific Mobility' (2011) 15 *Law, Text, Culture* 187, 200.

sometimes they involve 'direct transposition' of the treaty formulations of what should be criminalised. More often they involve 'indirect' transposition of the treaty provisions, which involves the decoding of the essence of the norm to fit it into the national legal system's structures, principles and existing criminal laws.[39] Intrinsic to this system is cooperation under the auspices of international law and mutual recognition of other laws that are the product of that cooperation. It is a substitute for codification at an international level: the suppression conventions provide a normative outline, but so much space is given to national discretion in implementation as to undo any claim to codification. It may be useful to think of it as 'conformal' national law, an idiosyncratic representation of different features or elements of those horizontal obligations in a number of different pieces of national legislation.[40]

The third challenge for the concept of transnational criminal law is posed by those national crimes like murder that occur transnationally (the much loved hypothetical from criminal law textbooks of the murderer shooting across the border) or where the fugitive from some entirely intraterritorial crime flees abroad. In both types of situations the alleged offenders are the subject of international procedural arrangements like extradition or mutual legal assistance but are not the product of any substantive international treaty obligations to criminalise. Are these crimes and the national laws for criminal cooperation part of transnational criminal law? After all, these crimes can be transnational in nature or effect and these procedural laws do provide for transnational cooperation. In my view, however, they are simply national crimes subject to transnational criminal procedures. An alleged murderer who shoots someone across a border and who is then subject to an extradition request based on a bilateral treaty engages only a national criminal prohibition on murder and a transnational criminal procedure for murder rather than transnational criminal law, because the criminalisation of murder is left to national law. Currie subtly overcomes this problem by referring to crimes like this cross-border murder as 'crimes under domestic law which involve, in some way, more than one state' as 'transnational crimes of domestic concern', which he distinguishes from 'transnational crimes of international concern' falling under transnational criminal law.[41] It seems that some distinction is necessary, as the absence of substantive international obligations to criminalise does make a difference because of the absence of a promise by states to include within the scope of their coercive powers certain behaviour not simply to assist that other state procedurally but to denounce it and punish it themselves. Without this element, a prohibition regime does not come into being which suppresses that

[39]Celina Nowak, 'The Internationalization of Polish Criminal Law: How Polish Law Changed under the Influence of Globalization' (2013) 59 *Crime, Law and Social Change* 139, 144.

[40]In the same way that the Mercator Projection is a conformal representation of the Earth's surface.

[41]Currie (n 7) 19–20.

particular crime and creates a system of criminal cooperation for that particular crime. Most civil law systems, for example, consider international criminal law an overarching term which contains within it separate systems of international criminal law relating to extraterritorial jurisdiction, mutual legal assistance, and so forth. Clauss Kress makes this kind of distinction when he defines transnational criminal law as the 'body of international treaties dealing with crimes of a transnational character' as opposed to 'international criminal law as the law governing the prescriptive criminal jurisdiction of States', 'international criminal law as the law of international cooperation in criminal matters', namely extradition law, and 'international criminal law *stricto sensu*' as the law establishing individual criminal responsibility directly under international law.[42]

D. *The relationship between the vertical and transversal components*

Although distinct in source (agreement vs national legislative authority), nature (tortious vs criminal) and in terms of subjects (states vs individuals), the horizontal, international and vertical national components of transnational criminal law can be said to be 'transversal' in combination. Importantly, these components provide the normative boundaries of transnational criminal law, at least when viewed from a traditionalist perspective.

III. Expanding the transnational legal space

Is there more to transnational criminal law than this synthesis of international obligation and national criminal law? National judicial decisions such as *Liangsiriprasert v US*,[43] where the Privy Council held that effects-based jurisdiction could be established over an inchoate conspiracy that had no actual impact on the territory of the state establishing jurisdiction,[44] have long had normative effects elsewhere.[45] This kind of normative transferability appears to be an unstated premise of the rationale of transnational criminal law. But is something more going on in the emergence of decisions originating in transnational legal space that serve as a rapidly developing *lingua franca* of transnational crime suppression? The fourth challenge for transnational criminal law is whether it is composed, at least in part, of what Jessup classed as 'other rules' in some way autonomous from international and national sources of legislative authority.[46]

One of the concerns of transnational legal theory is to break assumptions about the nexus of state and law or the nexus of territory and law, or, to put it more

[42] Kress (n 7) para 6.
[43] [1990] 2 All ER 866.
[44] *Ibid*, 878.
[45] *R v Sansom* [1991] 2 All ER 145.
[46] See Scott (n 12) 873–5.

simply, assumptions that laws are only promulgated by, and apply within, states. Scott argues that transnational law also includes 'transnationalized legal decisionism', which suggests that transnational criminal law may also consist in the result of national and international decisions (diplomatic, administrative, judicial, etc.) made about a particular transnational criminal situation. Sieber talks of the privatisation of law through the development of functional equivalents to law by private actors, and a return to the pre-modern pre-state era.[47] He argues that interaction between similarly situated parties in different states in pursuit of the suppression of the same crimes denationalises law, degrades sovereign territorial control and weakens the hegemony of the state, causing problems of legitimacy.[48]

There is no doubt that norms and rules of transnational criminal law are emerging from unfamiliar sources of authority. There has been a proliferation of transnational law enforcement networks composed of non-state actors which engage in normative activity directed at states and at individuals. The normative actions of intergovernmental organisations like the Financial Action Task Force (FATF) set up by the Organisation for Economic Co-Operation and Development (OECD), for example, often appear detached from any justifying legislative national or international source.[49] Central bankers, securities commissions,[50] transnational corporations,[51] NGOs,[52] transnational intergovernmental law enforcement agencies[53] – all enjoy (within transnational interstices where the state is

[47]Ulrich Sieber, 'Legal Order in a Global World: The Development of a Fragmented System of National, International and Private Norms' (2010) 14 *Max Planck Yearbook of United Nations Law* 1, 17.

[48]*Ibid*, 19.

[49]See Kenneth S Blazejewski, 'The FATF and its Institutional Partners: Improving the Effectiveness and Accountability of Transgovernmental Networks' (2008) 22 *Temple International and Comparative Law Journal* 1.

[50]See, for example, Basel Committee on Banking Supervision (BCSB), International Association of Insurance Supervisors (IAIS) and International Organisation of Securities Commissions (IOSCO), *Initiatives by the BCBS, IAIS and IOSCO to Combat Money Laundering and the Financing of Terrorism* (June 2003), www.bis.org/publ/joint05.pdf.

[51]See, for example, the anti-tobacco smuggling agreements signed benwteen major tobacco products manufacturers such as Philip Morris International and the European Commission Anti-Fraud Office (OLAF), which contain a wealth of normative content and provision for working together on the problem of the illicit trade in tobacco. Commission, 'Cigarette Smuggling' (16 January 2015), http://ec.europa.eu/anti_fraud/investigations/eu-revenue/cigarette_smuggling_en.htm.

[52]Transparency International's work as the UNCAC Coalition Secretariat, a coalition of more than 300 NGOs working to pressure state compliance with the UNCAC, is just one of many examples of NGOs taking normative action. Transparency International, 'Turkey and Western Balkans: National Integrity Systems', www.transparency.org/whatwedo/activity/our_work_on_convention.

[53]The US Drug Enforcement Agency is just one of many significant national agencies operating at a transnational level – see Ethan A Nadelmann, *Cops Across Borders: The Internationalization of US Criminal Law Enforcement* (Pennsylvania State University Press, 1993), 189 ff, recounting the introduction of covert policing into Europe.

almost absent) some measure of *de facto* independence to suggest, interpret and sometimes make rules in their areas of expertise. Does this mean that the neat transversal structure of transnational criminal law is dissolving into multiple nodes of unrecognisable legal authority unjustified by any participatory process?

In attempting to answer this question, we should not ignore the fact that these actors work within the framework of treaty obligations like those in the 1988 Drug Trafficking Convention and the UNTOC. These major multilateral suppression conventions provide a space for governance in which various actors try to hammer out tighter obligations on states, and thus indirectly on individuals, by establishing baseline criminalisation of conduct. Take for example Recommendation 3 of the 2012 FATF Recommendations: 'Countries should criminalize money laundering on the basis of the Vienna Convention and the Palermo Convention.'[54] Further investigation of these recommendations reveals multiple examples of 'soft' (formally non-binding) transnational criminal law. Soft law such as the FATF's recommendations on money laundering is becoming increasingly attractive as a tool for the suppression of transnational crime. Recommendation 4 provides, for example, that 'Countries should consider adopting measures that allow such proceeds or instrumentalities to be confiscated without requiring a criminal conviction (non-conviction based confiscation)', whereas non-conviction based forfeiture is only indirectly suggested in the conventions themselves. For proselytisers of globalisation like the OECD, soft law of this kind directed at states is the way to go. While treaty provisions are coupled with only very weak powers for enforcement of implementation, soft law is faster and cheaper to make than treaty law and is thus more adaptive, and can be combined with fairly coercive name and shame tools to ensure implementation. This recommendation also provides an example of a trend towards provisions of a quasi-penal or regulatory nature such as civil forfeiture within transnational criminal law.

There has been a discernible shift from criminalisation towards faster and cheaper administrative and regulatory penalties that avoid the *ne bis in idem* rule, impose a milder degree of censure – making them less likely to draw public attention, and involve a less formal process and less rigorous standards of proof. Their penal nature obscured, these civil provisions increase coercive public power, while eroding individual rights and executive accountability. The transnational normative space is expanding, but a number of points can be made about this expansion: it is directed at states rather than individuals, and the state must mediate these expressions of authority. Thus transnational criminal law retains its transversal structure, and it is only the participants in the horizontal level that include non-state entities. It is also doubtful whether these developments

[54]FATA, 'The FATF Recommendations: International Standards on Combating Money Laundering and the Financing of Terrorism and Proliferation' (2013), www.fatf-gafi.org/media/fatf/documents/recommendations/pdfs/FATF_Recommendations.pdf, 12.

signal the triumph of the functional ends of transnational criminal law over its national (statist) origins. The activities of criminal justice IGOs, such as the UN Office of Drugs and Crime, reflect states' interests rather than their own interests.[55] Transnational criminal law remains a modernist project: the state may be in retreat elsewhere, but not here. In any event, the opposition is false, as the dominant state interest is in the function of suppressing crime. Transnational criminal law is an example of legality blurring into executive power operating within a juridical space.[56] Both the softening and 'civilising' of transnational criminal law indicate not a diminution of state power, but the growth of state power.

IV. Transnational criminal law as a pluralist legal order

The various different kinds of rules that I have argued fall within transnational criminal law - treaty relations, national criminal laws, and 'other' norm of transnational origin - make for a confusion or normative orders. The fifth challenge for transnational criminal law is whether this massive diffusion of norms from law-making authorities can be called a system. The system is loose, and there is not a uniform reproduction of horizontal obligations in each state party's vertical obligations directed at individuals. One alternative is to ignore issues of systematicity. At a general level, Zumbansen suggests that 'transnational law' is best conceived of as a methodological approach in the sense of providing a lens through which the transformation of legal institutions can be studied in an evolving globalising society.[57] It provides a tool to 'bridge the experience of legal pluralism in the nation state with that of the emerging transnational space',[58] to 'allow us to study such regimes not as entirely detached from national political and legal orders, but as emerging out of and reaching beyond them'.[59] There is much to be said for eschewing the debate about the systematicity of transnational criminal law and simply using transnational criminal law as a lens for revealing what the terms 'international criminal law' and 'crimes of international concern' obscure. It allows us to avoid searching fruitlessly for the supranational connotations associated with the former term and yet reveals something of the nature of the criminal activity and normative space not revealed by either term. Most

[55]This is revealed, for example, in the donation by states of funds for earmarked special projects rather than into the general purpose funding, which allows donor parties to dictate the direction of UNODC activity, rather than leaving the UNODC to plot its own course. United Nations Office on Drugs and Crime, 'Fundraising Strategy 2012–2015' (September 2012), www.unodc.org/documents/donors/Fundraising.Strategyv._final_print_version.5_Sep.2012.pdf.

[56]See Giorgio Agamben, *State of Exception* (Chicago University Press, 2005) 26.

[57]Peer Zumbansen, 'Defining the Space of Transnational Law: Legal Theory, Global Governance and Legal Pluralism' (2012) 21 *Transnational Law & Contemporary Problems* 305, 307.

[58]*Ibid*, 312.

[59]*Ibid*, 330.

prominently, it enables us to focus more clearly on the peculiar social, political, economic and normative contexts in which different transnational crimes emerge and are implemented. It reveals the nature of the social construction of prohibition regimes, and the structured diffusion of legal norms through socialisation processes marked by emulation and persuasion, and sometimes by manipulation and coercion. In plotting this diffusion, scholarship on legal pluralism provides a useful magnifier. Berman notes that

> [t]he pluralist framework captures a dialectical and iterative interplay that we see among normative communities in the international system, an interplay that rigidly territorialist or positivist visions of legal authority do not address.[60]

Legal pluralism is the 'situation in which two or more legal systems coexist in the same social field'.[61] Transnational criminal law can thus be understood as an example of an area or field within transnational legal pluralism that only becomes fully visible if one examines domestic legal systems with a view to identifying their transnational features. Interstate, state and non-state systems for the suppression of crimes overlap and govern the same compound normative situation. Thus, for example, when someone engages in the act of money laundering within a particular state's territorial jurisdiction, her action may engage the extraterritorial jurisdiction of more than one state and be the kind of situation contemplated by the obligations contained in a suppression convention. Each state will proceed using its own selection of jurisdictional principles and its own version of the money laundering offence. (Given the absence of an operative principle of *ne bis in idem* in these situations, she may be proceeded against multiple times.) However, given the provenance of the crime in Article 3(1) of the 1988 Drug Trafficking Convention, that legislation is likely to exhibit marked similarities. A closer examination of the history of law reform in each state with respect to money laundering is likely to reveal a web of links between states leading all the way back to the first formulation of the offence in section 1956 of the US Money Laundering Control Act.[62] Only a thorough investigation of the history of particular norms in particular contexts, and of the dialectical way in which they have been constituted and reconstituted under the influence of other norms, whether by radical reform or by incremental adjustment and reinterpretation,[63] will reveal these extraterritorial influences and make it possible to judge the weight of their impact. The lens of transnational criminal law thus reveals that

---

[60] Paul Schiff Berman, *Global Legal Pluralism: A Jurisprudence of Law Beyond Borders* (Cambridge University Press, 2012) 25.

[61] Sally Engle Merry, 'Legal Pluralism' (1988) 22 *Law and Society Review* 869, 870 (and works cited therein).

[62] Money Laundering Control Act of 1986 (Subtitle H of Title I of the Anti-Drug Abuse Act of 1986), Pub L No 99-570.

[63] Merry (n 61) 889.

alleged criminals are members of multiple normative communities, local, territorial, extraterritorial and non-territorial in nature.[64]

A. *Cui Bono?*

Transnational criminal law can take on an instrumentalist hue. Its cultural and political authority can appear highly questionable, mainly because of scepticism about who benefits from it. The sixth question for transnational criminal law is how it can escape the stain of Western hegemony. Transnational criminal law expresses domestic concerns such as drugs, money laundering and intellectual property. Through the prohibition regimes, states seek the cooperation of other states to overcome the territorial limits on their own coercive power. They try to convince other states that this interest is mutual and that other states should adjust their domestic laws to suppress these threats internally and make it possible to cooperate internationally.[65] But as Nye notes, in international relations, '[c]ontrary to some rhetorical flourishes, interdependence does not mean harmony. Rather, it often means unevenly balanced mutual dependence'.[66] This imbalance arises out of the greater capacity of some states to project their self-interest. Historically, Western states – in particular Great Britain in the nineteenth century and even more spectacularly the United States in the twentieth – have driven the development of transnational criminal law to suit their interests, using their national legislation as models for treaty provisions and thus for law reform in other states.[67] In many instances, transnational criminal law has been a vehicle for denationalising and renationalising criminal law norms. The 'forerunner' legislation for the OECD Anti-Bribery Convention,[68] for example, is the US Foreign Corrupt Practices Act.[69] It is not surprising that this happens, as drafting experts from Western states know their own law well, they work with it, and they usually have neither the time nor the inclination to examine the merits of competing approaches (if they exist). However, this influence often arises out of more than just the prestige, shared legal tradition or accessibility of this forerunner legislation.[70] In many cases it is domestic

[64]Berman (n 60) 11.
[65]Barbara M Yarnold, 'The Doctrinal Basis for the International Criminalization Process' in MC Bassiouni (ed), *International Criminal Law: Crimes* (Transnational, 2nd edn 1999) 131; Erin Creegan, 'A Permanent Hybrid Court for Terrorism' (2011) 26 *American University International Law Review* 237, 246–51.
[66]Joseph S Nye, 'Soft Power' (1990) 80 *Foreign Policy* 153, 158.
[67]See Peter Andreas and Ethan Nadelman, *Policing the Globe: Criminalization and Crime Control in International Relations* (Oxford University Press, 2006) 17, 105.
[68]Convention on Combating Bribery of Foreign Public Officials in Transnational Business Transactions (adopted 17 December 1998, entered into force 5 March 2002) 37 ILM 1.
[69] Foreign Corrupt Practices Act of 1977 (15 US § 78dd-1 ff).
[70]For conditions for transferability, see Alan Watson, 'Legal Change: Sources of Law and Legal Culture' (1982) 131 *University of Pennsylvania Law Review* 1121, 1147.

policy to extra-territorialise this law, and technical assistance is a useful inducement.[71] Delmas-Marty comments:

> Many international conventions providing for the rapprochement of domestic criminal systems in various areas linked to globalisation, such as bribery, money laundering, organised crime and terrorism, have been drafted on the initiative of the United States and generally result in the transplant of the American Model.[72]

At a macro level, developed states give the law and developing states take it.[73] But this framework is fleshed out at meso- and micro-levels, where the bulk of the actual 'technology transfer' of policy, domestic model laws, practical know-how, administrative arrangements and institutions takes place. Consumption of criminal 'goods' takes place in the global 'North' and in the 'South'. Thus, in certain transnational crimes such as drug trafficking, the inhabitants of developed 'consumer states' consume illicit products originating in developing 'producer states'. With respect to other transnational crimes such as the corruption of foreign public officials, individuals and corporate entities in developed 'producer states' produce illicit products to be consumed by the inhabitants of developing 'consumer states'. The process of normative transfer, however, tends to be unidirectional from developed states to developing states. This raises unavoidable questions about the democratic deficit in the development of transnational criminal law. First, the conclusion of the suppression convention itself – usually entirely in executive hands – reifies the global legitimacy of the suppression of that transnational crime through the consent of nominally equal negotiating parties. Second, the fact that renationalisation takes place through democratic institutions that legitimise the adoption of these norms of foreign origin ignores the many inducements for local political elites to agree to the treaty obligations mainly through technical assistance. Third, ignorance, political incapacity to resist diplomatic pressure, and a complete absence of democracy at a national level are features of the process of legislative implementation. Fourth, states have an incentive to join the regime because transnational criminal law strengthens state power through more

[71] A recent example of this is the role the EU's agreements with tobacco companies played as blueprints for much of the content of the Protocol on the Illicit Trade in Tobacco Products (Conference of the Parties to the WHO Framework Convention on Tobacco Control, *Draft Protocol to Eliminate Trade in Tobacco Products*, FCTC COP/5/6, 11 May 2012). See Neil Boister, 'Recent Progress in the Development of a Protocol on the Illicit Trade in Tobacco Products' (2010) 5(1) *Asian Journal of WTO and International Health Law Policy* 53, 59.

[72] Mireille Delmas-Marty, *Ordering Pluralism: A Conceptual Framework for Understanding the Transnational Legal World*, trans Naomi Norberg (Hart Publishing, 2009) 107 citing her own work, *Les Forces imaginantes du droit (I): le relatif et l'universel* (Seuil, 2004).

[73] See Susan Silbey, '1996 Presidential Address: "Let Them Eat Cake": Globalization, Postmodern Colonialism, and the Possibilities of Justice' (1997) 31 *Law and Society Review* 207, 221.

substantive criminal laws and greater procedural powers. The capacity of developed states to resist these donations depends on a range of factors including the lack of domestic legal capacity, the recalcitrance of local political elites, the basic incompatibility of their criminal laws, and the national margin of appreciation permitted by the suppression conventions which differs from regime to regime. The point is that there are conflicting state interests within the system. Thus, for example, while US commentators may feel that they are sufficient to address crimes such as drug trafficking,[74] President Evo Morales of Bolivia considers the drug conventions and international drug strategy to be a failure.[75] Ironically, where states comply with these hegemonic demands, transnational criminal law becomes more systematic, with the hegemon as the centre of authority. However, the negative consequences of compliance for developing states include the potential distortion of their legal systems, which may, for example, possess up-to-date money laundering legislation flanked by dated colonial legislation or no legislation at all for suppressing activities of more pressing domestic concern. Moreover, the impact of using these new laws at the behest of other states may overburden the already creaking criminal justice systems of developing states (Kenya's struggle to cope with Somali pirates comes to mind).[76] Finally, suppression of supply-sided activities in their jurisdiction can have considerable negative impacts without any reciprocal suppression of demand in developing states (the mayhem in Mexico is the obvious current example).[77] A transnational criminal law that remains part of the Western *mission civiliatrice*, enforcing the contingent, parochial morality of its authors, is of questionable effectiveness and doubtful legitimacy.

How can it be ensured that states cooperate against the truly harmful but do not subordinate themselves and become instruments of other states, or of interest groups within those states? One way is to counterpoise international obligation with an authentic margin of national appreciation. For Delmas-Marty, arrangements like transnational criminal law should hover somewhere between world disorder (a disorder of states of equal status and capacity in relationships of horizontal 'coordination' based on reciprocity, which seldom achieves efficiency in this case in suppressing transnational crime) and an externally imposed order (a hegemonic vertical relationship that attempts to 'unify' the systems of subordinate states but

[74]See Stewart M Patrick, 'International Efforts Not Up to Combating Criminals, Shows CFR Interactive' (10 July 2012), www.cfr.org/international-crime/international-efforts-not-up-combating-criminals-shows-cfr-interactive/p28684.

[75]'Opening statement at the 56th Session of the UN Commission on Narcotic Drugs, UN Centre Vienna' (12 March 2012), www.cndblog.org/search/label/plenary%20sessions?updated-max=2013-03-12T14:59:00%2B01:00&max-results=20&start=40&by-date=false.

[76]See James Gathii, 'Kenya's Piracy Prosecutions' (2010) 104 *American Journal of International Law* 416.

[77]It has been characterised as an armed conflict to which international humanitarian law applies. See Craig A Bloom, 'Square Pegs and Round Holes: Mexico, Drugs and International Law' (2012) 34 *Houston Journal of International Law* 345.

which is illegitimate and inefficient because it is resisted by states) in a middle ground that she terms 'ordered pluralism', where states accept a vertical relationship to a set of principles rather than other states – a system of 'harmonisation'.[78] These principles would have to govern the process of substantive criminalisation and procedural cooperation in the suppression of transnational crime. A transnational criminal law governed by such a clear set of principles would be a mosaic of systems which do not necessarily conform to a particular model but are compatible because they are consistent with governing international principles in such a way that their systemic nature is clear.[79] A number of points can be made with regard to the establishment of such a set of principles: first, the development of transnational criminal policy should be governed by an outcomes-based principle which would test each new policy to ensure a measurable equal benefit for all. Second, transnational criminal law should be governed by a precautionary principle, a willingness to question criminalisation as a response to certain practices and to question certain forms of procedural arrangements as a mechanism for effective implementation of criminalisation. Third, the deep grammar of the extant transnational criminal law (principles of material and mental culpability, participation in crime and so forth)[80] has been shaped so fundamentally by dominant common law states that it does not provide an incontestable set of grammatical principles. Establishing a complete common grammar would be difficult, and suggests a move from inter- to supra-state relations,[81] which further hints at universalism and the unlikely transformation of transnational criminal law into international criminal law in a strict sense. Fourth, transnational criminal law requires a more sophisticated regulatory concept than coordination or cooperation in procedural matters that preserves the flexibility needed at a national level to adjust to the international obligations.[82] There are many potential candidates, including functional equivalence, mutual recognition and graded compatibility, to mention but a few.[83] Fifth, legality and the protection of human rights must be recognised as a governing framework. Any system of extraterritorial enactment and enforcement of criminal laws immediately runs into problems of legality in imposing criminal proscriptions on individuals in other states who may have no warning of the criminality of their actions.[84] Although the suppression conventions do make occasional direct reference to human rights,[85] this is usually under domestic

---

[78]Delmas-Marty (n 72) 14, 17 ff.
[79]*Ibid*, 46.
[80]See Boister (n 6) 125.
[81]Delmas-Marty (n 72) 75.
[82]*Ibid*, 159.
[83]*Ibid*, 161, citing JF Coste and M Delmas-Marty, *Le Genre humain* (Seuil, 1998) 135.
[84]Universal Declaration of Human Rights (adopted 10 December 1948) GA Res 2174 (III), UN Doc A/810, 71 (UHDR), Art 11(2).
[85]See for example the United Nations Convention against Corruption (adopted 31 October 2003, entered into force 14 December 2005) 2349 UNTS 41 (UNCAC), Art 30(5), which

law[86] and there is little direct reference to the international human rights instruments.[87] Cooperation against transnational crime frequently takes place in an extraterritorial legal space that enables the avoidance of human rights.

V. Conclusion: bringing transnational criminal law clearly into view

This piece has tried to provide greater conceptual clarity with regard to transnational criminal law. It has argued that it consists of the transversal elements of international treaty and domestic crime (both with transnational elements and without transnational elements but of transnational concern), but it has expanded its scope to include norms originating in the transnational space. It has been careful to exclude parochial national law and procedure. It has avoided the debate about the systematic nature of transnational criminal law, by arguing that transnational criminal law can serve as a lens to reveal the relationships between seemingly unrelated national criminal laws. It is suggested that the use of this lens makes it possible to see the normative cross-pollination between the different regimes within transnational criminal law that put, for example, a law on human trafficking in one country in relationship with such a law in another. It makes it possible to examine the transnational criminal procedures and law enforcement structures that have grown up in the 'transnational legal space' to service these regimes. Finally, it is submitted that transnational criminal law should be seen as a whole – as an agglomeration of all these rules, procedures and practices. If it is not, many of its features will be lost to sight, the programmatic nature of the development of the system will be obscured, and the systemic absence of concern for legality and human rights will be hidden. The ignorance of the principles of legality which control substantive criminal law (certainty, fair warning, fair labelling, the individualisation of guilt and so forth) would be overlooked. Finally, in order to, *inter alia*, escape accusations that transnational criminal law is an exercise in Western hegemony, this piece has backed the call for a set of governing principles for transnational criminal law. Work on a set of principles for transnational criminal law has already begun.[88]

---

speaks of having due regard to the rights of the defence when imposing obligations on states parties to take measures to ensure the presence of the accused at proceedings.

[86]See e.g. Art 16(13) UNTOC.

[87]An exception is the rights of victims under Art 2(b) of the Protocol to Prevent, Suppress and Punish Trafficking in Persons, Especially Women and Children, supplementing the UNTOC.

[88]Professor Sabine Gless is undertaking a project at the University of Basel to identify the general principles underpinning transnational criminal law, which she considers to be, *inter alia*, the principle of legality, the principle of guilt as a prerequisite of criminal liability, fair trial rights and procedural safeguards, an internationalized *ne bis in idem* principle, judicial control and the right to an effective remedy. See http://tcl.ius.unibas.ch/ (accessed 20 January 2015).

Transnational counter-terrorism law: law, power and legitimacy in the 'wars on terror'

Cian C. Murphy[a,b*]

[a]*Academic Co-Director, Center for Transnational Legal Studies, London, UK;*
[b]*Senior Lecturer in Law, The Dickson Poon School of Law, King's College London, UK*

The transnationalisation of counter-terrorism law is a key feature of law after 11 September 2001. The development of a 'transnational counter-terrorism law' has been led by efforts through the UN Security Council, in particular in its resolution 1373 (2001) and 2178 (2014). This paper uses these examples of transnational law to critique the idea of transnational criminal law and to examine the extent to which the transnationalisation of law poses new questions for the legitimacy of the criminal law. The paper argues that efforts to categorise and contextualise the law need to be undertaken alongside critical projects to understand changes in state power and in the use of that power to regulate politics across the globe.

'One must imagine Sisyphus happy'[1]

The rise of terrorism as an object of transnational law has been one of the most remarkable features of twenty-first-century global governance. The commencement of a 'war on terror' in response to the attacks in New York and Washington DC on 11 September 2001 was, at first, (mis)understood as a temporary and extraordinary state. Today, the claim that we are in the middle of 'wars on terror' appears a prescient if somewhat pessimistic prediction.[2] We are in a post-'war on terror' world insofar as the excesses of the immediate reaction to 11 September 2001 have been the subject of extensive examination and, in the case of certain

---

*All websites accessed April 2015.

[1]Albert Camus, *The Myth of Sisyphus* (Penguin Modern Classics, 2013). Sisyphus was punished by the gods by having to push a boulder up a mountain only to have to do it over and over again as it would roll back to the bottom each time. Camus uses the myth to argue that life, whatever its struggles, is better than the alternative.

[2]Philip Bobbitt, *Terror and Consent: The Wars for the Twenty-First Century* (Allen Lane, 2008). On the rise of the group known as Islamic State see Patrick Cockburn, *The Jihadis Return: ISIS and the New Sunni Uprising* (OR Books, 2014).

actions, statements of regret.[3] However, despite acknowledgements that the Bush administration and governments across the world took excessive action in response to the attacks, recent developments suggests that it is the recalibration of counter-terrorism powers, rather than their repeal, that is now the order of the day.

It is remarkable that counter-terrorism, previously amongst the most divisive fields in international law, has come to be emblematic of transnational law in the twenty-first century. It is trite to highlight the contestability of the term 'terrorism', to suggest that use of the term turns not on objective taxonomies or classifications, but rather on judgements about the validity of a particular cause or the morality of particular tactics.[4] It was this subjectivity that made counter-terrorism cooperation so difficult in the past. Each state's desire to preserve its prerogative to recognise one violent uprising as legitimate, and yet denounce another, led the international community to an intellectual and political impasse in its search for a definition.[5] And yet today, despite the contestability of the term and the inherent subjectivity its use entails, many multilateral efforts to combat terrorism rely on a denial of its political nature. It is as if governmental responses to the politics inherent in 'terrorism' and 'counter-terrorism' must deny that politics least contestability make action impossible. The law in this field exists in an 'indistinct fuzzy middle zone' wherein states attempt to evacuate 'any antagonistic sense of politics'.[6] The extent to which this is occurring not just in national law, but also in transnational law, is the subject of a small but growing literature.[7]

The focus in this symposium is on transnational criminal law, and in particular on the efforts by Neil Boister to define that field. This paper's central analytical criticism of that definitional work, at least as it applies to counter-terrorism, is that it misdirects our attention and its focus is at once too narrow and too vague. Boister's treatise on the subject explores, in the context of counter-

[3]Note, for example, President Obama's response to the US Senate Intelligence Committee's 500-page report into the use of torture by the CIA in the aftermath of 11 September 2001. The President said that 'these harsh methods were not only inconsistent with our values as a nation, they did not serve our broader counter-terrorism efforts or our national security interests'. See 'Obama Pledges No Repeat of Harsh U.S. Interrogation Methods' *Reuters* (9 December 2014).

[4]It is not necessary to define terrorism here as the paper's subject is 'counter-terrorism' (i.e. action by states and international organisations to combat what they consider to be terrorism). For a discussion of the political problems in the definition of terrorism, see Noam Chomsky, 'International Terrorism: Image and Reality' in Alexander L George (ed), *Western State Terrorism* (Polity Press, 1991).

[5]Ben Saul, *Defining Terrorism in International Law* (Oxford University Press, 2006).

[6]Matthew Stone, Illan rua Wall and Costas Douzinas, 'Law, Politics, and the Political' in Matthew Stone, Illan rua Wall and Costas Douzinas (eds), *New Critical Legal Thinking: Law and the Political* (Birkbeck Law Press, 2012).

[7]See Cian C Murphy, 'The Dynamics of Transnational Counter-Terrorism Law: Towards a Methodology, Map, and Critique' in Federico Fabbrini and Vicki Jackson (eds), *Constitutionalism across Borders in the Struggle against Terrorism* (Edward Elgar, 2015).

terrorism, 'the criminalization of aviation offences, hostage-taking, attacks on UN personnel, nuclear terrorism, maritime security crimes and offences, terrorist bombing, and terrorist financing'.[8] This law was part of pre-September 11 action by the United Nations. Boister's work also references 'the unusual and precedent-setting criminal-law-making role of the UN Security Council'.[9] However, contemporary transnational counter-terrorism law requires us to move beyond a narrow view of the field towards one that involves civil and administrative law, and so transnational counter-terrorism law must be broader than transnational criminal law, or, in the alternative, transnational criminal law must be broader than Boister's definition allows. A more complete account of the field would capture both the juridical and disciplinary power found in contemporary transnational counter-terrorism law as they manifest across categories of criminal, civil and administrative law.

The paper illustrates its argument using the example of UN Security Council action on 'foreign terrorist fighters' serving Islamic State in Iraq and Syria.[10] This action involves the use of a Chapter VII resolution under the authority of the UN Charter to require states to adopt certain measures against Islamic State. The resolution can be understood as a successor to the earlier UN Security Council Resolution 1373 (2001) and other counter-terrorism resolutions adopted in the decade after 11 September 2001.[11] The former resolution was undertaken by the Security Council to set a legislative agenda across the globe.[12] Boister's work on transnational criminal law misses the extent to which it is this form of action, and not the pre-September 11 conventions, which best characterises contemporary transnational counter-terrorism law. This misstep is, at least in part, a consequence of Boister's commitment to a categorical approach to the field instead of a contextual one. Although a commitment to categorisation to improve legal doctrine can be useful, efforts at categorisation are counterproductive if they obscure reality rather than reveal it, and Boister's definition is closer to the former than the latter.

The paper next moves from analytical considerations about what transnational (criminal or counter-terrorism) law is to an analysis of a key challenge to transnational law – the challenge of legitimacy. Boister raises this challenge but it requires further elaboration. To do so, this paper considers three forms of legitimacy: the formal legitimacy that derives from valid legal authority; the democratic legitimacy that derives from the consent of those subject to legal rules; and the procedural legitimacy that accrues when legal process is respectful of the rights of its subjects. The paper argues that the formal legitimacy of transnational

---

[8]Neil Boister, *An Introduction to Transnational Criminal Law* (Oxford University Press, 2012) 62.

[9]*Ibid.*

[10]UNSC Res 2178 (2014).

[11]UNSC Res 1373 (2001).

[12]José E Alvarez, 'Hegemonic International Law Revisited' (2003) 97 *American Journal of International Law* 873.

counter-terrorism law is contestable and that the democratic and procedural legitimacy of such law is deeply problematic. Overall, the effect may be to shrink the space for political action within and across states, through exercises of juridical and disciplinary power that deny the politics inherent in counter-terrorism law.

In the final section, the paper draws attention to the limits of transnational counter-terrorism law as a field of study and reflects on the need for work that seeks to categorise the law, engage in theoretical reflection, and test hypotheses using empirical legal methods. There is a Sisyphean task here for transnational counter-terrorism lawyers, but one that is necessary if the realities of law under globalisation are to be better understood. To begin, it is necessary to consider the relationship between terrorism and the (criminal) law.

1. Terrorism and (criminal) law

In some states, terrorism has long been an object of criminal law.[13] The consequences of the specific criminalisation of terrorism, rather than reliance on offences such as damage to property, kidnapping, false imprisonment and murder, are significant. First, the criminal law represents the state's most prohibitive action against social deviance. To criminalise behaviour is to subject it to the strongest disapproval and to impose upon perpetrators severe infringements of their liberty, often through incarceration, as punishment. The criminal justice system has safeguards for persons under suspicion and those subject to prosecution, so as to ensure that any infringements of liberty are not done lightly – or in error. Although particular criminal law rules and procedures differ across legal systems, there is, in Europe for example, a common standard deriving from the European Convention on Human Rights.[14] The standard of protection may be eroded when the state takes extraordinary action to combat terrorism. Thus, insofar as the operation of the criminal justice system entails a balance between the state's interest in prosecution and punishment and the defendant's right to due process, the invocation of terrorism tends to shift that balance, often rather significantly, in favour of the state.[15]

Second, given the strong popular and political will to act against terrorism, the designation of behaviour as such may empower the state over individuals and the population as a whole. The designation of certain behaviour as terrorism may give rise to extraordinary preventative powers for the state if there is insufficient (admissible) evidence to secure the conviction of those under suspicion. As a

[13]For example, in the UK, see Clive Walker, *Terrorism and the Law* (Oxford University Press, 2011).
[14]Sarah Summers, *Fair Trials: The European Criminal Procedural Tradition and the European Court of Human Rights* (Hart Publishing, 2007).
[15]See Lucia Zedner, 'Securing Liberty in the Face of Terror: Reflections from Criminal Justice' (2005) 32(4) *Journal of Law and Society* 507.

result there has been a rise in the use of administrative law measures to address terrorism, as a form of socio-political deviance, alongside the rise in the use of administrative law measures against deviance in general. The impact of the 11 September 2001 attacks was therefore to prompt governmental shifts that 'complement already existing shifts in criminal justice policies and ideologies brought about by adjusting to globalisation, economic neo-liberalism and the shift away from the post-war liberal welfare settlement'.[16] These trends suggest a relationship between the globalisation of governance and its bureaucratisation – a matter to which this paper will return.

In more particular terms, the response to terrorism exemplifies trends in criminal law and criminal justice during the latter half of the twentieth century. This paradigm of counter-terrorism is 'preventative' or even 'pre-emptive' in nature. Under a pre-emptive paradigm of counter-terrorism, the state seeks to take action not on the basis of evidence of actual deviance, but on the basis of suspicion of possible deviance, and the action tends not to result in prosecution and punishment, but rather in incapacitation of those under suspicion.[17] This approach is seen in Europe's counter-terrorism law and policy.[18] A consequence of a pre-emptive approach, and the shift in criminal law and criminal justice that it signifies, is that much counter-terrorism law is not criminal law, or at least not in the traditional sense of the term.

It is illustrative to examine UK action against foreign nationals under suspicion of involvement in terrorism, but whose extradition would be unlawful under human rights law. The state first sought to incarcerate such foreign nationals without trial, then to use 'control orders', and now 'terrorism prevention and investigation measures', to restrict their personal liberty.[19] A further example is that it is now possible, through a combination of national, European and international law, to impose restrictive measures on individuals under suspicion of

[16]Bernadette McSherry, Alan Norrie and Simon Bronitt, 'Regulating Deviance: The Redirection of Criminalisation and the Futures of Criminal Law' in Bernadette McSherry, Alan Norrie and Simon Bronitt (eds), *Regulating Deviance: The Redirection of Criminalisation and the Futures of Criminal Law* (Hart Publishing, 2008).
[17]Cian C Murphy, *EU Counter-Terrorism Law: Pre-emption and the Rule of Law* (Hart Publishing, 2012) 7–13.
[18]See Murphy, *ibid*, for a case study using the European Union. See further M de Goede, 'The Politics of Preemption and the War on Terror in Europe' (2008) 14 *European Journal of International Relations* 161. For an analysis of pre-emption in US counter-terrorism after September 11, see David Cole and Jules Lobel, *Less Safe, Less Free: Why America is Losing the War on Terror* (The New Press, 2009).
[19]The relevant law is found in Part IV of the Anti-Terrorism, Crime and Security Act 2001, in the Prevention of Terrorism Act 2005 (following *A v Secretary of State for the Home Department* [2004] UKHL 56), and in the Terrorism Prevention and Investigation Measures Act 2011. For a discussion see Adrian Hunt, 'From Control Orders to TPIMs: Variations on a Number of Themes in British Legal Responses to Terrorism' (2014) 62(3) *Crime, Law and Social Change* 289.

financing terrorism. The consequences of such measures are severe – individuals are subject to indefinite freezing of their assets and organisations effectively shut down.[20]

The rights of due process, the burden of proof, and other procedural rules in the operation of these administrative systems tend to offer inferior protection to that found in criminal justice systems. One key example here is the erosion of due process rights owing to the use of secret evidence in court proceedings.[21] Despite much evidence that such action is contrary to rule of law principles, it remains, nevertheless, government by law, or at least 'government with law'.[22] Thus, legal power, in both juridical form (law that prohibits wrong-doing) and disciplinary form (law that constrains wrong-doing through incapacitation) work together as tools of governmental action without the safeguards we associate with classic legality.[23]

The necessary conclusion is that counter-terrorism law is criminal law insofar as it sets out certain offences in criminal law. It might also be understood as such, albeit through a broader use of the term, insofar as it entails powers for the institutions and agencies of the state responsible for criminal justice. However, counter-terrorism law is also much more. To understand, in meaningful terms, the 'constitution of counter-terrorism law',[24] it is necessary to see it as a field of law that transcends classic divides between criminal and civil law, between criminal and administrative measures, and even between ordinary and constitutional law. If this is correct at national and European levels, then the question for this paper is whether it is also correct when we consider transnational criminal law. The question is in two parts. First, we might ask whether the same shifts in criminal law and criminal justice are occurring in transnational law. Second, if the same shifts are occurring, we might consider whether they are having the same detrimental effect on the rule of law at a transnational level. This paper will answer the first part of the question, but will only begin to explore the second part, as a more complete answer is not possible here.[25]

---

[20]See the contributions to Iain Cameron (ed), *EU Sanctions: Law and Policy Issues Concerning Restrictive Measures* (Intersentia, 2013).

[21]Cian C Murphy, 'Counter-Terrorism and the Culture of Legality: The Case of Special Advocates' (2013) *King's Law Journal* 19.

[22]Ben Bowling and James Sheptycki, 'Global policing and transnational rule with law', this volume.

[23]For an early discussion of Foucault's ideas on juridical and disciplinary power in legal form see Victor Tadros, 'Between Governance and Discipline: The Law and Michel Foucault' (1998) 18 *Oxford Journal of Legal Studies* 75.

[24]Cian C Murphy, 'The Constitution of EU Counter-Terrorism Law' (*EJIL: Talk!*, 16 July 2012), http://www.ejiltalk.org/the-constitution-of-eu-counter-terrorism-law/.

[25]I will come closer to a more complete answer in Cian C Murphy, *Control Beyond the State: Transnational Counter-Terrorism Law* (Hart Publishing, forthcoming 2016).

Two caveats are appropriate before the focus shifts to transnational law. First, the claims made about developments in criminal law and criminal justice draw heavily from Anglo-American criminology.[26] Insofar as transnational counter-terrorism law is not just about the law and policy of the UK and US but also of other states, it is reasonable to ask whether these claims are generalisable. The contention here is that it is possible to generalise, at least in the field of counter-terrorism law, because of the significant influence of both the UK and the US on counter-terrorism policy across the globe before and after the 11 September 2001 attacks. The UK has long been an exporter of policy in this field owing to its history of legislation against terrorism as a result of conflicts in Northern Ireland and elsewhere.[27] The role of the US as an agenda-setter in counter-terrorism law after the 11 September attacks is also well established.[28] Thus, it would not be surprising to find trends in Anglo-American criminal justice practices emerging in transnational law against terrorism.

Second, it is appropriate to ask whether the Euro-centric nature of the second example above, drawing from EU counter-terrorism law, is appropriate. There is a risk that the analysis falls into a not uncommon trap in literature on transnational law: to see the EU as the pre-eminent transnational legal order and therefore to argue that claims as to transnationalisation of law are generalisable from the European to the global levels of governance.[29] The claim here is not, therefore, that Europe's experience of counter-terrorism cooperation is determinative of how transnational counter-terrorism law will develop in the wider world, but rather that there are lessons from the European experience from which any advocate of transnational law would do well to learn.

2. Terrorism and transnational (criminal) law

Transnational law, as a field, remains deeply controversial, insofar as it challenges the dominance of existing philosophies of law, such as Western analytical jurisprudence, without necessarily offering a coherent alternative to that intellectual tradition. The contribution of law and legal studies to globalisation, and the effect of globalisation on law and legal studies, has taken longer to be subject to significant

[26]See Richard V Ericson and Kevin D Haggerty, *Policing the Risk Society* (Oxford University Press, 1997); Malcolm M Feeley and Jonathan Simon, 'The New Penology: Notes on the Emerging Strategy of Corrections and Its Implications' [1992] *Criminology* 499.
[27]Kent Roach, 'The Post-9/11 Migration of Britain's Terrorism Act 2000' in Sujit Choudhry (ed), *The Migration of Constitutional Ideas* (Cambridge University Press, 2007).
[28]See in general Kent Roach, *The 9/11 Effect: Comparative Counter-Terrorism* (Cambridge University Press, 2011); see also Kim L Scheppele, 'The Migration of Anti-Constitutional Ideas: The Post-9/11 Globalisation of Public Law and the International State of Emergency' in Choudhry (n 27).
[29]See in general David D Caron and Cian C Murphy, (eds), *Transnational Law* (Edward Elgar, forthcoming 2016).

exploration than has been the case in disciplines such as economics or international relations.[30] However, over the past decade, there has been a proliferation of literature that seeks to make up the ground lost to other disciplines. Key fields in which law's role in and response to globalisation have been the subject of examination include human rights law, international refugee law, environmental law and international economic law, to name but a few of the most prominent examples.[31]

In contrast, scholars of national criminal law, at least in common law legal systems, have been slow to address the transnationalisation of their field.[32] Of course some of the post-World War II development of international law related to crime – the crimes against humanity of the Nazi regime across Europe for example. Nevertheless, scholarship and practice in this field of international criminal law was, and remains, set apart from the more mundane field of national criminal law.[33] Until Boister's 'Transnational Criminal Law?'[34] there was little in between these distinct realms – in stark contrast to the discipline of criminology which was already coming to grips with globalisation.[35] This may in part be because of the close associations between the state and the criminal law and the resultant conceptual challenge that criminal law 'beyond the state' appears to pose.[36] If to add 'transnational' to the term 'law' is 'like adding a question mark' then there are few, if any, fields in which this is more true than criminal law and criminal justice.[37] This field represents 'the means by which the state, in collaboration with many other social institutions, seeks to make civil society

[30]For two early contributions on law see William Twining, *Globalisation and Legal Theory* (Cambridge University Press, 2000), and Michael Likosky, *Transnational Legal Processes: Globalisation and Power Disparities* (Butterworths, 2002).

[31]Peer Zumbansen, 'Transnational Law, Evolving' in J Smits (ed), *Elgar Encyclopedia of Comparative Law* (Edward Elgar, 2nd edn 2012).

[32]To evidence an absence is difficult – but take a crude illustration: a search on 30 January 2015 found that, in the *Criminal Law Review*, between 1986 and 2014, there were only 28 articles with a mention of the term 'transnational' and only 16 articles with a mention of the term 'globalisation'. The *Journal of Criminal Law*, between 2004 and 2014, returns 8 articles with a mention of 'transnational' and 8 articles with a mention of 'globalisation'. Of course, national criminal lawyers writing about transnational law and globalisation may well publish elsewhere, but at the very least we can say is that national journals of criminal law are not paying it much attention.

[33]Kevin Jon Heller, *The Nuremburg Military Tribunals and the Origins of International Criminal Law* (Oxford University Press, 2011).

[34]Neil Boister, '"Transnational Criminal Law"?' (2003) 14(5) *European Journal of International Law* 953.

[35]For an early contribution, see Malcolm Anderson, *Policing the World: Interpol and the Politics of International Police Co-operation* (Clarendon Press, 1989). See also the discussion of the literature in Bowling and Sheptycki's contribution to this symposium.

[36]As readers of this journal will know, law 'beyond the state' is the classic description of transnational law. See also Philip C Jessup, *Transnational Law* (Yale University Press, 1956).

[37]On the addition of the question mark see Roger Cotterrell, 'What is Transnational Law?' (2012) 37 *Law and Social Inquiry* 500.

sustainable'.[38] And yet, even in this field, the presumption of the state's pre-eminence has long been open to question.[39]

The idea of transnational law, law 'across' or 'beyond' states, necessarily involves a challenge to the pre-eminence of the state, and of state law, in the analytical philosophy of law that dominates Western jurisprudence.[40] The focus on state law – at national and international levels – provides clear categories of analysis in which scholars may explore the development of legal doctrine. These categories have largely been dependent on the state's dominance (if not monopoly) over the making of law. One possible response to the challenge which now arises, as the state's dominance becomes more uncertain, is to replace or to complement existing categories of analysis, such as state law and international law, with new ones (to categorise). An alternative response to the challenge is to argue that transnational law is a means to understand law in a way that is not bound by such categories (to contextualise).[41] Thus, a tension exists in debates about transnational law between those who seek to categorise and those who seek to contextualise. To a certain extent this is a continuation of the debate between methodologies of legal studies such as analytical jurisprudence and doctrinal legal studies on the one hand, and socio-legal studies, law and economics and critical legal studies on the other.

Thus far, perhaps in part because of the strong influence of economics, political economy and sociology in more general efforts to explain globalisation, those working to develop contextual analyses of law in contemporary global society appear to have the upper hand. However, there is a risk that amidst debates on 'post-national law' and 'pluralist structures' the intrinsic value of law, and of legal institutions, is lost.[42] It is unsurprising then that recent years have seen some reaffirmation of that value.[43] What is useful, therefore, is to situate legal studies

[38]Lucia Zedner, *Criminal Justice* (Clarendon, 2004) 2.

[39]David Garland, 'The Limits of the Sovereign State: Strategies of Crime Control' (1996) 36 *British Journal of Criminology* 445.

[40]Joseph Raz, 'Why the State?', King's College London Law School Research Paper No 2014-38. On the problems of 'Western Jurisprudence', see Tim Murphy, *Western Jurisprudence* (Round Hall, 2004).

[41]Note, for example, Halliday and Shaffer's work on transnational legal ordering: Terence C Halliday and Gregory Shaffer (eds), *Transnational Legal Orders* (Cambridge University Press, 2015); see also Gregory Shaffer (ed), *Transnational Legal Ordering and State Change* (Cambridge University Press, 2014); Gralf-Peter Calliess and Peer Zumbansen, *Rough Consensus and Running Code: A Theory of Transnational Private Law* (Hart Publishing, 2010).

[42]See, for example, the discussion in Gregory Shaffer, 'A Transnational Take on Krisch's Pluralist Postnational Law' (2012) 23(2) *European Journal of International Law* 565, which reviews Nico Krisch, *Beyond Constitutionalism: The Pluralist Structure of Postnational Law* (Oxford University Press, 2010).

[43]See Thomas Schultz, *Transnational Legality: Stateless Law and International Arbitration* (Oxford University Press, 2014); A Harel, *Why Law Matters* (Oxford University Press, 2014); see also Raz (n 40).

so as to benefit from the perspective of other disciplines without losing sight of 'why law matters', not just as a human institution, but also as a field of study.

It is against this backdrop that it is necessary to examine the work of Neil Boister to define transnational criminal law. In his early work Boister sought to distinguish between crimes against the international community (international criminal law) and crimes that the international community cooperate to suppress (transnational criminal law). This transnational criminal law has, he claims, two aims: the suppression of transnational crime; and the diffusion of criminal offences through the medium of international law.[44] It consists of 'horizontal treaty obligations between states' and 'the vertical application of criminal law by those states to individuals in order to meet their treaty obligations'.[45] The core of the concept is therefore a rather formalistic one with reliance on both a treaty element and national criminal law to constitute the field.

Boister offers a number of arguments in favour of his approach. The first argument is the need to focus the attention of scholars on the phenomenon he identifies. He claims this law is 'the most significant existing mechanism for the globalisation of substantive criminal norms', that there has been neglect of the study by the existing scholarship (as of 2003), and that any conflation of this concept with international criminal law is incorrect.[46] Whether as a result of Boister's call for attention, or independent of it, there has indeed been a surge of interest in transnational criminal law over the past decade.[47] However, at least in the field of transnational counter-terrorism law, Boister's work misdirects our attention and its focus is at once too narrow and – despite his intentions – too vague.

Terrorism is an apt example. The most significant action against terrorism by the international community in the decade after 11 September 2001 did not come through suppression treaties but rather through UN Security Council resolutions. As a result it is difficult to comprehend why Boister's chapter on terrorism gives so much space to the earlier treaties and so little to Security Council resolutions such as 1373. When Boister does give attention to the role of soft law, in his treatise's chapter on anti-money laundering and counter-terrorist finance, the analysis places too great an emphasis on the phenomenon's novelty (the Financial Action Task Force, the principal site of rule making in this field, pre-dates his first effort at definition of transnational criminal law). The analysis is also, strangely, somewhat isolated – kept somewhat apart from the remainder of his work to define transnational criminal law. The result is the misdirection of our attention and the persistence of a definition that is too narrow and categorical in its formalistic conception of transnational criminal law.

---

[44] Neil Boister, 'Further reflections on the concept of transnational criminal law', this volume.

[45] Boister (n 8) 13.

[46] Boister (n 34) 956.

[47] This symposium itself is evidence of this claim, as too is the literature Boister and others reference herein.

The second argument Boister presents is the need for doctrinal coherence in transnational criminal law. It is necessary, he claims, 'to find a doctrinal match for … "transnational crime"'.[48] The latter term is 'a criminological rather than a juridical term'[49] and its corollary, transnational criminal law, refers to 'indirect suppression by international law through domestic penal law of criminal activities that have actual or potential trans-boundary effects'.[50] It is worthwhile to strive for doctrinal coherence. This form of legal research can improve knowledge of, and even the operation of, legal principles and rules by clearing up ambiguities and by resolving apparent conflicts between rules. However, despite its narrowness, Boister's approach may be too vague in its focus to garner these benefits of legal doctrine and the field itself may render it impossible to do so.

In terms of sources of transnational criminal law, Boister's definition focuses on national implementation of suppression conventions, but he also admits that transnational criminal law may be established by custom, and that its normative content may emerge, as set out above, from soft law.[51] The quest for doctrinal coherence may be lost from the outset if the system of rules is not the subject of clear definition, and in this respect Boister's conception of transnational criminal law remains too vague. It is as if Boister's awareness of the broader normative context causes him to take it into account but his decision to do so, and manner of doing so, risks losing the benefits of a narrow categorical approach.

These benefits may not be possible even with a more rigorous application of a categorical approach. Transnational criminal law, understood as a field of legal doctrine, would require the progressive elaboration and clarification of principles and rules of law. This is difficult, if not entirely impossible, when the rules in question depend on transposition into national law by legislatures and subsequent interpretation and application by courts. As long as transnational criminal law involves national criminal justice systems in a non-hierarchical relationship with each other, and as long as there is no ultimate arbiter of the meaning of principles and rules of transnational criminal law, then the law cannot achieve the systematicity necessary for a coherent legal doctrine to emerge.[52]

Transnational counter-terrorism law does accord with the two aims Boister identifies for transnational criminal law. It entails the suppression of crime (terrorism) that is often, if not necessarily, transnational. It also involves the diffusion of

---

48 Boister (n 34) 953.
49 *Ibid,* 954.
50 *Ibid,* 955.
51 Boister (n 34) 963.
52 This criticism is not blind to claims, often from European human rights lawyers or 'global constitutionalism' scholars, that there is a slow convergence of legal rules around the world. See, for example, the work of Krisch (n 42). However, the emergence of global legal norms is far less certain than these accounts allow, and the persistence, even in Europe, of rather different systems of criminal justice procedure does not give cause for optimism on this front.

certain criminal offences through international law into the law of all states. Thus, counter-terrorism law may be understood as a field of 'transnational criminal law'. However, to understand transnational counter-terrorism law only in relation to criminal offences set out in the suppression treaties and subject to transposition and enforcement in national law would miss too much that is salient. In terms of legal power, Boister captures only the law's juridical power, and not its disciplinary effects.

In particular, it is not clear that such a formalistic approach is appropriate to capture the civil and administrative law measures, measures that Boister refers to as 'quasi-criminalisation', that constitute much transnational counter-terrorism law. If transnational criminal law against terrorism refers, in a narrow sense, to the introduction of criminal offences into national law so as to give effect to treaties and resolutions, then the broader measures, involving quasi-criminalisation, should, strictly speaking, be excluded. This is wrong-headed and Boister does include references to them – albeit in too cursory a manner. On the other hand, if the quasi-criminalisation measures fall within the scope of transnational criminal law, then that term must have a broader meaning than that first set out in Boister's early work. To understand transnational counter-terrorism law it is necessary to consider different manifestations of legal power, in juridical and disciplinary forms and across categories such as criminal, civil, and administrative law.

The re-examination by Boister of his concept of transnational criminal law in this symposium suggests that he is aware of the challenges to the seemingly straightforward systematicity of transnational criminal law in his earlier work. The discussion, in particular, of the 'transnational legal space' and transnational criminal law as 'a plural legal order' appears to acknowledge, and even to concede, that the categorisation in his earlier work has its limits. It may well be that he is shifting his efforts from categorisation to contextualisation. This shift would have its merits, but would mark a dramatic departure from his initial approach. The goals of categorisation and contextualisation are different, just as the goals of analytical jurisprudence and socio-legal studies are different. One cannot purport to do one while doing the other – or achieve the goals of one through the methods of the other. The lack of clarity in Boister's approach undermines its ability to achieve the goals of both categorisation and contextualisation.

It is possible to draw out the need for clarity through an example of the most recent UN action in this field. Until the adoption of UN Security Council Resolution 2178 in late 2014, it was UN Security Council Resolution 1373 that was the principal example of transnational counter-terrorism law. An earlier resolution, 1368, adopted on 12 September 2001, was the Security Council's condemnation of the 11 September attacks, but it was Resolution 1373 that saw the Council take legislative action.[53] In total, from the adoption of Resolution 1368 to the adoption

[53]PC Szasz, 'The Security Council Starts Legislating' (2002) 96(4) *American Journal of International Law* 901.

of Resolution 2178, the Security Council agreed 34 resolutions whose principal concern was terrorism.[54] This UN action involves the combination of the most forceful mechanism for the exercise of juridical power in international law (UN Chapter VII resolutions) with perhaps the most powerful apparatus for the exercise of disciplinary power (the work of the Counter-Terrorism Committee).[55] Today's global governance in the field of counter-terrorism therefore involves quite a lot of transnational criminal law and criminal justice with none of the clarity or coherence that Boister sought for the field.

3. Resolution 2178 as transnational counter-terrorism law

The nature and potential breadth of transnational counter-terrorism law are demonstrable through the example of the recent UN Security Council resolution. The resolution is chosen for examination because it demonstrates that even after the recalibration of counter-terrorism law in the post-'war on terror' world there remains political willingness to use UN Charter powers with hegemonic effect to adopt new law in this field. That willingness is made clear when we consider that Resolution 2178 was adopted on 24 September 2014 in a meeting under the chairmanship of US President Barack Obama. This was only the sixth occasion on which the UN Security Council had met at the Head of State level.[56] The resolution calls for states to take a broad range of action against individuals known as 'foreign terrorist fighters'. The idea of the 'foreign terrorist fighter' has arisen owing to the conflict in Iraq and Syria. In Iraq, control of large parts of the northern state territory has been lost to Islamic State, while in Northern Syria, it is Islamic State, rather than the Assad government or the rebels fighting against it, which controls much of the territory. Journalist reports also suggest an Islamic State presence in Egypt and the organisation may pose an even greater threat to international peace and security in the region that Al-Qaeda did at the time of the 11 September 2001 attacks.[57]

Nevertheless, the adoption of Resolution 2178, with its broad obligations on states, is a remarkable response from the UN Security Council. It is too close to

[54] In chronological order: 1368 (2001), 1373 (2001), 1377 (2001), 1438 (2002), 1440 (2002), 1450 (2002), 1452 (2002), 1455 (2003), 1456 (2003), 1465 (2003), 1516 (2003), 1526 (2004), 1530 (2004), 1535 (2004), 1566 (2004), 1611 (2005), 1617 (2005), 1618 (2005), 1735 (2006), 1787 (2007), 1805 (2008), 1822 (2008), 1904 (2009), 1963 (2010), 1988 (2011), 1989 (2011), 2082 (2012), 2083 (2012), 2129 (2013), 2133 (2014), 2160 (2014), 2161 (2014), 2170 (2014), 2178 (2014).

[55] See I Roele, 'Disciplinary Power in the UN Counter-Terrorism Committee' (2014) 19(1) *Journal of Conflict and Security Law* 49.

[56] Tanya Somanader, 'President Obama Chairs the UN Security Council Meeting on Foreign Terrorist Fighters' (24 September 2014), https://www.whitehouse.gov/blog/2014/09/24/president-obama-chairs-un-security-council-meeting-foreign-terrorist-fighters.

[57] Khalil al-Anani, 'ISIS Enters Egypt: How Washington Must Respond' *Foreign Affairs* (4 December 2014).

the resolution's agreement and too early in its implementation to make strong claims about its substantive impact on counter-terrorism law and policy across the globe. It is, however, notable that the resolution does not define 'foreign terrorist fighter' – thus making the term facilitative of enforcement action without giving its subjects the protection of precise legal categories. The exposition here sets out the transnational counter-terrorism law found in the resolution: including criminal law measures, civil and administrative law measures, and measures on criminal justice cooperation. The aim is to illustrate the breadth of transnational counter-terrorism law so as to demonstrate the limitations of an approach that focuses only on the use of international and national law to set out criminal offences in a transnational exercise of juridical power.

The criminal law in the resolution is rather easy to spot. Although the resolution itself does not, it appears, directly criminalise acts of terrorism, it does require states to do so.[58] The clearest example is found in Article 6. That Article 'decides that all States shall ensure that their domestic laws and regulations establish serious criminal offenses sufficient to provide the ability to prosecute and to penalise in a manner duly reflecting the seriousness of the offence … ' before going on to set out a range of actions. The range of actions is very broad and includes travel to perpetrate, plan or prepare 'terrorist acts', providing or receiving training for such a purpose, funding, or facilitating the funding of, actions for such a purpose, and organising the travel of others for such a purpose. The use of criminal law is necessary to implement Article 6, but its use is also possible in respect of several other articles. Thus, Article 5 'decides that Member States shall … prevent and suppress' a range of activities in relation to terrorist acts. This language of prevention and suppression may provide the basis for criminalisation in national law. Nevertheless, it may also be subject to implementation through civil and administrative law. The ambiguity may be necessary to make it possible for states with very different systems of criminal law and criminal justice to agree on measures. However, it undermines the coherence of transnational criminal law as a field of legal doctrine.

The resolution does not restrict itself to criminal law. There is also much civil and administrative law in its 27 articles. These provisions relate to travel to and from theatres of war in the Middle East, the provision of training and support to actual or potential 'foreign fighters', and incitement or radicalisation of others to engage in terrorism. For example, Article 2 'reaffirms that all States shall prevent the movement of terrorists or terrorist groups by effective border controls'. The article also

[58]Anne Peters, 'Security Council Resolution 2178 (2014): The "Foreign Terrorist Fighter" as an International Legal Person Part I' (*EJIL: Talk!*, 20 November 2014), www.ejiltalk.org/security-council-resolution-2178-2014-the-foreign-terrorist-fighter-as-an-international-legal-person-part-i/; 'Security Council Resolution 2178 (2014): The "Foreign Terrorist Fighter" as an International Legal Person Part II' (*EJIL: Talk!*, 21 November 2014), www.ejiltalk.org/security-council-resolution-2178-2014-the-foreign-terrorist-fighter-as-an-international-legal-person-part-ii/.

'encourages Member States to employ evidence-based traveller risk assessment and screening procedures'. In a similar vein, Article 8 'decides that Member States shall prevent the entry into or transit through their territories' of individuals where there are 'reasonable grounds to believe' that he or she seeks to engage in a range of activities in relation to terrorist acts. Article 4 calls upon states to prevent

> the radicalization to terrorism and recruitment of foreign terrorist fighters, including children, preventing foreign terrorist fighters from crossing their borders, disrupting and preventing financial support to foreign terrorist fighters, and developing and implementing prosecution, rehabilitation and reintegration strategies for returning foreign terrorist fighters.

This is a broad and onerous obligation that raises the possibility of the regulation of political speech in a way that is impossible in the US (in constitutional terms) but may be possible in Europe. Thus, the prospect of universities in the UK serving as sites of governance, with obligations to report on radical students, is once more a feature of public debate in that jurisdiction.[59] Implementation of these provisions may involve the enactment of criminal law offences but is more likely to involve systems of surveillance and administrative reporting that represent disciplinary rather than juridical power.

The third type of measure found in the resolution relates to cooperation between law enforcement authorities in different states. This increase in cooperation takes several forms, including the exchange of data, operational cooperation, and capacity building through the provision of technical assistance. On data exchange, Article 3 calls for states to 'intensify and accelerate the exchange of operational information regarding actions or movements of terrorists or terrorist networks'. In particular, in connection with travel surveillance, the resolution calls for the collection of traveller data and its exchange with other states.[60] States are also to exchange information to enable the identification of 'foreign terrorist fighters'.[61] There are references to operational cooperation found throughout the resolution, including on counter-radicalisation,[62] in criminal investigations on terrorist financing – including evidence exchange,[63] and through cooperation with Interpol to 'monitor and prevent' the transit of foreign terrorist fighters.[64] Article 17 declares that states should cooperate in efforts to prevent the exploitation of technology for the incitement of terrorism. Article 18 calls upon states to 'cooperate and

[59]Paul Peachy, 'Government Wins Power to Intervene in Schools and Colleges to Prevent Radicalisation' *The Independent* (24 November 2014), www.independent.co.uk/news/uk/politics/government-wins-power-to-intervene-in-schools-and-colleges-to-prevent-radicalisation-9879753.html.

[60]UN Security Council Resolution 2178 (24 September 2014), Art 9.

[61]*Ibid*, Art 11

[62]*Ibid*, Art 4.

[63]*Ibid*, Art 12.

[64]*Ibid*, Art 13.

consistently support each other's efforts to counter violent extremism'. Article 14 refers to capacity building on the prevention of travel by foreign terrorist fighters, and Article 24 requests that the Counter-Terrorism Committee assess states' capacities to implement Security Council resolutions, and to facilitate technical assistance. These references to 'technical assistance', 'capacity building' and implementation in general reveal the bureaucracy that is key to contemporary global efforts to counter terrorism and the disciplinary power it entails.[65]

Even this brief overview of the resolution makes clear that the Security Council does not just legislate, it also acts as a key site for the diffusion of transnational counter-terrorism law around the world. The promotion of capacity building through technical assistance is not an exercise in juridical power (although it can lead to exercises of juridical power when states enact new criminal offences on the basis of technical assistance) but it is an exercise in disciplinary power. These two forms of power together ensure the diffusion of norms into legal systems across the globe. In one sense this is to the law's benefit. It may promote the convergence of rules across different legal systems and might, as a result, benefit the development of legal doctrine. If this were the case then problems of coherence in legal doctrine would, however, be overtaken by problems of legitimacy, as the discussion below explores.

The use of technical assistance to build capacity can be deeply problematic because it relies on the depoliticisation of the law in a field that is intrinsically political.[66] Furthermore, there is an imbalance of power between more powerful states and less powerful states. States that are more powerful, with greater capacity, may be donors of technical assistance, or may at the very least not require technical assistance from other powerful states, and may therefore develop measures to implement their international obligations consistent with their national interests and their domestic legal culture. States that are less powerful are likely to have less capacity and will be recipients of technical assistance – such states may adopt counter-terrorism law that accords with the Counter-Terrorism Committee's priorities, or with a donor state's, but which is out of step with their national interests and legal culture. The political contestability of measures becomes subordinate to the state's need to have 'capacity' to act and ensure that there is 'technical' compliance with international law. The seemingly neutral language of bureaucracy masks the exercise of legal power with hegemonic effect.

The adoption of Resolution 2178 is therefore further evidence of the fundamental shift in international law and politics after 11 September 2001. Although the adoption of Resolution 1373 could, in part, be attributable to the collective shock of that day, the adoption of Resolution 2178 comes at a time when there

[65]Isobel Roele, 'Disciplinary Power in the UN Counter-Terrorism Committee' (2014) 19(1) *Journal of Conflict and Security Law* 49. Note also H Hegemann, *International Counter-terrorism Bureaucracies in the United Nations and the European Union* (Nomos, 2014).
[66]*Ibid, passim.*

is a reasonable expectation of a more sober response to terrorism. There has been some recalibration in the resolution's approach in comparison to the earlier Resolution 1373. Resolution 2178, while in some respects broader than Resolution 1373, also contains a number of references to international law measures that seek to safeguard individuals from excessive law enforcement. Whereas Resolution 1373 was subject to strong criticism for its lack of attention to international human rights law, international humanitarian law and international refugee law, Resolution 2178 does include references to these bodies of international law. Whether states take these aspects into account, and whether UN bodies such as the Counter-Terrorism Committee and technical assistance donor states seek the diffusion of these rules on a par with rules of enforcement, remains to be seen. Some scholars see the process of transnationalisation as having the potential to reinforce, rather than undermine, constitutional values such as the rule of law.[67] On this view, the imposition of requirements to comply with international human rights law, for example, might curtail what would otherwise be excessive counter-terrorism action by states.

If, on the other hand, the shifts in criminal law and criminal justice found in national (UK) and European law are also present in transnational law, then there is a danger that the transnationalisation of counter-terrorism law and policy, and the bureaucratisation that facilitates that transnationalisation, will shrink the space for lawful political action across the globe.[68] Thus, one critique of the recent UN Security Council resolution suggests that it may be used by 'authoritarian states to have their repression of internal opposition rubber-stamped at the highest level of international law'.[69] In this regard transnational counter-terrorism law may be a form of governance that focuses on 'control beyond the state'.[70] This is control in a sense that echoes the work of social control theorists in Anglo-American criminology but also critical governance theorists in other traditions.[71] A full development of this thesis is beyond the

[67]For a case study in counter-terrorism law see Fiona de Londras, *Detention in the 'War on Terror': Can Human Rights Fight Back?* (Cambridge University Press, 2011). In broader terms see Harold Hongju Koh, 'Transnational Legal Process' (1996) 75 *Nebraska Law Review* 181.

[68]Inspiration for the dystopia that follows is drawn from Hannah Arendt, *On Violence* (Harcourt, 1969).

[69]Kai Ambos, 'Our Terrorists, Your Terrorists? The United Nations Security Council Urges States to Combat "Foreign Terrorist Fighters", But Does Not Define Terrorism' (*EJIL: Talk!*, 2 October 2014), www.ejiltalk.org/our-terrorists-your-terrorists-the-united-nations-security-council-urges-states-to-combat-foreign-terrorist-fighters-but-does-not-define-terrorism/. See also Connor Gearty, *Liberty and Security* (Polity Press, 2013).

[70]This idea combines Jessup's 'law beyond the state' with Garland's 'culture of control'. See David Garland, *The Culture of Control: Crime and Social Order in Contemporary Society* (Oxford University Press, 2002).

[71]The recent trend towards Foucauldian studies of public international law, and of counter-terrorism law, are relevant here. See, for example, Roele (n 65); see also the symposium in (2012) 25 *Leiden Journal of International Law* 603.

scope of this paper. It suffices here, before the discussion turns to legitimacy, to imagine a dystopia: that national political agency becomes subject to circumscription by discipline through technical assistance, that the potential for political contestation diminishes within states and across them, and that transnational counter-terrorism law evolves beyond a prohibition regime into a mode of global governance.[72]

4. The legitimacy of transnational counter-terrorism law

The discussion thus far demonstrates that transnational counter-terrorism law involves transnational criminal law, in accordance with a formalistic definition of the latter term, but it also involves much more. It is more than merely criminal, civil or administrative law. There is potential for this law to be deeply regressive, as the above dystopian images highlight, but a full exploration of the substantive effects of the law are for another day. In the remainder of this paper attention turns to the question of the effects of transnationalisation on the legitimacy of the law. Three forms of legitimacy are pertinent: first, formal legitimacy that derives from valid legal authority; second, democratic legitimacy deriving from the consent of those subject to legal rules; and third, procedural legitimacy that accrues when legal process is respectful of the rights of its subjects. This section examines the implications for legitimacy when the site of governance shifts from the national level, to the EU, and then to the UN.

At national level it is necessary to rehearse some basic principles of constitutional law. In the UK, for example, the formal legitimacy of the criminal law comes from the valid legal authority of the Queen in Parliament. This legitimacy pre-dates the shift to democratic government. However, today it is understood that the legitimacy of the criminal law is found, at least in part, in the fact that the criminal law is the product of a democratic Parliament.[73] This claim to democratic legitimacy may be open to challenge, in particular in the field of counter-terrorism law, as it may be the case that the 'majority' agrees to repressive counter-terrorism law and policy in the knowledge that its use in practice will be against a 'minority'.[74] Thus, the quality of democratic legitimacy of counter-terrorism may vary across states, and at different times, and is contingent upon the quality of democracy in general. The procedural legitimacy in criminal law and criminal justice derives from the due process of law. This legitimacy comes under strain in the context of counter-terrorism. The trend towards a crime control model of

---

[72]See, for example, the work of Jonathan Simon on governance through crime: Jonathan Simon, *Governing through Crime: How the War on Crime Transformed American Democracy and Created a Culture of Fear* (Oxford University Press, 2007).

[73]Nicola Lacey, 'What Constitutes Criminal Law?' in RA Duff, Lindsay Farmer, SE Marshall, Massimo Renzo and Victor Tadros (eds), *The Constitution of the Criminal Law* (Oxford University Press, 2013).

[74]See the literature that flows from Paddy Hillyard, *Suspect Community: People's Experience of the Prevention of Terrorism Acts in Britain* (Pluto Press, 1993).

criminal justice at the cost of due process predates the rise of administrative law measures to regulate deviance such as terrorism, but that trend is even more evident today.[75] The impact of the pre-emptive paradigm on criminal law and criminal justice has therefore been to erode procedural legitimacy within national legal systems, as the earlier example of the use of secret evidence demonstrates.

If the site of governance shifts from the national to the European level then legitimacy may come under further strain. The EU Framework Decision on Combating Terrorism, which implements, in part, UN Security Council Resolution 1373, is a useful example.[76] The EU had valid legal authority to adopt the measure – Articles 29, 31(e) and 34(2)(b) of the Treaty on European Union – and therefore the measure may be said to have formal legitimacy.[77] However, the democratic legitimacy is more problematic. The Council of the EU agreed the measure through a unanimous vote in accordance with the EU Treaties. The Council consists of Member State executive branches of government, executives that have, of course, both formal and democratic legitimacy as each derives its power from a national constitution and is accountable to its electorate. However, the existence of that democratic legitimacy may in fact obscure the poor quality of the legitimation in practice. Furthermore, although modern democracies involve checks and balances across organs of government, it is notable that the executive branch of government is often subject to less stringent constitutional controls, or may receive a greater degree of deference from the legislature and judiciary, in foreign relations, and in national security matters. Insofar as the adoption of EU criminal law against terrorism falls, to an extent, within both categories, then the de facto deference may be even greater.

The question of procedural legitimacy at EU level is more difficult to unravel. The EU does not have a criminal justice system and so its measures depend on national criminal justice systems for their operation. Thus, the development of counter-terrorism law and policy at European level may pose no greater threat to procedural legitimacy than exists at national level.[78] However, the imposition of criminal justice priorities by the EU on national criminal justice systems might increase the political pressure on those systems, and exacerbate existing tendencies towards crime control and away from due process. Furthermore, there is an absence of 'transnational procedure' to safeguard suspects as a corollary to the increasing power of law enforcement across EU borders.[79] Thus, the increase

[75]Herbert L Packer, *The Limits of the Criminal Sanction* (Stanford University Press, 1968).

[76]Council Framework Decision 2002/475/JHA of 13 June 2002 on combating terrorism (FDCT).

[77]See, in general, Valsamis Mitsilegas, *EU Criminal Law* (Hart Publishing, 2009).

[78]A caveat here is that the operation of measures such as the European Arrest Warrant has seen an increase in enforcement cooperation without a correlative increase in transnational procedural protections for individuals. See Murphy (n 17) ch 7 for a discussion.

[79]CC Murphy, Aldo Zammit Borda and Lucy Hoyte, 'The Perspectives of Counter-Terrorism Operatives on EU Counter-Terrorism Law and Policy' in Fiona de Londras and

in geographic scale of law enforcement as a result of the shift to EU level, and the increase in complexity as multiple jurisdictions become involved, may impact upon legal process and, as a consequence, affect procedural legitimacy.

If the site of governance shifts, once more, to the UN level, then the nexus between the citizen and their state's executive is even more tenuous than at EU level. There is a difference here between pre-September 11 action by the UN and the organisation's post-September 11 efforts. Prior to the attacks on that day, the principal forum for counter-terrorism cooperation at the UN was the General Assembly, the principal form of cooperation was the agreement of international conventions, and the principal mode of action in those conventions was agreement to criminalise certain acts – such as hostage-taking or aircraft hijacking – and to operate an 'extradite or prosecute' rule in respect of perpetrators.[80] The use of international conventions was respectful of states' right to consent, or not to consent, to cooperation. States could choose whether or not to accede to the conventions and were only bound to implement a convention if they so choose. The result was that the formal legitimacy of the action was secure because of the legal validity of international agreements between states. The democratic legitimacy of the action was also, on the face of it, secure – although the challenge of holding the executive to account for its actions in foreign relations should not be forgotten. Reliance on the principle that states should extradite or prosecute was respectful of national criminal justice systems and therefore the action's procedural legitimacy was not necessarily better or worse than in those systems.

The action taken by the UN since the attacks on 11 September 2001 has involved institutional and methodological shifts. The UN Security Council has overtaken the UN General Assembly's role in counter-terrorism cooperation. Key UN action since that day has been taken by the Security Council, in the form of UN Charter Chapter VII resolutions, and therefore requires the adoption by all states of new criminal, civil and administrative law measures. The formal legitimacy of this action is open to dispute as the Security Council's authority to adopt measures affecting individuals is not clear.[81] In terms of democratic legitimacy, the post-September 11 action is not respectful of states' right to consent to cooperate as the Security Council resolutions involve obligations that are mandatory under international law. Furthermore, after the shift in locus of action from the General Assembly to the Security Council, the majority of the world's citizens do not have any representation in the law-making process. Furthermore, the post-September 11 resolutions oblige states not only to adopt criminal offences against the

---

Josephine Doody (eds), *The Impact, Legitimacy and Effectiveness of EU Counter-Terrorism* (Routledge, 2015) 176.

[80] For a full exegesis of the relevant action see Ben Saul (ed), *Research Handbook on International Law and Terrorism* (Edward Elgar, 2014).

[81] Andrea Bianchi, 'Assessing the Effectiveness of the UN Security Council's Anti-Terrorism Measures: The Quest for Legitimacy and Cohesion' (2006) 17(5) *European Journal of International Law* 881.

commission of acts of terrorism, but also to adopt criminal offences against inchoate behaviour with a link to terrorism, and to take administrative action against individuals on the basis of mere suspicion. The procedural legitimacy of the resulting law will come under strain if transnational law proves to be a vector for the transmission of anti-constitutionalist tendencies in, for instance, UK and US law.

The formal legitimacy of transnational counter-terrorism law requires deeper interrogation, in particular as to the role of the Security Council when international peace and security is under threat not only from states, but also from non-state organisations and individuals. The democratic legitimacy and procedural legitimacy of counter-terrorism law may, of course, be subject to erosion even within national legal systems. The claim here is not, therefore, that in the absence of the transnationalisation of law the operation of counter-terrorism law would be unproblematic. Rather, the claim is that the process of transnationalisation exacerbates already apparent trends in the law to the detriment of democratic legitimacy and perhaps also of procedural legitimacy. If these exercises of juridical and disciplinary power tend towards dystopia then the problems of legitimation may be difficult to resolve because law that aims to asphyxiate violent extremist politics may also render it difficult to engage in the sorts of political debates that are necessary to facilitate democratic legitimation. In this way one effect of transnational counter-terrorism law might be to prevent its own contestation.

There is much work to do to properly explore these questions. Boister notes that the early UN efforts sought to avoid the politicisation found in, for example, the UK and EU definitions of terrorism.[82] However, this depoliticisation is neither possible nor desirable. The very concept of terrorism is political, and efforts to deny that political nature may worsen rather than improve political realities.[83] To deny the politics inherent in terrorism and counter-terrorism does not resolve political antagonisms – it merely seeks to prevent their manifestation through an evacuation of the political space in which those antagonisms would otherwise come to the fore.

Thus, it is unhelpful to ask whether transnational criminal law can 'escape the stain of Western hegemony'.[84] In relation to counter-terrorism, at least, the hegemonic position of the UN Security Council is constitutive of the field. The power

---

[82]Boister (n 8) 98.

[83]Note, for example, the attempts by Margaret Thatcher as UK Prime Minister to deny the politics inherent in the violence of Irish republicans when she said: 'Once again we have a hunger strike at the Maze Prison in the quest for what they call political status. There is no such thing as political murder, political bombing or political violence. There is only criminal murder, criminal bombing and criminal violence. We will not compromise on this. There will be no political status.' Margaret Thatcher, speech delivered in Belfast (5 March 1981). Resolution of the conflict in Ireland ultimately required acknowledgement of the political nature of the violence. See, for an introduction, David McKittrich and David McVeigh, *Making Sense of the Troubles: A History of the Northern Ireland Conflict* (Penguin, revised and updated edn 2002).

[84]Boister, this volume.

relationships amongst the five permanent members of the UN Security Council are key to the Security Council's rule-making process. Also relevant are the relationships between those five permanent members and the 10 additional members of the UN Security Council. As a result, the aim for scholars (and practitioners) of transnational counter-terrorism law should not be to wash the law of a 'stain', but rather to make clear these power relationships so that their effect on the law can be better understood.

In this respect, perhaps one of the most problematic aspects of transnational counter-terrorism law is its role in setting a global agenda.[85] The Security Council has principal responsibility for international peace and security. If groups like Islamic State pose a threat to international peace and security, as that group certainly does in the Middle East, then it is appropriate for the Security Council to act. However, the choice by the Security Council to focus on counter-terrorism, and to use Chapter VII resolutions to mandate action by states, sets a legislative agenda not just in international law but also in national legal systems across the globe. Thus, even in states where other legislative priorities may be more pressing, it is terrorism that those in government must address.[86] The hegemonic effect of transnational law, as a result of its juridical and disciplinary power, can be to dictate national legislative and executive priorities to states for whom other concerns – public health, economic deprivation, climate change – may be more urgent. This may be the most significant problem of legitimacy: not the form or substance of transnational counter-terrorism law, but rather the fact that finite resources are spent on this problem rather than others.

5. Transnational counter-terrorism law: a boulder on the mountain

This paper has sought to address transnational counter-terrorism law as a field of law and as a field of scholarship. The danger with such an effort is that it too serves an agenda-setting role, giving counter-terrorism the same problematic priority in the academy that it has in policy making. However, the potential implications of transnational counter-terrorism law for national and international politics, as well as the broader insights that the field may provide into law under globalisation, demands our attention. There are significant limitations to existing research into transnational counter-terrorism law. The sheer volume of new soft and hard law, and the multiplicity of sites of governance, legal processes, and public and private actors can leave even the most energetic researcher gasping for breath as

[85]The idea of agenda setting as a form of power can be found in Steven Lukes, *Power: A Radical View* (Palgrave Macmillan, 2nd edn 2004).

[86]The gap between public goods and governmental priorities can also occur in powerful states. A note in the 2011 Annual Report of the UK Independent Reviewer of Terrorism Legislation merits attention. David Anderson QC notes that, in the twenty-first century, 'terrorism has been an insignificant cause of mortality in the United Kingdom'. David Anderson QC, *The Terrorism Acts in 2011* (The Stationery Office, June 2012) 27.

they push their boulder up the mountainside.[87] In reality no one project can capture the full breadth of the field, which requires diverse projects with distinct, if overlapping, goals. These goals involve efforts to categorise, to theorise, and to examine through empirical legal research.

This paper has set out the limits of one categorical approach to the definition of transnational criminal law – that of Neil Boister – at least insofar as it applies to terrorism. An alternative effort at categorisation might be to describe the 'dynamics of transnationalisation' and thereby to explore the ways in which rule making and enforcement transcends national legal systems. This effort has been begun elsewhere in relation to transnational counter-terrorism law. The relevant dynamics can be understood as the emergence of global governance, regional government, bilateral and multilateral agreements with implications for national law, the diffusion of rules across legal systems, an increase in extraterritoriality, and the rise of private rule making and enforcement.[88] This map of the dynamics does not seek to define a field of law but rather to describe categories of legal phenomenon that may be subject to study.

There has already been much effort, not least in the pages of this journal, to explore new theories of the authority and legitimacy of law in the context of globalisation. Despite the globalisation of law, 'states face change but not displacement', and state law remains 'the most comprehensive legal system with [its] domain'.[89] Surveys of contemporary counter-terrorism law suggest that states remain exercisers of power and sites of rule enforcement. Thus, theories of authority and legitimacy of transnational counter-terrorism law need to take account of the endurance of, and reshaping of, state power. It is the state's role as the primary site of rule making that transnationalisation alters. It may therefore be useful to re-examine the foundations of public law and reconsider whether the deference shown by the legislature and the judiciary towards the executive's actions in international relations remains appropriate given the significant role of those external relations in internal rule enforcement. These questions are as much about law as they are about politics – but in this field the two domains are not easily distinguishable.

The most pressing need in transnational counter-terrorism law may well be the need for empirical legal research on the operation of the law in practice. Whether, and in what way, transnational (criminal or counter-terrorism) law entails the evolution of existing systems of law is, in part, an empirical question. The answer to that question requires more than categories of analysis or theoretical hypotheses – it requires empirical evidence. There has not been much empirical legal research

[87] On the challenges in this field see Murphy (n 7) and Victor V Ramraj, 'The Impossibility of Global Anti-Terrorism Law?' in Kent Roach, Michael Hor, Victor V Ramraj and George Williams (eds), *Global Anti-Terrorism Law and Policy* (Cambridge University Press, 2nd edn 2012).
[88] See further Murphy (n 7).
[89] Raz (n 40) 18.

on transnational counter-terrorism law to date, although some work in this field is beginning to emerge.[90] For the field to progress beyond its current state will require the recent turn towards empiricism in international legal scholarship to be brought to bear on transnational counter-terrorism law.[91] Useful projects would consider the emergence of epistemic communities among policy makers and law enforcement officials in this field; the development of a legal culture in those communities;[92] and the extent to which capacity building through technical assistance is used to emphasise safeguards for suspects, and the population as a whole, as much as it seeks to facilitate better law enforcement.

One final reflection comes to mind on the Sisyphean task of research in this field. The discipline of criminology has been called a 'rendezvous discipline': 'a subject where other disciplines meet and its very liveliness and, at its best, intellectual interest is because of this position on the busy crossroads of sociology, psychology, law and philosophy'.[93] The same sentiments ring true of transnational counter-terrorism law. It is a field of study that sits across the boundaries of legal jurisdictions, academic disciplines and research methodologies. Insofar as it involves transnational criminal law and criminal justice, those policy domains, and their academic study, can only serve to emphasise the interstitial nature of the field. Our responsibility then, as transnational counter-terrorism lawyers, is to be clear about our epistemological assumptions, methodological choices and intellectual commitments. If we do so, then we may not be happy, but it will be worthwhile to keep pushing on up the mountain.

Acknowledgements

I am grateful to Ben Bowling, Stephen Coutts, David Nelken, Marcel Niggli, Nicola Palmer, Joseph Raz, Thomas Schultz, and Peer Zumbansen for conversations to clarify the thoughts herein, to the anonymous reviewers for their insights, and to Maryam Khalid for her editorial work. Any errors and eccentricities are my own.

Funding

This article draws on research supported by the British Academy and the Fulbright Commission.

[90]Note the striking effort in Gavin Sullivan, 'Transnational Legal Assemblages and Global Security Law: Topologies and Temporalities of the List' (2014) 5(1) *Transnational Legal Theory* 81. Note also the work of the SECILE Research Consortium on EU counter-terrorism law and policy: www.secile.eu.

[91]Gregory Shaffer and Tom Ginsburg, 'The Empirical Turn in International Legal Scholarship' (2012) 106(1) *American Journal of International Law* 1.

[92]On the culture of legality see Murphy (n 24).

[93]Jock Young, 'In Praise of Dangerous Thoughts' (2003) 5(1) *Punishment and Society* 97. Young attributes the term to David Downes – the elaboration is Young's own.

Rethinking the 'international law of crime': provocations from transnational legal studies

Prabha Kotiswaran and Nicola Palmer

Dickson Poon School of Law, King's College London, UK

Neil Boister's distinction between international and transnational criminal law offers a valuable first step in delineating two fields of enquiry. Drawing on transnational legal studies, however, we show in section I how Boister engages with international criminal law in an idealised form, yet in practice this area of law faces many of the same challenges that plague transnational criminal law. In section II we challenge the stability of the category of 'transnational crime' and pluralise the international regulatory matrix beyond the use of criminal law to address the fall-outs of globalisation, expanding, in the process, the horizontal, vertical and temporal dimensions of transnational criminal law. We argue against reifying international and transnational criminal law and draw on the critical orientation of transnational legal studies manifest in its invocations of legal realism, legal pluralism and socio-legal scholarship to articulate a wide-ranging agenda for rethinking the theoretical and empirical dimensions of the 'international law of crime'.

Introduction

The most recent wave of globalisation inaugurated in the late 1980s has produced a crisis for lawyers everywhere. As we regroup to reconfigure, even overhaul entire bodies of legal theory and rework conceptual schema in discrete legal fields, criminal law is no exception. Neil Boister's opportune intervention in 2003 to delineate the field of transnational criminal law (TCL) as a juridical counterpart to 'transnational crimes' resulting from the negative externalities associated with the liberalised movement of products, goods, services and indeed human beings is one such attempt.[1] Boister defines TCL as 'the indirect

[1]Neil Boister, '"Transnational Criminal Law"?' (2003) 14(5) European Journal of International Law 953, 955. Similarly, scholars at Tilburg University Law School are proposing the concept of 'global criminal law' as a way for criminal lawyers to account for crimes that are strongly related to globalisation. This is worth mentioning here, even if only to highlight

suppression by international law through domestic penal law of criminal activities that have actual or potential trans-border effects'.[2] Central to this definition is the existence of an international treaty directed at suppressing conduct that is subsequently criminalised through domestic law. In this article we explore the underlying assumptions that Boister makes in calling this field of TCL into being. In doing so we show how challenging and rethinking these assumptions opens up valuable new research pathways.

The point of departure for Boister's work is the distinctions between TCL and international criminal law (ICL). In particular, he highlights the institutional, doctrinal and teleological distinction between these two bodies of criminal law. At a doctrinal level, ICL and TCL both draw on the legal sources of public international law, however they display different levels of 'institutional density'. International criminal law imposes responsibilities directly on individuals and can punish violations through international mechanisms. Thus, international crime refers to those criminal offences over which international courts or tribunals have been given jurisdiction under general international law. They comprise the so-called 'core crimes' of genocide, crimes against humanity, war crimes and, subject to sufficient ratifications, the crime of aggression. As a result the majority of doctrinal scholarship in ICL focuses on the development of this body of law through the decisions handed down by these international institutions.[3] In contrast, for Boister, TCL offers a doctrinal match for the criminological term 'transnational crime' and, rather than the existence of a supranational court, the core component of TCL is a crime suppression treaty, whether agreed bilaterally, regionally or through a large UN-backed multilateral convention. He describes this as the 'horizontal' component of TCL. Following this,

> [t]he vertical component in transnational criminal law involves domestic criminalisation of the specified conduct of individuals and the enactment of allied procedures and provisions for cooperation in regard to those individuals by the states parties to the particular suppression convention.[4]

---

that the starting point for any endeavour to name a legal field into being determines its frame of analysis and trajectory. To the extent that global criminal law is committed to understanding the field as a response to the dark side of globalisation, it brings a broader set of methodologies into the conversation (e.g. attention to the role of non-state actors). For an exposition of the idea of global law, see Neil Walker, *Intimations of Global Law* (Cambridge University Press, 2015).

[2]Ibid.

[3]For an interesting discussion on the use and validity of different legal sources in the development of the doctrine within the ICC see Claus Kress, 'On the Outer Limits of Crimes against Humanity: The Concept of Organization within the Policy Requirement. Some Reflections on the March 2010 ICC Kenya Decision' (2010) 23 *Leiden Journal of International Law* 855; Matt Halling, 'Push the Envelope – Watch it Bend: Removing the Policy Requirement and Extending Crimes against Humanity' (2010) 23 *Leiden Journal of International Law* 827.

[4]Neil Boister, 'Further reflections on the concept of transnational criminal law', this volume.

At first glance, such distinctions may appear to simply highlight the absence of any international courts with jurisdiction over transnational crimes. However, at a teleological level, Boister builds the distinction between ICL and TCL around their differing objectives. He argues that the principal purpose of ICL is to protect 'international interests like international peace and security or the most important basic common values of mankind like life and human dignity'.[5] In other words, ICL makes claims to common interests and values that can be realised through common institutions. In contrast, 'the central purposes of the suppression conventions is to build a foundation in national law in order to make international cooperation in the suppression of the particular form of conduct effective'.[6] The agreements in TCL on substantive criminalisation and procedural cooperation serve specific individualised state interests.

Having articulated the need for this concept of TCL, Boister draws attention to what he sees as the major issues facing this area of law. He identifies six central challenges: the first centres on inconsistencies in the principles that justify criminalisation at the supranational level; the second on the political legitimacy of those formulating TCL; the third and fourth on the resultant doctrinal and human rights weaknesses when the law is domestically enacted; and the fifth and sixth on concerns of Western hegemony at the points of both enacting and enforcing TCL.[7] These critiques lead Boister to argue for a need to adopt a clear set of principles for transnational criminalisation, which would include 'an authentic margin of national appreciation'[8] while developing a more harmonised system of law.

In his contribution to this Special Issue, Boister revisits his 2003 article to further elaborate the definition and boundaries of TCL by explicitly taking into account the insights of transnational legal studies. He extends his definition of TCL to include criminal activities that have 'transboundary moral impacts',[9] expanding the scope of TCL to include norms originating in the transnational space. In an apparent relaxation of the purposive distinctions between ICL and TCL, he concedes that 'the horizontal diffusion of criminal law norms from state to state without the agency of a suppression convention'[10] could possibly fall within the purview of TCL as long as they 'address an issue of transnational conduct, effect or concern'.[11] Despite raising this possibility, Boister continues to focus his definition on the role of crime suppression treaties and in doing so situates TCL as a subset of international law that is related to, but distinct from, ICL in a strict sense.

Boister's delineation of the institutional and resultant doctrinal distinctions between ICL and TCL is valuable from a descriptive point of view and has

[5]See Boister (n 2) 965.
[6]*Ibid*, 967.
[7]*Ibid*, 957–8.
[8] Boister, this volume.
[9]*Ibid*.
[10]*Ibid*.
[11]*Ibid*.

found resonance.[12] However, his distinguishing of ICL and TCL as a means to draw 'the normative boundaries of transnational criminal law'[13] is more problematic. We argue that working out the implications of the full range of insights from transnational legal studies requires us to not only challenge the assumptions Boister makes in drawing this distinction, but to fundamentally rethink the very conceptual core of both ICL and TCL. Thus, in section I we show how Boister engages with ICL in an idealised form, juxtaposing it with the 'real-world' Vittelian constraints that TCL faces. We argue that in practice the development of ICL faces challenges that are similar to those within TCL. ICL is fragmented at the domestic level. Its justifications for international criminalisation show subtle inconsistencies and the legal interpretation of complementarity by the International Criminal Court (ICC) has resulted in growing numbers of domestic trials operating in concert and at times in competition with cases at the international level. A legal pluralist turn in the scholarship offers an avenue for better understanding these vertical practices in ICL, taking seriously the possibility that domestic courts may offer very different justifications for the use of criminal law than those articulated at the international level. This pluralist account draws attention to the constraints on Boister's proposal for establishing distinct international governing principles for TCL and questions the weight that he ascribes to the teleological distinctions between ICL and TCL.

In section II of this article, we interrogate some of Boister's assumptions in relation to TCL. We challenge the stability of the very category of 'transnational crime'. We complicate the horizontal aspect of TCL by adopting a legal realist approach to the use of criminal law to address the fall-outs of globalisation. Consequently, we highlight the contingency of a criminal law response while bringing to the fore a range of background legal rules that facilitate the very conditions for the material and discursive production of the phenomenon that we call transnational crime. We bring to bear on TCL the rich debates within global governance and transnational legal theory on the decentring of formal state law and the full range of technologies of governance, including social norms, codes of conduct, naming and shaming measures, ranking mechanisms and social indicators that non-state actors increasingly articulate in order to address transnational social problems. With a view to deepening the vertical dimension of TCL, we call for TCL to engage with domestic conversations that revisit the shifting contours of 'criminal law'. Further, we suggest an expansion of the theoretical lens on TCL along synchronic and diachronic lines to embrace comparative criminal law and colonial criminal law respectively.

By pursuing the insights of transnational legal studies alongside a methodological commitment to legal realism, legal pluralism, socio-legal studies and

[12]See e.g. Rob Cryer *et al*, *An Introduction to International Criminal Law and Procedure* (Cambridge University Press, 2nd edn 2010) 6.
[13]*Ibid*, 10.

legal ethnography, the article proposes that the purposive distinctions between ICL and TCL become more blurred and the points of theoretical overlap are made visible. It is only through a conversation between the two fields that the 'international law of crime' and international law more generally can cure its legitimacy deficits in addressing transnational social problems.

I. An ICL less ideal; and some similarities with TCL

It has been a turbulent 13 years for the International Criminal Court, and for the practice of ICL more broadly, since the Courts' founding treaty document, the Rome Statute, came into effect in 2002.[14] This section reviews the current practice of ICL in light of Boister's criticisms of TCL. Specific attention is drawn to the justifications for international criminalisation. The doctrinal developments in ICL are at times in tension with both the liberal principles often drawn on to justify the use of criminal law in the domestic sphere and those principles drawn on to demarcate the boundaries of public international law at the supranational level. In addition, as Boister highlights with regard to TCL, ICL continues to face democracy deficits that have impacted on how the law has been drafted and interpreted. Finally, a transnational, legal pluralist gaze realised through legal ethnographic work illuminates the fragmentation of ICL when domestically enacted, highlighting the notable variance in objectives of international and domestic criminal courts. Undertaking such a review, which maps onto the specific criticisms raised by Boister in the transnational context, challenges Boister's idealised account of ICL. In doing so this section argues that ICL, while a distinct area of study, would benefit from understanding and engaging more deeply with the horizontal, vertical and temporal dimensions of the 'international law of crime' made visible in the emerging study of TCL as outlined in detail in section II.

A. *International criminalisation*

As his first step in conceptually demarcating TCL, Boister focuses on how such a term would enable an examination of 'the social construction of transnational

[14]Rome Statute of the International Criminal Court (adopted 17 July 1998, entered into force 1 July 2002) 37 ILM 1002. There are important overlaps in the formation and practice of the ICC and that of the other international criminal law institutions, namely the International Criminal Tribunal for Rwanda (ICTR), the International Criminal Tribunal for the former Yugoslavia (ICTY), the Special Court for Sierra Leone (SCSL) and the Extraordinary Chambers in the Courts in Cambodia (ECCC). As Halley correctly describes, the courts are not hermetically sealed off from one another and a focus on the creation and practice of ICC occurs in concert, sometimes supporting and sometimes in tension with the activities occurring before the other supranational criminal courts. Janet Halley, 'Rape at Rome: Feminist Interventions in the Criminalization of Sex-Related Violence in Positive International Criminal Law' (2008) 30 *Michigan Journal of International Law* 1, 10.

threats and the appropriateness of transnational penal responses'.[15] He is particularly concerned that the rhetorical assertion of a transnational threat may 'presume a common interest in suppression where none exists, and may lead to legal overkill'.[16] As discussed above, it is precisely the existence of a broad, and Boister goes so far as to claim universal, common interest in suppressing international crimes that he sees as a distinguishing feature of ICL and TCL. For Boister, specific and varied states' interests underpin TCL while ICL draws on a common moral interest in condemning war crimes, crimes against humanity and genocide. So with ICL's strong normative claims, is it less vulnerable to these concerns about criminal overreach? And if it isn't, then is it necessary to explore the horizontal dimensions of ICL in which criminal law is but one of the multiple possible responses to extreme violence?

A closer look at the rapid doctrinal development of ICL, in part made possible due to the institutional density that characterises this field, highlights how ICL encounters similar challenges to TCL in determining the principles that demarcate the boundaries of this coercive law. Faced with the severity of the harm and the difficulties of holding senior leaders individually accountable, ICL has struggled, particularly with regard to its modes of liability and defences, to interpret the law in a manner that draws on a consistent set of constraining principles. This has been lucidly discussed by Darryl Robinson, who was himself heavily involved in the drafting of the Rome Statute. Robinson is concerned that in bringing together criminal law, international human rights law and international humanitarian law, ICL has absorbed contradictory assumptions and methods of reasoning, leading to 'sweeping modes of liability, expanding definitions of crimes, and reticence towards defences'.[17]

To some extent, concerns over the potential for expansive interpretations of ICL are inherent to an area of law that ascribes individual criminal responsibility to crimes developed through international legal sources. As Dapo Akande notes, there is a breadth of interpretation with regard to treaty law, one of the principal sources of ICL that often encourages broad phrasing to allow for case-by-case interpretation or arguments of analogy. However, when these treaties relate to the attribution of individual criminal responsibility this breadth of interpretation is in tension with the liberal constraints on criminal law. Rather than a broad interpretation that draws on analogy, liberal constraints would suggest that any ambiguity in the text should be read in favour of the accused.[18] Article 22(2) of

---

[15]See Boister (n 2) 956.

[16]*Ibid*, 956–7.

[17]Darryl Robinson, 'The Identity Crisis of International Criminal Law' (2008) 21 *Leiden Journal of International Law* 925, 927.

[18]Dapo Akande, 'Sources of International Criminal Law' in Antonio Cassese (ed), *The Oxford Companion to International Criminal Justice* (Oxford University Press, 2009) 41, 44.

the Rome Statute tackles this issue head on with regard to the definition of crimes, stating:

> The definition of a crime shall be strictly construed and shall not be extended by analogy. In the case of ambiguity, the definition shall be interpreted in favour of the person being investigated, prosecuted or convicted.[19]

However, more subtle interpretive issues remain at play, particularly when ICL makes broader claims to be protecting human rights through criminal law. Robinson argues that these claims to realising human rights permeate the interpretive approach of the judges in international criminal courts. In human rights law a wide purposive reading of the rights of citizens against the state are generally viewed as progressive. However, a similar breadth of interpretation in ICL faces the same challenges of interpreting treaty law (albeit less immediately visible) and becomes decidedly illiberal in the context of exercising coercive control over a specific individual. The contradictions in human rights reasoning and that of criminal law are particularly visible when the courts have interpreted the general parts of ICL relating to modes of liability and defences. The supranational criminal law institutions have consistently offered a wide reading of what constitutes co-perpetration, command responsibility and joint criminal enterprise, offering purposive justifications focusing on realising victims' rights in their reasoning. The outcome has been a stretching of how individuals can participate in international crimes and a narrowing of the defences that are available to them.[20]

Robinson argues that ICL's expansive interpretive approach is further exacerbated by its utopian aspirations to 'end impunity' and eradicate the occurrence of the crimes themselves. His discussion of the defence of duress is particularly illuminating. Before the ad hoc Tribunals, the defence of duress was not included in the Statute; there was no clear customary law on the issue and there were contradictory approaches at the national level. The *Erdemovic* case before the ICTY, concerning a member of a firing squad who was threatened with death if he did not participate in the murder of Bosnian Muslim men who had surrendered or been captured after the fall of Srebrenica, provided a perfect moment to apply the

---

[19] Rome Statute of the International Criminal Court (adopted 17 July 1998, entered into force 1 July 2002) 37 ILM 1002, Art 22(2).

[20] These two developments have come under increasing criticism in the scholarship. See Jens Ohlin, 'Three Conceptual Problems with the Doctrine of Joint Criminal Enterprise' (2007) 5 *Journal of International Criminal Justice* 67; Harmen G van der Wilt, 'The Continuous Quest for Proper Modes of Criminal Responsibility' (2009) 7 *Journal of International Criminal Justice* 307; Alexander KA Greenawalt, 'The Pluralism of International Criminal Law' (2011) 86 *Indiana Law Journal* 1063. Other authors suggest that the liberal principles argued for at the domestic level cannot automatically be aggregated up and applied to the exceptional circumstances of mass violence. See Mark Osiel, *Making Sense of Mass Atrocity* (Cambridge University Press, 2009); Mark Drumbl, *Atrocity, Punishment and International Law and Policy* (Cambridge University Press, 2007).

leniency required by reading such ambiguity in favour of the accused. However, in contrast, the majority, in rejecting the defence, adopted a purpose-based or teleological reading of the ICTY Security Council mandate, finding that such a defence was inconsistent with the stated objective to 'halt and effectively redress' the widespread and flagrant violations of international humanitarian law.[21] In the interests of such a bold utopian endeavour, the structural constraints on the choices open to Erdemović, between an unavoidable murder and his own death, were sidestepped through the Chamber's approach to legal reasoning.[22] As discussed in the next section, such structural concerns are much more readily taken into account when such readings extend the reach of the law. However, what is clear from the outset is that the rapid expansion of ICL's material scope, like that of TCL, continues to need to be, in Boister's own words, 'complemented (or complicated) by general discussion of coherent principles justifying or constraining criminalization, like individual autonomy, welfare, harm and minimalism'.[23]

Recognising these more subtle doctrinal tensions in the justifications for international criminalisation also opens up the possibility of acknowledging horizontal dimensions of ICL that take account of when, and how, other regulatory regimes are responding to the same conduct. As discussed below, political and criminological writing on the topic has touched on this issue. However, ICL would equally benefit from examining the actors and legal intersections set out in section II in relation to TCL.

While political scientists have described the increasing use of ICL as a 'justice cascade',[24] at the same time there is clear empirical evidence showing the continued use of amnesties in the wake of political violence.[25] Following the establishment of the ICC, a wealth of scholarship emerged around whether amnesties for international crimes would still fit within the Statute, as the domestic use of amnesties was not explicitly excluded in the wording of the treaty.[26] More recently,

[21]See Robinson (n 17) 945.
[22]More recently Robinson has asked, as part of a larger project focused on developing a cosmopolitan liberal account of ICL, whether the ICTY could have justifiably imposed a higher standard of behaviour on Erdemović because he was acting in the role of a soldier. Darryl Robinson, 'A Cosmopolitan Liberal Account of International Criminal Law' (2013) 26 *Leiden Journal of International Law* 127.
[23]See Boister (n 2) 957.
[24]Ellen Lutz and Kathryn Sikkink, 'The Justice Cascade: The Evolution and Impact of Foreign Human Rights Trials in Latin America' (2001) 2 *Chicago Journal of International Law* 1; Kathryn Sikkink, *The Justice Cascade: How Human Rights Prosecutions are Changing World Politics* (WW Norton, 2011).
[25]Louise Mallinder, *Amnesty, Human Rights and Political Transition: Bridging the Peace and Justice Divide* (Hart Publishing, 2008).
[26]Max Pensky, 'Amnesty On Trial: Impunity, Accountability and the Norms of International Law' (2008) 1 *Ethics and Global Politics* 1; Darryl Robinson, 'Serving the Interests of Justice: Amnesties, Truth Commissions and the International Criminal Court' (2003) 14 *European Journal of International Law* 481.

criminologists have called for a radical reconceptualisation of what constitutes 'accountability', drawing on interdisciplinary writings to establish a broader set of characteristics that moves beyond the narrow deployment of the term as synonymous with criminal trials.[27] Such a reading is a welcome development as it offers a much wider set of possible responses to international crimes, but – as discussed below – these developments are almost certainly constrained by the ICC's current interpretation of its own 'margin of appreciation', that of the principle of complementarity. As a result it will become increasingly necessary in ICL scholarship to look at the vertical intersections, more common in TCL, those of the relationship between ICL and the existing and often long-standing domestic criminal law regimes. In addition, the transnational provocations raised in section II might ask us to look at whether the justifications for international criminalisation may extend outside the exclusive focus on extreme forms of physical violence to include more emotively mundane but nonetheless pressing social problems, such as the regulation of the arms trade or environmental pollution.

B. *Legitimacy in the development of the system*

The international courts from which much ICL doctrine has developed are established through international treaty law.[28] As a result, in a very similar manner to the TCL suppression conventions, institutions face the challenge of operating with a democratic deficit. One major effect of this deficiency that is immediately visible in the establishment of the ICC is that specific non-state actors have played a very prominent role in determining particular offences that are included in the Rome Statute, at times stretching the boundaries of the traditional constraints on both criminal responsibility in public international law and domestic criminal law.

Echoing Boister's concerns about the drafting of suppression treaties, Immi Tallgren described in her observations of the Rome Conference that led to the establishment of the ICC how the specific state delegates, NGO representatives and academics who engaged in the negotiations were not elected to participate in this legislative drafting of ICL. She noted at the time of the drafting of the Statute that 'any democratic control … will at best be retroactive, at the point

[27]Louise Mallinder and Kieran McEvoy, 'Rethinking Amnesties: Atrocity, Accountability and Impunity in Post-Conflict Societies' (2011) 6 *Contemporary Social Science: Journal of the Academy of Social Science* 107.

[28]As noted, the ICC was established through the Rome Statute, a multilateral treaty. The ICTY and ICTR, whilst established through Security Council Resolutions 827 (1993) and 955 (1994), were adopted pursuant to the Security Council's powers under Chapter 7 of the United Nations Charter, and thus find their binding force in Art 25 of the Charter, a multilateral treaty. Similarly, the SCSL and the ECCC were established through bilateral treaty obligations between the UN and the host country.

of ratification'.[29] In addition, as Janet Halley notes, many of the specific actors involved in the Rome Conference had overlapping roles, advocating for particular positions while publishing academic papers on those positions and being actively involved in the actual drafting.[30] Halley goes on to provide a fascinating account of the homogenising impact of these overlapping functions for feminists who participated as NGO representatives, academics and state delegates. She argues that the internal divides within feminism, particularly as they relate to the capacity of individuals to exercise autonomous choice and the structural constraints on the validity of such choices, were papered over in order to put forward a highly structuralist consensus position on what the law should be. As a result, the distinct crimes of rape, sexual slavery, enforced prostitution, forced pregnancy and enforced sterilisation were included as both war crimes, if committed as part of an armed conflict, and as crimes against humanity, if committed as part of a widespread or systematic attack against a civilian population. This was done, not in an effort to recognise that some consent to sexual activity between members of opposing groups may be possible, but rather to ensure that a narrow reading of any one of the terms could be mitigated through including 'as many sexual wrongs as possible under the most stigmatic terms that they could find'.[31] The domestic constraints on criminalising sexual offences were more comfortably dismissed once operating at an international level and applied in times of armed conflict or systematic attack.

In the drafting process, the constraints on extending individual criminal liability offered by public international law proved to be similarly elastic on key issues. Rhetorically, the core crimes included in the Rome Statute were to reflect existing customary international law. However, due to the elite political bargaining at Rome, some of them, such as the prohibition under war crimes of the use of both chemical weapons and starvation as a means of warfare, were not included in the ICC's exhaustive list of war crimes.[32] Other conduct, most notably relating to the use of child soldiers, offered an easier opportunity for consensus. Both the conscription *and* enlistment of child soldiers were included as war crimes in international and internal armed conflict. The drafters were not constrained by existing criminalised prohibitions in public international law and extended the definition of the crime to include non-enforced conscription (i.e. enlistment).[33] The outcome of the Rome negotiations was a treaty, so – in and

[29]Immi Tallgren, 'We Did It? The Vertigo of Law and Everyday Life at the Diplomatic Conference on the Establishment of an International Criminal Court' (1999) 12 *European Journal of International Law* 683, 685.
[30]See Halley (n 14) 12.
[31]*Ibid*, 96.
[32]Claus Kress, 'War Crimes Committed in Non-International Armed Conflict and the Emerging System of International Criminal Justice' (2001) 30 *Israel Yearbook on Human Rights* 1, 37 and 39; Cryer *et al* (n 12) 278 and 304.
[33]*Ibid*, 309.

of itself – this was legitimate as States retained the choice to become signatories; however, it did show that public international law was not consistently used to set the boundaries of determining what conduct was criminalised. This raises the question of what principles are constraining the development of ICL.

The extension of criminalisation of child soldiering to include both conscripting and enlisting young people could be read in a similar fashion to Halley's critique of the expansive drafting of sexual offences. Including both conscription and enlistment simply ensured that consent on the part of a young person to participate in hostilities could not be raised as a defence, due to the structural conditions under which such a decision would have been made. Such a claim is supported by the interpretation of this law in the *Lubanga* judgment, the first to be handed down by the ICC, in which the Court found no need to draw a distinction between enlistment and conscription.[34] Mark Drumbl argues that this reading further entrenches a view of child soldiers as passive victims who are unable to exercise any free choice. He argues that the predominance of this view in the 'international legal imagination' fails to take account of the different gradients of child participation in violence, undermining valuable re-integrative processes for the children themselves, while distorting the reparatory processes available to the people harmed by their actions.[35]

Elite actors claiming specifically directed legal expertise drove the drafting process of the Rome Statute. This enabled the subtle extension of ICL beyond the general constraints on criminal law argued for by liberals in many domestic spheres or those that could be drawn on in public international law. This was most visible at points of universalised moral consensus relating to the capacity of women and children to make choices during conflict. Yet at the same time, other areas potentially warranting the use of criminal law as a means of final regulatory recourse, such as those relating to corporate conduct, were explicitly excluded.[36] In addition, the possibility of democratising this drafting of ICL at the stage of ratification has raised further challenges for the ICC, in a similar vein to Boister's concerns regarding doctrinal weakness in TCL.

C. *Doctrinal weakness in the system*

A major area of concern in public international law has been the potential for fragmentation of the law.[37] Recent detailed doctrinal and institutional studies on this

[34]Trial Chamber Judgment, *Prosecutor v Thomas Lubanga Dyilo* (ICC-01/04-01/06).
[35]Mark Drumbl, *Reimagining Child Soldiers in International Law and Policy* (Oxford University Press, 2012).
[36]Wolfgang Kaleck and Miriam Saage-Maass, 'Corporate Accountability for Human Rights Violations Amounting to International Crimes' (2010) 8 *Journal of International Criminal Justice* 699.
[37]This issue came to prominence via Martii Koskenniemi's report to the International Law Commission and has resulted in the development of an extensive body of scholarship.

question suggest that such fragmentation has indeed occurred, most notably between the International Court of Justice (ICJ) and the ICC.[38] Boister similarly warns of doctrinal fragmentation in TCL, but his focus is nationally oriented, looking at the domestic enactment of suppression treaty crimes. When turning this TCL gaze back to the practice of ICL, similar issues are visible. The Rome Statute has generally, although not exclusively, resulted in the domestic enactment of criminal legislation. This incorporation of international crimes into domestic law offers an example, prevalent in the practice of TCL, of 'denationalising and renationalising criminal law norms'.[39] While many scholars have argued for this domestic enactment as a crucial step towards both harmonisation and enforcement of ICL,[40] the result has simultaneously been one of fragmentation. The motivations for domestically criminalising international crimes have been mixed. For some states, such as Australia and Slovenia, it offers an opportunity to assert their jurisdictional primacy over the ICC, while for others, such as Belgium, it has been used to actively assert the primary of the ICC by ceding domestic jurisdiction to the international court.[41] This 'renationalising' of international crimes has also led to differences in the definitions of the actual crimes themselves. For example, in Sudan, which is not a signatory to the Rome Statute but subject to the ICC's jurisdiction following a Security Council referral, at the national level international crimes have been intentionally and controversially reframed, to include, for example, adultery 'within the framework of a methodical and widespread attack' in the list of conduct constituting crimes against humanity.[42] The

---

See Martti Koskenniemi and Päivi Leino, 'Fragmentation of International Law? Postmodern Anxieties' (2001) 15 *Leiden Journal of International Law* 553; Martti Koskenniemi, *Fragmentation of International Law: Difficulties Arising from the Diversification and Expansion of International Law*, Report of the Study Group of the International Law Commission' International Law Commission, United Nations General Assembly, 58th Session, 13 April 2006, A/CN.4/L.682; Larissa van der Herik and Carsten Stahn (eds), *The Diversification and Fragmentation of International Criminal Law* (Brill, 2012); Cesare PR Romano, 'Patterns, Possibilities, and Problems: Deciphering the Grammar of International Jurisprudential Dialogue' (2009) 41 *New York University Journal of International Law and Politics* 755; Larissa van der Herik and Carsten Stahn (eds), *The Diversification and Fragmentation of International Criminal Law* (Brill, 2012).

[38] Philippa Webb, *International Judicial Integration and Fragmentation* (Oxford University Press, 2013).

[39] See Boister, this volume.

[40] Olympia Bekou, 'Crimes at Crossroads: Incorporating International Crimes at the National Level' (2012) 10 *Journal of International Criminal Justice* 677.

[41] Olympia Bekou, 'In the Hands of the State: Implementing Legislation and Complementarity' in Carsten Stahn and Mohamed M El Zeidy (eds), *The International Criminal Court and Complementarity: From Theory to Practice* (Cambridge University Press, 2011).

[42] A December 2007 amendment to the Armed Forces Act 1986, applicable to members associated with the armed forces, incorporated genocide and crimes against humanity into Sudanese law and reintroduced war crimes. In addition, the Criminal Act 1991 was amended in 2008 to include genocide, war crimes and crimes against humanity. For a detailed discussion of points at which this law differs from that of the Rome Statute and

domestic enactment of international crimes has been undertaken not only to reassert traditional claims to sovereignty, but also to make plural claims to the types of wrongs that warrant classification as 'international crimes'.

D. *Legitimacy in the control of the system and the place of pluralism*

Finally, in drawing on transnational methodologies, a legal pluralist approach to ICL suggests that this national fragmentation has not been confined to the doctrine. It has also occurred inside the legal institutions themselves and is evident when examining the objectives driving the judges and lawyers involved in decision-making. Rwanda provides an early example of international criminal justice operating in concert with national and localised criminal trials through the concurrent operation of the ICTR, the national courts and the localised *gacaca* community courts.[43] Legal ethnographic work conducted by one of the authors, inside all three of these post-genocide courts, shows that although the courts do not exercise any jurisdictional challenge to one another, the judges and lawyers working within these institutions have interpreted their actions very differently. For the international judges and lawyers, the ICTR has been principally concerned with the development of international criminal case law. While the Rwandan lawyers argued that the national courts had focused on internal legal reform, the personnel inside *gacaca* view their central contribution as having been towards obtaining a better local understanding of the conflict. It is arguable that, on this reading, the three courts could still complement one another, with the ICTR contributing to a global legal order, the national courts to the development of domestic judicial capacity, and *gacaca* to providing a local mechanism of truth-telling and accountability. However, the empirical data from within each court indicates that how one process is internally justified affects how the others are viewed and understood by the personnel working inside that particular post-genocide court. How the judges and lawyers understand their own work elucidates aspects of each institution's legal culture. It is within this specific legal culture that the work of the other courts is assessed. The common interpretations within the institutions, and the divergences among them, highlight conflicting legal cultures that have led to competition between the jurisdictions and failures in effective collaboration.

---

customary international law see Sarah MH Nouwen, *Complementarity in the Line of Fire: The Catalysing Effect of the International Criminal Court in Uganda and Sudan* (Cambridge University Press, 2013) 284–91.

[43] *Gacaca* is a state-implemented but locally administered transitional justice process that draws its name and some of its procedural aspects from a traditional Rwandan process of dispute resolution. Organic Law No 40/2000 of 26/01/2001 Setting Up *Gacaca* Jurisdictions and Organizing Prosecutions for Offences Constituting the Crime of Genocide or Crimes against Humanity Committed between 1 October 1990 and 31 December 1994, Official Gazette of the Republic of Rwanda, March 2001 (*Gacaca* Law 2001). This initial legislation has been amended on five occasions, most notably in 2004 and 2008.

This competition has been particularly marked at points of formal interaction, such as the transfer of cases between two jurisdictions or where the use of evidence raised in one court is later introduced in another.[44]

Such a legal pluralist view shows how, at the level of the law and the legal institutions, legal fragmentation and resistance to the overstretched claims to universal objectives have marked the renationalisation of international criminal law. Boister's solution to these concerns of over-criminalisation, democracy deficits, doctrinal weaknesses and Western hegemony in the TCL context is to counterpoise any international obligations with a margin of national appreciation at the stage of national implementation. Similar ideas underpinned the legal notion of complementarity recognised under the Rome Statute. Within broader scholarship, complementarity is held up as an effective example of 'global legal pluralism'.[45] In practice, complementarity, rather than harmonising the law, has shifted towards harmonising the investigation of international crimes. This severely restricts the exercise of domestic prosecutorial discretion where no such restrictions are imposed upon the ICC itself and at best highlights an increasing need to be able to accommodate concurrent domestic and international trials that may be underpinned by very different ideational goals.

Within the structure of the ICC, the principle of complementarity is generally understood to establish the Court as a subsidiary to national jurisdictions through Article 17 of the Rome Statute. For a case to be admissible at the international level, the Pre-Trial Chamber of the ICC must first determine whether the same case has been, or is being, investigated or prosecuted by a state with the necessary jurisdiction. Under the current case law, at the national level the conduct need not be charged as an international crime. However, the case must concern the same accused and 'the substantially same conduct',[46] including partial overlap on specific factual incidents. Once the Pre-Trial Chamber has determined that there are domestic proceedings in the same case, the Rome Statute requires under

[44]For a more thorough discussion of this argument see Nicola Palmer, *Courts in Conflict: Interpreting the Layers of Justice in Post-Genocide Rwanda* (Oxford University Press, 2015).

[45]Paul S Berman, *Global Legal Pluralism: A Jurisprudence of Law beyond Borders* (Cambridge University Press, 2014).

[46]*Prosecutor v William Samoei Ruto and Joshua Arap Sang*, Judgment on the appeal of the Republic of Kenya against the decision of Pre-Trial Chamber II of 30 May 2011 entitled Decision on the Application by the Government of Kenya Challenging the Admissibility of the Case Pursuant to Article 19(2)(b)) ICC-01/09-01/11, A Ch (30 August 2011), para 47; *Prosecutor v Saif Al-Islam Gaddafi*, Judgment on the appeal of Libya against the decision of Pre-Trial Chamber I of 31 May 2013 entitled Decision on the admissibility of the case against Saif Al-Islam Gaddafi, ICC-01/11-01/11 A Ch (21 May 2014), para 72; *Prosecutor v Abdullah Al-Senussi*, Judgment on the appeal of Mr Abdullah Al-Senussi against the decision of Pre-Trial Chamber I of 11 October 2013 entitled Decision on the admissibility of the case against Abdullah Al-Senussi, ICC-01/11-01/11-57, A Ch (24 July 2014), para 75.

Article 17 an examination of whether the state is either 'unwilling or unable' to genuinely undertake these proceedings.

Sarah Nouwen argues that the ICC's reading of what constitutes a case, while sound in terms of the Statute, is underpinned by a broader 'anti-impunity' push within the Court itself. The same conduct/same person test means that

> if the ICC prosecutes a person who has been or is being investigated or prosecuted domestically for different conduct, or for the same conduct but [substantially] different incidents, it does not compete with the national jurisdiction; all it does is to 'complement' the national jurisdiction to ensure that there is less impunity.[47]

Robinson, in supporting the same person/same conduct reading of Article 17, argues that a 'conviction for one crime … does not and should not legally insulate a person from future proceedings for a completely different crime'.[48] When applying this interpretation of the law to instances of mass violence where an individual could be connected to multiple specific violent acts, this reading is strongly in line with the general anti-impunity drive noted by Nouwen.

The practical outcome of this approach is that, despite the inclusion of a national margin of appreciation in the current structure of ICL, the ICC's restrictive reading of what constitutes a case means that there will be increasing numbers of international and domestic trials for international crimes running concurrently. In addition, while there is certainly scope for a broader notion of accountability at the domestic level, the predominance of the automatic resort to criminal trials at the international level will make it increasingly necessary to find legal, institutional and cultural mechanisms to accommodate the plural objectives that are ascribed to these processes.

The above discussion highlights how Boister's insights into TCL can be used to shine a critical light on ICL. At the same time, these insights challenge Boister's idealised account of ICL and question whether general principles established at the international level, with sufficient margins of national appreciation, will offer a solution to the problems facing TCL. ICL clearly faces similar challenges to those faced by TCL regarding criminalisation, democracy deficits, fragmentation and hegemony. While supporting Boister's claim that it is necessary to distinguish between ICL and TCL as two discrete areas of study, a deeper and wider engagement with TCL may offer avenues for research into the 'international law of crime' that has greater diachronic and synchronic nuance and offers potential for a more critical and effective engagement with the current use of both ICL and TCL to respond to transnational social problems.

---

[47]See Nouwen (n 42) 70.

[48]Darryl Robinson, 'Three Theories of Complementarity: Charge, Sentence, or Process' (2012) 53 *Harvard International Law Journal* 166, 179.

II. 'Transnational' criminal law: further provocations from transnational legal studies

Section I highlighted how many of the problematic features of TCL afflict ICL as well, yet drawing a distinction between the two may offer a productive avenue for thinking through these afflictions. Section II largely agrees with the basic thrust of Boister's naming of the field of TCL as 'a lens for revealing what the terms "international criminal law" and "crimes of international concern" obscure'.[49] In particular, we welcome his recent attempts to take seriously the insights of transnational legal theory so as to gradually broaden the ambit of TCL – whether in terms of the notion of 'transnational' or the 'law' – while questioning the presumed centrality of the state. Thus, Boister accepts that *transnational* criminal law might include crimes that may have no phenomenological transnational 'hook' but merely a transnational normative hook. He further concedes that a horizontal treaty element is not necessary for TCL. In terms of his understanding of transnational criminal *law*, he visualises TCL as a 'non-hierarchical normative' legal field rather than as a legal order 'with an identifiable legislative source of a hierarchical system of legal norms'.[50] He further acknowledges the role of non-state actors in the field of TCL, although he ultimately believes that they operate within the parameters of international law where the state reigns supreme. While on board with many of the conceptual moves Boister makes in 2015, this section attempts to untether TCL from its sole preoccupation with suppression treaties and further open up the field of TCL to the full range of substantive and methodological innovations that transnational legal studies has to offer.

In particular, this section draws on the example of human trafficking and the TCL architecture that it has spawned in the form of the 2000 United Nations Protocol to Prevent, Suppress and Punish Trafficking against Persons, Especially Women and Children (Palermo Protocol)[51] supplementing the 2000 United Nations Convention against Transnational Organized Crime.[52] As one of the first criminal law interventions on an international scale in the wake of globalisation, anti-trafficking law is a paradigmatic case study illustrating in the field of criminal law all the challenges and complexities facing global governance that transnational legal scholars seek to theorise. Fifteen years on from the negotiation of the Palermo Protocol, we are also able to productively map the shifting discursive registers in which trafficking is discussed as well as interpreted by domestic legal jurisdictions. In an effort to expand the horizontal dimensions of TCL, we use the trafficking example to demonstrate the radical contingency of its construction in terms of a 'transnational crime'. The regulatory corollary of such reframing

---

[49]See Boister, this volume.
[50]*Ibid.*
[51]UN GAOR, 55th Sess, Supp No 49 at 60, UN Doc A/55/49 (23 December 2000).
[52]United Nations Convention against Transnational Organized Crime, 15 November 2000, TIAS No 13, 127, 2225 UNTS 209.

draws on a legal realist approach to reconceptualise anti-trafficking law and displaces the centrality of the criminal justice response inherent in the Palermo Protocol. The range of non-state actors engaged in the trafficking debates and their role in governance agendas outside of and in conjunction with formal state law also queries Boister's insistence of their ultimate subordination within TCL to state interests and the suppression of crime.

In an attempt to deepen our understanding of the vertical dimensions of TCL, this article proposes that TCL engage closely with domestic criminal law scholarship, especially when the very nature of criminal law as well as its regulatory universe – particularly in relation to socio-economic offences – is up for grabs. Further, if, as Boister acknowledges, TCL need not be limited to crimes arising from states' commitment to criminalise under a suppression treaty, but can instead emerge from transnational norms, then we can agree that TCL must be concerned with crimes under domestic law that might derive from a universal commitment to eradicate pressing social problems such as violence against women. This paves the way for a renewed research agenda in comparative criminal law within TCL.

This section concludes by introducing a diachronic dimension to TCL, by considering legal transplants that have travelled under the aegis of colonialism so that transnational criminal lawyers can readily compare the colonial substrata of criminal law, which is common across jurisdictions and over which domestic criminal laws have evolved.

A. *Expanding the horizontality of TCL*

(i) *Problematising 'transnational crime'*

While Boister is open to alternate formulations of the 'transnational' and 'legal' aspects of the TCL, he is less critical of the underlying notion of transnational 'crime' itself. It is true that he is primarily interested in conceptualising a juridical counterpart to 'transnational crime', yet he takes for granted the ontological reality of a transnational crime. The unspoken assumption is that crime is an exceptional phenomenon to otherwise normal circuits of exchange of goods and services warranting the heavy, corrective hand of the criminal law. There is however a steadily increasing body of scholarship that offers critical insights into the very construction of 'transnational crimes', and this has significant normative and regulatory implications for TCL. Kal Raustiala, for instance, has offered a powerful critique of states' desire to section off the legal from the illegal. He eloquently maps how the 'legal, technological, and administrative changes implemented to foster licit world trade will also foster illicit word trade'.[53] Conversely, he argues in the context of drug trafficking that casting the criminal law network widely in a bid

[53]Kal Raustiala, 'Law, Liberalisation & International Narcotics Trafficking' (1999) 32 *New York University Journal of International Law and Politics* 89, 116.

to counter drug trafficking may increasingly constrain legal trade and financial liberalisation.[54] Beyond mapping this recursive relationship between the legal and illegal, he critiques the predominant construction of the problem of drug trafficking in terms of crime and morality (plague, evil, pollution and invasion),[55] considering instead the alternate – albeit less influential – public health framing of drug trafficking. Similarly powerful critiques have become *de rigueur* in relation to the transnational crime of human trafficking, particularly the prominence of the paradigmatic trafficking episode etched in our minds by the media of the young female teenager duped into sex work in a foreign country. Trafficking lends itself to several alternative framings, including those of 'modern slavery, globalization of crime, problems posed by transnational organized criminals, prostitution and migration'.[56] How then does the law select between these competing paradigms? Law, we are told, plays an active role in producing selected frames. Jo Doezema thus powerfully demonstrates through her ethnography that the Palermo Protocol negotiations were not inspired or influenced by the myth of trafficking (namely of the young female sex slave) but in fact produced this very myth.[57] She was hard-pressed to find in the course of the Protocol negotiations mention even once of the stock anti-trafficking episode proliferating in the news media. Instead, she claims,

> the narrative was indeed present: it appeared, fragmented, out of sequence, disguised in legalese or hidden in human rights language … in synecdochal splinter … Thus a word such as 'consent' or a phrase such as 'sexual exploitation' is able to conjure up the entire corpus of the myth.[58]

Further, feminists have drawn on the sociology of moral panics to demonstrate the significant parallels between the contemporary anti-trafficking movement and its historical antecedents in the anti-white slavery campaigns at the turn of the twentieth century.[59] They have argued that the intense activity around sex trafficking seeks to allay fears arising from globalisation. Women's bodies become the site where anxieties about the changes ushered in by globalisation are sought to be managed, reflecting a yearning for a familiar race and gender order.[60] Hence, where women are increasingly migrating across borders, anti-trafficking

[54] *Ibid*, 92.
[55] *Ibid*, 137.
[56] David Nelken, 'Transnational Legal Processes and the (Re)construction of the "Social": The Case of Human Trafficking' in Dermot Feenan (ed), *Exploring the 'Socio' of Socio-Legal Studies* (Palgrave Macmillan, 2013) 137–56.
[57] Jo Doezema, *Sex Slaves and Discourse Masters: The Construction of Trafficking* (Zed Books, 2010) 107.
[58] *Ibid*.
[59] *Ibid*, 16.
[60] Rutvica Andrijasevic, 'Beautiful Dead Bodies: Gender, Migration and Representation in Anti-Trafficking Campaigns' (2007) 86 *Feminist Review* 24, 27.

campaigns seek to discourage such migration[61] and are organised around the gendered dichotomy of innocent female victims and dangerous male Eastern European and Russian criminals. By conflating women's migration with trafficking for forced prostitution, anti-trafficking campaigns convey the danger of leaving home and project the home as a haven of safety, thus discouraging women from migrating or leaving home.[62] The patriarchal state keeps non-Western migrant women in their home countries rather than allowing them to take the risks of migration for better pay.[63] This shrouds women's economic decision making while the home state benefits from their labour in a system marked by inequality.[64] Constructing human trafficking as sex trafficking also allows the Christian Right to reinvigorate its ideological positions equating loose sexuality with criminality,[65] while advocating for the family, promoting abstinence and rescuing women from work outside the home.[66] In the process, as Emma Goldman reminded us as far back as in 1910, attention and action are diverted from the underlying causes of women's oppression, namely marriage, the family and political economy.[67] Anti-trafficking discourse also shores up social hierarchies – especially in Europe, where 'trafficking in women has become a site marked by phantasmic fears of foreigners, immigrants, criminals, terrorists and globalisation'.[68] States' attempts to recuperate the border and their sovereignty by arresting migrants and deporting women back to their proper homes also bolsters nationalism.[69] As the definitional import of trafficking has increasingly expanded to include not only trafficking for sex work but also labour trafficking, similar arguments have been made to reiterate that the focus on the most severe instances of trafficking draws attention away from the endemic conditions of dull exploitation and precarious labour in the globalised economy. For the purposes of TCL, these interventions point to the contingent and ideologically driven construction of social phenomena in terms of transnational crime.

---

[61]Rhacel Parreñas, 'Trafficked? Filipina Migrant Hostesses in Tokyo's Nightlife Industry' (2006) 18(1) *Yale Journal of Law and Feminism,* 145, 178, citing Agustín.
[62]Andrijasevic (n 60) 26.
[63]Laura María Agustín, 'A Migrant World of Services' (2003) 10(3) *Social Politics: International Studies in Gender, State and Society* 377, 392.
[64]Jacqueline Berman, 'Biopolitical Management, Economic Calculation and "Trafficked Women"' (2010) 48(4) *International Migration* 84, 86 (special issue on *Human Trafficking*).
[65]Jacqueline Berman, 'The Left, the Right, and the Prostitute: The Making of US Antitrafficking in Persons Policy' (2006) 14 *Tulane Journal of International and Comparative Law* 269, 278.
[66]*Ibid*, 276.
[67]Carole S Vance, 'Thinking Trafficking, Thinking Sex' (2010) 17(1) *GLQ: A Journal of Lesbian and Gay Studies* 135.
[68]Berman (n 64) 85.
[69]*Ibid*, 86.

(ii) *Toward a legal realist reorientation of TCL*

Closely intertwined with the conceptualisation of transnational social problems in terms of transnational crime are the regulatory repertoires invoked to counter it. Just as transnational crimes are socially constructed phenomena, states also make a contingent choice and thereby default to criminal law as an effective way of countering transnational crime. To return to Boister, he articulates how the horizontal component of TCL in international law and the vertical component in domestic law produce a conformal national law where there is an international normative outline in the suppression conventions but national discretion undoes any claim to codification.[70] However, the contingent frames used to describe transnational social problems suggests the need to revisit the horizontality of TCL beyond suppression treaties. Interestingly, certain areas of TCL are more porous to this provocation than others. Thus, despite the overwhelming influence of the US-driven prohibitionist model against drug trafficking, supply states and scholars actively debate the full range of options implicating (and often dispensing with) the criminal law, namely criminalisation, decriminalisation and legalisation.[71] In relation to human trafficking, on the other hand, the criminal law has reigned supreme in the scholarly and activist literature until very recently.

To elaborate, at least three phases of anti-trafficking law since the negotiation of the Palermo Protocol 15 years ago can be discerned: a phase between 2000 and 2009, which was the heyday of sex work exceptionalism; a phase between 2009 and 2014, when closer attention was paid to labour trafficking which rendered visible the competing frames of 'modern slavery' and 'forced labour'; and a phase from 2014, during which legal interventions framed in terms of slavery and forced labour begin to be enacted.[72] We deal with each of these phases in turn.

The sex work exceptionalism that marked the first phase of anti-trafficking law and policy has been well documented.[73] Migration experts like James Hathaway pointed to the high human rights cost of mainstreaming trafficking into international law by coupling the Palermo Protocol to the UN Convention against

---

[70]Boister (n 2) 9.

[71]See e.g. Justin Shapiro, 'What are they Smoking?! Mexico's Decriminalization of Small-Scale Drug Possession in the Wake of a Law Enforcement Failure' (2010–11) 42 *University of Miami Inter-American Law Review* 115; Michael P O'Connor and Celia M Rumann, 'Market Solutions to Global Narcotics Trafficking and Addiction' (2011–12) 5 *Phoenix Law Review* 123.

[72]For example, the UK Modern Slavery Act 2015 and the 2014 ILO Protocol supplementing the Forced Labour Convention of 1930.

[73]Michael Dottridge, *Collateral Damage: The Impact of Anti-Trafficking Measures on Human Rights around the World* (2007), www.gaatw.org/Collateral%20Damage_Final/singlefile_CollateralDamagefinal.pdf, 1, 4 (accessed April 2015); see also Janie Chuang, 'Rescuing Trafficking from Ideological Capture: Prostitution Reform and Anti-Trafficking Law and Policy' (2010) 158 *University of Pennsylvania Law Review* 1655.

Transnational Organized Crime.[74] In other words, the criminal law was consciously used to further the agenda of border control, motivated in turn by the sovereignty and security concerns of states, thus undermining the rights of migrants, asylum seekers, sex workers and undocumented migrants.[75] The effects of the Palermo Protocol were furthered by the policies of the Bush administration, which was keen to abolish the sex industry and named and shamed countries through the annual Trafficking in Persons Report issued under the Victims of Trafficking and Violence Protection Act 2000. By 2009, however, with the change in regime, the US State Department was beginning to re-focus its attention on labour trafficking in place of its sole preoccupation with sex trafficking and sex work. The definition of trafficking in Article 3 itself is fairly broad,[76] and various aspects that emerged in the amalgamated definition of trafficking such as slavery, practices similar to slavery and forced labour had been dealt with earlier (albeit ineffectively) by the international human rights system. Thus, the International Labor Organization, stunned by the attention and resources that trafficking was garnering, revisited its mandate to eliminate forced labour. While its several reports on the extent of forced labour published since 2005 do not identify the precise definitional relationship between trafficking and forced labour, its estimates have been freely used by anti-trafficking activists. The entry of forced labour into the activists' vocabulary has brought with it an attention to non-criminal law mechanisms for dealing with trafficking. Indeed, the 2014 Protocol and Recommendation to the Forced Labour Convention adopted by the International Labour Conference put on the table a range of labour law mechanisms for reducing vulnerability to trafficking and forced labour. Similarly, a major reframing of trafficking in terms of modern-day slavery has been undertaken by activist-scholars like Kevin Bales, major philanthropic organisations like the Walk Free Foundation, and states like the UK, which has adopted the Modern

[74]James C Hathaway, 'The Human Rights Quagmire of "Human Trafficking"' (2008) 49 *Virginia Journal of International Law* 1, 46; for a response see Anne T Gallagher, 'Human Rights and Human Trafficking: Quagmire or Firm Ground? A Response to James Hathaway' (2009) 49 *Virginia Journal of International Law* 789, 789–91.

[75]Anne Gallagher, 'Human Rights and the New UN Protocols on Trafficking and Migrant Smuggling: A Preliminary Analysis' (2001) 23 *Human Rights Quarterly* 975, 977; see also Dottridge (n 73).

[76]Art 3: '(a) "Trafficking in persons" shall mean the recruitment, transportation, transfer, harbouring or receipt of persons, by means of the threat or use of force or other forms of coercion, of abduction, of fraud, of deception, of the abuse of power or of a position of vulnerability or of the giving or receiving of payments or benefits to achieve the consent of a person having control over another person, for the purpose of exploitation. Exploitation shall include, at a minimum, the exploitation of the prostitution of others or other forms of sexual exploitation, forced labour or services, slavery or practices similar to slavery, servitude or the removal of organs; (b): The consent of a victim of trafficking in persons to the intended exploitation set forth in subparagraph (a) of this article shall be irrelevant where any of the means set forth in subparagraph (a) have been used.'

Slavery Act, 2015. 'Modern slavery' is being used to describe phenomena such as the use of forced labour in supply chains.

This decentring of the criminal law in anti-trafficking struggles has been exacerbated by definitional problems around trafficking itself. Many of the terms used in Article 3 of the Palermo Protocol, including key ones relating to the means of trafficking (such as abuse of power or of a position of vulnerability, coercion) and the purpose of trafficking (exploitation), have been unclear even to the United Nations Office on Drugs and Crime (UNODC) and have in turn been interpreted by domestic criminal law regimes in rather varied ways. The instability of the definition of trafficking and its ability to address a vast continuum of social possibilities has meant that activists, scholars and international organisations like the UNODC and International Labour Organization are coming round to the realisation that the most effective ways of dealing with trafficking would involve a broad regulatory mix, including some combination of criminal law and civil law.

As anti-trafficking law continues to evolve dynamically, we argue for a legal realist re-assessment of the horizontality of TCL. We take as a starting point, like many others have,[77] the work of American legal realist Robert Hale. His critique of the so-called free economy and numerous conceptual trappings that accompanied the idea of the free market (such as 'freedom of contract' and 'market value') is wide-ranging. Significantly, he shows that the role of the state is not as ephemeral as it appears but that the state is an active player in maintaining inequality. Thus he notes:

> We live in what is known as a free economy. We did, at least, before it was subjected to the controls necessitated by the war, or, as some would say, before the advent of the New Deal. Government and law did not tell us what part each of us must play in the process of production, or assign to each of us our respective rations of coffee, gasoline or other materials. What work we should do and how much we might consume were determined by a process known as freedom of contract. Yet in that process there was more coercion, and government and law played a more significant part, than is generally realized.[78]

---

[77]See, for example, Chantal Thomas, 'Immigration Controls and "Modern-Day Slavery"' (2013), http://papers.ssrn.com/sol3/papers.cfm?abstract_id=2294656 (accessed April 2015), arguing that a highly significant legal factor influencing modern-day slavery is the presence of immigration controls. Other influential articles drawing on Hale in other contexts include Duncan Kennedy, 'The Stakes of Law, or Hale and Foucault!' in his *Sexy Dressing etc: Essays on the Power and Politics of Cultural Identity* (Harvard University Press, 1993) 83–125; Fleur Johns, 'Performing Power: The Deal, Corporate Rule, and the Constitution of Global Legal Order' (2007) 34(1) *Journal of Law and Society* 116; Peer Zumbansen, 'The Law of Society: Governance through Contract' (2007) 14(2) *Indiana Journal of Global Legal Studies* 191.

[78]Robert Hale, 'Bargaining, Duress, and Economic Liberty' (1943) 43 *Columbia Law Review*, 603.

Further, Hale significantly demonstrated how the bargaining power of parties to a contract is determined not just by the terms of the contract itself but importantly by background legal rules, such as the laws of property. Thus, as he notes,

> In our industrial society, an employee works in order to make a bargain with his employer and thus obtain the money with which to free himself from some of the restrictions which other people's property rights place on his freedom to consume … Those who own enough property have sufficient liberty to consume, without yielding any of their liberty to be idle. Their property rights enable them to exert pressure of great effectiveness to induce people to enter into bargains to pay them money. The law endows them with the power to call on the governmental authorities to keep others from using what they own.[79]

The legal realists also understood the role that criminal law played in backing up these unequal bargaining arrangements. This understanding of the force of background legal rules furthermore led legal realists to demolish the private law/public law binary that lawyers hold onto somewhat dearly. Thus, as another legal realist, Morris Cohen, has noted,

> The law of contract, then through judges, sheriffs, or marshals puts the sovereign power of the state at the disposal of one party to be exercised over the other party … [T]he law of contract may be viewed as a subsidiary branch of public law, as a body of rules according to which the sovereign power of the state will be exercised as between the parties to a more or less voluntary transaction.[80]

Legal realists did not hesitate to claim contract law to be a branch of public law. Indeed, if contract law can only be understood in relation to property law and criminal law, we are invited as legal realists to understand the true remit of anti-trafficking law (currently operationalised predominantly in terms of criminal law) with reference to varied sets of background legal rules. So far, labour law has been a crucial background rule in the anti-trafficking literature such that there is now a strong argument for a labour approach to trafficking.[81] As descriptions of the political economy of several migrant work sectors become available, rather more unexpected sets of laws as wide-ranging as immigration law, contract law, tort law, corporate law and even banking law seem to be increasingly relevant.[82]

---

[79]*Ibid*, 626–7.

[80]See Zumbansen (n 77) 199.

[81]James Gray Pope, 'A Free Labor Approach to Human Trafficking' (2010) 58 *University of Pennsylvania Law Review* 1849, 1871–4; Hila Shamir, 'A Labor Paradigm for Human Trafficking' (2012) 60 *University of California Law Review* 76, 105–19 (arguing that a labour rights approach would provide more effective strategies to combat trafficking than the human rights approach).

[82]See, for example, a news article on the plight of Indonesian domestic workers migrating to Hong Kong and the debts they are required to take from large banks: Sheridan Prasso and Cathy Chan, 'Indentured Servitude of Women in Hong Kong Abetted by Loan Firms',

So, as far as Boister's claims as to the nature of TCL are concerned, we can say that, at the very least, there are competing frames to the conceptualisation of transnational crime as well as to regulatory alternatives to the use of the criminal law. In other words, a legal realist approach to TCL would require us to trouble the conventional divisions of labour between public law and private law, adopt a highly contingent view of the use of the criminal law, provide a more detailed account of its interaction with other sets of legal rules, and assess the material benefits and costs (including unintended ones) of deploying criminal law. Some legal realists would in fact go so far as to argue that the contract–crime dyad in addressing trafficking in fact has legitimating effects as well. By viewing crime as an exception to the contractual realm, and defining criminal behaviour rather narrowly (as involving, say, physical force or extreme exploitation), and using anti-trafficking law only against such cases in fact legitimates a whole range of contracts supposedly voluntarily entered into but involving precarious working conditions.

B. ***Deepening the verticality of TCL***

(i) *TCL's encounter with domestic criminal law*

One of the motivating factors for carving out the field of TCL and pressing for its rationalisation is that TCL until now has been a pale shadow of its domestic law counterpart. Devoid of doctrinal coherence and unable to reveal its deep internal grammar, Boister argued in 2003 that TCL struggles to meet the high standards of justification for criminalisation that any domestic criminal law would need to satisfy.[83] Consequently, TCL suffers from a democratic deficit and becomes an instrument of unabashed Western hegemony. While one can hardly disagree with this powerful critique of TCL, one must pay closer attention to the context in which Boister makes this critique, namely, in order to call a field into being. Given this context, if TCL aspires to be more like domestic criminal law, then this section argues that it must engage more deeply with how domestic criminal law theorists understand its contemporary role in society. There is at the outset a pragmatic need to do so given the importance of national criminal law to TCL. But it becomes all the more crucial if we are to take seriously the theoretical challenges posed by transnational legal studies. In an effort to bridge global governance discourse with a range of interdisciplinary interventions on thinking about governance within the nation state given the latter's radical restructuring in recent

---

Bloomberg News (on file with author). See Rhacel Salazar Parreñas, *Illicit Flirtations: Labor, Migration and Sex Trafficking in Tokyo* (Stanford University Press, 2011) for a similar account of the indentured labour of Filipina entertainers who migrate to Japan as hostesses in the entertainment sector.

[83] Boister (n 2) 957.

decades,[84] Zumbansen persuades us to view globalisation not as an endpoint of legal development but as an opportunity to reflect on 'law's proximity to self-destruction' and law's relationship to its Other.[85] Even while endorsing the need to carve out the field of TCL, we argue that it needs to be porous so that in attempting to infuse TCL with analytical rigour, we do not reify long-held assumptions about the proper remit of criminal law which are coming undone even in the much-fetishised locale of domestic criminal law.

To take Zumbansen's call seriously, how does domestic criminal law's 'Other' look? Consider, for this purpose, current debates in English criminal law. The first-year law school curriculum and its engagement with theories of criminalisation offer a touchstone opportunity for considering the state of the field. First-year English criminal law students typically encounter the canonical liberal texts of Joel Feinberg which were inspired by J. S. Mill and other utilitarians and learn how liberal Western democracies criminalise (or certainly ought to criminalise) behaviour only in exceptional circumstances when they are harmful and offensive to others. Quickly thereafter, students experience a doctrinal drip-feed of general principles of criminal liability and the study of core offences such as homicide, non-fatal offences against the body, sexual offences, property offences, and an overview of defences to criminal liability. They have at best one combined class on strict liability offences and corporate criminal liability wherein the inability of conventional criminal law to deal with so-called socio-economic offences relating to drugs or offences by large complex organisations like corporations become apparent. This reiterates the holy grail of English criminal law which is that criminal law must properly be invoked only against substantial wrongdoing by an individual wherein his or her *mens rea* is proved before affixing criminal liability; that liability for omissions remain exceptional; and that the prosecution bear the burden of proving guilt, all of which presume adjudication through a criminal trial process with adequate safeguards for the rights of the defendant.

For the most part, however, law students are oblivious to the raging debate amongst criminal law scholars as to the very boundaries of criminal law. Scholars like Andrew Ashworth and Lucia Zedner warn against the crisis of overcriminalisation[86] brought on in the late twentieth century wherein the almost 8000 offences animating English criminal law impinge on individual liberty with no coherent overarching bases for justification in their view. They call for the state's carceral powers for use only against 'paradigm crimes'. In a wide-

[84] Peer Zumbansen, 'Defining the Space of Transnational Law: Legal Theory, Global Governance, and Legal Pluralism' (2012–13) 21 *Transnational Law and Contemporary Problems* 305, 307.

[85] *Ibid*, 321.

[86] Andrew Ashworth, 'Is the Criminal Law a Lost Cause?' (2000) 116 *Law Quarterly Review* 225; Andrew Ashworth and Lucia Zedner, 'Defending the Criminal Law: Reflections on the Changing Character of Crime, Procedure and Sanctions' (2008) 2 *Criminal Law and Philosophy* 21.

ranging critique of this liberal position, Jeremy Horder calls for a fundamental reconceptualisation of the proper remit of criminal law in light of the seismic changes in both the nature of the economy and the role of the welfare state since the 1920s. Drawing on historical data, he demonstrates that the vast expansion of English criminal law was undertaken in the first half of the twentieth century with the rapid growth of the regulatory state, resulting in what he calls 'regulatory criminal law'.[87] Instances of regulatory criminal law include several statutes passed in 1920 alone, such as the Census Act 1920, the Dangerous Drugs Act 1920, the Ready Money Football Betting Act 1920, the Seeds Act 1920, the Roads Act 1920, the Firearms Act 1920, the Official Secrets Act 1920 and the Employment of Women, Young Persons and Children Act 1920.[88] In a criminal law universe where teaching and scholarship are almost exclusively preoccupied with crimes that are *malum in se* and deeply disconnected with the practical effects of the criminal law, Horder prioritises crimes that are *mala prohibita.* He argues against an essentialist understanding of crime,[89] challenging an understanding of a criminal law system that is necessarily tethered to the police machinery (as opposed to professional bodies, officials and employers), individual offenders (as opposed to corporations big and small and sole proprietorships)[90] and *ex post* punishment in terms of imprisonment for harm already done (as opposed to preventative offences aimed at risk reduction or the use of monetary administrative penalties). Interestingly, Horder traces two of these 1920 statutes to international law obligations of Great Britain, suggesting the recursive relationship between TCL and domestic criminal law and how both registered changes in the global political economy and states' regulatory responses to such changes.[91] To the extent that TCL is most often concerned with *mala prohibita*, arising ostensibly from the ills of globalisation, an understanding of crime and the criminal law in terms of *regulation* as well as the distinct nature of transnational *offenders* (who could well be corporations) offers TCL a flexible regulatory repertoire that a conventional criminal law approach lacks.

In turn, TCL offers a unique opportunity to reconsider the use of the criminal law (including at the domestic level) to counter socio-economic problems such as firearms trafficking, drug trafficking, human trafficking, corruption, cybercrime, hijacking and counterfeiting. The transnational scale of these problems introduces

[87]Jeremy Horder, 'Bureaucratic "Criminal" Law: Too Much of a Bad Thing?', LSE Law, Society and Economy Working Papers 1/2014.
[88]*Ibid*, 15.
[89]*Ibid*, 13, suggesting that seriousness of wrongdoing by itself offers no meaningful yardstick and that wrongs can vary dramatically in terms of their seriousness, rendering any attempt to discern a tipping point at which they become truly criminal doubtful. See also *ibid*, 27.
[90]For instance, he claims that in 2008, 440 offences were legislated, of which 30 were aimed at individuals and the rest at business activity. *Ibid*, 17.
[91]*Ibid*, 15.

a level of intractability that could reinforce a strong commitment to the criminal law (as evident in US prohibitionism in relation to drug trafficking).[92] Yet TCL also allows for the emergence of alternate views of the criminal law, as evident in say Mexico's legalisation of the possession of certain drugs[93] and the recent call by the Global Commission on Drug Policy to fundamentally rethink global and national drug policies.[94] This ongoing debate on the use of the criminal law to counter drug trafficking and the varied economic consequences on a transnational scale of complete criminalisation, partial criminalisation, decriminalisation and legalisation offer deep insights into the interplay between market forces and the criminal justice system and the intended and unintended consequences of criminalisation thus rendering the role of the criminal law in addressing complex problems even more contingent.[95] TCL's potential to complicate the somewhat weak conceptual vocabularies of criminalisation could in turn inform domestic debates, which are too often preoccupied with the harmful behaviour of individuals.[96] A feedback loop between TCL and domestic criminal law can thus substantially enrich both fields.

(ii) *TCL's synchronic life and renewed prospects for comparative criminal law*

Another way of deepening the vertical dimension of TCL is through the adoption of a comparative lens. Interestingly, however, comparative criminal law is a field that has yet to take off. As Dubber notes, its invisibility within the canons of comparative jurisprudence can be traced back to its 'peculiar parochialism ... [which] is deeply bound up with the history of criminal law itself'.[97] Although punctuated by the attempts of influential criminal law thinkers like PJA Feuerbach and George Fletcher to theorise universal principles of criminal law, comparative criminal law,

---

[92]Fernando Avelar, 'Alternative Drug Policies in the Americas' (2012) 18 *Law and Business Review of the Americas* 403, 405.

[93] Shapiro (n 71).

[94]*War on Drugs: Report of the Global Commission on Drug Policy* 2 (2011), www.globalcommissionondrugs.org/Report (accessed April 2015).

[95]O'Connor and Rumann (n 71); Andrew Sunter 'The Harm of Drug Trafficking: Is there Room for Serious Debate?' (2006–8) 32(1) *Manitoba Law Journal* 174; Marshall B Lloyd, 'Conflict, Intervention, and Drug Trafficking: Unintended Consequences of United States Policy in Colombia' (Summer 2011) 36(2) *Oklahoma City University Law Review* 293; Matthew S Jenner, 'International Drug Trafficking: A Global Problem with a Domestic Solution' (2011) 18(2) *Indiana Journal of Global Legal Studies* 901.

[96]The stock analyses in this regard are the works of Joel Feinberg: *The Moral Limits of the Criminal Law, Volume 1: Harm to Others* (Oxford University Press, 1984); *The Moral Limits of the Criminal Law, Volume 2: Offense to Others* (Oxford University Press, 1985); *The Moral Limits of the Criminal Law, Volume 4: Harmless Wrongdoing* (Oxford University Press, 1984).

[97]Markus D Dubber, 'Comparative Criminal Law' in Mathias Reimann and Reinhard Zimmermann (eds), *Oxford Handbook of Comparative Law* (Oxford University Press, 2006) 1287–325.

according to Dubber, has been a lacklustre field with sporadic attempts to either narrowly and ahistorically compare specific doctrinal legal principles between two jurisdictions or to offer elaborate compendia of snapshots of foreign criminal law without any serious theoretical attempt at comparison.[98] Shifts are discernable, yet we continue to be exposed to a wide range of domestic criminal laws in need of further comparative theorising[99] or rather more in-depth and meaningful comparisons of a minute number of jurisdictions.[100] Given the challenges of attempting deep, historical, critical and nuanced comparative scholarship, it is no surprise that comparative criminal law as a field suffers from a breadth–depth trade-off. As Dubber astutely observes, this further produces a bias within the comparative project wherein there is likely to be a far greater elaboration of criminal procedure and punishment theory across jurisdictions than a comparison of substantive criminal law doctrine which is likely to be theoretically ambitious. There is then the further bias that even sophisticated comparisons of criminal law doctrine will focus on paradigmatic crimes rather than the vast panoply of crimes that are *mala prohibita*.

This snapshot view of comparative criminal law has to be considered against the backdrop of comparative law more generally, wherein transnational legal developments have triggered a sense of crisis and disciplinary anxiety.[101] As comparative lawyers who have been preoccupied with horizontal comparisons of national legal systems race to build up their study of the vertical dimension of law 'beyond' the nation state, lawyers working in TCL have a unique opportunity to undertake comparative criminal law scholarship. Although it may seem that TCL should be properly concerned only with a given international suppression treaty and its operationalisation through domestic criminal law, there in fact exists, across a range of issues, a robust practical sphere of comparative criminal lawyering wherein lawyers, consultants, policy makers and NGOs, as well as members of epistemic communities (such as feminists), actively compare and borrow from the domestic criminal laws of other jurisdictions. They often deal with matters of transnational moral concern. This alone calls for a redefinition of TCL to include comparative criminal law. Legal academic scholarship has been slow to capture these developments, yet scholars from other disciplines including sociology, political science and criminology have been actively engaged in the comparative study of the distinct crimes that comprise TCL. It may be useful to think of such scholarship in sectoral terms. On sex work for example, several special issues of journals grapple with the governance and

[98] *Ibid*, 1291, 1293, 1304, 1305.

[99] Kevin Jon Heller and Markus D Dubber (eds), *The Handbook of Comparative Criminal Law* (Stanford University Press, 2010).

[100] Markus Dubber and Tatjana Hörnle, *Comparative Criminal Law* (Oxford University Press, 2014).

[101] Mathias Reimann, 'Beyond National Systems: A Comparative Law for the International Age' (2001) 75 *Tulane Law Review* 1102.

regulation of sex work and allied sectors in numerous domestic jurisdictions.[102] However, the lack of comparative legal theorising in such sectoral inter-disciplinary collaborations has all too often translated into ambiguous policy vocabularies relating to criminalisation, decriminalisation and legalisation which are used in contrary ways even within a particular sector and most certainly have different connotations across sectors.[103] Worse still, the lack of a sophisticated legal vocabulary on policy questions and an account of the dynamic interactions between criminal law and other sets of legal rules in any given sector[104] leads social scientists unfamiliar with the nuances of law and legal theory to declare the law irrelevant![105]

For TCL lawyers undertaking such comparative work, the transnational legal 'hook' is likely to vary in intensity. The three examples we consider briefly relate to a widely ratified international legal instrument (trafficking), a weakly ratified legal instrument (sex work), and a case where no suppression treaty exists (domestic violence). Thus in the case of the Palermo Protocol on Trafficking, which has been widely ratified, there is considerable scope for comparing how countries have operationalised the various elements of the Article 3 definition of trafficking. Indeed, the UN Office on Drugs and Crime recently commissioned three issue papers on 'abuse of power or of a position of vulnerability', 'consent' and 'exploitation' with a view to gauging definitional consistency in the operationalisation of the Protocol. Each of these reports has involved comparing the anti-trafficking laws of numerous countries. Significant differences appear. In the Netherlands, for instance, irregular Chinese migrants working for less than half the Dutch

---

[102] (2010) 37(1) *Journal of Law & Society*, special issue on *Regulating Sex/Work: From Crime Control to Neo-Liberalism*, ed Teela Sanders and Jane Scoular; (November 2014) 14(5) *Criminology and Criminal Justice,* special issue on *The Governance of Commercial Sex: Global Trends of Criminalisation, Punitive Enforcement, Protection and Rights*, ed Teela Sanders and Rosie Campbell; (2012) 20 *Feminist Legal Studies*, special issue on *Sex Work and the Regulation of Vulnerability(ies)*, ed A FitzGerald and Vanessa E Munro.

[103] For example, in the context of sex work, regulation is usually used to connote the repeal of any special anti-sex work criminal law allowing the usual laws governing economic activity to govern sex work. Where the criminal law continues to remain on the books but a certain aspect of the industry is decriminalised, that is referred to as partial decriminalisation. In the drug trafficking context, meanwhile, the decriminalisation of a certain activity (such as possession) might be considered regulation. Legalisation in this context might mean the repeal of any criminal laws dealing with drugs.

[104] See P Kotiswaran, 'Born Unto Brothels: Toward a Legal Ethnography of Sex Work in an Indian Red-Light Area' (2008) 33(3) *Law & Social Inquiry* 579 for an account of such interactions. See, more generally, P Kotiswaran, *Dangerous Sex, Invisible Labor: Sex Work and the Law in India* (Princeton University Press, 2011) for the need to reconceptualise anti-sex work criminal laws in light of their economic effects. See also Dubber's bold call for domesticating comparative criminal law by elaborating on the relationship between criminal law and the law of torts, contract and property: Dubber (n 97) 1301.

[105] Laura Agustín, 'Sex and the Limits of Enlightenment: The Irrationality of Legal Regimes to Control Prostitution' (December 2008) 5(4) *Sexuality Research & Social Policy* 73.

minimum wage are considered exploited and trafficked. In Switzerland, on the other hand, all migrant sex workers are considered vulnerable to trafficking even if they have entered this form of work voluntarily. In other instances, where the suppression treaty is less widely ratified, as in the case of the 1949 UN Convention on the Suppression of Prostitution,[106] fewer countries share a family resemblance in the structure of their anti-sex work laws but where they do, the similarity is remarkable. Often, however, the domestic laws of certain countries wield considerable *international* influence, exceeding that of an international legal instrument. At the prohibitionist end of the spectrum, for example, many countries have sought to incorporate into their domestic laws the Swedish model, as it has come to be called, which criminalises customers who buy sexual services. At the non-prohibitionist end, meanwhile, the Canadian litigation in the *Bedford* case[107] has been closely followed in several countries, spurring sex worker groups in particular to test the constitutionality of their respective anti-sex work laws. Similarly, the New Zealand approach has long been held up as sex worker-friendly and therefore worthy of import. Even where a given suppression treaty is poorly ratified, TCL needs to take account of domestic criminal law, as it may be crucial for the implementation of a different suppression treaty. Thus, given the conflation of trafficking with sex trafficking and sex work in the early years after the adoption of the Palermo Protocol, a state could claim that it had met its obligations under the Palermo Protocol by amending the domestic criminal law on sex work.

In the third instance, where the transnational legal hook might appear the weakest, the domestic impulse to criminalise comes not from a suppression treaty but from a human rights instrument, such as the Convention on the Elimination of Discrimination against Women and the mainstreaming of women's human rights within the international human rights movement. Legal ethnographers like Sally Merry have eloquently mapped the negotiation of transnational norms around violence against women in spaces of transnational modernity such as the UN and the complex translation of these norms by national elites into domestic criminal law. Similarly, Keck and Sikkink track how feminists used UN world conferences to build a global network against sexual violence.[108] TCL cannot afford to neglect these developments, particularly because often changes in domestic law and international law emerge contemporaneously[109] and also influence each other.[110]

[106]This Convention has only 25 signatories and 82 ratifying states.

[107]*Canada (Attorney-General) v Bedford* 2013 SCC 72.

[108]Margaret E Keck and Kathryn Sikkink, *Activists beyond Borders: Advocacy Networks in International Politics* (Cornell University Press, 1998).

[109]The US Victims of Trafficking and Violence Protection Act 2000 (VTVPA) came into being around the same time as the negotiation of the Palermo Protocol.

[110]The influence of American feminists in the negotiation of the Protocol has been well documented: see Chuang (n 73); similarly the effect of the VTVPA and the Trafficking

(iii) *TCL's diachronic possibilities: colonial criminal law as TCL par excellence*

We now deal briefly with the need for a diachronic extension of TCL's comparative lens. A foundational anxiety for TCL is the taint of Western hegemony that characterises the negotiation and implementation of several suppression treaties despite the formal equality of nation states as subjects of international law. Yet at least some of these power imbalances that continue to haunt TCL can be traced back to when several non-Western countries were subjects of colonial rule. The export of criminal law to these jurisdictions back then hardly required the mediation of international law. As colonial powers often used the imposition of criminal law in colonies across continents as the key means to consolidate their own sovereignty, it is colonial criminal law that qualifies as 'transnational' criminal law *par excellence*. Beyond acknowledging this historical fact, what use is the study of colonial criminal law to contemporary TCL? After all, it may be that the Indian Penal Code 1860 (IPC) found its way not only to India but also to Singapore, Malaysia, Kenya, Uganda, Tanzania, Somalia, Sudan and Aden.[111] The IPC in these jurisdictions would have then evolved to suit the distinct needs and political formations of these postcolonial nation states, taking off on their own peculiar trajectories of independence.[112] Yet we suggest two motivations for creating a pathway within TCL for the study of colonial criminal law.

At a pragmatic level, the historical depth that an understanding of colonial criminal law offers means that we have a fuller understanding of how triggers from international suppression treaties for the creation of new offences become absorbed in domestic law, building upon layers of pre-existing laws often aimed at countering the very problem that the suppression treaty aims to resolve. Take, for example, the Indian law on trafficking. According to recent statistics, of the 35.8 million victims of modern slavery around the world, 61 per cent – almost two-thirds – live in India, China, Pakistan, Russia and Uzbekistan.[113] India has the highest absolute numbers of slaves in the world. If countries like India and Pakistan are 'hotspot' areas according to NGOs such as Walk Free and the Thomson Reuters Foundation, any serious response to trafficking would be meaningless without a historical understanding of their criminal law regimes (both having inherited the IPC), and their relationship to constitutional mandates and

in Persons Report on the domestic criminal law regimes has been well documented. See Anne T Gallagher, 'Improving the Effectiveness of the International Law of Human Trafficking: A Vision for the Future of the US Trafficking in Persons Reports' (2011) 12 *Human Rights Review* 381, 390–7.

[111] Thomas Metcalfe, *Imperial Connections: India in the Indian Ocean Arena, 1860–1920* (University of California Press, 2008) ch 1.

[112] At least on the face of it, India developed as a democracy post-independence while Singapore is an authoritarian regime; although the IPC operates in both, the trajectory of its development and use varies.

[113] Hope for Children Organization Australia Ltd, *Global Slavery Index* (2014).

subsequent layers of postcolonial labour laws with penal sanctions. In other words, no analysis of the anti-trafficking offence introduced by the Indian Criminal Law Amendment Act 2013 is complete without an understanding of offences against forced labour mandated by the adoption of the Indian Constitution in 1950 and, prior to that, a slew of offences in the IPC on slavery, unlawful compulsory labour and prostitution. It is only against this backdrop that crucial omissions (relating to both the means and purpose under Article 3) in the definition of trafficking in the Criminal Law Amendment Act 2013 make sense. Organisations like UNODC do commission comparative work[114] but without the full benefit of a historically informed theoretical approach that would consider prior attempts to counter 'trafficking' as we have set out above. A similar exercise can be carried out for anti-corruption offences. Indeed, prosecutions under the IPC of corrupt public officials had long been hampered by its requirement to seek prior permission from the executive for prosecution – clearly a requirement meant to suit colonial needs. A substantial number of developing countries use the IPC or some version deriving from it and to that extent share a common criminal law infrastructure. This makes the work of the comparative criminal lawyer more feasible and offers the transnational criminal lawyer an unparalleled vantage point from which to map patterns in the adoption, enforcement and development of a suppression treaty.

At a theoretical and methodological level, the invitation to consider colonial criminal law as part of TCL also brings to the law the rich insights of postcolonial theory. There is already a renaissance amongst legal historians of South Asia as they unpack several areas of colonial law. There is in particular a renewed interest in the IPC and its trans-oceanic travels.[115] Legal historians have sought to demolish the civilisational biases inherent in colonial law exports by destabilising the 'modern English law' – 'despotic traditional Indian law' dyad. David Skuy, for instance, 'provincialises'[116] English criminal law by demonstrating how English criminal law in the first half of the nineteenth century was not modern and that the reason that Macaulay chose it was because he was most familiar with English law and not on account of its inherent superiority. Similarly, Iza Hussin departs from a simplistic view of the IPC as an instrument of empire that simply travelled from metropole to colony to focus on its various 'ports of call',

[114]United Nations Office on Drugs and Crime, *Responses to Human Trafficking in Bangladesh, India, Nepal and Sri Lanka Legal and Policy Review* 2011; see http://traffickingroundtable.org for my review of the report.

[115]David Skuy, 'Macaulay and the Indian Penal Code of 1862: The Myth of the Inherent Superiority and Modernity of the English Legal System Compared to India's Legal System in the Nineteenth Century' (1998) 32(3) *Modern Asian Studies*, 513; Iza Hussin, 'Circulations of Law: Colonial Precedents, Contemporary Questions' (2012) 2(7) *Oñati Socio-Legal Series* 18.

[116]We use this in the sense proposed by Dipesh Chakrabarty in his *Provincialising Europe* (Princeton University Press, 2000).

the complex processes of translation, negotiation, domestication and all-out war that accompanied its reception[117] and the networks of institutions and people who made it possible. Interestingly, she finds significant parallels between the travels of colonial law and the contemporary export of the rule of law project. This examination through colonial law of 'nodes in the worldwide circulation of law' resonates with current attempts to map transnational legal processes and as such contributes both to transnational legal studies in general and to the travels of the criminal law in particular.

Conclusion

In this article, we have argued that Boister's 2003 article has been a crucial intervention in the naming of a sub-field of the international law of crimes, i.e. transnational criminal law. The distinctions between ICL and TCL are useful to a limited extent in affording transnational and international criminal lawyers the discursive space to analyse in greater detail the fast-changing nature of criminal law instruments being ushered in by states to address the effects of globalisation. The nature of transnational criminal law in general, its sources and boundaries and its logics in responding to particular 'transnational crimes' thus need continued clarification. TCL is like a mansion with a shiny new door and Boister's invitation to explore the riches of this (until now) obscure and under-theorised field of law is very appealing. Needless to say, we are attracted. After all, for the most part, we are embedded in the study and teaching of domestic criminal law doctrine while grappling with its all-too-familiar and often narrow scholarly and political trappings. Yet we are essentially ethnographers of criminal law and cross the threshold of the 'international law of crime' with our own prior and eclectic commitments to legal history, legal realism, socio-legal studies, postcolonial theory and transnational legal studies. From this viewpoint, reifying ICL and TCL hardly seems productive. Instead, we find within the relatively new edifice of the international law of crime an extraordinary maze of back doors, interconnecting rooms and even alternative entrances to a variety of private and public legal orders at every scalar unit of transnational legal analysis – the international, regional, domestic and local, as well as the tunnels of history, some alive and others in various states of disrepair. As we have shown in this article, embracing the messiness and contradictions of transnational and international law opens up research pathways linking the 'international law of crime' to private law but also to domestic criminal law, comparative criminal law and colonial criminal law. It is only through this undertaking that we can query the true nature and role of criminal law under conditions of neo-liberal globalisation.

We conclude with a note on the institutional locations and circumstances that make our own critical elaboration of the nascent fields of international and

[117]Hussin (n 115) 18.

transnational criminal law possible. Many of our ideas expressed in this article arose out of teaching in experimental institutional spaces fostered by the increased visibility of transnational legal studies as a field. Our first attempt at teaching what we call Transnational Criminal Law was at the Centre for Transnational Legal Studies (CTLS) based in London, made up of faculty from 14 law schools around the world. The second opportunity we have had to teach the course has been as part of a dedicated LLM Pathway on Transnational Law at King's College London under the aegis of the newly established Transnational Law Institute. As enriching as the classroom has been for our research, particularly the ideas expressed in this article, any effort at truly transnational legal education requires the bridging of numerous legal pedagogical traditions. Students at CTLS, for instance, were undergraduate law students but brought to the classroom a panoply of civil law and common law traditions of thinking about criminal law, which we as common law trained lawyers might have been papering over. Similarly, in drawing students from the Law School and the War Studies department, the Masters level course at King's offered us the opportunity to engage not only with different legal traditions but also with varied disciplinary orientations in a bid to locate the novelty of the transnational legal method and map parallel developments in international relations, peace and security studies. We grappled with the varied expectations of us – to both teach doctrine to the public international lawyers who were eager to join the ranks of the profession while also using the opportunity to broaden the intellectual horizons of those could quite easily end up as consultants for the various international organisations working on transnational criminal law. While the journey towards truly transnational legal education has only just begun, these venues afforded us an opportunity to reflect on the various aspects of our interests in the highly dynamic field of the international law of crime.

The 'elephant in the room' in debates about universal jurisdiction: diasporas, duties of hospitality, and the constitution of the political

Frédéric Mégret*

Associate Professor, Faculty of Law and Canada Research Chair in the Law of Human Rights and Legal Pluralism, McGill University, Canada

Universal jurisdiction is typically understood by reference to the interstate world: for example, as a cosmopolitan institution transcending the limitations of sovereignty. This article highlights instead the concrete role of victim diasporas in bringing claims under universal jurisdiction. Transnational criminal law as a paradigm can also help one understand how the transnational movement of persons is shaping the prosecution of those responsible for atrocities. In addition to being a better descriptive theory of universal jurisdiction, transnationalism has the potential to provide a better normative theory. This article focuses on the extent to which the provision of universal jurisdiction can be understood as fulfilling a duty of hospitality towards those who have suffered harm abroad but are now on the territory of a new state. Universal jurisdiction is part of the constitution of political bonds in migrant societies and should be understood as a manifestation of forms of rooted cosmopolitanism.

Introduction: 'I know who you are!'

In one of the most famous scenes in the film *Marathon Man*,[1] an old woman in Manhattan recognises Dr Szell, a former Nazi dentist known as the 'White Angel of Auschwitz', on the other side of the street, in the heart of the diamond district. Dr Szell, sufficiently sure of his impunity to venture out in this centre of New World Jewish life but nonetheless clearly a bit edgy, is there to get some diamonds appraised. She pursues him, slowly at first, but gradually faster, all the while muttering to herself in German or in strongly accented English as if having trouble believing that it is him. As passers-by part to let her pass, the camera zooms out and shows them to be alternatively intrigued or amused by

*All websites accessed April 2015.

[1] dir John Schlesinger (Paramount Pictures, 1976).

her admonitions of 'My God, stop him! He's a murderer, he's a beast'. No one seems to take her particularly seriously or to want to intervene, some vaguely smiling at the sight of her apparent folly. The street is classic (1970s) Manhattan: full of cars and pedestrians, busy, minding its own business. All the while, Dr Szell uses this indifference to press forward, barely turning back and trying to look composed. As the scene builds to a climax, the old woman, now half-screaming and pointing an accusatory finger at him, crosses the street to incoming traffic and is hit by a car. The crowd rush towards her, at last seemingly concerned. Dr Szell uses this moment of respite to accelerate his pace. As he distances himself from the crowd, we notice that he is being followed, this time by a tall, bold, middle-aged jewellery shop employee (and former concentration camp inmate, as revealed by the tattoo visible on his wrist) who had harboured suspicions about him as he tried to sell his diamonds. The man catches up with him and confronts him: 'I know who you are you murderer, I know who you are!' Dr Szell activates a retractable blade hidden in his sleeve and in one swift blow neatly cuts his confronter's throat. He promptly escapes in a taxi, never to be seen again, as the man lies dying.

This cinematic theme – of the encounter between the victim of a crime and her tormentor in some distant location to which both have resettled but which seems incapable of comprehending the nature of their relation – is the starting point of this article. The unheeded 'I know who you are!' cry embodies a form of tragic encounter. It expresses problems of indifference and untranslatability, as well as the tragic consequences that accompany them: the solitude of the victim, the impunity of the criminal, the missed opportunity for society to condemn, etc. As such, it is powerfully evocative of a range of issues that trials based on universal jurisdiction (UJ) arguably seek to address, albeit in ways that are still remarkably unrecognised, by mixing the distant and the local, the international and the domestic, indifference and concern. Trials of UJ are the place where the two diasporas (perpetrator and victim) meet, where their narratives compete, and where the host society is called upon to arbitrate a conflict that implicates its own becoming and evolving political constitution. This encounter provides a powerful opportunity to reconceptualise UJ at a time when it is largely seen as *passé* – a brief adventure straddling the mid-1990s and early 2000s. Instead, the article will suggest that, properly conceptualised, the practice may have more future than is commonly thought.[2]

The goal of this article is to devise an overarching theory of UJ that is ambitious as a normative theory but also arguably better grounded in the actual processes of UJ than competing theories. In doing so, I give a particular twist to the notion of transnational criminal law that is distinct from the broad portrayal offered by Boister's piece in this issue. The dominant understanding of transnational criminal law is that it deals with largely private crimes of international

[2]Julien Seroussi, 'La Cause de la compétence universelle' (2008) 173 *Actes de la recherche en sciences sociales* 98.

concern whose distinctness is that they are not criminalised as such, as opposed to international criminal law (ICL, which might be more appropriately described as supranational criminal law) understood as 'criminal law applicable in international criminal tribunals where individual criminal responsibility [is] directly applied under international law'.[3]

Although this is not the place to criticise the distinction generally, the opposition between the private and the public, the vertical and the horizontal, the transnational and the inter- (or supra-) national, arguably does not do justice to the fundamental unity of ICL, and the rather contingent and fluid distinction between its transnational and supranational variants. At the very least, I proceed from the background intuition that transnational law and ICL are joined at the hip or possess significant tools in common. Not least of those is the whole apparatus of judicial cooperation and extradition (most supranational crimes are, in the end, treated through domestic or transnational means), as well as jurisdictional rules concerning domestic criminal trials, themselves deeply embedded in public international law.

For example, typical transnational crimes might very well be the object of traditional ICL enforcement (e.g. terrorism before the Special Tribunal for Lebanon, the early proposal of drug trafficking as a crime entering a then hypothetical International Criminal Court [ICC] Statute).[4] More importantly, characteristically supranational crimes (war crimes, genocide, crimes against humanity) are also the object of significantly transnational modalities of crime repression. In this context, UJ may not cover transnational crimes strictly speaking but it is itself a form of transnational criminal *practice*. This makes it a particularly interesting transnational-supranational hybrid, one that combines the horizontal and vertical dimensions of ICL to a remarkable degree and that in itself challenges too rigid a distinction between the two. One might say that universal jurisdiction sits somewhat uneasily between *droit pénal international* and *droit international pénal.*

There is more to this, however, than the intrinsically transnational nature of UJ. The sort of systemic thought that informs the classification of various practices as characteristic of transnational or supranational criminal law often privileges substance (the crimes themselves) over procedure, and at any rate is quite doctrinal in nature. Instead, I argue that transnational criminal law needs to be understood

[3]Neil Boister, 'Further reflections on the concept of transnational criminal law', this volume.

[4]Similarly, there is no reason in principle why UJ as a technique of enforcement should be restricted to supranational crimes. This merely reflects a contingent compromise that UJ should be used sparingly and restrictively given its implications for sovereignty. Longstanding practices of UJ for acts of piracy, admittedly an offence that is caught uneasily between the transnational and supranational paradigms, suggest that UJ can clearly be extended at least beyond the ICC's core crimes.

in a way that benefits from the best insights of transnational legal theory,[5] and that goes beyond the doctrinal or typological to evaluate transnational criminal law in context, as a set of social as well as legal practices. In addition to being intrinsically transnational, I will argue that UJ is used in particularly and distinctly transnational ways that reinforce the notion that transnational criminal law as a paradigm has real social heuristic and not just formal explanatory power.

The article proceeds in three quite distinct methodological steps. First, it focuses on various standard *discourses* that are deployed to justify UJ and that rely on a mix of descriptive and normative claims. It will argue that these discourses largely miss the potential of UJ trials, often because they proceed from grand narratives rather than studying the practice of UJ from the ground up. In particular, UJ has been very much embedded in a model of public international law that emphasises either its cosmopolitan basis, its potential to disrupt interstate relations, or that sees it as a manifestation of the rise of global society, but fails to understand UJ as having much to do with something more domestic and intimate. Second, drawing on the notion of transnational criminal law as seen through transnational legal theory more generally, the article seeks to better understand the actual practice of universal jurisdiction as the product of transnational strategies of justice. These transnational strategies are not, as is often understood, the product of global society but, much more discreetly and powerfully, the product of the flow of peoples across borders and in particular what I refer to as 'victim and perpetrator diasporas'. It is truly such diasporas that provide the missing link in attempts to explain both the potential and limits of UJ in the world today. Third, drawing on this new reality, the article seeks to imagine how it might form the basis of an actual normative theory. Rather than deduce the theory from the necessities and particular constraints of an existing normative system (e.g. public international law), it teases it out by stylising actual normative practices and radicalising their implicit moral claim. UJ is reinterpreted as manifesting a certain concept of hospitality to strangers, an ideal of a functioning democracy vis-à-vis its citizens, and a more general transnational right to remedy for victims. The article concludes with a few thoughts on how such a theory of UJ based on diasporas is strongly supportive of UJ whilst providing at the same time built-in limitations when most necessary.

Three models of universal jurisdiction

In this section, I describe three 'models' of UJ that are proposed as stylised accounts of the facticity and normativity of the practice. By 'model' I understand something specific, namely a combination of both descriptive and normative claims that typically work hand-in-hand as part of set-discourses of the 'is' and

[5]Peer Zumbansen, 'Defining the Space of Transnational Law: Legal Theory, Global Pluralism' (2012) 21 *Transnational Law & Contemporary Problems* 305.

'ought' ('this is how UJ works and how it should/should not work'). This combination of the descriptive and the normative is of course quite characteristic of international legal argument and responds to the need for law practices to be seen as both grounded (apologetic) and normative (utopian).[6] The descriptive part of such discourses gives an air of plausibility to the claims made (UJ as it is understood actually exists as a practice); the normative part rescues UJ from the suspicion that it might be nothing else than a manifestation of power (UJ is not imperialistic). The debate on UJ evident in these models is a debate that is ultimately, I will argue, less about UJ itself taken seriously as a socio-legal practice than about the continued relevance of the public international law framework as prescribing the 'normal' questions that can be asked about it.[7]

The cosmopolitan model

The cosmopolitan model of UJ is arguably the dominant and most ambitious one, having been very influential in the rhetorical genesis of UJ. It is principally concerned with proposing a theory of why UJ is legitimate in a world of states and, in particular, defending UJ against misgivings based on jurisdiction's normal association with sovereignty. Given the tremendous breadth of the exception it proposes to carve, it needs to provide a convincing theory of the exceptionality of UJ. As a result, it frames UJ as a form of jurisdiction exercised against crimes that are so serious as to be considered crimes committed against all – crimes that are, in other words, themselves universal.[8] The central tenet is that certain international crimes are so heinous that they 'shock the conscience of mankind'[9] and that those who commit them are '*hostes humanis generis*' (enemies of mankind).

The exercise of UJ is then typically understood as a form of decentralised enforcement of universal values, wherein certain states stand in for the 'international community', notably (although not only) in the absence of any international criminal tribunal. As expressed recently by the Supreme Court of

[6]Martti Koskenniemi, *From Apology to Utopia: The Structure of International Legal Argument* (Cambridge University Press, 2006).
[7]Mitsue Inazumi, *Universal Jurisdiction in Modern International Law: Expansion of National Jurisdiction for Prosecuting Serious Crimes under International Law* (Intersentia, 2005).
[8]*National Commissioner of the South African Police Service v Southern African Human Rights Litigation Centre* 485/2012 [2013] ZASCA 168 (27 November 2013), para 39: the 'basis for [universal] jurisdiction is not tied to the state's territory or some other traditional connecting factor, but is rather grounded in the universal nature of the offence committed'.
[9]Adducing an absolutely exceptional rationale for universal jurisdiction is of course not the only way in which UJ is kept within the bonds of sovereign propriety. Immunities, for example, retain an essential role. See Chandra L Sriram, 'Human Rights Claims vs. the State: Is Sovereignty Really Eroding?' (3 December 2005), bepress Working Paper 874, http://law.bepress.com/cgi/viewcontent.cgi?article=4379&context=expresso.

Appeals of South Africa, '[international crimes] are crimes in whose suppression all states have an interest as they violate the values that constitute the foundation of the world public order'.[10] States in a sense contribute their judicial system and good will to try individuals 'for the sake of the international community'. States have no particular jurisdictional interest of their own in prosecuting international crimes, only an interest as 'good citizens' of the international community who come to have custody over 'international criminals'.

This theory is made somewhat plausible by the artisans of universal jurisdiction typically invoking its language. Moreover, it is a jurisdictional language that narrowly emulates the language of ICL more generally as a legal order based on the cosmopolitan idea that there is such a thing as crimes against humanity and which sees through sovereigns to target individuals as moral agents directly. There is at least a superficial plausibility to the notion that, in this post-Holocaust age, certain crimes 'shock the conscience of mankind', and pressure from public opinions has occasionally had a role in furthering the cause of UJ. After a while, this creates the notion that UJ is not just normatively *justified* in such a way, but also *operates* as a form of cosmopolitan institution.

However, the cosmopolitan model's weakest spot is as descriptive theory of what goes on when UJ is exercised. In practice, what shocks some does not necessarily shock others, and the delayed use of UJ, sometimes many years after a crime was committed, often belies the notion that the world was 'shocked'. The simple fact that states, judges and activists invoke and speak the language of 'Humanity' does not mean that this is effectively what guides them. In fact, the invocation of 'Humanity' largely fails to tell us why UJ is used in some cases and not others, a decision that must surely be based in something else than pure universalist good citizenship.[11] The idea that states have obligations *erga omnes*, for example, is more a permissible ground than a constraining one. In practice, states invoke the *erga omnes* discourse when they do not want to be faulted for being imperialistic, not as something that 'tied their hands' and left them no choice but to prosecute. If and to the extent that UJ is exercised, it is almost never noticeably for the reasons that the cosmopolitan model of UJ suggests.

This then weakens the cosmopolitan account of UJ as a *normative* theory, rendering it vulnerable to several accusations, all of which have in common a critique of its artificiality and, therefore, illegitimacy. Concretely, the cosmopolitan theory suggests, for example, that the prime beneficiary of UJ is 'global society'. Having set this as its standard, UJ is then often found wanting. The 'international community' is (at best) the most imagined of imagined communities, one whose prioritisation (or even significant influence) as against the ties that bind the local, the national and the interstate is always going to be problematic. For realists, for

[10] *National Commissioner of the South African Police* Service (n 8) paras 23–24.

[11] Itamar Mann, 'The Dual Foundation of Universal Jurisdiction: Towards a Jurisprudence for the "Court of Critique"' (2010) 1 *Transnational Legal Theory* 513.

example, UJ is dangerous for international relations because it risks disrupting normal foreign and diplomatic interaction.[12] For anti-imperialists, UJ is almost always used as part of existing relations of power, particularly relations that espouse old colonial ties. For judicial nationalists, UJ is a waste of precious domestic resources in a context where the state should not be expending significant resources to prosecute foreign criminals for foreign crimes.[13] For liberals, UJ threatens comity at the international level and democracy domestically, since it risks undermining deliberation and transition in the territorial state.[14] For international lawyers, the common critique is that UJ, by targeting individuals as fig leaves for states, bypasses the limitations of interstate adjudication (for example, the International Court of Justice (ICJ)) in ways that are unwarranted.

The interstate model

The interstate model is a less normative and more descriptive and critical theory of UJ and tries to bring a measure of realism to the cosmopolitan theory. This view is particularly prevalent in states whose nationals have been the targets of UJ and who accuse the state exercising it of undue interference in their own affairs. The central tenet here is that it is, above all, *states* that exercise UJ against other states for reasons that, if anything, have much to do with state interest. The model thus predicts that 'disinterested' exercises of UJ when it comes to 'atrocity crimes' (as opposed, for example, to piracy) are highly unlikely because there is no interest in states investing the effort for what is essentially a collective good.[15] Normatively, the model does seem to be able to countenance a limited use of UJ in conditions in which it is seen as corresponding with sovereign interest.

From a public international law perspective, the emphasis on states is an appropriate description of the legal reality. It is of course states that adopt the laws on UJ, without which courts would be most unlikely to exercise it. Moreover, even if courts are independent, they are technically agents of the state and, as a result, every exercise of UJ independently arrived at by a prosecutor or a judge is in effect attributable to the state under international law. UJ is also always, in

[12]Henry A Kissinger, 'The Pitfalls of Universal Jurisdiction' (July/August 2001) *Foreign Affairs* 86.
[13]On this debate (the point having been made on talk radio in Québec at the time with even more intensity), see 'Procès Munyaneza: les frais atteignent les 1,4 Million' *Le Devoir* (14 December 2007), www.ledevoir.com/societe/justice/168463/proces-munyaneza-les-frais-atteignent-les-1-4-million.
[14]For a useful summary rather than endorsement of the argument, see Diane Orentlicher, 'Whose Justice: Reconciling Universal Jurisdiction with Democratic Principles' (2003) 92 *Georgetown Law Journal* 1118–23.
[15]Eugene Kontorovich, 'A Positive Theory of Universal Jurisdiction' (2004) 80 *Notre Dame Law Review* 211.

some way or other, exercised against other states rather than simply individuals. When Ariel Sharon, George Bush or Hu Jintao are the object of arrest warrants, those who seek to have them prosecuted do not really see them as pure individuals in a cosmopolitan world. Rather, they see them as the embodiment of typically sovereign policies and practices that are nefarious and which they seek to fight as such. The interstate model thus 'calls the bluff' of cosmopolitans. UJ is more likely to be seen as 'merely a form of intervention into another state's domestic jurisdiction'.[16]

It is clear that international law as a law (mostly) of states still generally sets out the parameters of UJ. To the extent that it defends UJ at all, this model militates for a sober use of UJ, justified more on functional grounds such as the fact that the *fori delicti* courts are unable and unwilling to exercise their jurisdiction. Its inspiration would be at best Grotian rather than Kantian. Indeed, it strongly argues that international criminal justice should be rendered in the territorial state, which should have priority in prosecuting its nationals. Several states, for example, have made it clear that they have a 'no safe haven' policy and that the default rule is that war criminals should be tried in their country of origin rather than prosecuted under UJ. The interstate model is most likely to tolerate UJ to the extent that it is entirely steeped and integrated within the sovereign order; for example, because there is agreement on both sides that someone should be prosecuted.[17] The credibility of the model has been reinforced superficially by the fact that states and the producing and receiving sides of UJ have fought out their disputes before the ICJ. The ICJ, in turn, has obliged, by reaffirming the status of immunities.[18] This attests to public international law as a traditional arbiter of disputes about the proper cosmopolitan reach of international criminal justice.

There are, however, significant flaws with the interstate model. First, it typically fails where its claim is supposed to be strongest, namely as a descriptive theory. The economic-rationalist claim that exercises of UJ when it comes to 'atrocity crimes' should be extremely rare because of the lack of national interest[19] fails to explain why those cases that have arisen (relatively few in number but involving

---

[16]Anthony Sammons, 'The Under-Theorization of Universal Jurisdiction: Implications for Legitimacy on Trials of War Criminals by National Courts' (2003) 21 *Berkeley Journal of International Law* 114.

[17]Note that this is not an impossibility and UJ need not arise in conditions of state hostility. For example, Senegal and Chad have concluded a treaty following the decision by Senegal to exercise UJ over Hissen Habré, which shows that UJ might not be opposed by the state whose nationals committed the crimes or on whose territory they were committed. Rwanda has also welcomed the presence of a special mission of the French judiciary to investigate genocide crimes on its territory. 'Génocide au Rwanda: l'arrivee d'une mission de la justice française saluee par Kigali' *Jeune Afrique* (6 July 2012), www.jeuneafrique.com/Article/ARTJAWEB20120706184102.

[18]*Arrest Warrant of 11 April 2000 (Democratic Republic of the Congo v Belgium)*, Judgment, [2002] ICJ Rep 3.

[19]Kontorovich (n 15).

an outlay of significant resources) did arise. Moreover, if it is states that are technically liable internationally for uses of UJ, and typically states that are seen as the players in international relations, it is significant sociologically that much of the energy for prosecutions has come from independent magistrates, often with the disapprobation or reluctance of authorities. Indeed, even though legislatures may have passed laws allowing UJ, executives and in particular foreign ministries have often been aghast at the consequences, notably in terms of disruption of foreign policy. There is scant evidence that states are the driving force behind actual uses of UJ, and considerable evidence that both states that are on the receiving *and* producing end of the practice have displayed significant ambivalence towards it. By and large, the forces that lie behind UJ do not see it as falling within a traditional state paradigm, and although some uses are subsumable within that paradigm, they are the exception rather than the rule.

Normatively, the interstate model is problematic. In the best of cases and in refocusing attention on the polities in which crimes were committed, it emphasises the extent to which UJ may displace local transitional and democratic processes, and dispossess societies of cases that ought to be prosecuted in the *locus comissi delicti*. More importantly, it is of course not much of a theory of UJ at all. It basically eviscerates UJ in ways that ask us to sacrifice too much of the idealism of the practice and fails to account for the normative enthusiasm it attracts. In fact, the interstate 'model' of UJ might, at some level, just be reframed as the interstate 'critique of universal jurisdiction', one not particularly inclined to its use except in the rarest of cases. Ultimately, UJ ought to be exercisable even against the wishes of the territorial state and, as will be explored in the last section of this article, arguably even at times when that state is able and willing to try the individuals in question.

The global civil society model

In an attempt to transcend the limitations of both the cosmopolitan and the interstate models of UJ, some scholars have argued that UJ is best understood as a manifestation of global civil society. Global civil society – principally in the form of non-governmental organisations (NGOs) but also including international legal entrepreneurs[20] – carries forward the promise of UJ, pushing cases here and there, creating common platforms for its encouragement and ultimately scoring cosmopolitan points against the interstate world.[21] In that context, the local and the global are being co-constituted through what has been described as a

[20]Carly Nyst, 'Solidarity in a Disaggregated World: Universal Jurisdiction and the Evolution of Sovereignty' (2012) 8 *Journal of International Law and International Relations* 36.

[21]Naomi Roht-Arriaza, *The Pinochet Effect: Transnational Justice in the Age of Human Rights* (University of Pennsylvania Press, 2005).

process of 'recursive cosmopolitanization'.[22] There is an element of international solidarity at work; for example, when Argentine NGOs pressed UJ-based cases concerning the Spanish Civil War, after Spain itself brought cases against the Argentine junta. Civil society essentially nudges the state to rise up to its cosmopolitan role, arguing that UJ is increasingly not just an option but an obligation.

It is certainly true that some NGOs have been at the forefront of some UJ cases and the account probably fares better as a descriptive account than either the cosmopolitan or the state models. NGOs have often deployed UJ strategies on a global basis in which knowledge is shared, best practices are encouraged and transnational NGOs serve as a bridge between different initiatives. Some of the evidence suggests a certain 'justice cascade'[23] so that trials in Spain, for example, have an impact in Argentina or Chile and vice versa. The advantage of focusing on civil society is that it makes the cosmopolitan promise of UJ seem less abstract since it is now carried by real social actors, while not conceding that UJ should be reducible to states' whims. The role of civil society also helps to enhance the legitimacy of UJ in relation to abstract cosmopolitanism or sovereign whim, by reframing democracy as partly tied to transnational processes. As Diane Orentlicher has argued, 'to suggest that Chile should determine Pinochet's fate without hindrance from outsiders misses a crucial point: how Chileans exercise their moral autonomy is partly a function of their participation in transnational normative processes'.[24] By focusing on the transnational element, the focus on civil society is also clearly a step in the right direction.

The problem with the global civil society model is that it is still largely intended as a validation of the cosmopolitan model. Civil society groups do not and of course cannot invoke their own interests as a basis for legitimising UJ, so they speak the language of 'Humanity'. As a result, normative theories based on the idea of global civil society often run into problems of legitimacy and representativeness, as it is not always clear from whom they derive their mandate and whether they are a match for powerfully expressed sovereign or democratic opposition to particular exercises of UJ. Moreover, the elite character of international civil society is not particularly appealing as a normative basis for justifying UJ. The theory does not fully explain why certain cases of UJ occur rather than others. There is still little sense of the forum state actually having an interest of its own in exercising UJ, or of UJ having much connection to local political life and democracy. Theories of global society tend to foreground elements of global consensus among elite transnational actors and typically miss the crucial role played by those actually bringing UJ cases.

---

[22]Daniel Levy, 'Recursive Cosmopolitanization: Argentina and the Global Rights Regime' (2010) 61 *British Journal of Sociology* 579.
[23]Ellen Lutz and Kathryn Sikkink, 'Justice Cascade: The Evolution and Impact of Foreign Human Rights Trials in Latin America' (2001) 2 *Chicago Journal of International Law* 1.
[24]Orentlicher (n 14) 1128.

In conclusion, both the cosmopolitan and state models reinforce each other despite their apparent opposition by suggesting implicitly that whatever else may be true, the debate is one about locating UJ specifically within dilemmas characteristic of the international legal order. For cosmopolitan defenders of UJ, it should be defended because cosmopolitan duties exist; for interstate sceptics of UJ the problem is precisely a cosmopolitan ethos that will often only be a pretext. The civil society model seeks to bridge the gap between these discourses, as well as between normative and descriptive accounts, suggesting that UJ emerges from the practices of global civil society that are both idealistic and grounded. This is a step in the right direction, but it is, as the next section argues, the wrong step.

Another model: the role of diasporas

The significant common problem with all three of the models outlined is their apparent agreement that the state exercising UJ has no particular interest of its own in exercising it. They differ only in the consequences that they attribute to this: for cosmopolitans, merely servicing the 'international community' should be a sufficient motivation; for interstatists there is not much point in trying to encourage states to exercise UJ unless they have a real national interest reason for doing so; and civil society enthusiasts see the possibility of, willy-nilly, nudging the state to see itself in more cosmopolitan terms. Here it seems that the theory of UJ is constantly at risk of confusing its legal definition – the form of jurisdiction exercised by a state that has no evident territorial or personal connection to the persons tried – for a theory of when and why states exercise UJ (or not). Could there be an alternative to these models that shows a way forward and does not simply reproduce the questions implicit in its questioning?

What is striking is the degree to which the dominant descriptive and normative theories of UJ have, in practice, ignored the 'elephant in the room', namely the extent to which UJ is not primarily the result of some abstract invocation of humanity, state interest or, for that matter, global or even domestic civil society. UJ is almost never exercised in a pure supranationalist void by states 'sacrificing themselves' for the global public good; instead it almost always follows existing patterns of transnational interaction between states (for example, between Rwanda and Belgium). This is very occasionally noted in passing as a pertinent sociological variable, but one that is without effect on the descriptive, let alone normative, theory of UJ. I suggest that, on the contrary, this transnational societal factor should be a central element in a wholesale reconstruction of the theory of UJ. Specifically, in this section, I want to focus on the role of 'victim diasporas'[25] as the crucial variable in understanding the evolving practice of UJ as it actually unfolds in reality. Although the existence of an institution of *parties civiles* as a

[25]See Robin Cohen, *Global Diasporas: An Introduction* (Routledge, 2008) 39–60.

trigger for UJ cases is sometimes noted, this must be seen in conjunction with the ability of actual victims, typically in the country itself, to constitute themselves as such.

The reconstitution of polarised communities

Mass crime typically create considerable population flows as individuals flee the site of atrocities, often to faraway destinations. In practice, it seems that there has not been a single use of UJ that was not framed in some way by the residence of victims in the forum state (to mention but a few, Chilean and Argentine victims living in Spain and France; Rwandan victims living in Belgium, France and Canada; Zimbabwean victims living in South Africa; and Chinese/Tibetan victims living in Spain). The existence of diasporas frames the continued relevance of international crimes in subtle but significant ways, helping us to understand that crimes have not spent their entire potential in far-flung locations, but rather continue to have very intense transnational effects. Diasporas in a sense 'bring the crime' to the forum state, sensitise it to its existence and, often, demand some form of recognition. This is evident, for example, in the way the Armenian diaspora has mobilized for decades to obtain recognition of the genocide in every country where it is implanted.

Of course, from a strictly legal point of view, the crime is traditionally understood to have been committed once and for all 'at the time and place' where it was physically executed. However, in practice, if not in strict law, many atrocity crimes have a scope that extends far beyond the moment of commission. Some of the consequences of mass crimes live on in the minds and bodies of those who flee. Atrocities have a way of inscribing themselves in the bodies of their victims, as wounds and trauma, both physical and psychological, that prolong their effects and travel with their bearers. This is particularly the case for crimes that evidence a veritable willingness to mark the body and soul of their targets (rape, torture). In such cases, as feminist political geographers have emphasised, the 'body', acting as a substitute for the group or the nation, describes the 'place' of crime much better than, say, the territory of a state.[26]

Perhaps even more significantly, diasporas often reconstitute in the forum country some of the very tensions and polarities that were characteristic of the state of origin, and therefore some of the conditions that created criminality. That is because, in practice, both victims and perpetrators flee, and both often follow the same routes – routes that typically espouse postcolonial trajectories.

[26]Tamar Mayer, 'Embodied Nationalisms' in Lynn A Staeheli, Eleonore Kofman and Linda Peake (eds), *Mapping Women, Making Politics: Feminist Perspectives on Political Geography* (Psychology Press, 2004) 160 (pointing out that '[a]lthough the location of the rapes can be identified in geographical terms, the site of the rapes was always the woman's body').

Emigration after mass crime is often constrained by availability and practicality, but also quite often historic ties: Turks and Armenians moving to Germany, Jews and former Nazis moving to the Americas,[27] Tutsis and Hutus moving to Brussels or Paris. Arriving at their destination, they then often head straight to some of the very same neighbourhoods that have been more or less implicitly assigned by the host society to recent immigrants, encouraged by a common culture despite their antagonism. This significantly increases the chances that victims' and perpetrators' paths will intersect again, bringing them face to face, in ways that powerfully perpetuate some of the residual energy of the crime that set them on their respective roads, opening old wounds and reigniting past trauma. In the societies to which communities associated with perpetrator and victim emigrated, the legacy of the crimes continues to affect local reality in ways that have sometimes defined processes of 'dealing with the past abroad',[28] as well as leading to more concrete efforts at accountability.[29]

The risk of further victimisation

The 'encounter' between former victims and perpetrators can sometimes take a literal, even ominous character. Consider, for example, the following description of one encounter that eventually led to the opening of an investigation:

> When Hiram Gahima unexpectedly encountered a childhood friend from Rwanda on a Windsor city bus six years ago, he immediately knew something was wrong.
>
> Jacques Mungwarere seemed uncomfortable.
>
> He avoided eye contact with Gahima and dodged questions about what he'd been up to since the two had last seen each other nearly 15 years earlier. Mungwarere 'mumbled and jumbled' his way through the brief conversation and declined to give Gahima his contact information. Gahima was stumped …
>
> Alarm bells went off and Gahima began asking around. He came across stories of Mungwarere's alleged involvement in the 1994 Rwandan genocide, including tales of three survivors and witnesses who now live in Michigan.[30]

---

[27]Ignacio Klich, 'The Nazis in Argentina: Deconstructing Some Myths' (1995) 29 *Patterns of Prejudice* 53.

[28]Alexander Freund, 'Dealing with the Past Abroad: German Immigrants' Vergangenheits-bewaltigung and their Relations with Jews in North America since 1945' (2002) 31 *Bulletin of the German Historical Institute* 51; Karen Quintiliani, Susan Needham, Robert Lemkin and Thet Sambath, 'Facilitating Dialogue between Cambodian American Survivors and Khmer Rouge Perpetrators' (2011) 23 *Peace Review* 506.

[29]Harold Troper and Morton Weinfeld, *Old Wounds: Jews, Ukrainians and the Hunt for Nazi War Criminals in Canada* (University of North Carolina Press, 1989).

[30]'Genocide Suspect Arrested' *Edmonton Journal*, 9 November 2009. A 'letter from the community' was subsequently written to Immigration Canada and the police, reporting concerns. He was arrested and prosecuted under the Canadian Crimes against Humanity and War Crimes Act, SC 2000, c 24.

The chance encounter of victim and perpetrator in some accidental space created by dispersion is a recurrent motif in the movies, and its potential for suppressed violence is significant. Films and novels like *Marathon Man*, *The Odessa Files*[31] and *The Boys from Brazil*[32] helped to sensitise a broad public to the existence of Nazi fugitives throughout the world. Although the image of Nazis conniving in the Amazon to relaunch the Third Reich may owe more to the imagination of Hollywood, Simon Wiesenthal's *The Murderers Among Us*, and countless incidents of former Nazi criminals being found living in impunity, show that enduring presence to be a reality.[33] Tensions have frequently flared up in Brussels, within the Rwandan diaspora in what is known as 'little Kigali':

> In Brussels, more than in any other European city, the separation between victims and executioners is physically incarnated in bars, restaurants, associations, and even dance groups. Insults are exchanged, drunken patrons fist fight. Vandalized several times, the Rwandan cultural center had to close its doors.[34]

Violence has also erupted in the same city on several occasions between Rwandans and Congolese in relation to violence in Eastern Congo.[35] In the 1920s, the failure to punish the Armenian genocide led some Armenians to execute some of those responsible who were then resident in Germany. The danger is not only that victim communities might take justice into their own hands but, more basically, that social peace will be significantly disrupted.[36] There is a symbolic violence to the presence of perpetrators in the same diasporic space as victims, which provides ample opportunity for revictimisation. The idea that this qualifies as a form of permanent insult is quite widespread in testimony from within victim diasporas.[37] At a certain level, the very presence of tormentors is seen as an affront to the memory of victims, and as a concrete threat to their peace of mind. For example, Torontonian Holocaust survivors were said to have felt powerfully insulted by the fact that Imre Finta owned a fashionable downtown restaurant.[38]

---

[31]dir Ronald Neame (Columbia Pictures, 1974).

[32]Ira Levin (Random House, 1976); and the subsequent movie adaptation directed by Franklin J Schaffner (20th Century Fox, 1978).

[33]Simon Wiesenthal, *The Murderers Among Us* (Heinemann, 1967).

[34]Léna Mauger, 'Bruxelles, l'autre terre des divisions rwandaises' *M, le magazine du Monde* (4 April 2013), www.lemonde.fr/afrique/article/2013/04/04/bruxelles-l-autre-terre-des-divisions-rwandaises_3153748_3212.html.

[35]Dan Damon, 'Congo-Rwanda Dispute Hits Heart of Europe' BBC News (29 January 2013), www.bbc.com/news/world-africa-21204861.

[36]Piotr H Kosicki, 'Sites of Aggressor–Victim Memory: The Rwandan Genocide, Theory and Practice' (2007) 37 *International Journal of Sociology* 24.

[37]Tristana Moore, 'How One Nazi War Criminal's Case Could Bring Others to Justice' *Time* (12 May 2011), http://content.time.com/time/world/article/0,8599,2071241,00.html.

[38]James E McKenzie, *War Criminals in Canada* (Detselig Enterprises Ltd, 1995) 139: 'His celebrity as a restaurant operator, and the way in which he deliberately drew attention to

The failure of diaspora studies to take on the question of universal jurisdiction

It is one thing to notice the existence and identity of diasporas as being linked to mass crimes and processes of reckoning with them, but it is quite another to understand how diasporas might actually help to challenge ideas about jurisdiction. The broader idea that the rise of diasporas has the potential to profoundly transform international law is not new and has now become the object of significant research. The work of several scholars, notably in North America, including Adenos Addis,[39] Kim Barry[40] and Anupam Chander,[41] comes to mind. Diasporas have emerged in the minds of some as one of the crucial ways of bridging sovereign and cosmopolitan theories of international law:

> In a world that is increasingly diasporan, full of crisscrossing loyalties, transborder mobility, multinational political states, and transnational communities, neither the statist nor the cosmopolitan paradigm fits. Diasporas require a reconceptualization of the nation-state and the international system. They challenge both the Westphalian cartography of territorially defined sovereigns and the cosmopolitan utopia of a united mankind. The diaspora model begins with the recognition that diasporas exemplify the contemporary condition ... The diaspora model thus offers an intermediate point between the exclusivity of statism and the universality of cosmopolitanism. The lived experience of diasporas demonstrates the possibility of negotiating such divided feelings in a way that allows diasporas to contribute to their homelands and adopted lands simultaneously.[42]

The implications of such an intuition for changing concepts of jurisdiction generally have not been missed. The main focus of the scholarship has been, however, on what is typically described (perhaps ambiguously) as the 'home' state, namely the one from which diasporas emigrated, leading, for example, to the exploration of a notion of 'diasporic jurisdiction'.[43] In other words, the scholarship is largely interested in 'the domestic abroad' rather than 'the foreign at home'.[44] As a result, diaspora scholars have largely missed the relevance of

---

himself, made it seem to the Jews as if he was flaunting his war crimes. The Jews were keen to see him prosecuted ... '

[39] Adeno Addis, 'Imagining the Homeland from Afar: Community and Peoplehood in the Age of the Diaspora' (2012) 45 *Vanderbilt Journal of Transnational Law* 963.

[40] Kim Barry, 'Home and Away: The Construction of Citizenship in an Emigration Context' (2006) 81 *New York University Law Review* 11.

[41] Anupam Chander, 'Diaspora Bonds' (2001) 76 *New York University Law Review* 1005.

[42] *Ibid.*

[43] Addis (n 39). As the title suggests, the emphasis is on imagining the 'homeland' (understood as the country of origin), not imagining the country of destination as something that diasporas actively participate in.

[44] Latha Varadarajan, *The Domestic Abroad: Diasporas in International Relations* (Oxford University Press, 2010).

UJ.[45] The one incident that came close historically to recognising a link between diasporas and UJ was of course the trial of Adolf Eichmann, but this represents a very peculiar set of circumstances in which jurisdiction was exercised by Israel for crimes committed against Jews.

This focus on the state of origin rather than the state of destination is quite at odds with what this article is interested in. It seems to assume that only the state of origin can legitimately exercise jurisdiction because only it can assert a significant link to the populations in question, whereas the state of destination has no particular jurisdictional connection to crimes committed against some of its immigrant population. It is as if the trauma, the pain, the demand for justice were left at the door of the host state upon arrival and could not continue to have legal consequences beyond the state where the crimes were committed. This ignores the fact that diasporas are defined not solely by their country of origin but also by their country of choice, specifically by the choice of having left one for the other, and often of inhabiting mental and sentimental spaces between both. Moreover, it also ignores, perhaps more crucially for our purposes, the fact that diasporas live and breathe in their state of destination and aspire to conditions of decency and the good life there.

Finally, it ignores the fate and ambitions of the society of reception and what may be its own irreducible interest in behaving in certain just ways towards its immigrant populations. Indeed, there has long existed in international law a sense that the *judex deprehensionis* has an interest of its own in not tolerating the presence of persons guilty of certain crimes.[46] As the United States Supreme Court put it, 'A political community has an interest in the law-abiding qualities of its new members, and in deterring repetition of prior misconduct'.[47] War criminals may engage in a range of activities that will create even greater social harm, such as the encouragement of revisionism, the silencing of others through intimidation, or even some sinister plot that is the continuation of their crimes. Indeed, who knows what someone once capable of past atrocities might yet be capable of in his adoptive country (we need only think of Klaus Barbie, the former Gestapo chief in Lyon reinventing himself as security adviser to the Banzer regime in Bolivia). At a certain level, therefore, while the victim refugee seems to be saying, 'Take care of me, provide my remedy for a harm that you did not cause and may not feel responsible for', she is also saying, 'We know this person, believe us you do not want her roaming freely among you'. As a

[45]Interestingly, although Adeno Addis, one of the leading scholars on diasporas, has also written one of the most interesting articles on UJ to date, he does not connect both themes. Adeno Addis, 'Imagining the International Community: The Constitutive Dimension of Universal Jurisdiction' (2009) 31 *Human Rights Quarterly* 129.

[46]Donnedieu de Vabres, 'The System of Universal Jurisdiction: Historical Origins and Contemporary Forms' (2011) 9 *Journal of International Criminal Justice* 534.

[47]As quoted in Centre d'étude et de recherche de droit international et de relations internationales, *La Justice pénale internationale* (Martinus Nijhoff, 2002).

trajectory, this seems immensely preferable to immigrant victims keeping their wounds to themselves in the sullen resignation that their host society can never understand their suffering, never feel empathy towards them, and could not care less about their close encounters with their tormentors.

The idea that the state of origin is the only relevant community is therefore a gross simplification. Affirmation of its relevance cannot take away from another society's grounded affirmation of the relevance of the same crimes to its own community and destiny, albeit for different reasons. Nor can one simply find that the prosecution of X in Rwanda is more important to Rwanda than it is if X is prosecuted in Canada for Canada. We simply do not have an unproblematic metric to compare such things, and there is no reason why Canada as a sovereign concerned with its own political destiny should *a priori* and always cede jurisdiction to Rwanda. It may well be that X is a forgotten *génocidaire* in Rwanda, which already has hundreds of thousands to prosecute, whereas he is a visible community leader in Canada whose presence is seen as taunting the survivors of the genocide and creates a huge commotion there. Attempts to rank the claims of states to a particular case, such as the Princeton Principles,[48] are only soft law suggesting solutions 'all other things being equal'.

'Travelling' harms, human rights and cosmopolitan duties of hospitality

In this final section, I seek to propose a normative theory of UJ that takes seriously the role of diasporas in precipitating exercises of UJ. Drawing on scholarship that has begun examining the impact of migrations on the reframing of 'domestic' human and civil rights issues,[49] and more generally the role of what Harold Koh has referred to as 'agents of internalization' of international law,[50] I seek to conceptualise UJ as an encounter between the host society and its ambiguous 'other' incarnated by the migrant. The 'other' is ambiguous because the decision to resort to and actual use of UJ is about, as I will argue, constitutively determining his or her status. The encounter typically begins with a demand that is made by the 'other' for recognition and possibly inclusion, expressed as a demand for justice in the form of an exercise of UJ (against an alleged perpetrator in the host country).

[48]Princeton Project on Universal Jurisdiction, *The Princeton Principles on Universal Jurisdiction* (Program in Law and Public Affairs and Woodrow Wilson School of Public and International Affairs, Princeton University, 2001).
[49]Kevin R Johnson, 'The End of Civil Rights as We Know It: Immigration and Civil Rights in the New Millennium' (2002) 23 *Immigration and Nationality Law Review* 587.
[50]Koh has described internalisers as 'those individuals, international organizations, or governments that provoke these interactions and dialogues aimed at inducing state compliance with international law'. Although Koh surprisingly did not include diasporas amongst such internalisers, they are arguably an obvious choice. See Caleb J Stevens, 'Hunting a Dictator as a Transnational Legal Process: The Internalization Problem and the Hissène Habré Case' (2012) 24 *Pace International Law Review* 198.

As such, it puts in sharp relief not just abstract cosmopolitan duties to 'Humanity', but much more concrete ones to immigrants and citizens of foreign origin. Moreover, it goes on to raise issues that are as much the victims' as they are those of the society of reception.

The 'other' and universal laws of hospitality

The starting point is that, as has been seen, victims of atrocities travel and bring their trauma and suffering to their country of adoption. That trauma, then, continues to unfold as part of the 'long tail' of mass crime in the host country. More importantly, victim diasporas have legitimate expectations to be treated with decency, if only because the state in question has accepted them, often as refugees and on the very basis of their persecution at the hands of the other government. Victims may thus expect to be treated with dignity, respect for their individuality, and the past that defines them. Specifically, they have at the very least the right not be revictimised by the spectacle of the impunity of perpetrators in their vicinity.

The use of UJ can then be reframed as fundamentally an exercise in creating a safe, welcoming and hospitable society. Kant famously saw a universal duty of hospitality as one of his three articles for a cosmopolitan association. Hospitality arguably corresponds to the most 'grounded' facet of Kant's cosmopolitanism. The obligation of hospitality is seen as deriving directly from the notion that, under conditions of cosmopolitanism, 'violation of right on one place of the earth is felt in all'.[51] Whatever that case may be (and we have expressed moderate scepticism about its descriptive character today), that violation of the law is or should be, at least, felt with greatest intensity at the point of intersection between the universal, the foreign and the local. It is there that the traveller reveals his wounds, as the host opens his door to him. In that respect, victim diasporas can be seen as cosmopolitanism's 'wake up call', putting a local face on an abstract idea, and grounding cosmopolitan obligations in the immediacy and intimacy of an encounter.

Benoît Frydman, in this context, is one of the very few authors to have spotted the potential of theories of hospitality to understand and justify UJ.[52] He has emphasised the usefulness of David Hume and Adam Smith's description of justice as a sentiment of indignation of the spectator. In the encounter with the other that is immigration, the pain and suffering of the diasporic victim, his crossing paths with his former tormentor, or at least knowing that they occupy the same space on the globe, strikes at the core of the observer's intuitions about justice. It is

[51]Immanuel Kant, *Practical Philosophy* (Cambridge University Press, 1999) 330.
[52]Benoît Frydman, 'L'hospitalité judiciaire', Séminaire de Philosophie du Droit 2006–2007, 'Justice et cosmopolitisme', 11ème Séance, Institut des Hautes Etudes sur la Justice (21 May 2007), www.philodroit.be/IMG/pdf/frydman_21_05_07-2.pdf.

this encounter, I would argue, that, more than anything, contributes to actualise cosmopolitan sentiment in concrete ways: not as a result of general sad stories of people being massacred in far-flung locations (which is easily dismissed as distant and not something one can do much about), but of the realisation that the hapless survivors of such events are now in our care. This means that we can no longer be allowed to turn a blind eye, and that, perhaps more concretely, puts victims in a position to make demands on our institutions of justice and democracy.

Frydman goes beyond Kant's own insistence on the rather minimal obligation not to treat the other as an enemy, which is evidently out of tune with contemporary conceptions of how to treat refugees, to specifically include the provision of justice. He speaks of an obligation of 'judicial hospitality': the obligation 'to not close the door of the tribunal to the victim who seeks justice and has no other place to make herself heard'.[53] To close the door to the diasporic victim, in such circumstances, would be incompatible with the duty of hospitality. One cannot, as a host society, decide to ignore some of the characteristics of the diasporic victim or to ask her to renounce them – for example, invite her in only on the condition that she not mention her trauma or, worse, that she not seek the justice to which she is entitled. The obligation is to accept the individual for what he is, as he is, and it is an unconditional one. Derrida's own work on hospitality lamented the extent to which in the West hospitality had become characterised as a form of conditional hospitality, limited by the law. Derrida insisted that the principle of hospitality 'demands, it even creates the desire for, a welcome without reserve and without calculation, an exposure without limit to whoever arrives [*l'arrivant*]'.[54] One might think that access to UJ mechanisms would be a remarkable way of circumventing the law's exclusions, of treating the newcomer as if he were already a citizen.

In fact, the denial of such justice might be considered to be a form of revictimisation, or at least a trivialisation of 'their' suffering, that is incompatible with the very refugee status that they have been granted. As Farber pointed out, '[e]fforts by successive Canadian governments to get rid of Nazi war criminals living in Canada have been "shameful"' to the point where 'allowing these men to live in Canada alongside Holocaust survivors is an insult'.[55] It is noteworthy that in some political discourses on UJ, the presence of international criminals is presented less as an affront to humanity or a violation of international obligations than as an unbearable way of behaving vis-à-vis local victim communities. As one French Senator put it during the debate on the French law of UJ:

[53] *Ibid*, 12 (my translation). The original reads: 'qu'on ne ferme pas la porte du tribunal à la victime qui réclame justice et qui n'a pas d'autre lieu pour se faire entendre.'
[54] Jacques Derrida, 'The Principle of Hospitality' (2005) 11 *Parallax* 6.
[55] Laura Striker, 'Bring War Criminals to Justice, CJC Urges' (2007) 37 *Canadian Jewish News*.

> Is it acceptable that, outside any diplomatic justification, war criminals are quietly sojourning on our soil, free to go shopping or enjoy holidays? Can we remain indifferent to this situation, even as our country welcomes and gives protection to more than 10,000 asylum seekers each year, some of whom are victims of those very crimes?[56]

Similarly, the Dutch Immigration and Naturalization Service emphasises on its website that '[i]t should not be the case that victims who have been granted protection still feel unsafe by the presence in the Netherlands of those who are actually responsible for the fact that they were forced to leave behind hearth and home'.[57] The exercise of UJ may be merely an option under international law, but seeing it as an integral part of the normal process of welcoming refugees and migrants may give it a particular moral urgency. Moreover, migrants who 'put the state before its responsibilities' are effectively doing the host state a service, contributing to the detection, investigation and prosecution of war criminals whose very presence on the territory of the state is a looming threat to public order.

In this context, the willing exercise of UJ is also, in the framework of unconditional hospitality, 'about allowing the self to be interrupted or questioned by the welcome of the other'.[58] In the best of cases, it may involve hearing and accepting stories, for example, about how one's state was also implicated in the far-flung genocide. It should be fairly evident that this is a goal to which democracies should aspire as a way of making sense of their place and responsibilities in the world. Conversely, there are many traces in the public discourse, the sentiment being that a society that fails to provide justice against criminals in its midst 'demeans' itself.[59]

---

[56]Jean-Yves Leconte, République française, Sénat, Séance du 26 février 2013 (compte rendu intégral des débats) (my translation). The original reads: 'Pouvons-nous accepter que, sans aucun motif de nature diplomatique, des responsables de crimes de guerre séjournent tranquillement sur notre sol pour y faire leurs courses ou y passer des vacances? Pouvons-nous rester indifférents à cette situation, alors que notre pays accueille chaque année plus de 10 000 demandeurs d'asile et qu'il leur accorde sa protection, à eux qui ont parfois été victimes de ces crimes?'

[57]'The Netherlands Not a Refuge for War Criminals and Human Rights Offenders', Immigratie-en Naturalisatiedienst, https://ind.nl/EN/organisation/themes/1F/Pages/default.aspx. Of course, there has long been a certain ambiguity about 'no safe haven' policies that seem more concerned with insulating the country from war criminals than actively prosecuting those that nonetheless have made it in. However, the notion that victims should not have to run into their former tormentors can stand as a justification both for exclusion of war criminals from the asylum process and for prosecution of those who have managed to dodge immigration filters.

[58]Karima Laachir, 'Hospitality and the Limitations of the National' in Sarah Gibson and Jennie Germann Molz (eds), *Mobilizing Hospitality: The Ethics of Social Relations in a Mobile World* (Ashgate, 2012) 178.

[59]Mark Aarons, 'No Refuge for War Criminals' *The Australian* (25 April 2005), www.theaustralian.com.au/business/legal-affairs/no-refuge-for-war-criminals/story-e6frg986-1111116156771.

From migrants to citizens: universal jurisdiction as part of the democratic process

There remains one problem with the intuition that universal laws of hospitality are the key lens with which to assess states' obligations to articulate UJ regimes as articulated by Frydman on the basis of Kant: namely that Kant was only concerned with the transient visitor. He did not imagine a world of mass migrations in which migrants would be allowed to stay as a matter of right and would more often than not decide to remain in their country of immigration. Nor was he (nor perhaps could he have been) interested in the constitution of complex multicultural societies with very peculiar symbolic and legal needs. What is interesting in this respect is that, within the loose category of victim diasporas, the distinction between foreigners and citizens (first, second or third generation) is increasingly blurry. In fact, one way of reconstructing claims to the assertion of UJ by victims is not as a demand from 'without' (as in the case of Rigoberta Menchu literally travelling from Guatemala to Spain to start a UJ case and then returning home) but increasingly very much a demand from 'within' (as in the case of the grandchildren of Holocaust victims born and raised in North America mobilising for action to seek reparations).

This applies, perhaps most interestingly, at the point of transition from immigrant to citizen. The choice to bring a case in the host country is not misguided and, apart from the fact that it is constrained by all kinds of practicalities, should be seen as a normative, even deeply political one. What migrant victims are doing, in an act symbolically founding of their new citizenship (or at least their aspiration to it), is fundamentally deciding that, at least in this particular instance, they would rather their case be pursued in their host society than in their home state.[60] Therefore, in seeking the assistance of institutions of justice in their country of immigration, victims are not burdening it with an illegitimate task or engaging in 'judicial tourism' (to draw on the tiresome 'welfare tourism' metaphor often used in the tabloid press). In fact, their choice of the host state is fundamentally an act of integration within their host society and a vote of confidence in its judicial system. In choosing a particular host society, diasporas have inscribed their political existence within its evolving constitution. To press the case for justice in that society is already to experience it as citizens, citizens who make a claim for their suffering to be taken seriously, and not settling for bare acceptance. Far from being primarily a vindication of cosmopolitan citizenship (as theories of global civil society seem to suggest), then, the pressing of UJ claims is much more *an expression of a traditional aspiration to be integrated within the bounded community of a particular polis.*

[60]This latter option may well remain a possibility, but one almost never voiced. The Rwandan diaspora in Canada insist that Munyaneza be prosecuted back in Rwanda in order to protect Rwandan sovereignty, for example.

Seen from the point of view of the host society, the question that the victim claimants ask is also a fundamentally political one, and one that must be confronted: to whom exactly does the host state owe its obligation of hospitality? Indeed, the victim seems to be saying: 'You cannot have both of us here – I who suffered at the hands of him, and he who tormented me.' Confronted with this stark choice, a hospitable society must choose one or the other. 'If one of the two of you has to leave (or be prosecuted),' the host should surely then reply, 'then it should be he who has killed and not he who has suffered.'[61] The answer can only be, at least from the perspective of democratic theory and cosmopolitan justice, that hospitality is owed to the victims and not to the perpetrators. Indeed, much of the efforts of states have been directed at withdrawing citizenship from those who have committed international crimes (leading to their expulsion). This at least addresses the fact that an individual probably should never have been accepted on the territory of the state in the first place.

However, the better position is that they should be tried locally. In not simply 'ridding itself' of individuals suspected of atrocity crimes through expulsion, the forum state accepts that their crimes have had a local incidence and that their lies have affected the bonds of citizenship, and gives the implicit assurance to victims that their lives will not be poisoned by the presence of their tormentors. The exercise of UJ for the benefit of victim diasporas at home is therefore a form of symbolic reaffirmation of a community of destiny encompassing migrant citizens' pasts as victims, as if to say 'your suffering is now our own'.[62] As one Rwandan-Canadian activist put it, UJ 'allows victims and survivors to feel protected by a justice system that is prepared to seek accountability for the harm they have suffered'.[63] As a result, the obligation to grant access to justice arguably goes far beyond the minimum obligations of hospitality. It also extends in time to travellers who have long rested their metaphorical suitcase and become part of the community within which they seek justice; indeed, often those who have become *citizens*. It is important to understand that in practice the plaintiffs or *parties civiles* in UJ cases often do not appear principally as 'foreigners' or even refugees or migrants. Rather, they typically bring their case as members of the forum

[61]This is worth pointing out because of the way in which the laws of hospitality have at times been invoked in a twisted way to defend the fugitives themselves. '[Habré's lawyers] argue prosecution would be contrary to traditional Senegalese hospitality. This discursive strategy relies on *teranga* [hospitality] when calling attention to the fact that, since he arrived in Senegal, Habré has lived in peace as a good Muslim, married a Senegalese woman from a prominent Tijaniya family, had Senegalese children, and used his wealth to become an important supporter of local businesses'. Stevens (n 50) 229.

[62]There are other contexts where this is evident – for example the way in which certain countries with significant Armenian diasporas have become champions both domestically and internationally of the recognition of the Armenian genocide.

[63]Richard Nsanzabaganwa, cited in Canadian Centre for International Justice, 'As Sentencing Hearing Opens in Historic War Crimes Trial, Experts Say More Can Be Done' (14 September 2009), www.ccij.ca/media/news-releases/2009/index.php?WEBYEP_DI=21.

society. The 'stranger', in other words, is much more familiar than the UJ-hospitality mystique might suggest. He is very much 'one of us', perhaps a neighbour – different only in that at an earlier point in his life he was victimised as part of a campaign of human rights abuses, but otherwise our equal and, most importantly, our co-citizen. As the 'other' morphs into the 'citizen', this evidently reframes his right of access to justice no longer as just part of the management of the peripheral reaches of the polity, but very much as part of the lived life of democracy.

When it comes to existing citizens, UJ might be seen as the political equivalent of a renewal of vows, one designed to affirm that the social compact remains and is as strong as ever, regardless of the diverse origins of the participants in the life of the city. In this intriguing line of thought, UJ would be less about the global fight against impunity than about the affirmation of equality between citizens. Here the lines between criminal and constitutional law become blurred as the criminal law becomes a way of *constituting the political.* In a quite different yet relevant context, Leora Bilsky has shown how, in some criminal trials (of terrorists, in her case), 'instead of working within the well-known boundaries of a political community from which it draws its legitimacy, the court itself participates in the act of drawing the boundaries of the political discourse community to which it belongs', highlighting the extent to which the 'relation between criminal law and a political community ... is a dynamic and a constitutive one'.[64]

Courts exercising UJ, I would argue, are also very much engaged in this exercise of 'boundary drawing', albeit in different ways and for different ends than terror trials.[65] The exercise of UJ is the manifestation and perhaps the act of constitution of a community composed of both native-born and immigrant, of those whose lives have been unperturbed by mass crime and those whose lives have been defined by it. It affirms, in a sense, a community of destiny, that we are 'all in this together', and that 'although asking us to feel the suffering of the whole of humanity may exhaust our sympathy and be work fit for a saint, your suffering as neighbour, friend, colleague, and fellow citizen is our suffering too'. Fundamentally, therefore, it inscribes citizenship within an act of empathy, solidarity and equality, which expresses the highest political virtues.

---

[64]Leora Bilsky, 'Strangers Within: The Barghouti and the Bishara Criminal Trials' in Austin Sarat, Lawrence Douglas and Martha Umphrey (eds), *Law and the Stranger* (Stanford University Press, 2010) 97.

[65]Although Bilsky is interested in terror trials characterised by 'radical difference' between two groups, there is a sense in which UJ trials also exhibit such a 'radical difference' between the part of a diaspora associated with victims and that associated with perpetrators (possibly reinforced by indigenous sectors of local public opinion taking the side of one or the other). The difference is that, unlike terror trials, the domestic courts are less strongly implicated in this radical difference and are therefore perhaps better placed to comment on it.

The human rights obligations of the host state: do victims have a right to universal jurisdiction?

To what extent is this reasoning implicitly recognised in existing positive international law? Could it be used to press the normative case further? The theoretical idea that diasporic victims should be 'welcomed' as parties in UJ cases at least has the potential to mesh well with certain notions taken from international human rights law. Where the legal debate on UJ has typically, following a broad public international law inspiration, focused on the presence of the accused on the territory proposing to exercise jurisdiction, one might consider that a human rights perspective on UJ would instead focus on the presence of migrant or diasporic victims on that territory. Three rights come to mind that might support strategies claiming that under international human rights law one has a right to the availability and exercise of UJ: the right to an 'effective remedy'; the right to access a court; and the right to reparation.

Individuals who are victims of crimes that are also grave human rights violations have a recognised right under international law to a remedy, which is largely understood as involving access to justice and judicial remedies (i.e. courts). This remedy is also understood as involving the investigation, search, arrest, prosecution and, as the case may be, conviction of the individuals who committed such crimes. In other words, the repression of international crimes is not simply an obligation owed to the international community as such; it is, in the human rights framework, concretely and directly owed to the victims. The right is a right to an effective remedy that is directed at the state, but it is not entirely clear that this is necessarily the state in whose territory the crime was committed. The issue of the right to an effective remedy has increasingly come up in transnational contexts, in which the issue was whether a victim of human rights violations had been deprived of her right to an effective remedy in another jurisdiction.

In *Al-Adsani v United Kingdom*, the European Court of Human Rights found that the UK had not breached its obligation to provide a civil remedy by failing to waive the immunity of Kuwait and Kuwaiti nationals – but it did thereby seem to accept the principle that the UK might have otherwise 'inherited' Al-Adsani's right to a remedy, because of his presence in the UK. More revealingly, the UN principles on the Right to a Remedy and Reparation for Victims of Gross Violations of International Human Rights Law and Serious Violations of International Humanitarian Law state that:

> 4. In cases of gross violations of international human rights law and serious violations of international humanitarian law constituting crimes under international law, States have the duty to investigate and, if there is sufficient evidence, the duty to submit to prosecution the person allegedly responsible for the violations and, if found guilty, the duty to punish her or him …

> 5. To that end, where so provided in an applicable treaty or under other international law obligations, States shall incorporate or otherwise implement within their domestic law appropriate provisions for universal jurisdiction.[66]

As can be seen, the principles move seamlessly from (i) prescribing an obligation of states (in the plural) to investigate to (ii) incorporating UJ, as though the two are intimately tied. This reinforces the sense that UJ is the natural prolongation of the right to an effective remedy and to reparations. Finally, perhaps the clearest signal to date has come from the Committee against Torture, which has emphasised on numerous occasions when considering state reports that states parties should establish UJ in cases of torture. In *Suleymane and others v Senegal*, the Committee reaffirmed that position.[67] The emphasis has also been on the obligation to provide jurisdictional remedies so that victims of torture can obtain reparations in their host country.[68]

In fact, nothing in existing international human rights instruments suggests that the state where or by whose nationals the crime was committed should necessarily be the one providing justice,[69] and there is certainly an argument that victims should not be forced to seek an improbable or impractical remedy there. The right to an effective remedy is framed in broad terms and as a general right. Presumably most victims will want to seek a remedy against or in the state that they accuse of violating their rights but, provided the forum state has a realistic opportunity of providing a remedy (e.g. because a suspect is on its territory), and especially if the victims reside in the forum state, it does not seem that they should be prevented from obtaining it there. We can thus see the contours of a 'transnational right to an effective remedy' appearing, entailing, essentially, the exercise of the state's criminal law prerogatives for the victim's benefit through the medium of UJ.

It is important to note that conceptualising the 'right to UJ' in that way both strengthens and limits its status. It strengthens it because UJ is as a result portrayed as a human right of victims and not simply a right/prerogative of states; it limits it because only persons with significant ties to the jurisdictional state have a right to seek an effective remedy, thus guarding against forum shopping. In accepting them as residents or even citizens, the host country has consented to those

---

[66]Basic Principles and Guidelines on the Right to a Remedy and Reparation for Victims of Gross Violations of International Human Rights Law and Serious Violations of International Humanitarian Law, GA Res 60/147, UN Doc A/RES/60/147 (16 December 2005).
[67]*Suleymane Guengueng et al v Senegal*, Communication No 181/2001, UN Doc CAT/C/36/D/181/2001 (2006).
[68]Christopher Keith Hall, 'The Duty of States Parties to the Convention against Torture to Provide Procedures Permitting Victims to Recover Reparations for Torture Committed Abroad' (2007) 18 *European Journal of International Law* 921.
[69]On this technical point, I disagree with the more prudent position expressed by Frydman (n 52) 12–14. I see more potential for a broad right to reparation and effective remedy as exercisable wherever the victims have some significant connection – which of course need not be the state where the crimes were committed.

victims' presence on its territory, including the degree to which that presence is a continuation of a traumatic past. They therefore fall under its jurisdiction from the point of view of international human rights law. Seeing UJ as part of a domestic public service of justice and reparations to victims wherever their victimhood has been experienced helps to connect jurisdiction to the state in which victims have elected to live and which becomes by virtue of this election their *obligé* in terms of human rights. It gives true resonance to the cosmopolitan moorings of UJ: not so much the abstract defence of humanity as the honouring of the discrete rights of persons seeking justice on one's territory.

Conclusion

This article has sought to propose a radical reframing of the theory of UJ based on a closer inspection of its practices and an articulation of its ethos. It contrasted several typical 'models' of UJ, which ultimately were all criticised for having been forged in a different age and with a view to solving normative riddles (how international order and justice can be sustained simultaneously) that are no longer the most relevant. These discourses ultimately have several problematic features in common: a neglect of actual micro-socio-legal practices of UJ and in particular a relative neglect of the way in which transnational flows, notably as illustrated by diasporas, powerfully reshape both the demand for and offer of UJ. Instead, diasporas were presented as truly the missing link in understanding how UJ actually functions. It is they who not only press for cases but, in a sense, bring the distant to the local, and help to demonstrate through their lived experiences that crimes committed in faraway countries may continue to have significant repercussions on others.

This then sets the groundwork for a quite different understanding of the *normative* theory of UJ, one seeking to make the case that these practices should be taken seriously as normative practices. UJ may be defended or opposed on the broad basis of a defence of 'Humanity', but in practice it can be understood as defending a much more specific form of 'Humanity': that which lies in the encounter between a host society and the victim 'other'. In that respect, I have shown that the line between extending universal laws of hospitality to migrants and integrating citizens is a thin one and that, in practice, victims bringing cases under UJ simultaneously constitute themselves as citizens rather than merely guests. They give the local justice system a vote of confidence and hold it worthy of their demand for justice. As such, the exercise of UJ should be seen not as a net liability for the state that exercises it – a more or less abstract service rendered to the international community – but very much a part of the ongoing constitution of multicultural societies and politically democratic institutions based on the rejection of the presence of free war criminals 'in our midst'.

The theoretical work suggested in the article has implications concretely for when UJ cases should be accepted, and it militates very much for a case-by-case approach. To the extent that there is an increasing 'public interest' test in determining whether prosecutions should be launched, factors that are worthy of significant deferral are the presence of victims as residents or citizens within the host state and the fact that they decided to bring their case there. However, the public discussion should be very much informed by issues of *national* politics involving the ongoing questioning of society, the proper delimitation of the bonds of citizenship and foreignness, and the choice that a society makes about its inscription in the global. The resulting theory is doubly unorthodox in that it is more expansive than sovereignists would want in some cases, and more internationalist than cosmopolitans would ideally wish it to be. On the expansive side, rather than always presuming that the territorial state is the one that should be competent unless it is found unable or unwilling – as is very much the emerging dogma – we should recognise that the forum state has an interest of its own in bringing prosecutions on the basis of UJ that is quite independent from the territorial state's, and that it should not be shy about defending that interest. The main idea seems to be that the territorial/national state (i.e. the one in which the crimes were committed) has no monopoly on cases in a world in which crimes often continue to have effects far beyond the place where they originally occurred. This means, for example, that there is no strong reason why the forum state's jurisdiction should necessarily be subordinate to that of the territorial state; it also means, for example, that not even the territorial state's amnesties should bind the forum state, for the forum state's interest in exercising jurisdiction is its alone.

On the restrictive side, the theory is far from being a free-for-all, and does rise to the challenge of setting clear limits on UJ that guard against overreach. For example, contrary to the views of many 'cosmopolitans', the theory would militate quite strongly for the presence of perpetrators on the territory of the forum state as creating a situation that is fraught with domestic tension with local victim groups and therefore warrants exercise of UJ. Conversely, it would tend to typically ignore more virtual assertions of *in absentia* jurisdiction that seem to be based largely on some quixotic concept of abstract justice not based on any meaningful encounter. The priority is to prosecute cases that cause social alarm at home, not to engage in international feuds based on opportunistic forum shopping. In practice, this is largely what has happened, which may explain why UJ has defied the fears of critics that it would become excessively politicised.[70] In effect, situations in which a diaspora becomes cognisant of the presence of war criminals in its midst and decides to and has the ability to do something about it, are relatively limited instances.

In saying this, this article does propose a radical rethink of the very basis of jurisdiction. By grounding it in attention to one's neighbours and friends from

[70]MH Morris, 'Universal Jurisdiction in a Divided World: Conference Remarks' (2000) 35 *New England Law Review* 357 (noting that 'if the potential for improper use of universal jurisdiction is so great, then it is perplexing that we do not see more examples of its misuse').

afar (the 'victims' rather than the 'criminals' in our midst) – whether citizens, residents, or even temporary refugees – and by making it a part of the constitution of a just society at home, it hopes to have fundamentally shifted the case for UJ away from an abstract cosmopolitan gaze. The vision of UJ as conducted 'for' or 'against' others at a distance, on which both proponents and opponents converge, has failed to notice what is in a sense staring observers in the face, namely the much more intimate mixture of the local, transnational and global that in practice provides the fuel for actual UJ strategies. As such, the argument provides resources for those who seek to advocate for UJ, but expands that constituency beyond, say, human rights NGOs to include citizens with an interest in democracy: all those interested in the fate of migrants and the politics of integrating new citizens.

To conclude, this article presents an opportunity to think about the relationship between public international law, ICL and the paradigm of transnational law. I have shown that the public international law model and its symbolic construction are part of the problem: an obstacle to understanding what UJ actually involves, and therefore to being open about its normative potentialities. ICL itself, for all its claims to disciplinary renewal, is heavily dependent on this public international legal model. Understanding the full sociological and normative dynamics of UJ requires attention to issues that are typically swept aside by public international lawyers and are better understood as falling under a broad transnational law label. Transnational criminal law allows us to break open new paths of exploration that better connect different temporalities and spaces, and fundamentally make better sense of the complex legal worlds that we inhabit.

By the same token, it is clear that transnational law and ICL do not exist in a state of complete disconnectedness. International law still helps us understand how UJ, all other things being equal, impacts on the problem of maintaining order and relations between states. Admitting the relevance of such concerns is not the same thing as saying that they exhaust the debate, though. In effect, transnational legal flows continue to be embedded in the public international world that defines them (after all, the very definition of a diaspora is mediated by the notion of states and borders), even as they seek to manipulate and transform it. Transnational criminal legal theory, then, is neither entirely external to nor subsumed by ICL, but can help to bridge the gap between its domestic, interstate and cosmopolitan components.

Acknowledgements

I gratefully acknowledge the invaluable research assistance of Allison Rhoades.

Bird's-eye view and worm's-eye view: towards a defendant-based approach in transnational criminal law

Sabine Gless*

Professor of Criminal Law and Criminal Procedure, Faculty of Law, Basel University, Switzerland

While the classic approach to transnational law provides a valuable tool for identifying the legal frameworks governing transborder occurrences, it falls short of covering all relevant aspects of transnational criminal law (TCL). This article argues that criminal law – unlike other areas of law – is fundamentally a state-oriented concept, leading to unique problems when implemented across state borders, especially for the individual facing penal power. A theoretical concept of TCL must therefore not only map extensions of state powers from high above, but also look for the individual's position in the possibly overlapping normative orders on the ground. The current predominant bird's-eye view must be modified according to the worm's-eye view. In doing so, the specific features and resulting problems of TCL will emerge. From this modified point of view, a main challenge is the establishment of a globally recognised coordination scheme, which will protect the legal position of individuals – particularly defendants – affected by states exercising their *ius puniendi* across borders.

I. Introduction

For several decades now, scholars have been debating the emergence and consequences of legal frameworks providing the structure necessary to exercise the *ius puniendi* in a transnational setting.[1] The historical dimension is central to this discussion: the founding and consolidation of state jurisdiction rests upon the Westphalian model of a state, based on territoriality and a monopoly of force,[2] which is

*All websites accessed 16 February 2015.

[1]Neil Boister, *An Introduction to Transnational Criminal Law* (Oxford University Press, 2012) 3–23; Kai Ambos, *Internationales Strafrecht* (CH Beck, 4th edn 2014) 2–5; Helmut Satzger, *International and European Criminal Law* (CH Beck, 2012) 2.

[2]Daniel-Erasmus Khan, 'Territory and Boundaries' in Bardo Fassbender and Anne Peters (eds), *Oxford Handbook of the History of International Law* (Oxford University Press, 2012) 225, 233–5.

well-established in Europe and elsewhere and accompanied by the transfer of prosecuting power from the victim to the public.[3] This development has not only proven favourable for building state power but has also granted defendants a guarantee of due process when being charged with a crime.[4] The phenomenon, however, did not turn out to be a win-win situation for everyone involved, since some defendants lost domestic privileges[5] and some victims lost control over the conflicts that aggrieved their rights.[6] The adoption of criminal codes and the establishment of state courts, as well as the appointment of governmental judges and subsequently of public prosecution services ('*Staatsanwaltschaften*'), have been key factors in the rise of the Westphalian state because they allowed specific state organs to exercise the monopoly of force according to public law within a given territory.[7] The concept translates into different forms of jurisdiction – prescriptive, adjudicative and enforcement – which all originate from a state's interest in maintaining its legal order.[8]

The emergence of transnational criminal law (TCL) – a special branch of transnational law pertaining to transnational criminal cases[9] – calls into question the basic features of criminal law, namely the monopoly of force within a given territory, since it rests on the assumption that states may exercise power across borders in the field of criminal law. This explains the fierce political struggle, as well as the legal debate, over a possible transfer of the *ius puniendi* from the state level to the supranational level. In Europe, the debate surrounding a broad European Union

[3]For a recent analysis of criminal laws being public laws, see e.g. Malcolm Thorburn, 'Criminal Law as Public Law' in RA Duff and Stuart P Green (eds), *Philosophical Foundations of Criminal Law* (Oxford University Press, 2014) 21.
[4]See Frederick Mark Gedicks, 'Originalist Defense of Substantive Due Process: Magna Carta, Higher-Law Constitutionalism, and the Fifth Amendment' (2009) 58(3) *Emory Law Journal* 585.
[5]Sabine Gless, 'Transnational Cooperation in Criminal Matters and the Guarantee of a Fair Trial: Approaches to a General Principle' (2013) 9 *Utrecht Law Review* 90.
[6]Nils Christie, 'Conflicts as Property' (1977) 17(1) *British Journal of Criminology* 1, 7–9.
[7]See, for example, from a historical point of view: Hinrich Rüping and Günter Jerouschek, *Grundriss der Strafrechtsgeschichte* (CH Beck, 2007) 26–29, 97–99; Frank Meyer, *Strafrechtsgenese in Internationalen Organisationen* (Nomos, 2012) 601–11; from a philosophical point of view: RA Duff, 'Responsibility, Citizenship, and Criminal Law' in Duff and Green (n 3) 125, 131–41; from an international criminal law point of view: Danielle Ireland-Piper, 'Prosecutions of Extraterritorial Criminal Conduct and the Abuse of Rights Doctrine' (2013) 9 *Utrecht Law Review* 68, 69–72.
[8]On the various forms of jurisdiction in the context of criminal law, see Michiel JJP Luchtman, 'Towards a Transnational Application of the Legality Principle in the EU's Area of Freedom, Security and Justice?' (2013) 9 *Utrecht Law Review* 11, 17–23; Anna Petrig, 'The Expansion of Swiss Criminal Jurisdiction in Light of International Law' (2013) 9 *Utrecht Law Review* 34.
[9]I.e., acts that are not international core crimes but are committed in or affect more than one jurisdiction. See Sabine Gless and John A.E. Vervaele, 'Editorial: Law Should Govern. Aspiring General Principles for Transnational Criminal Justice' (2013) 9 *Utrecht Law Review* 1.

(EU) mandate on shaping and adopting criminal law and criminal procedure serves as a prominent example.[10]

By and large, little attention has been given to a theory of TCL up until now. The various fields – such as law flowing from 'suppression conventions' adopted within the United Nations (UN) framework, rules governing mutual legal assistance and European criminal law – have instead sprouted in their own peculiar ways with little connection to each other. Only recently has the growing interest in the basics of TCL led to new discussions about its theoretical underpinnings. For some scholars, the crucial question is: *What is the nature of transnational criminal law?* This question moves beyond the traditional distinction between two bodies of law we can define quite clearly: national criminal law, and international criminal law *stricto sensu*, i.e. the core crimes codified in the Rome Statute of the International Criminal Court (ICC Statute) and grave breaches of international humanitarian law.[11] For others, it seems more important to consider *what transnational criminal law actually does*, especially with regard to the individuals affected by it.[12] The divide is not, as one might initially think, between theorists striving to categorise and practitioners handling the impact. The divide is rather between the particular legal approaches to TCL: on the one hand, classic state-oriented, international public law scholars see TCL as the international 'suppression conventions and the consequences for state policies in criminal justice'.[13] Scholars of criminal law, on the other hand,[14] look rather for the effects of TCL enforcement on particular individuals, such as procedural rights and criminal defence on the side of the defendant in practice, or a possible powerlessness on the side of the victim to file a private claim on its own merits.[15] What may seem an insignificant difference

---

[10]See, for example, the 'Lisbon judgment' of the German Bundesverfassungsgericht: BVerfG, 2 BvE 2/08 vom 30.6.2009, Absatz-Nr (1-421), www.bverfg.de/entscheidungen/es20090630_2bve000208en.html, paras 252–5; Daniel Halberstam and Christoph Möllers, 'The German Constitutional Court says "Ja zu Deutschland!"' (2009) 10 *German Law Journal* 1241, 1250; Petter Asp, *The Substantive Criminal Law Competence of the EU* (Skrifter utgivna av Juridiska fakulteten vid Stockholms, 2012) 43–69.

[11]Rome Statute of the International Criminal Court, 17 July 1998, 2187 UNTS 90 (entered into force 1 July 2002); see Neil Boister, '"Transnational Criminal Law"?' (2003) 14(5) *European Journal of International Law* 953; Claus Kress, 'International Criminal Law' in Rüdiger Wolfrum (ed), *Max Planck Encyclopedia of Public International Law* (Oxford University Press, 2009) 6–9.

[12]For early contributions see Albin Eser, Otto Lagodny and Christopher L Blakesley, *The Individual as Subject of International Cooperation in Criminal Matters* (Nomos, 2002).

[13]But 'suppression conventions' are not blind to individual rights either; see e.g. International Convention against the Taking of Hostages, 17 December 1979, 1316 UNTS (entered into force 3 June 1983), Art 8(2).

[14]Classic textbooks on transnational or international criminal law include Boister (n 1) and Christine Van den Wyngaert, *International Criminal Law* (Kluwer, 2nd rev edn 2000).

[15]See e.g. Malin Thunberg Schunke, *Whose Responsibility?* (Intersentia, 2013); Ester Herlin-Karnell, *The Constitutional Dimension of European Criminal Law* (Hart Publishing, 2012).

at first glance translates into various aspects of how TCL is seen: is the concern that one state will infringe the *ius puniendi* of another? Or does the concern lie with the individual facing numerous states all expanding their penal powers? This article advocates an individual-based approach that acknowledges the individual's position in TCL, and especially pays attention to the legal position of the defendant. Such an approach requires a reassessment of our understanding of the *ius puniendi*'s impact in a transnational setting, and an evaluation of the consequences for individuals. The plea for an adequate coordination scheme among cooperating states – one that protects the legal position of the interests of individuals – is at the centre of a new individual-based approach to TCL.

II. Definitions of transnational criminal law (TCL)

When academic discussions consider the concept of TCL, the first question is: How is TCL defined? While there are quite clear notions of *national* criminal law, as well as of international criminal law *stricto sensu*, a commonly shared definition of *transnational criminal law* does not yet exist.

A. *The classic definition of transnational law – and its application to criminal law*

In attempting to define transnational law, a natural starting point is the classic definition as provided by *Philip Jessup* in the 1950s: transnational law is law that regulates actions or events that transcend national frontiers.[16] This definition can be refined for the criminal law context, as, for instance, *Neil Boister* does in the current volume when he assigns to TCL the area of 'crimes established through treaty obligations in multilateral crime suppression conventions such as the 1988 Vienna Convention – the so-called "treaty crimes" or "crimes of international concern"'.[17] Such a definition is based on a law enforcement approach and holds a public international law perspective but, at first glance, works well for the identification of emerging legal areas of transnational crime control where new rules transcend national jurisdictions and are thus 'concerned with governance of transnational criminal actions', such as UN conventions aimed at the criminal prosecution of certain conduct ('suppression conventions') or – more intensified – the EU areas of freedom, security and justice.[18] According to Boister, the specific criminal law branch of transnational law, i.e. TCL, involves 'the indirect suppression by international law through domestic penal law of criminal activities that have (i)

[16]Philip Jessup, *Transnational Law* (Yale University Press, 1956) 2.
[17]Neil Boister, 'Further reflections on the concept of transnational criminal law', this volume.
[18]Annika Suominen, 'What Role for Legal Certainty in Criminal Law within the Area of Freedom, Security and Justice in the EU?' (2014) 2(1) *Bergen Journal of Criminal Law and Criminal Justice* 1, 3–6.

actual or (ii) potential transboundary effects or (iii) transboundary moral impacts'.[19] This approach to defining and assessing TCL, however, is primarily concerned with the governance of transnational criminal actions by way of international 'suppression conventions' or other forms of cooperative law.

Therefore, the question is: does a continuation of the classic definition provide an adequate lens through which the transformation of legal institutions can be studied in an evolving, globalising society?[20] The history, substance and effect of criminal law suggest that it needs a slightly different approach: one more tailored to the peculiarities of criminal law, since this legal field stands out with regard to its outcomes, namely a possible punishment. Criminal law therefore appears to be state-fixed because of its particular purpose of authorising a society's response to alleged crimes.[21] The classic justification for a harsh reaction, such as public prosecution or punishment of certain conduct, is that such conduct runs counter to society's will and therefore stands in opposition to the law of the land.[22] This fundamental rationale can justify the grave consequences of government action that the alleged wrongdoers face – such as search and seizure, imprisonment or even execution.[23] These distinctive features have determined longstanding principles of criminal law and criminal procedure, shaped the legal frameworks surrounding these areas of law, and influenced how we think about the *ius puniendi*.

B. *The bird's-eye view of TCL*

In a manner of speaking, Boister's approach in this volume to defining and assessing TCL represents the bird's-eye view of the global landscape of normative frameworks.[24] The focus is on rule-making and rule-enforcement, essentially taking a top-down approach.

Boister[25] uses the example of cross-border money laundering to illustrate how the origin of a particular asset is often concealed when moved across state

[19] Boister, this volume.

[20] Peer Zumbansen, 'Defining the Space of Transnational Law: Legal Theory, Global Governance and Legal Pluralism' (2012) 21 *Transnational Law & Contemporary Problems* 305, 307 et seq.

[21] See Andrew Ashworth, *Sentencing and Criminal Justice* (Cambridge University Press, 2010) 74; Duff (n 7) 131–41; Anne Schneider, 'The Basic Approach to Jurisdiction in Private and Criminal Law' in Martin Böse, Frank Meyer and Anne Schneider (eds), *Conflicts of Jurisdiction in Criminal Matters in the European Union, Vol II: Rights, Principles and Model Rules* (Nomos, 2014) 227.

[22] Duff (n 7) 125, 131–41. For further information on the implications of the 'principle of legality' or '*Gesetzlichkeitsprinzip*' for TCL, see e.g. Sabine Gless, *Internationales Strafrecht* (Helbing Lichtenhahn Verlag, 2011) 291–5; Luchtman (n 8) 23–26.

[23] On the part of the victim the consequence of state prosecution is the inability or rather restriction to accuse in one's own name or a collection of damages.

[24] Boister, this volume.

[25] *Ibid.*

borders.[26] Today, and more so than in the past, the rules applicable to tracing a 'dirty' money trail, as well as the rules governing whether a certain act will be deemed money laundering, are not solely within the competence of a national system but are rather issued by many different players.[27] For instance, international law adopted within the UN system obligates state parties to criminalise money laundering on the basis of, among other UN instruments, the so-called Palermo Convention.[28] However, no thought was given to the question of how to safeguard individual rights at the international level. The national lawmaker must then translate the international standards into national law, properly phrasing the mandate placed on the individual by such standards. In addition, regional bodies, such as the Organization for Economic Cooperation and Development (OECD) and its Financial Action Task Force (FATF),[29] set standards regarding how to handle assets that cross borders.[30] Institutions handling money transfers, and the bodies controlling them, may establish soft law by way of self-regulation, like the Basel Committee on Banking Supervision (BCSB)[31] or the International Association of Insurance Supervisors (IAIS)[32].

This unsorted coexistence of international, national and even private rule-setting accounts for the legal pluralism[33] typical of certain transnational law settings, opening doors to adaptable models. However, in the field of criminal law, it may lead to a dangerous conflict of laws. When 'two or more legal systems coexist in the same social field',[34] they may offer a flexible solution to newly emerging problems in cross-border situations, but this eventually leads to a minefield for the individual who must abide by such (possibly conflicting) laws. Legal pluralism in TCL is, to some extent, the result of a paradox. On the one hand, the adoption of national criminal law, as a conceded claim of sovereign statehood in

[26]See, for different scenarios, Mark Pieth and Gemma Aiolfi, *A Comparative Guide to Anti-Money Laundering* (Edward Elgar, 2004).

[27]Mark Pieth, 'Vor Art. 305bis Siebzehnter Titel: Verbrechen u. Vergehen gg. die Rechtspflege.' in Marcel Alexander Niggli and Hans Wiprächtiger (eds), *Basler Kommentar, Strafrecht II, Art. 305bis, 305ter inkl. Vorbemerkungen* (Helbing Lichtenhahn Verlag, 2013) 2671, Art 305, nos 18–43.

[28]UN General Assembly, 'United Nations Convention against Transnational Organized Crime' (8 January 2001), Res/55/22.

[29]FATF Recommendations: Financial Action Task Force, *International Standards on Combating Money Laundering and the Financing of Terrorism and Proliferation* (2012), www.fatf-gafi.org/media/fatf/documents/recommendations/pdfs/FATF_Recommendations.pdf; for case studies see e.g. Herlin-Karnell (n 15) 146–222.

[30]Pieth (n 27) 23–32.

[31]The Basel Committee is a regulating body for banks, setting standards and providing a forum for cooperation on banking supervisory matters. See www.bis.org/bcbs/about.htm.

[32]The Joint Forum, Initiatives by the BCBS, IAIS and IOSCO to Combat Money Laundering and the Financing of Terrorism (June 2008), www.bis.org/publ/joint05.pdf.

[33] For definitions, see Sally Engle Merry, 'Legal Pluralism' (1988) 22 *Law and Society Review* 869, 870–4.

[34]Boister, this volume.

the Westphalian tradition, stands as a self-contained punitive power inflexible to other states' wishes. Yet, on the other hand, such autonomous exercise of state power may easily foil the Westphalian state promise of 'one jurisdiction, one law'. When, for instance, states establish jurisdiction to prosecute crimes committed against their citizens abroad, they *de facto* extend their state borders in order to protect their own nationals extraterritorially.

The individual will not only wish to be subject to the law of one land alone, but will also hope to rely on the Westphalian promise of legal certainty and clear direction on how to act in order to avoid punishment.[35]

Going back to the current debate surrounding TCL, the problem of conflicting laws is neither surprising nor new. Jessup has previously discussed the ideal of legal certainty as a possible obstacle to defining transnational law as a valid concept, stating that

> one purpose of law is certainty. Individual persons, corporations, states, and international organizations must know the rules by which they should govern their conduct from day to day; such certainty cannot exist if decisions are to be rendered according to the whim of the judge who in his travels may have become fascinated by the tribal customs of Papua.[36]

Thus, from the beginning, transnational law has involved a struggle between the promise of Westphalian state order and the need for transborder implementation of certain norms. By now, one would therefore expect an abundance of theories focusing on the legitimate expectation of individuals as the addressees of multiple state powers in a situation of transnational law and how to sort out incoherent normative orders. One would especially expect such theories in the realm of TCL, since it places individuals in a precarious position. Theories that focus on individual interests in TCL, however, are virtually nonexistent. Only recently, when new ideas of global constitutionalism spilled over into areas of transborder criminal justice, has the debate about the individual's position in TCL begun to inch towards the spotlight.[37] However, the relationship between human rights and judicial entitlements, or rather the tangible implications for an individual affected by transnational criminal proceedings, remains unresolved in the overall scenery of multiple sovereign claims for criminal jurisdiction.

---

[35]See e.g. Mark Pieth, 'Synthesis: Comparing International Standards and their Implementation' in Pieth and Aiolfi (n 26) 445–52; Ingeborg Zerbes, 'Transnationales Korruptionsstrafrecht Gestaltungsmacht privater Akteure hinter staatlichem Regelungsanspruch' in Gralf-Peter Calliess (ed), *Transnationales Recht* (Mohr Siebeck, 2013) 539–54. For a more general discussion in light of EU criminal law, see Sabine Gless, 'A New Test for Mens Rea? Safeguarding Legal Certainty in a European Area of Freedom, Security and Justice' (2011) 2 *European Criminal Law Review* 114; see also Suominen (n 18).

[36]Jessup (n 16) 107.

[37]See e.g. Herlin-Karnell (n 15) 232–9; Schunke (n 15) 131–4.

C. *The worm's-eye view of TCL*

The TCL landscape changes considerably as soon as one zooms in on a situation of alleged cross-border crime and sees it through the eyes of an alleged wrongdoer. The laws governing the investigation and prosecution of transnational offences have emerged in parallel, yet uncorrelated, systems of cooperation between states (such as UN 'suppression conventions' or within the EU or Schengen frameworks) or even cooperation between states and private actors (like the Basel Committee on Banking Supervision, BCSB).[38] The prosecution side has driven cross-border cooperation, and the interests of defendants have rarely been taken into account equally.[39] One reason for this shortfall may be that transnational law is traditionally perceived as being addressed to states only (or other lawmakers) and not to individuals.[40] The initial focus and the current development are illustrated for instance by the Palermo Convention,[41] which merely obligates states to criminalise certain conduct, as do many of the OECD rules, while recent forms of self-regulation (like FATF and BCSB recommendations) pay attention to implementing mechanisms, yet still centre on crime control. The point of view of the individual, who must sort out the potentially differing orders set in disparate rules, is seldom taken into account.[42] Legal certainty and the right not to be subjected to arbitrary punishment, however, are judicial liberties based on human rights.[43] Yet human rights protection rarely forms a central part of newly emerging international frameworks of cross-border cooperation. Traditionally human rights

---

[38]For case studies see Herlin-Kamell (n 15) 146–222; Pieth and Aiolfi (n 26).

[39]Gless (n 5); Ilias Anagnostopoulos, 'Criminal Justice Cooperation in the European Union after the First Few "Steps": A Defence View' (2014) 15 *ERA Forum* 9.

[40]Anna Petrig argues, that various suppression conventions contain provisions addressing the right to consular assistance. Such provisions can according to Anna Petrig arguably be interpreted as containing international individual rights, similar to those enshrined in Vienna Convention of Consular Relations, 18 April 1961, 500 UNTS 95, Art 36(1). She refers, for example to Article 7 of the Convention for the Suppression of Unlawful Acts against the Safety of Maritime Navigation (10 March 1988, 1678 UNTS 221, 27 ILM 668) as well as to Article 6 of the International Convention against the Taking of Hostages (17 December 1979, 1316 UNTS 205). See on the individual rights enshrined in the Vienna Convention e.g. Anne Peters, 'Membership in the Global Constitutional Community' in Jan Klabbers, Anne Peters and Geir Ulfstein (eds), *The Constitutionalization of International Law* (Oxford University Press, 2009) 153, 168–9.

[41]Pieth (n 27) 23–32.

[42]Gless (n 35); Suominen (n 18) 6; for an account in international criminal law *stricto sensu*, see Stefanie Bock, 'The Prerequisite of Personal Guilt and the Duty to Know the Law in the Light of Article 32 ICC Statute' (2013) 9 *Utrecht Law Review* 184.

[43]Granted for instance in the European Convention on Human Rights (ECHR), 3 September 1953, 213 UNTS 222, Arts 6 and 7: *Silver and others v United Kingdom*, App nos 5947/72; 6205/73; 7052/75; 7061/75; 7107/75; 7113/75; 7136/75 (ECtHR, 25 March 1983), [88]; *Sunday Times v United Kingdom*, App no 6538/74 (ECtHR, 26 April 1979), [48]–[49]; *EL, RL et JO v Suisse*, App no 20919/92 (ECtHR, 29 August 1997), [51]–[53]; Robert Esser, *Auf dem Weg zu einem europäischen Strafverfahrensrecht* (De Gruyter, 2002) 744.

belong to the individual versus state context, and appropriate remedies are rather hard to achieve when a state's power crosses a border.[44]

It is, however, the individuals possibly violating the law who are most affected by TCL. If they find themselves in the position of a defendant, they may face severe consequences. If an action triggers criminal proceedings across borders, a defendant may be confronted with the claim of validity of a foreign law, he or she may be arrested with the aim of extradition and held abroad, and may be subjected to unfamiliar procedures in a language he or she does not speak or understand.[45] In a situation where different criminal laws conflict, individuals face a dilemma that – unlike conflicts of law in international private law – they cannot easily resolve. Such dilemmas can arise in quite different situations and may sometimes be rather surprising for the actors involved. For example, in the border region of Germany and Switzerland, where nationals from both countries cooperate in frontier traffic, such dealings may on occasion include the transfer of money from one country to the other. Laws against money laundering on the two sides of the border, however, differ substantially. According to Swiss law, only concealment of profits gained from the commission of a *felony* is deemed to be money laundering,[46] whereas in Germany the mere concealment of profits gained by certain *misdemeanours* may qualify as money laundering.[47] Therefore, not only cross-border commuters but also bankers and other agents who never leave their own country must prudently assess the possible legal consequences of transferring money, since the validity of German law does not end at the border. And while bankers (being part of a world-wide industry) may be obliged to act with due diligence, conflicts of laws arise on all scales. If, for instance, a group of both Swiss and German nationals participate in a music-swapping club for newly registered local songs on both sides of the border, they may quickly learn that their respective neighbouring home countries might evaluate their business model quite differently, and that while their choice of corporate residence may be important, it will not necessarily save them from (possibly harsh) legal consequences depending on the specific details of the business set-up. The music-swapping club may infringe copyright laws on one side of the border but not necessarily on the other, since Swiss law allows copyrighted music to be

[44]Interestingly enough, rather early TCL frameworks with reference to human rights intend to protect the victim's interests, which often is not primarily directed against the state but the alleged criminal individual. See Jonathan Dock, *Victims' Rights, Human Rights and Criminal Justice* (Hart Publishing, 2008).

[45]Gless (n 5).

[46]See Article 305bis subpara 1 Schweizerisches Strafgesetzbuch (Code pénale Suisse, SR 311.0, http://www.admin.ch/opc/de/classified-compilation/19370083/index.html; for an English translation see http://www.admin.ch/opc/en/classified-compilation/19370083/index.html).

[47]See Section 261 subpara 4 lit b Deutsches Strafgesetzbuch (StGB), www.gesetze-im-internet.de/stgb/__261.html; for an English translation see www.gesetze-im-internet.de/englisch_stgb/index.html.

downloaded for personal use,[48] yet German law criminalises it.[49] Furthermore, according to German law, the concealment of gains resulting from a possible infringement of copyright law can qualify as money laundering.[50] Therefore, certain financial transactions with regard to the 'local music sharing' may qualify as an act of money laundering only within a particular jurisdiction, but not necessarily in the state of residence of the (alleged) wrongdoer. In Europe, with its mix of states and justice systems, numerous areas of criminal law differ across borders.

Moreover, it is worth mentioning that defendants may not only be affected by TCL when committing an act with consequences across borders. Individuals in their home jurisdictions may, in certain situations, be expected to align their conduct to rules set by foreign lawmakers or international self-regulating bodies in order to avoid criminal liability.[51] For example, the Swiss Penal Code criminalises 'insufficient diligence in financial transactions' for persons who accept assets as part of their profession.[52] If they 'fail to ascertain the identity of the beneficial owner of the assets with the care that is required in the circumstances', they may be held criminally liable. However, in order to determine the level of 'care that is required' in a particular situation, Swiss judges will rely on FATF or BCSB recommendations, amongst other considerations.[53]

Therefore, TCL should not be defined from the bird's-eye view of a suppositional lawmaker alone, but must also incorporate the perspective of the affected individual.[54]

D. *Towards a modified bird's-eye view of TCL*

In sum, TCL is not simply a field shaped by treaty obligations of multilateral crime suppression conventions, but a landscape with pitfalls and safe harbours for individuals. A useful definition of TCL must therefore not only focus on states' interests when allowing for a cross-border *ius puniendi*, but include all aspects crucial to criminal justice. When Boister (and many others) consider the crucial

[48]Christoph Gasser, 'Art. 19 URG' in Barbara K. Müller and/Reinhard Oertli (eds), *Urhebergesetz – Stämpflis Handkommentar* (Stämpfli Verlag, 2012) paras 5 et seq.

[49]Michael Heghmanns, 'Musiktauschbörsen im Internet aus strafrechtlicher Sicht' [2004] *Multimedia und Recht, Zeitschrift für Informations-, Telekommunikations- und Medienrecht* 14–18.

[50]See Section 261 subpara 4 lit b Deutsches Strafgesetzbuch; Section 106 Deutsches Gesetz über Urheberrecht und verwandte Schutzrechte (Urheberrechtsgesetz, http://www.gesetze-im-internet.de/urhg/; for an English translation see http://www.gesetze-im-internet.de/englisch_urhg/index.html).

[51]Foreign criminal law can, however, be relevant in various ways: see Böse, Meyer and Schneider (n 21) 223–9.

[52]Article 305ter Schweizerisches Strafgesetzbuch.

[53]Pieth (n 27).

[54]Gless and Vervaele (n 9).

points of TCL to be that 'the actions and ideas of those who clarify, normativise and apply the norms transcend territorial boundaries' and that '[t]he actions of the lawmakers are as transnational as the actions of the lawbreakers',[55] they place too much emphasis on the power of rule-making and the enforcement capability across borders within the 'suppression conventions' framework.[56] The (ostensibly) transnational consensus on the punishability agreed upon by contract among states, however, may only feign a legal order. If one zooms in on the realities from the point of view of affected individuals, TCL looks very different. From the point of view of a defendant, TCL is not yet a coherent, clear-cut legal framework but rather a patchwork of laws,[57] made up of overlapping subsystems of national *ius puniendi*.[58] A definition that relies on an approach that focuses only on crime control by international law might merely gloss over the real problems of transnational prosecution. TCL must therefore – as a first step – be defined in a way that merges the bird's-eye view with the worm's-eye view, in order to provide ground for an individual-based or rather a defendant-based approach. This new, modified bird's-eye view seeks the big picture, but rather from the perspective of the individual facing the situation of overlapping normative frameworks.

III. A defendant-based approach to TCL: coordination scheme grounded on general principles

The basic challenge for an approach that addresses the problems of legal pluralism and conflicts of laws in TCL from the perspective of the defendant is the introduction of a coordination system – one which protects the interests affected when states exercise their *ius puniendi* across borders.

By mounting cross-border cooperation on the one hand, while still holding on to separate, independent powers to prosecute on the other, individuals could find themselves caught in a diffusion of states' responsibilities.[59] Without a coordination system binding the use of the *ius puniendi* (for instance, how to implement jurisdictional principles or a general rule on *ne bis in idem* across borders) individuals may be left without protection. Boister contends in his

---

[55] Boister, this volume.

[56] Traditionally, textbooks on international criminal law are often organised around 'suppression conventions': see e.g. Wyngaert (n 14).

[57] Boister, this volume.

[58] See Wolfgang Schomburg, Otto Lagodny, Sabine Gless and Thomas Hackner, 'Einleitung' in Wolfgang Schomburg, Otto Lagodny, Sabine Gless and Thomas Hackner (eds), *Internationale Rechtshilfe in Strafsachen, Mutual Legal Assistance in Criminal Matters* (CH Beck, 5th edn 2012) 11 ('Vertragsgestrüpp').

[59] See for a prominent example the discussion about law enforcement on the internet: Teresa Scassa and Robert J Currie, 'New First Principles? Assessing the Internet's Challenges to Jurisdiction' (2010–11) 42 *Georgetown Journal of International Law* 1017.

paper in this volume that, as a consequence of TCL, alleged criminals become 'members of multiple normative communities, local, territorial, extraterritorial, and non-territorial in nature'.[60] What sounds like empowerment in Boister's paper may in fact turn out to be disadvantage, which is apparent when following up on the example of the music-swapping club in the Swiss–German border region: instead of gaining more protection, the entrepreneurs are exposed to greater penal power. They seem to fall through the cracks, since criminal charges could be brought against them in Switzerland or Germany, or both at the same time, and for the same act.[61] Even if Swiss authorities perceive the group to be based on Swiss territory but refuse to initiate proceedings by claiming that the deed is compliant with Swiss law, German authorities could nevertheless proceed.[62]

A. *Balancing interests through a coordination scheme*

As explained above, public prosecution is an important element of state power, which affects individual interests in various ways and manifests itself in many respects: the jurisdiction to prescribe, the jurisdiction to adjudicate and the jurisdiction to enforce must all add up in order to exercise the *ius puniendi* effectively.[63] In exercising its penal power, a state's condemnation of criminalised conduct may not be directed at the wrongdoer alone. It can furthermore carry a message for society as a whole.[64] Criminal law is intrinsically linked to the state authority of prosecution and penal power.[65]

When states extend their *ius puniendi* across state borders, it may lead to numerous unresolved problems. For example, is it only one state or can all states prosecute and impose a punishment if they get their hands on the (alleged) wrongdoer? Today, even if states cooperate closely, there is rarely a

---

[60]Boister, this volume.

[61]For the question whether Schengen Implementing Convention Art 65 applies, see Andreas Eicker, *Transstaatliche Strafverfolgung – Ein Beitrag zur Europäisierung, Internationalisierung und Fortentwicklung des Grundsatzes ne bis in idem* (Centaurus Verlag Herbolzheim, 2004) 84–130.

[62]However, given the legal framework governing cross-border *ne bis in idem* between these two countries, the Swiss authorities could save the group from prosecution if they were to initiate proceedings and then formally terminate them, which would be a rather inefficient, but consistent, approach given the Westphalian rationale of non-intervention among sovereign states. See *ibid.*

[63]On the various forms of jurisdiction in the context of criminal law, see Petrig (n 8).

[64]See Markus D Dubber and Tatjana Hörnle, *Criminal Law: A Comparative Approach* (Oxford University Press, 2014) 4–5; Tatjana Hörnle, 'Gegenwärtige Strafbegründungstheorien: Die herkömmliche deutsche Diskussion' in Andreas von Hirsch, Ulfrid Neumann and Kurt Seelmann (eds), *Strafe – Warum?* (Nomos, 2011) 11, 21–23.

[65]Asp (n 10) 76–78.

binding legal rule[66] regarding how to pick the jurisdiction.[67] The EU Member States, for instance, form one 'legal space that include[s] actions and events that transcended boundaries'.[68] In this novel area of freedom, security and justice,[69] central agencies interact with national law enforcement authorities: the EU's Judicial Cooperation Unit (Eurojust) and the European Police Office (Europol) support national prosecution services and police forces to coordinate mutual legal assistance, provide legal and factual information, or gather evidence abroad.[70] Using their resources, the EU agencies may even seek out the 'best jurisdiction' for a given case. Naturally, from the perspective of the defence, such forum shopping constitutes an abuse of power, especially since defence lawyers have no direct access to such transboundary support services.[71] Furthermore, the principle of mutual recognition, according to which a decision taken by a judicial authority in one EU country must be recognised (and enforced) in other EU countries, may curtail individual rights accorded in a defendant's home state.[72] The European Arrest Warrant, for instance, which secures arrest and extradition throughout the EU almost automatically,[73] has substantially expanded the reach of law enforcement authorities across Europe. It establishes one 'implementing area' that is, however, based on different substantive criminal laws. Only quite recently has the EU lawmaker acknowledged that mutual recognition may lead to a 'unilateral increase of punitiveness',[74] meaning that the state with the harshest criminal laws may ask for extradition of alleged perpetrators (subject to the establishment of jurisdiction). During this piercing of the Westphalian promise of 'one jurisdiction, one law', individual rights have been sidelined. Today various legal scholars and the EU Commission all advocate respect for and inclusion of individual

[66]There is soft law, however, like the Eurojust Guidelines for deciding which jurisdiction should prosecute, published in the *Eurojust Annual Report 2004* (2004), www.eurojust.europa.eu/doclibrary/corporate/eurojust%20Annual%20Reports/Annual%20Report%202004/Annual-Report-2004-EN.pdf, 92 et seq.

[67]See e.g. Böse, Meyer and Schneider (n 21).

[68]See Jessup (n 16) 2; see also Böse, Meyer and Schneider (n 21) 59 et seq.

[69]See, for example, from the criminal law point of view, Luchtman (n 8) 14–17.

[70]See e.g. Alexandra de Moor and Gert Vermeulen, 'The Europol Council Decision' (2010) 47 *Common Market Law Review* 1089, 1107.

[71]For similar problems in cases of ICC prosecutions, see Elena A Baylis, 'Outsourcing Investigations', *Legal Studies Research Paper Series*, Working Paper No 2010-20, 145.

[72]Annika Suominen, *The Principle of Mutual Recognition in Cooperation in Criminal Matters* (Intersentia, 2011); Valsamis Mitsilegas, 'The Constitutional Implications of Mutual Recognition in Criminal Matters in the EU' (2006) 43 *Common Market Law Review* 1277.

[73]André Klip, *European Criminal Law* (Intersentia, 2nd edn 2012) 294–5.

[74]See e.g. Silvia Allegrezza, 'The Interaction between the ECJ and the ECHR with Respect to the Protection of Procedural Safeguards after Lisbon' in Katalin Ligeti (ed), *Towards a Prosecutor for the European Union*, vol 1 (Hart Publishing, 2013) 905, 941–2; Klip (n 73) 305–6.

rights in cross-border cooperation.[75] The reasoning behind such initiatives appears to be evident: if, in national systems, authorities in criminal investigations, prosecutions and subsequent trials have to abide carefully by precise procedures and respect constitutional guarantees and human rights, all the while balancing the different interests at stake, corresponding standards should apply on a supranational level of cross-border crime fighting as well as in situations of TCL. In transnational cases, the aspiration of adhering to General Principles ought to be the same, simply because the exact same individual interests are at stake. There is no valid justification for the protective gaps that appear on the side of the alleged wrongdoer or that of the supposed victim. This is the point where constitutionalism and TCL intersect, and the states that pierce through sovereignty by way of cooperation must provide a functional equivalent to protect all exposed citizens.[76]

The demand for a strict rule dictating where to bring charges is one result of such reasoning, aiming at a clear and coherent handling of transnational criminal cases with formal protection for the individuals affected.[77] Such a claim is asking for a resurgence of the bird's-eye view – that is, towards a modified bird's-eye view. Instead of looking for a set of rules aimed at 'indirect suppression by international law through domestic penal law of criminal activities that have actual or potential transboundary effects',[78] one seeks a structure for a protective coordination scheme.

In theory, different solutions seem feasible here. Each legal community involved could put forth a protection scheme of its own – one which safeguards individuals' interests within the respective national legal system. Such a 'national solution' would support an individual-based approach to TCL, but in each state separately. Such a national solution is at the extreme end of the range of possible answers and rather adheres to a worm's-eye view, since the focus is on a purely national answer (to a cross-border problem). At the other end of the spectrum of possible approaches is the postulation of a common uniform framework – one that considers individual rights in a cross-border scheme, for all states involved in cooperation in a coherent and concerted way. Choosing this approach is, as

[75]See on the part of the defendant: Directive 2010/64/EU of 20 October 2010 on the right to interpretation and translation in criminal proceedings, OJ L280 of 26.10.2010, 1; Directive 2012/13/EU of 22 May 2012 on the right to information in criminal proceedings, OJ L142 of 1.6.2012, 1; Directive 2013/48/EU of 22 October 2013 on the right of access to a lawyer in criminal proceedings and in European arrest warrant proceedings, and on the right to have a third party informed upon deprivation of liberty and to communicate with third persons and with consular authorities while deprived of liberty, OJ L294 of 6.11.2013, 1. On the part of the victim: Directive 2012/29/EU of 25 October 2012 establishing minimum standards on the rights, support and protection of victims of crime, and replacing Council Framework Decision 2001/220/JHA, OJ L315 of 14.11.2012, 57.

[76]Gless and Vervaele (n 9) 5; Schunke (n 15) 131–4; Herlin-Karnell (n 15) 232–9.

[77]See Juliette Lelieur, '"Transnationalising" *Ne Bis in Idem*: How the Rule of *Ne Bis in Idem* Reveals the Principle of Personal Legal Certainty' (2013) 9 *Utrecht Law Review* 198, 204–5.

[78]Boister, this volume.

has been pointed out above, analogous to looking for a modified bird's-eye view striving for a protective coordination scheme safeguarding individuals' interests.

Legal scholars have considered both the national approach and the common approach. An example of the national approach would be a specific test for *mens rea* in transnational cases that each nation-state would have to establish on its own,[79] while the more recent initiatives in the EU's legal framework illustrate the possibilities of a common approach.[80] And the latter proposal indeed appears to be the better approach: where states formed close coalitions, which in turn created specific bodies for implementing TCL, such as Eurojust, the EU's Judicial Cooperation Unit or Europol, or other national bodies within the Schengen cooperation framework, scholars quickly realised that penal power marching in unison with state sovereignty is a thing of the past. The policy driving TCL must ensure that individuals' interests are included, which means that they must be accounted for at the supranational level. And in fact, this reasoning is precisely behind numerous initiatives demanding a strict rule stipulating how to decide on the forum in cases of conflict of jurisdiction or how to implement a cross-border scheme for *ne bis in idem* that is in line with an individual-based approach to overlapping jurisdictions.[81]

B. *General principles and the common denominator*

In arguing that a new concept of TCL must include a coordination scheme for safeguarding the interests of individuals, only the notional question of structure has been answered, i.e. that it needs a common ground to protect certain interests, while the question of substance remains open.

In criminal law, state power threatens individuals with harsh consequences in situations where an individual, or the public, has been wronged by violation of a (morally substantiated) norm. The state claims a monopoly on the prosecution and possible punishment of the wrongdoer (with the promise of a criminal justice system applied fairly and equally), putting citizens on the witness stand, and taking away the entitlement of victims to proceed on their own (i.e. no 'vigilante justice').

In order to establish a shared coordination system, one must therefore find a strong common denominator which represents the essence of the relevant rules in criminal law and criminal procedure protecting individual interests in modern states. Put differently, one must strive to identify the general principles that determine the relevant rules in national law, which will eventually be capable of

[79] Gless (n 35); Suominen (n 18).
[80] See Schunke (n 15) 69–117; Gless (n 5); Ilias Anagnostopoulos, 'The Right of Access to a Lawyer in Europe: A Long Road Ahead?' (2014) *European Criminal Law Journal* 3.
[81] See e.g. John Vervaele, '*Ne Bis in Idem*: Towards a Transnational Constitutional Principle in the EU' (2013) 9 *Utrecht Law Review* 211, 217–27.

generating adequate rules for TCL, even if those rules amount to little more than a coordination system. A tradition of determining such aspirational principles, however, is lacking, as is consensus on a method for identifying general principles in international legal frameworks. Therefore, in searching for a strong common denominator as a base for a coordination system, one can either turn to basic ideas from legal philosophy or examine existing practice.

(i) *Drawing inspiration from legal philosophy*

A promising approach in legal philosophy is to differentiate between general principles and mere rules; this approach was used even before Ronald Dworkin refined it.[82] His theory distinguishes axioms from working mechanisms and has been used and adjusted by scholars in manifold fields,[83] including international criminal law.[84] Whilst this approach has met with some criticism,[85] it has been accepted as a structure for establishing principles and rules in international law. For instance, when applying Article 38 of the ICC Statute, one of the most prominent examples of a reference to 'general principles', the statutory rule uses the term 'general principles of law recognized by civilized nations'.[86] It does not, however, provide further explanation for identifying the content or implications. While the question of how to identify and justify general principles is contentious,[87] it is clear that a body of TCL must be based on a common denominator of elementary regulations for criminal law and criminal procedure, and that at the same time one must try to avoid a web of principles, which – at a high level of abstraction – cannot gain substance and will thus only feign a collective foundation.[88]

According to Dworkin, the necessary difference between legal principles and legal rules can be achieved logically in the following way:

[82]Ronald Dworkin, *Taking Rights Seriously* (Harvard University Press, 1977) 22–28.
[83]See, for a discussion of rules and standards in US constitutional law, Kathleen M Sullivan, 'Foreword: The Justices of Rules and Standards' (1992) 106 *Harvard Law Review* 22, 56–59.
[84]See e.g. Lelieur (n 77) 202.
[85]With regard to the fact that a differentiation between principles and rules is difficult – and maybe sometimes impossible, see Carl-Friedrich Stuckenberg, 'Rechtsfindung und Rechtsfortbildung im Völkerstrafrecht' (2007) 154 *Goltdammer's Archiv für Strafrecht* 80, 94; see further Alain Pellet, 'Article 38' in Andreas Zimmermann, Christian Tomuschat, Karin Oellers-Frahm and Christian J Tams (eds), *The Statute of the International Court of Justice: A Commentary* (Oxford University Press, 2nd edn 2012) 731, 834.
[86]'The Court, whose function is to decide in accordance with international law such disputes as are submitted to it, shall apply: a. international conventions, whether general or particular, establishing rules expressly recognized by the contesting states; b. international custom, as evidence of a general practice accepted as law; c. *the general principles of law* recognized by civilized nations; … '
[87]See Pellet (n 85) 1–3, 250–69; M Cherif Bassiouni, 'A Functional Approach to "General Principles of International Law"' (1990) 11 *Michigan Journal of International Law* 768, 770–2.
[88]See Stuckenberg (n 85) 94.

> Both sets of standards point to particular decisions about legal obligation in particular circumstances but they differ in the character of the direction they give. Rules are applicable in an all-or-nothing fashion. If the facts a rule stipulates are given, then either the rule is valid, in which case the answer it supplies must be accepted or it is not, in which case it contributes nothing to the decision.[89]

In contrast, principles operate differently: 'Even those [principles] which look most like rules do not set out legal consequences that follow automatically when the conditions provided are met'.[90] The distinction between principles and rules reveals a solution to the problems resulting from legal pluralism in the situation of cross-border prosecution. In cases of conflicting laws, one can search for, or rather establish, the underlying principle, which sets the overarching directive, but does not automatically determine the legal consequences following from it. Such an approach relies on a deductive method, which eventually ascertains a (prevailing) rule by way of a principle.

Going down that road, one can exemplify this abstract reasoning using our aforementioned case of the music-swapping nationals who want to conduct business across borders, and who eventually run into trouble because of the conflicting laws on the two sides of the border. According to the Dworkinian model, the two colliding rules can be resolved by retreating to an underlying principle, which here is legal certainty: 'If two rules conflict, one of them cannot be a valid rule. The decision as to which is valid, and which must be abandoned or recast, must be made by appealing to considerations beyond the rules themselves'.[91] Thus, one has to retreat to general principle when the national rules of *ne bis in idem* applied to a case – given the facts – lead to clear, but conflicting, legal obligations. For instance, such is the case when the national rule on one side of the border inhibits prosecution, whereas a different rule on the other side of the border compels prosecution of the same conduct. In such cases, it must be determined which rule will serve (a common understanding of) justice best and should therefore be applied; neither the defendant nor the prosecutor nor the victim has a right to the best of all possible worlds. Responding to individuals' interest in clarity, one must use the underlying principles in order to establish a system that will lead to legal certainty.[92] However, as Dworkin has correctly pointed out, the legal consequences flowing therefrom are not automatically spelled out. The question remains: How can the underlying principles be translated into a system that determines the relevant rules in a certain case and will allow for a working mechanism of the *ne bis in idem* principle? Or, to phrase the question more abstractly: How can the underlying

---

[89] Dworkin (n 82) 24.
[90] *Ibid*, 25.
[91] *Ibid*, 26–27.
[92] See, for a classic application, Duncan Kennedy, 'Form and Substance in Private Law Adjudication' (1976) 89 *Harvard Law Review* 1685, 1688–94; for an application in TCL, see Lelieur (n 77) 203–4.

principles be 'transnationalised' in order to establish rules that 'transnationalise' the protection of individuals affected by TCL?[93]

Returning to our bird's-eye/worm's-eye divide, with separating national rules implementing *ne bis in idem* from their traditional foundations and adapting the safeguard for the transnational level, one rather takes a modified bird's-eye view.[94] Eventually, a transnationalised *ne bis in idem* would be different from its national counterparts, because it must provide legal certainty for the individual in a system where different countries have different criminal codes. Thus, it must not only prevent double prosecution or double jeopardy, but also prevent *parallel* prosecutions, and determine the rules that serve justice best in all situations where one national lawmaker decides not to criminalise a certain type of conduct while other lawmakers decide differently.

(ii) *Drawing inspiration from practice*

Apart from drawing inspiration from legal philosophy, a glance at what happens in practice could also help identify general principles for TCL. Cooperation among states in the field of criminal law and the fragmentation of any legal system necessitates the identification of common principles in various situations.[95] Quite often such principles are needed as a fill-in;[96] for example, the 'general principles' referred to in Article 21(1) of the ICC Statute[97] serve as a subsidiary source filling in normative gaps.[98] The approach is empirical, and the task is to generate rules via a comparative process. In analysing national law, one must identify relevant regularities in the vast amount of regulations so as to define a new rule (relevant to international criminal law), while also sorting through irrelevant inconsistencies.[99] This task of establishing a valid 'substratum' and deducing a

[93]See Lelieur (n 77) 203–7.
[94]*Ibid*, 204–7; Vervaele (n 81) 219–26.
[95]See Stuckenberg (n 85) 93–94.
[96]See Bassiouni (n 87) 774.
[97]'The Court shall apply: (a) In the first place, this Statute, Elements of Crimes and its Rules of Procedure and Evidence; (b) In the second place, where appropriate, applicable treaties and the principles and rules of international law, including the established principles of the international law of armed conflict; (c) Failing that, general principles of law derived by the Court from national laws of legal systems of the world including, as appropriate, the national laws of States that would normally exercise jurisdiction over the crime, provided that those principles are not inconsistent with this Statute and with international law and internationally recognized norms and standards.'
[98]See e.g. Kai Ambos, *Treatise on International Criminal Law, Volume 1: Foundations and General Part* (Oxford University Press, 2013) 76.
[99]Jean-Marie Henckaerts, 'Study on Customary Rules of International Humanitarian Law: Purpose, Coverage and Methodology' (1999) 835 *International Review of the Red Cross*, https://www.icrc.org/eng/resources/documents/misc/57jq3k.htm; Stuckenberg (n 85) 93–96. For more information on comparative approaches for establishing general principles, see HC Gutteridge, 'Comparative Law and the Law of Nations' in William E

concrete rule therefrom is, as many scholars have pointed out, practically impossible, especially with regard to the vast amount of (and the differences between) legal systems of countries that are signatories to the ICC Statute.[100] Thus, the clear option is to turn to an evaluative process, weighing the laws in light of the objective of prosecuting core crimes. The empirical approach is modified by a normative element.[101] Again, if one wants to fit these approaches within the frame of bird's-eye view versus worm's-eye view, the empirical approach rather mirrors the worm's-eye view, or rather the worm's-eye view in adding up all the different rules governing the fate of individuals affected, whereas a more evaluative approach corresponds with the proposed modified bird's-eye view – recovering an overall picture of what is needed for a coordination system that actually safeguards individual interests. However, if a finding of general principles of TCL detaches itself too much from any empirical basis in the comparative process, it runs into problems with regard to legitimacy.[102] This struggle is apparent in the case law of all supranational courts intending to find general principles: they either resort to a more empirical approach or to a deductive testing. In the first case they look for a common denominator in national laws. In the second case they place the emphasis on a certain objective to be reached.

In European criminal law, for instance, the European Court of Justice (ECJ) has to find general principles of procedure defining rights of defence when European organs and agencies take part in investigations without a procedural code at hand. Here too, the ECJ first looks for a common denominator, namely the 'common traditions of the constitutions of the EU Member States', and – if the result lacks persuasiveness as such – points to European peculiarities often by reference to the case law of the European Court of Human Rights (ECtHR).[103]

The ECtHR has ventured down this path before by combining a comparative method with its two techniques of interpretation, namely the 'living instrument' doctrine and the 'practical and effective' doctrine.[104] In so doing, the Court first

---

Butler (ed), *International Law in Comparative Perspective* (Sijthoff & Noordhoff, 1980) 13 ff; Bassiouni (n 87) 785–7, 813–16; Hermann Mosler, 'General Principles of International Law' in Rudolf Bernhardt (ed), *Encyclopedia of Public International Law*, vol 2 (Max Planck Institute for Comparative Public Law and International Law, 1985) 89 ff, 97–103.

[100]See Claus Kress, 'Zur Methode der Rechtsfindung im Allgemeinen Teil des Völkerstrafrechts' (1999) 111 *Zeitschrift für die gesamte Strafrechtswissenschaft* 597, 608–13; Stuckenberg (n 85) 93–94.

[101]See e.g. *Prosecutor v Erdemovic* (Judgement) ICTY IT-96-22-A (7 October 1997), Separate and Dissenting Opinion of Judge Stephen, [25]: 'the prevailing number of nations within each of the main families of laws'.

[102]Stuckenberg (n 85).

[103]See e.g. Klip (n 73) 153–4.

[104]Sabine Gless and Jeannine Martin, 'The Comparative Method in European Courts: A Comparison between the CJEU and ECtHR?' (2014) 1(1) *Bergen Journal of Criminal Law and Criminal Justice* 36, 42–44.

establishes the validity of a principle, then points out a particular need, and then defines a new rule accordingly.[105]

Comparing the two European Courts, the practice of the ECJ appears to be more far-reaching. Not only does it rely on arguments drawn from history and from the objective of 'contextual harmonisation', it furthermore establishes 'general principles of law' in a creative manner, primarily by appraising the objectives of EU law.[106] The aspiration for new common ground corresponds with the consolidation of the policy framework at the EU level.[107] The need for a more aspirational approach when identifying the general principles can also be seen in international criminal law *stricto sensu*, which – as explained above – is bound to find general principles as a subsidiary source filling in (significant) normative gaps.[108] Obviously, one cannot adhere to a single method of sustaining international criminal law *stricto sensu* with general principles; rather, one must use a combination of techniques – including empirical and normative-deductive methods.[109]

(iii) *General principles and rules for TCL*

A more empirical approach would involve collecting the relevant regulations that are valid in the different areas of TCL, such as rules on the applicability of domestic criminal law to extraterritorial conduct, rules governing mutual legal assistance in criminal matters, rules of European criminal law, and rules in the various national and international legal frameworks.[110] Subsequently, one would have to compare and identify relevant convergences, patterns, etc., as well as any discrepancies, using a comparative-inductive method. Going down this road, one could, for instance, compare all EU Member States' laws on criminal jurisdiction, as well as rules established by EU institutions, like the Eurojust guidelines on jurisdiction,[111] in order to develop a prevailing pattern for settling jurisdictional

---

[105] *Ibid*, 44–45.

[106] Klip (n 73) 152–6.

[107] For discussion on a corresponding EU policy, see contributions in Mireille Delmas-Marty (ed), *What Kind of Criminal Policy for Europe?* (Kluwer, 1996); Asp (n 10) 70–76.

[108] For an illustration of the reasoning in the case against Dražen Erdemović (referred to at n 101), see 'Case Information Sheet: "Pilica Farm" (IT-96-22) Dražen Erdemović', International Criminal Tribunal for the former Yugoslavia, http://www.icty.org/x/cases/erdemovic/cis/en/cis_erdemovic_en.pdf, where the judges needed to define the requirements for duress as the defendant claimed that he had participated in the massacre at Srbrenica only because he was pressured to do so (under threat of death/at gunpoint). For a discussion see Kress (n 100).

[109] See Ambos (n 98) 78; Martino Mona, 'Strafrechtsvergleichung und Comparative Justice: Zum Verhältnis zwischen Rechtsvergleichung, Grundlagenforschung und Rechtsphilosophie' in Susanne Beck, Christoph Burchard and Bijan Fateh-Moghadam (eds), *Strafrechtsvergleichung als Problem und Lösung* (Nomos, 2011) 103–19.

[110] Gless (n 22) 290–1.

[111] Eurojust Guidelines for deciding which jurisdiction should prosecute: see Eurojust (n 66).

conflicts.[112] Ultimately, general principles could be inferred from similar sets of empirical findings. Such an approach is to a certain extent similar to the establishment of rules of customary international law.[113] By counting and comparing existing concrete and individual rules, one tries to establish a generally valid abstract principle. However, an approach which puts the empirical moment at the top will encounter certain difficulties. First, it must present a certain number of similar laws and practices in order to establish a pattern; second, this line-up must be evaluated. In comparative law, one must assess the spirit behind the rules – that is, search for the '*opinio iuris*'. Otherwise the finding will be too 'formal' and the basis of validity will lie primarily with the number of similar laws found in different criminal justice systems.

In contrast, one could also deduct basic principles *from the objective* of an individual-based approach to TCL: the achievement of justice by cross-border law enforcement while balancing the different interests involved, notably those of the individuals affected. Such an approach may, but will not necessarily, identify existing principles, in addition to locating principles that *ought* to be valid for transnational criminal cases. Thus, the determination of principles is more aspirational than deductive. Some general principles of TCL might not even have a counterpart in national law, as was explained with the transnationalisation of *ne bis in idem.*[114] In other words, this approach establishes 'aspirational' rules rather than merely reflecting the *lex lata.*[115] This method leans towards an approach used in comparative law, when scholars resort to a 'functional comparison' or to what is called '*wertende Rechtsvergleichung*' by combining the empirical method with an appraisal. The process involves looking at certain situations and comparing legal solutions provided by different national laws from a fixed point of comparison – the so-called *tertium comparationis* – which, in this context, could be a balanced resolution for the situation of a positive conflict of jurisdiction when an internet-based music-swapping service conducts business across borders. Such a method is widely used[116] – for instance, by scholars of EU law when drafting proposals on how to determine jurisdiction.[117] An approach that does not solely focus on the number of laws and cases, but also gives weight to 'good practice' and the '*opinio iuris*', leads to a formal-material basis of validity. A normative teleological approach,

[112]See Böse, Meyer and Schneider (n 21) 19.
[113]See Henckaerts (n 99); Kress (n 100) 608–13.
[114]See for similar approach in International Criminal Law Cassese's, *International Criminal Law* (Oxford University Press, 3rd edn., 2013) 9–15.
[115]Gless and Vervaele (n 9) 5.
[116]See Ambos (n 98) 78–79.
[117]Luchtman (n 8) 26–32; Arndt Sinn, *Jursidiktionskonflikte bei grenzüberschreitender Kriminalität, Conflicts of Jurisdiction in Cross-Border Crime Situations* (Universitätsverlag Osnabrück, 2012) 597–615; Frank Zimmermann, *Strafgewaltkonflikte in der Europäischen Union. Ein Regelungsvorschlag zur Wahrung materieller und prozessualer strafrechtlicher Garantien sowie staatlicher Strafinteressen* (Nomos, 2014) 369–454; Böse, Meyer and Schneider (n 21) 435–43.

which deducts principles *from the objective* of transnational criminal law, is justified only by the objective – i.e. the achievement of justice by cross-border law enforcement while balancing the different interests involved, in light of human rights norms. This is a purely material basis of validity, which, in turn, runs the risk that the result may only appeal to the eye of the beholder.

Both methods lead to core aspects of criminal law shared in modern societies, such as the principle that only competent authorities may hand down a verdict, that guilt must be established before criminal punishment, that each accused person has a right to a fair trial, and that one should not be punished twice for the same act.[118] Therefore, the two methods should be used in parallel, which can help reduce the risk of one-sided conclusions. The deduction of general principles by a judge may appear a risky operation as such an evaluation always reflects partly what is in the eye of the beholder. Such a threat may be balanced by a comparative overview of national principles, the concrete meaning and implications of which, however, will always differ somewhat in each national system.

C. *A defendant-based approach – backed by general principles*

In order to safeguard the interests worthy of protection that are affected by transnational criminal justice, we need more than a common scheme of coordination in transnational cases; the system must be based on a transnationally accepted set of general principles necessary to determine the relevant rules.

This finding may look mundane to some, but the debate surrounding TCL has a long way to go before it resolves the perception of transnational prosecution shaped by the tradition of Westphalian state order.[119] Transnational cases, in which one individual allegedly commits an act that affects different jurisdictions, have only recently been recognised as *one* form of transnational criminal proceeding conducted across borders by different states ('*international arbeitsteilige Strafverfolgung*').[120] For many years, even scholars of international criminal law saw these cases as a variety of co-existing national cases with little connection to and coordination with each other. The notional divide between the jurisdictions involved justified the situation of transnational cases being governed by different sets of self-contained rules, which derived from the respective national legal frameworks instead of a coherent transnational set of rules. Case studies,[121] however, suggest that if one examines the specific principles of

[118]See contributions in (2013) 9 (4) *Utrecht Law Review*, special issue, *Law Should Govern: Aspiring General Principles for Transnational Criminal Justice*.
[119]For a 19th-century opinion, see Julius Friedrich Heinrich Abegg, *Ueber die Bestrafung der im Ausland begangenen Verbrechen* (Franz Seraph Storno, 1819); Karl Binding, *Handbuch des Strafrechts* (Duncker & Humblot, 1885, reprint Scientia, 1991) 372–5.
[120]Schomburg *et al* (n 58) 22–30.
[121]*Soering v UK*, App no 14038/88 (ECtHR, 7 July 1989); *Stokjovic v France and Belgium*, App no 25303/08 (ECtHR, 27 October 2011).

criminal law as seriously as is necessary, cooperating states will be obliged to share the burden of protecting the interests of affected individuals. Such a shared burden mechanism must be based on general principles, which determine the rules that effectively transform traditional features of criminal law into TCL. Such general principles do not have a mere descriptive capacity, but must function as 'aspirational rules'. Therefore, in the future, one's aspiration must be to look for a set of principles aimed at protecting the interests of individuals and translating them into rules that compensate those whose interests are at stake when prosecution crosses borders, instead of identifying those sets of rules aimed at 'indirect suppression by international law through domestic penal law of criminal activities that have actual or potential transboundary effects'.[122] A theory for TCL must take the time-tested principles of criminal law and criminal procedure, which protect the individual, into account. The rationale is simple: when criminal prosecution carries harsh consequences for affected individuals, it must be bound by special safeguards and may be held to the different, sometimes even higher, standards resulting from the general principles governing rule-making in TCL.

IV. Conclusion

Having considered both the bird's-eye view and the worm's-eye view of TCL, a common pattern emerges. It centres on the need to take individuals' interests into account, or, as Boister himself explains in this volume: 'legality and the protection of human rights must be recognised as a governing framework. Any system of extraterritorial enactment and enforcement of criminal laws immediately runs into problems of legality … in imposing criminal proscriptions on individuals in other states who may have no warning of the criminality of their actions.'[123] Even though Boister gives some authority to the interests of individuals, such considerations are not immediately visible from the bird's-eye view of TCL. They remain hidden among other contentions, but they emerge as a pattern if one takes a worm's-eye view, working up to a new bird's-eye view that beholds an individual-based approach of TCL; the new perspective marks a continuum rather than a divide.

If we bear in mind the individual's perspective, two features will sit at the core of future debates on TCL. First, TCL requires a broad definition, one which places the necessary value on the individuals' interests affected. An individual-based approach to TCL must include a shared cooperation scheme so as to transform general principles of criminal law and criminal procedure from national frameworks into principles at the relevant transnational level, and thus safeguard the interests of the affected individuals. Secondly, legal frameworks of transnationally

[122] Boister, this volume.

[123] *Ibid*, with reference to the Universal Declaration of Human Rights (adopted 10 December 1948), UNGA Res 217 A(III), Art 11(2).

accepted basic rules protecting the interests of defendants must accompany the enhancement of legal frameworks of transnational crime control that transcend national jurisdictions. Only if this is achieved will Boister's vision for TCL come true, and alleged criminals will genuinely become 'members of multiple normative communities, local, territorial, extraterritorial, and non-territorial in nature'.[124]

[124]Boister, this volume.

Global policing and transnational rule with law

Ben Bowling[a] and James Sheptycki[b]

[a]*Professor of Criminology & Criminal Justice and Deputy Dean, The Dickson Poon School of Law, King's College, London, UK;* [b]*Professor of Criminology, Faculty of Liberal Arts and Professional Studies, York University, Toronto, Canada*

This paper advances the 'rule with law' concept. After a brief overview of the global policing field and its relationship with law, we use socio-legal theories of policing to examine four examples of law in action: (i) the global money system, (ii) transnational mobility, (iii) intellectual property, and (iv) high policing. These examples illustrate how legal instruments become tools in the hands of public and private social actors operating in the transnational sphere. The paper advances three arguments. First, we argue that global policing practices exemplify rule *with* law not rule *of* law. Second, we argue that attempts to codify transnational (criminal) law and procedure must recognise the distinction between 'law in the books' and the 'living law' as revealed in the practice of transnational policing. Third, we argue that the study of transnational policing should not be restricted to the response to transnational organised crime or defined as coterminous with transnational criminal law. Global policing practices deploy many kinds of public and private law as power tools in the governance of the global system.

Introduction

Policework is a curiously neglected subject in legal scholarship and education. Despite the long tradition of socio-legal research on policing,[1] contemporary legal scholars tend to focus on how legislative bodies make law, how judges use law in making decisions in court, or on doctrinal questions that arise from legal theory and history. By comparison, legal scholarship on the law in police hands is thin on the ground.[2] It is notable that of the hundred or so articles

[1]See Joseph Goldstein, 'Police Discretion Not to Invoke the Criminal Process: Low Visibility Decision in the Administration of Justice' (1960) 69 *Yale Law Journal* 543; Laurence Lustgarten, *The Governance of the Police* (Sweet & Maxwell, 1986); David Dixon, *Law in Policing* (Oxford University Press, 1997); Robert Reiner, *The Politics of the Police* (Oxford University Press, 4th edn 2010).

[2]Robert Baldwin and Richard Kinsey, 'Rules, Realism and the Police Act' (1985) 12 *Critical Social Policy* 89.

published in the first five volumes of *Transnational Legal Theory*, there is not a single article on policing or police and only two papers touch briefly on law enforcement in its broadest sense.[3] This paper fills a gap in the literature on transnational law by focusing on the current practices of transnational policing. We argue that today's police use a variety of legal instruments across national boundaries and that their decisions to do so tend to be low visibility ones that are not well understood. Transnational policing is carried out in a largely unregulated fashion in the name of law without being constrained by the rule of law. This, in our view, underlines the need for legal scholars to look more closely at the deployment of legal rules by police (broadly defined) in the transnational realm. The paper proceeds as follows. First, we set out an overview of global policing's origins, institutional architecture and contemporary practices. We then take up the challenge of this symposium by looking at legal tools in the context of transnational police work. Drawing on an interdisciplinary theoretical framework grounded in the socio-legal study of policing, we examine four examples of law in action concerning (i) the global money system, (ii) transnational mobility, (iii) intellectual property, and (iv) high policing. These examples illustrate how both public and private actors deploy legal instruments transnationally.

The paper advances three arguments. First, we argue that global policing practices do not exemplify rule *of* law, but rather rule *with* law. That is, technocratic 'legal engineers' use legal 'power tools' to achieve specific ends that usually uphold the existing global system dominated by seigneurial states and powerful private corporations. This examination of law in action under transnational conditions illustrates that the global social order is a rule with law system, not a rule of law system. Second, we argue that attempts to codify transnational (criminal) law and procedure must recognise the distinction between 'law in the books' and the 'living law' revealed in the practice of transnational policing. Rather than constraining state and corporate power, law is a tool available to police enabling intrusive surveillance and coercion to serve the interests of the powerful. Third, we argue that the study of transnational policing should not be restricted to responses to transnational organised crime or defined as coterminous with transnational criminal law. Global policing practices deploy many kinds of public and private law as power tools in the governance of the global system.

Global policing

The concept of global policing is a somewhat novel and controversial idea.[4] Our broad working definition of transnational policing (a more widely accepted term)

[3]Based on a search of article titles, keywords and abstracts.

[4]This section draws on Ben Bowling and James Sheptycki, *Global Policing* (Sage, 2012). See also Malcolm Anderson, *Policing the World* (Oxford University Press, 1989) ; Malcolm Anderson, Monica den Boer, Peter Cullen, William Gilmore, Charles Raab and Neil

is 'any form of order maintenance, law enforcement, peace-keeping, crime investigation, intelligence sharing or other form of policework that transcends or traverses national boundaries'.[5] Empirical evidence shows that this is a highly extensive, complex and costly social and legal process. It includes not only the detective function – investigating cross-border criminal activity and bringing alleged offenders before the courts – but also a wide range of other emergency order maintenance, social service and regulatory functions. Like their colleagues working in local police departments, the 'global cops' have an 'omnibus mandate' to secure social order. They respond to unregulated or undocumented migration, illicit financial movements, intellectual property violations, fraud, accidents and emergencies, sudden death, lost and stolen identity documents, terrorism and organised crime, illicit market transactions, smuggling and more. Transnational policing, unlike domestic policing, by definition, transgresses national boundaries.

Transnational policing is not new.[6] Borders define the territorial limits of states, but millions of tonnes of raw materials and manufactured goods, trillions of dollars in financial capital and countless people flow across them daily. When police are interested in the money, people or goods crossing borders, they too cross those borders.[7] Sometimes this is in 'hot pursuit' of a fleeing fugitive, but more frequently it involves routine visits to overseas counterparts to share information or collect evidence. Police organisations share information.[8] In the early years, they went on foot, bicycle and horseback, and later by planes, trains and automobiles. Now, many police agents spend their days in contact with overseas counterparts by internet and other forms of telecommunications.[9]

Academic research on transnational policing lags behind the practice it seeks to understand. The early works of Malcolm Anderson and Ethan Nadelmann

---

Walker, *Policing the European Union* (Oxford University Press, 1995); Ethan Nadelmann, *Cops Across Borders: The Internationalization of US Criminal Law Enforcement* (Pennsylvania State University Press, 1993) 470.

[5]See Bowling and Sheptycki (n 4) 3.

[6]Mathieu Deflem, *Policing World Society: Historical Foundations of International Police Cooperation* (Oxford University Press, 2004); HH Liang, *The Rise of Modern Police and the European State System from Metternich to the Second World War* (Cambridge University Press, 1992); Mike Brogden, 'The Emergence of the Police – The Colonial Dimension' (1987) 27(1) *British Journal of Criminology* 4; D Anderson and D Killingray, *Policing the Empire: Government, Authority and Control, 1830–1940* (Manchester University Press, 1991).

[7]Ben Bowling and James Sheptycki, 'Global Policing, Mobility and Social Control' in Sharon Pickering and Julie Ham (eds), *Routledge Handbook on Crime and International Migration* (Routledge, 2014) 57; see also Bowling and Sheptycki (n 4) 102–4, 114–18.

[8]Bernard Porter, *Plots and Paranoia: A History of Political Espionage in Britain 1790–1988* (Routledge, 1992) ch 6.

[9]Ben Bowling, *Policing the Caribbean: Transnational Security Cooperation in Practice* (Oxford University Press, 2010); James Sheptycki (ed), *Issues in Transnational Policing* (Routledge, 2000); Andrew Goldsmith and James Sheptycki (eds), *Crafting Transnational Policing* (Hart Publishing, 2007); Steven David Brown (ed), *Combating International Crime* (Routledge, 2008).

documented the development of transnational policing practice in Europe and North America, respectively.[10] Since then, more research has documented a range of policing agencies working transnationally.[11] One important early development was the creation of the British colonial police; individuals were selected in England or Ireland, trained, equipped and then deployed across the colonies from Australia to Zanzibar, taking in great swathes of Africa, the Caribbean, South East Asia, the Middle East and Canada.[12] Early transnational policing stemming from the United States included the pursuit of fugitive slaves and other so-called 'outlaws' and attempts to control smuggling (particularly alcohol).[13] A more global view shows that police conferences on international anarchism and the white slave trade in the late nineteenth and early twentieth centuries paved the way for the formation of Interpol in 1923.[14] Since then, transnational policing has grown in its capacity, geographical reach and impact. Fuelled by public anxiety about 'new security threats' such as transnational organised crime and international terrorism, and driven by a range of transnational actors and political interests, global policing is emerging as a key element in the governance of the global system.[15]

Today, Interpol is the best-known global policing brand.[16] Headquartered in Lyon and embedded within police agencies around the world, Interpol links police institutions through a global communications system that includes its own databases of wanted persons, fingerprints, police intelligence and other kinds of alerts.[17] The United Nations played a significant role in the development

[10]See Anderson (n 4); Anderson *et al* (n 4); Nadelmann (n 4) 470.

[11]Peter Andreas and Ethan Nadelmann, *Policing the Globe: Criminalization and Crime Control in International Relations* (Oxford University Press, 2006).

[12]Mike Brogden, 'The Emergence of the Police: The Colonial Dimension' (1987) 27(1) *British Journal of Criminology* 4; D Anderson and D Killingray, *Policing the Empire: Government, Authority and Control, 1830–1940* (Manchester University Press, 1991); Georgina Sinclair, *At the End of the Line: Colonial Policing and the Imperial Endgame, 1945–80* (Manchester University Press, 2006).

[13]See Nadelmann (n 4) 470; Andreas and Nadelmann (n 11).

[14]Mathieu Deflem, 'Bureaucratization and Social Control: Historical Foundations of International Police' (2000) 34(3) *Law & Society Review* 601; Richard Bach Jensen, 'The United States, International Policing and the War against Anarchist Terrorism 1900–1914' (2001) 13(1) *Terrorism and Political Violence* 15; see Deflem (n 6).

[15]See Bowling and Sheptycki (n 4); Ben Bowling and James Sheptycki (eds), *Global Policing and Transnational Law Enforcement*, vols 1–4 (Sage, forthcoming 2015); James Sheptycki, 'Transnational Policing and the Makings of a Postmodern State' (1995) 35(4) *British Journal of Criminology* 613.

[16]James Sheptycki, 'Brand Interpol', paper presented at the conference 'A Question of Trust: Socio-Legal Imperatives in International Police and Justice Cooperation', Oñati, Spain, 4–5 July 2013.

[17]Malcolm Anderson, *Policing the World: Interpol and the Politics of International Police Co-operation* (Clarendon, 1989); M Barnett and L Coleman, 'Designing Police: Interpol and the Study of Change in International Organisations' (2005) 49 *International Studies*

of transnational policing from its earliest days.[18] It has sponsored treaties and conventions, as well as creating police units to support peace operations. What started in Congo with a few hundred police officers in 1960 has grown into UNPOL, which by 2008 had recruited a force of 17,500 police officers, drawn from 98 countries, deployed to so-called weak, failing and failed states.[19] There are also global policing networks such as the World Customs Organization and Egmont Group, and intriguing developments in transnational policing within the prosecution divisions of the International Criminal Court.[20]

Officials from Interpol and the United Nations have long had global policing ambitions. In 1963, UN Secretary-General U Thant said he had 'no doubt that the world should eventually have an international police force which will be accepted as an integral and essential part of life in the same way as national police forces are accepted'.[21] Officials and legal scholars have set out proposals for an international or transnational police force on numerous occasions.[22] In October 2009, the 'global policing vision' was updated once again by transnational technocrats when Interpol and UNPOL brought together justice and foreign ministers from 60 countries (including the USA and China) to create a 'global policing doctrine'. The *New York Times* reported that Interpol and the UN were now 'poised to become partners in fighting crime by jointly grooming a global police force'.[23]

These are salient examples of what can be best termed 'global policing' because of its progenitors' ambition to create a policing network that covers the whole world. There are, however, myriad other forms of transnational policing occurring on a day-to-day basis. These include creating policing hubs to facilitate transnational activity, posting liaison officers overseas, creating joint investigation teams and coordinating operations to target fugitives and other forms of cross-border activity.[24] At the same time, it is clear that domestic policing is 'glocalising'

Quarterly 593; Fenton Bresler, *Interpol: A History and Examination of 70 Years of Crime Solving* (Sinclair-Stevenson, 1992); see Deflem (n 6).

[18]Beth Greener, *The New International Policing* (Palgrave Macmillan, 2009).

[19]Andrew Hughes (UN Police Adviser), at Interpol's 77th General Assembly, 'Organized Crime Threatens Peace Efforts, Top UN Police Official Warns Interpol', press release, St Petersburg, Russia, 8 October 2008.

[20]See Bowling and Sheptycki (n 4) ch 3.

[21]See Greener (n 18) 1.

[22]RC Johansen and SH Mendlovitz, 'The Role of Enforcement of Law in the Establishment of a New International Order: A Proposal for a Transnational Police Force' (1980) 6 *Alternatives: Global, Local, Political* 307; O Höffe, *Democracy in an Age of Globalisation* (Springer, 2007).

[23]'Interpol and UN Back "Global Policing Doctrine"' *New York Times* (11 October 2009) (emphasis added).

[24]Saskia Hufnagel, 'Strategies of Police Cooperation: Comparing the Southern Chinese Seaboard with the European Union' (2013) 61(4) *Crime, Law and Social Change* 377; see Andreas (n 11); Ersel Ayidinli and Hasan Yön, 'Transgovernmentalism Meets Security: Police Liaison Officers, Terrorism, and Statist Transnationalism' (2010) 24(1) *Governance: An International Journal of Political Administration, and Institutions* 55; Ben Bowling,

as local police agents are increasingly drawn into transnational networks of training and knowledge exchange predicated on the perceived need to control local manifestations of transnational crime and disorder.[25] What we call 'global policing' is a loosely coupled system of actors linked by various means. These agents operate in conditions of low visibility, act with considerable discretion and are largely unregulated by any superordinate form of authority, which brings us to consider the *relationship* between policing and law.

Transnational law and transnational policing

Policing and law intertwine domestically and transnationally. Police are referred to as 'officers of the law' or sometimes 'law enforcers'. Police agents stake a claim for legitimacy based on access to legal tools, and this is true in both civil code and common law systems. What police do – use coercive powers to stop and search, to maintain order, to restrain, arrest and hold people prisoner, to undertake intrusive surveillance – requires legal tools. Many, if not all, police actions would be serious criminal offences if they were not done under the cover of legality. In short, police rule with law. Policing is the *sine qua non* of legality; crudely put, what would law be if there were not agents authorised, equipped and capable of enacting it? Thus, in both criminal and civil law, policing activity is requisite to give it 'due execution'. Police investigate allegations or suspicions of wrongdoing (through surveillance, investigation or interrogation), bring parties before the courts, help to prepare cases for trial, pursue alleged wrongdoers, enforce fines and civil penalties, and ensure that convicted offenders go to jail or comply with their punishment. *A fortiori*, police agents protect the sources and repositories of legal instruments: legislators and judges, parliaments, government offices and courtrooms. The police use legal means in part to ensure the legitimacy and integrity of 'the law' itself.

It should come as no surprise to discover that contemporary scholarly debates about transnational law and transnational policing run in parallel. When Jessup coined the term 'transnational law' in 1956, he was interested in illuminating a transnational space wherein the attempt to regulate actions and events transcending national boundaries might involve the use of legal rules and practices.[26] Many police scholars, ourselves included, share Jessup's concern to understand the same

---

'Transnational Policing: The Globalization Thesis, a Typology and a Research Agenda' (2009) 3(2) *Policing* 149; see Nadelmann (n 4); see also Bowling and Sheptycki (n 4) for an overview.

[25]See Stuart Kirby and Sue Penna, 'Policing Mobile Criminality: Implications for Police Forces in the UK' (2011) 34(2) *Policing: An International Journal of Police Strategies and Management* 182; Bowling and Sheptycki (n 4).

[26]Philip Jessup, *Transnational Law* (Yale University Press, 1956) 2; Peer Zumbansen, 'Transnational Law, Evolving' in Jan Smits (ed), *Encyclopedia of Comparative Law* (Edward Elgar, 2nd edn 2012) 899; cf. Bowling and Sheptycki (n 4).

cross-border activities and events, differing only in the sense that we are focused on the role of police officers and how they use law and other legal tools. Transnational lawyers, criminologists and police researchers are working the same field and are united in the attempt to understand the regulation of the flow of people, goods, capital, services and information across national boundaries.

Both law and policing are complexly related to global social ordering. Understanding the law in books, treaties and conventions is one thing, but the logic of legal doctrine is not the same as law in action. Doctrinal legal study does not encompass the complex relationships of either legal practice or policing. The study of law and policing in the transnational realm heralds the end of the divide between domestic and international since they are 'both and neither'.[27] Law and policing inhabit the 'transnational space between',[28] existing in an organisational 'in-between state' reacting to the 'shifting balance between public administration and private execution, between government and governance'.[29] The changing nature of both law and policing represents challenges to participation and deliberation in a highly dispersed, fluid and fragmented global public sphere. The study of transnational law and policing coalesce around questions concerning the law in action.

In the spirit of engagement with this symposium issue on transnational criminal law, we focus here on the work of Neil Boister, who has given impetus to the conception of transnational law by conjoining it with a criminological issue: transnational crime.[30] Establishment of a principled basis for transnational criminal law remains in its infancy.[31] Boister has nevertheless established a view of a 'transnational legal space', perceptively arguing that the notion of transnational criminal law provides a conceptual lens through which to view a systemic whole.[32] It is worth understanding that whole, he argues, not least because, when the programmatic nature of the system of transnational criminal law remains hidden, so do concerns for legality and human rights. To us, this project involves understanding both law and policing.

Much policework is concerned with crime, and quite a bit of transnational policework is concerned with criminal law. For Boister, transnational criminal law is defined as law directed at suppressing criminal activities with actual or

---

[27]Peer Zumbansen, 'Transnational Law', CLPE Research Paper No 09, posted 14 March 2008, 743.
[28]See Bowling and Sheptycki (n 4).
[29]See Zumbansen (n 26) 745.
[30]Neil Boister, '"Transnational Criminal Law"?' (2003) 14(5) *European Journal of International Law* 953; Neil Boister, *An Introduction to Transnational Criminal Law* (Oxford University Press, 2012); Neil Boister, 'Further reflections on the concept of transnational criminal law', this volume.
[31]Sabine Gless and John AE Vervaele, 'Law Should Govern: Aspiring General Principles for Transnational Criminal Justice' (2013) 9(4) *Utrecht Law Review* 1.
[32]See Boister, this volume.

potential transboundary effects.[33] He argues that transnational criminal law is a 'system of law' that is both the province of 'law enforcement' specialists and the product of an international order dominated by a few powerful states jealously guarding their interests.[34] Boister raises a number of extremely important issues, such as problems of liability, jurisdiction, definitional coherence and ambiguity in the enforcement of criminal law in the transnational realm. He also points to the absence of clear regulation, enforcement and punishment polices as criminal justice becomes globally interconnected. He is also critical of the way transnational criminal law is created – in particular, the way in which legal tools are shaped by police actors, a point that we have made in our own work. The role of police officers in *making* domestic law has important implications for the nature of law and the practice of law enforcement in its general sense.[35] This also raises important questions about the legitimacy of the transnational policing enterprise, not least because of its impact on weak states.

Boister notes that current efforts in this area have encouraged a 'law and order attitude' in which, if human rights laws come into play at all, they are used in limited instances – usually only in national and international high courts – and then only retroactively. Some legal instruments are, of course, concerned with due process and the protection of human rights and civil liberties, but law can be used against law – for example, by creating state immunity and other legal lacunae because of the boundaries of jurisdictional competence.[36] One obvious point, which we address later, is that policing power may transgress territorial boundaries but human rights protections do not. As demonstrated by numerous well-known cases (e.g. Alvarez Machain[37] or Khalid El Masri[38]) and those that are less well-known (e.g. Derek Bond),[39] transnational policing can severely

---

[33]See Boister, '"Transnational Criminal Law"?' (n 30) 955.
[34]See *ibid*, 956.
[35]Richard V Ericson, *The Constitution of Legal Inequality* (Carleton University Information Services, 1983).
[36]Richard V Ericson, *Crime in an Insecure World* (Polity, 2007).
[37]Dr Alvarez-Machain was abducted by Mexican nationals under the direction of the US Drug Enforcement Administration (DEA), taken to the USA, tried and acquitted for his alleged role in the murder of a DEA agent. The US Supreme Court ruled in *Sosa v Alvarez-Machain*, 03-339, and *United States v Alvarez-Machain* 03-485 (29 June 2004), that the Federal Tort Claims Act prohibits claims for injuries occurring on foreign territory and that the Alien Tort Claims Act prohibits claims for arbitrary detention by US officials or their agents acting overseas.
[38]Khalid El Masri, a German and Lebanese citizen, was abducted in December 2003 by the Macedonian police, rendered by the CIA to a secret detention centre in Afghanistan, held for four months and tortured. Innocent of any offence, he was released on an open road in Albania in May 2004. In 2012, the European Court of Human Rights ruled that he had been tortured and abused by the CIA and Macedonian police and he was awarded compensation. *El-Masri v The former Yugoslav Republic of Macedonia*, Application 39630/09, 13 December 3012.
[39]Derek Bond, an English retiree on holiday in South Africa, was arrested in January 2003. Acting on an Interpol Red Notice, Bond's passport number and description matched an alias

impact supposedly fundamental legal human rights and freedoms, not to mention the physical well-being of the people affected. An intractable problem is that cross-border interventions that clearly breach human rights standards have frequently been deemed lawful by domestic courts.

When it comes to choices about using legal instruments, claims about effectiveness and expediency in responding to transnational threats tend to trump claims about democratic legitimacy, human rights and the rule of law. Boister observes that constitutional values concerning civil and human rights are not yet instilled transnationally and that cooperation among transnational policing agents is generally outside the purview of nationally based accountability mechanisms. His work attempts to address some of these problems and codify the legal instruments available to lawyers and police in the suppression of transnational crime. Boister seeks to provide a doctrinal basis for criminalisation and a fully transnational criminal law as distinct from either national or international criminal law. He delineates a list of substantive offences and seeks to construct a legal framework for enforcement in various spheres such as police cooperation, the high seas, mutual legal assistance, extradition, asset recovery and extradition, and he sets out a basis for transnational criminal procedure.[40]

Boister began to develop transnational criminal law doctrine early in the new millennium, optimistic that it could be tested against the benchmarks informing the penal function in domestic law, remedy doctrinal weaknesses in the system, introduce human rights considerations and establish legitimacy in systems of control.[41] A decade later, he has drawn the rather pessimistic conclusion that transnational crime control operates at the expense of justice.[42] Transnational criminal law, he laments, tends to be geared instrumentally to narrow definitions of effectiveness, deterrence, control and the engineering of social order. Driven by moral panics, it risks 'over-criminalisation', creates boundaries between insiders and outsiders, victims and scapegoats, citizens and suitable enemies, the mass and the usual suspects. Transnational criminal law and procedure, he says, tends to ignore the rights of alleged offenders to consular assistance: it does not guarantee a fair trial; it offers little protection against human rights abuse; and it offers no protection to victims or witnesses. The depressing conclusion of Boister's more recent work is that the future holds little prospect of creating a form of transnational criminal law that can deliver

used by Derek Lloyd Sykes, wanted for a $4.8 million fraud and the subject of an FBI arrest warrant issued in Houston, Texas. Bond was held without charge in Durban police station for three weeks until the FBI accepted that they had detained the wrong man, whereupon he was released. The FBI apologised but denied accountability in law for their error: *Daily Telegraph*, 26 February 2003; *The Guardian*, 26 February 2003; Bowling and Sheptycki (n 4) 10.

[40]See Boister, *An Introduction to Transnational Criminal Law* (n 30) 278; see also Gless and Vervaele (n 31).

[41]See Boister, '"Transnational Criminal Law"?' (n 30).

[42]See Boister, *An Introduction to Transnational Criminal Law* (n 30); Boister, this volume.

justice.[43] We share Boister's pessimism about the contention that transnational criminal law can provide a just and equitable basis for the foundation of transnational criminal justice. To take this debate forward, we turn now to socio-legal analysis of policing and introduce our central concept: rule with law.

Lessons from the socio-legal study of policework

A common starting point in discussions of justice is the ideal of the *rule of law*. This is the doctrine that citizens and state officials alike are bound by a set of known and settled written rules that are used in accordance with clear and known established procedures.[44] The rule of law claims to guard against the arbitrary use of state power because officials are bound by rules. The doctrine insists that the law binds governments and their officials just as much as it does everyone else. It is from the idea of rule of law that such principles as 'no punishment without the due process of law', 'equality before the law' and 'innocent until proven guilty' spring. As Boister observes, however, in the transnational realm, the 'system assumes rather than develops a rule of law framework'.[45] In our view, such an assumption is not merely unwarranted, it is directly contradicted by empirical evidence. We take the view that when we move to the '*what is*' from the '*what ought to be*' of how rules relate to policework a better description of policing in practice is 'rule with law'. To explain what we mean by this, we set out some key findings from the socio-legal study of policing. In the following subsections, we illustrate how police shape the substantive law, how legal permissiveness creates a space for police discretion to operate, how law is shaped by police occupational culture, and show law is a tool in the hands of the police.

Police shape the law in the books

The general tendency of domestic police officials to play a key role in law making at the national level is writ large in their activism in the transnational realm. Take, for example, the 2000 United Nations Convention on Transnational Organized Crime, known as the Palermo Convention. Jonathan Winer, US Deputy Assistant Secretary of State for International Law Enforcement from 1994 to 1999, observed that the harmonised legal standards in the Convention were designed by mid-level national and transnational technocrats mostly from Europe and the United States. These legal standards were designed 'to meet the new demands of cross-border enforcement activities, with minimal interference by domestic political

[43] See Boister, *An Introduction to Transnational Criminal Law* (n 30) 278; see also Gless and Vervaele (n 31).
[44] Tom Bingham, *The Rule of Law* (Penguin, 2011); Adam Tomkins, *Public Law* (Oxford University Press, 2003).
[45] See Boister, *An Introduction to Transnational Criminal Law* (n 30) 278.

constraints'.[46] As with many other legal instruments for transnational police cooperation, transnational policing actors themselves drafted the terms of the Convention. As Mathieu Deflem further observed, the relative autonomy of police institutions enables police knowledge systems, objectives and techniques to infuse into international partnerships.[47] Transnational criminal law, therefore, is a 'system of law' that is both the province of policing specialists and the product of an international order dominated by representation of a few powerful states who jealously guard their interests.[48] The role of police in making the law has been studied in detail by criminologists and has important implications for the nature of law and the practice of policing. The 'democratic deficit' that emerges when law is made not by democratic representatives but through the machinations of transnational police, customs, military, immigration, intelligence and other technocratic 'security specialists' raises important questions about the rule of law.

Legal permissiveness creates a space for police discretion

From early on, the socio-legal study of police focused on its discretionary nature. Until 1960, police discretion was an untheorised aspect of the law in practice; half a century later, socio-legal study of police discretion is well developed. Beginning with the obvious – that total law enforcement is a practical impossibility – Joseph Goldstein established that police agents frequently decide not to invoke the law.[49] This, he argued, was an example of 'low visibility decision making' in the criminal legal process.[50] Over time, the recognition of discretionary practice in police use of law led to the notion of the police officer's 'legal tool box'.[51] Robert Reiner coined the term 'blue letter law' to describe the police use of 'law in action' as a contrast to 'black-letter law' 'in the books'. Blue letter law refers to the police use of legal tools in managing an unpredictable variety of situational exigencies.[52] Related research showed that police use law as a 'presentational strategy' and charted the use of stock legal phrases that allow police agents to give legal cover for their actions after the fact.[53] In this sense, the

---

[46]Jonathon Winer, *Cops Across Borders: The Evolution of Transatlantic Law Enforcement and Judicial Co-operation* (1 September 2004), www.cfr.org/publication/7393/cops_across_borders.html, 2 (accessed April 2015).
[47]See Deflem (n 14) 634.
[48]Boister (2008) 956.
[49] Goldstein (n 1).
[50]S Bronitt and P Stenning, 'Understanding Discretion in Modern Policing' (2011) 35(6) *Criminal Law Journal* 319.
[51]Roger Cotterrell, *The Sociology of Law: An Introduction* (Oxford University Press, 2nd edn 1992) 272–85.
[52]See Reiner (n 1) 209.
[53]DJ Smith and J Gray, *Police and People in London* (Policy Studies Institute, 1985); Richard V Ericson, 'Rules in Policing: Five Perspectives' (2007) 11(3) *Theoretical Criminology* 367.

language of law functions as a rhetorical device to persuade audiences – including the general public, but also judges and other actors who are often called upon to ratify police decisions – of the legitimacy of police action. The idea of the police use of legal tools is captured in another way by Doreen McBarnet's aphoristic phrase, 'due process is for crime control', revealing that law is explicitly an enabling device.[54] Through these notions, some hard observations have been made about police use of legal tools:

> It is a cornerstone of orthodox legal theory that the police are, first and foremost, accountable to the law … However, 'rule of law' is an abstract concept that must be related to its expression in practice to be meaningful … law, police and court action cannot be separated. Rather than being directly accountable to the law, the existence of discretion in policing means that the law is permissive. The law defines when a police officer may act, but cannot direct a police officer to act or act in a particular way in a given instance … nor does it act as a control on police activity during encounters with the public … In practice, the law is frequently used as a resource by the police to achieve police-defined goals … For example, although the police may only stop and search someone if they have 'reasonable suspicion' or 'probable cause to believe' that an offence has been committed, these concepts are so permissive that, in practice, the police can stop and search anyone in almost any circumstance. Hence … abusive practices are facilitated by the law, rather than precluded by it.[55]

The police organisation has a special quality that police discretion increases as one moves down the hierarchy.[56] Reiner shows that the extent of police discretion means that 'the rank-and-file officer is the primary determinant of policing where it really counts: on the street'.[57] This observation has led police researchers to look at the norms, values and working practices of street-level police officers.[58]

Police occupational subculture shapes police discretion

We have argued elsewhere that understanding how the complex global policing system hangs together requires specific attention to the occupational subcultures

[54]Doreen McBarnet, *Conviction: Law, the State and the Construction of Justice* (Macmillan, 1981).
[55]Ben Bowling, Coretta Phillips, Alexandra Campbell and Maria Docking, 'Policing and Human Rights: Eliminating Discrimination, Xenophobia, Intolerance and the Abuse of Power from Police Work', United Nations Research Institute for Social Development, *Identities, Conflict and Cohesion*, Programme Paper 4, May 2004, 18.
[56]James Q Wilson, *Varieties of Police Behaviour* (Harvard University Press, 1968) 7.
[57]See Reiner (n 1) 116.
[58]Simon Holdaway, *Inside the British Police* (Basil Blackwell, 1983); Simon Holdaway, 'Discovering Structure: Studies of the Police Occupational Culture' in Mollie Weatheritt (ed), *Police Research* (Avebury, 1989); William Westley, *Violence and the Police: A Sociological Study of Law, Custom and Morality* (MIT Press, 1971); Michael Banton, *The Policeman in the Community* (Tavistock, 1964).

of policing.[59] There is now a large body of empirical evidence from both the domestic and transnational fields that shows how law is used by the constable on the street or by liaison officers and others in the transnational realm. This material shows how police make sense of their work and of the various enabling and constraining factors that shape the job.[60] A core feature of the police occupation lies in its relationship to coercion. The police capacity to use reasonable force rests on sociological and cultural expectations that evade the predicament of authority.[61] Policing subculture is a social space where agents actively create meanings of social order. The subculture of policing exhibits considerable local variation because local knowledge is relevant to policing. Nevertheless there remains a 'family resemblance' among subcultures of policing around the world. That kinship arises from common problems inherent in the use or threat of violence as a means to achieve peace and security. We refer to this as the *transnational subculture of policing*.

Through our empirical work, we have discovered that a novel *subculture of transnational policing* is emerging across the transnational security field.[62] This is the culture inhabited by police and 'law enforcement' technocrats including customs, immigration, border officers and others who work in the transnational space between.[63] As we noted above, police agents operate in many settings in the global system. The subculture of transnational policing shapes the global system in important ways. The policies and decisions these police agents make shape the transnational subculture of policing, which in turn shapes local policing around the world. Our argument is that police subculture adapts legal rules to create legal tools; these shape enforcement jurisdiction to suit operational requirements and, without reference to any form of democratic political authority, decisively shape the emergent transnational state system.

Legal engineering and law as a power tool

The importance of the occupational subculture for creating 'blue letter' law and in shaping global policing in practice becomes clear when it is placed in the context of the relationship between policing and other governance institutions. Policing practice becomes responsive to public welfare concerns and the general social good through democratic mechanisms of accountability and control. Gauging the extent of officers' autonomy in the transnational realm is therefore crucial to

---

[59] James Sheptycki, 'The Global Cops Cometh; Reflections on Transnationalization, Knowledge Work and Police Subculture' (1998) 49(1) *British Journal of Sociology* 57.
[60] Bethan Loftus, *Police Culture in a Changing World* (Clarendon, 2012).
[61] James Sheptycki, 'The Constabulary Ethic Reconsidered' in F Lemieux (ed), *International Police Cooperation; Emerging Issues, Theory and Practice* (Willan, 2010) 298.
[62] Sheptycki (n 59); see Bowling (n 9).
[63] Robert Reiner, 'Police and Policing' in M Maguire, R Morgan and R Reiner (eds), *Oxford Handbook of Criminology* (Oxford University Press, 2nd edn 1997) 1007.

understanding how subcultural norms and values fill the 'transnational space' within which policing decisions are taken. Because the laws governing policework and permissive and because policework has wide discretion and low visibility,[64] there is 'considerable leeway for police culture and the social and situational pressures on officers to shape police practice'.[65]

McBarnet describes this process as 'legal engineering'.[66] She shows that when law is a tool in the hands of social controllers, the attempt to control the controllers with law results in the emergence of new legal devices and the creative use of legal instruments. The people she calls legal engineers 'use whatever law is available at any given moment, sometimes drawing from areas of law and regulation not hitherto seen as relevant to the context in hand, in order to construct new ways of control'.[67] It is crucial to understand that *policing is not reducible to mere criminal law enforcement*. The police response to organised crime, for example, is not limited to the use of criminal law; on the contrary, a wide variety of other types of administrative and regulatory law (e.g. tax, immigration, licensing, health and safety) have been used in the police response to organised crime.[68] Philip Stenning, among others, has illustrated how property and contract law provide power tools in the context of private forms of policing and security. The literature concerning the public-private policing distinction has emphasised the interactions between different policing providers, some operating under private and some under public auspices.[69] Legal tools are used to configure these arrangements and empower the agents who constitute them.

The empirical study of the transnational practices of police agencies and police agents illustrates law in action in the transnational space between. A good example of this is 'jurisdiction shopping'[70]: policing agents operating in the transnational

[64] Wilson (n 56); Doreen McBarnet, 'Legal Form and Legal Mystification' (1982) 10 *International Journal of the Sociology of Law* 409.
[65] See Reiner (n 1) 117.
[66] Doreen McBarnet, 'Questioning the Legitimacy of Compliance: A Case Study of the Banking Crisis' in Adam Crawford and Anthea Hucklesby (eds), *Legitimacy and Compliance in Criminal Justice* (Routledge, 2013) 71.
[67] *Ibid*, 83.
[68] A Leong, *The Disruption of International Organised Crime: An Analysis of Legal and Non-Legal Strategies* (Ashgate, 2007); James B Jacobs, *Gotham Unbound* (New York University Press, 1999).
[69] P Stenning, 'Powers and Accountability of Private Police' (2000) 8 *European Journal on Criminal Policy and Research* 325; P Stenning, 'Governance and Accountability in a Plural Policing Environment: The Story So Far' (2009) 3(1) *Policing* 22; Les Johnston and Philip Stenning, 'Challenges of Governance and Accountability for Transnational Private Policing' in Frederic Lemieux (ed), *International Police Cooperation: Emerging Issues, Theory and Practice* (Taylor & Francis, 2010) 281; John Braithwaite, 'The New Regulatory State and the Transformation of Criminology' (2000) 40 *British Journal of Criminology* 222.
[70] Chantel Joubert and Hans Bevers, *Schengen Investigated: A Comparative Interpretation of the Schengen Provisions on International Police Cooperation in the Light of the European Convention on Human Rights* (Kluwer, 1996).

space between jurisdictions may pick and choose legal tools and legal forums.[71] As Boister observes, 'cooperation against transnational crime frequently takes place in an extraterritorial legal space that enables the avoidance of human rights'.[72] An example of this can be found in the words of a Dutch police officer speaking about cross-border police teams:

> If we arrest a drug dealer here in the Netherlands he will be given a penalty of a maximum of six months in prison. If we arrest him in Germany he will get a maximum of six years. We arrest them in Germany. It is better I think.[73]

The socio-legal study of policing practice reveals law to be a tool in the hands of a wide variety of policing agents in a complex web of interdependence.[74] As Ludwig Wittgenstein argued in *The Philosophical Investigations*, rule following is a social practice set in the context of taken-for-granted knowledge, assumptions and routines. Transposed into the context of our analysis, we could say that that form of life can be conceptualised in terms of an occupational subculture of policing situated within the global policing architecture.[75] Within that complex form of life, practical mastery of legal language is an important social competence. The decision to pick up and deploy legal tools shows the transformative power of legal discourse in which the taken-for-granted knowledge, assumptions and routines of the social world can be translated into authoritative terms and thereby shaped according to the dictates of the tool users. In this sense law is a tool in the hands of knowing actors and 'policework' resides in the mastery of a set of social practices and the language game that arises from it. We refer to this as 'rule *with* law'.

We understand governance generally as the practice of ruling with law, and this takes place in a world in which arguments about law and justice abound. The image of the goddess *Justice* – standing blindfolded with the sword of virtue in one hand and the scales of justice in the other – is suggestive of coercion and fairness. The socio-legal study of policing shows that, legal tools are used programmatically, but the systemic nature of their use often remains hidden to all but the most discerning observers. That is why the sociology of policing has carried within it an abiding interest in concerns for human rights.[76] The question is, in a world where transnational cultural, economic, political and social relations are

[71]James Sheptycki, 'Transnationalism, Crime Control and the European State System; A Review of the Literature' (1997) 7 *International Criminal Justice Review* 130; James Sheptycki, 'Review of Schengen Investigated' (1997) 1(4) *International Journal of Evidence & Proof* 46.
[72]See Boister, *An Introduction to Transnational Criminal Law* (n 30) 16.
[73]James Sheptycki, 'Law Enforcement, Justice and Democracy in the Transnational Arena: Reflections on the War on Drugs' (1996) 24(1) *International Journal of the Sociology of Law* 61.
[74]Jean-Paul Brodeur, *The Policing Web* (Oxford University Press, 2010).
[75]See Bowling and Sheptycki (n 4).
[76]James Sheptycki, 'Policing and Human Rights; An Introduction' (2000) 10(1) *Policing and Society* 1.

prevalent, how are policing agents employing legal tools in the pursuit of the general mandate to secure social order on a transnational basis?

Global governance and rule *with* law: some examples

The previous sections argued that the socio-legal study of policing has, over several decades, revealed patterns of police practice consistent with the idea of *rule with law*. The language of law provides a crucial set of policing tools – tools that are every bit as important as the coercive and surveillant technologies policing agents have at their disposal. Until recently, the socio-legal study of policing practice was more or less concerned with domestic governance and mostly focused on publically financed urban police agencies. We now turn to some examples that illustrate the evolution of transnational rule with law. Here we focus on examples of transnational policing practice beyond criminal law enforcement in order to broaden the conversation about policing and transnational law and to cast light on some general features and patterns of rule with law in global governance.[77]

In a world system, the transnational use of legal tools is significant in four important respects. First, legal tools configure institutions – both state-based and private – around particular mandates. Since policing is central to governance, the way policing agents use legal tools has consequences for the institutional architecture of global governance. The *policing of money* provides a good example of this. Secondly, rule with law establishes the patterned interactions of people and territories. A good example of this is *policing mobility* – the practice of controlling the transnational movement of people, goods and services within global markets, the legal construction of personhood through citizenship laws and the governance of physical movement more generally. Thirdly, the legal power tools in the hands of policing agents have implications for the institution of private property, and this affects processes of economic stratification and marginalisation. *Policing intellectual property* illustrates this process. Fourth, inter-state/intra-state and public-private distinctions have blurred, and the deployment of legal power tools originally intended to secure 'national interest' are articulated within a global system of governance that has become far more complex. This is illustrated by the *evolution of high policing*, that is, political policing historically concerned with matters of national security. In the following four sections, we explore each of these developments in turn.

Example one: policing the global money system

Concern over policing money began in the 1970s with the introduction of the term 'money laundering' into organised crime discourse.[78] Thereafter arose a new

[77]Neil Boister and Robert J Currie (eds), *Routledge Handbook of Transnational Law* (Routledge, 2014); see Boister, *An Introduction to Transnational Criminal Law* (n 30).
[78]Michael Levi and Peter Reuter, 'Money Laundering' in Michael Tonry (ed), *Crime and Justice, Volume 34* (Chicago University Press, 2006); Bill Gilmore, *Dirty Money: The*

paradigm and new legal tools for policing the global system of financial institutions. The 1988 UN Convention against Illicit Traffic in Drugs and Psychotropic Substances brought 'the confiscation of criminal proceeds' to the world stage, a kind of legal tool already developed in the United States. In the early years the worry was 'dirty money' – the proceeds of crime – entering the banking system. One problem was that the banking system was transnational but banking regulations were parochial. Tracing illicit funds was not only difficult, but it could easily end in an 'off-shore jurisdiction' where traditions of banking privacy were taken very seriously. Gradually, a global system for reporting suspicious transactions was established through political processes in the back rooms of transnational institutions and banks. This transnational effort was fostered by the Financial Action Task Force (FATF).

This transnational platform promulgated 40 'soft law' recommendations that eventually consolidated the legal toolkit for policing the global money system. Importantly, the FATF was an organisational offshoot of the OECD and membership was restricted to technocrats who represented institutional interests based in powerful states. These legal engineers were a mixture of police bureaucrats and officials from treasury departments. They fashioned the legal instruments for surveillance of the money system and freezing and forfeiture of 'criminal assets', constituting a system of international cooperation of banks and state agencies tied up in a transnational regime. As the tools were refined, the institutional basis for their deployment was elaborated into the Egmont Group of Financial Intelligence Units (FIUs).[79] The FIU network consists of nationally based units that gather information from the financial sectors within their jurisdiction and circulate these data transnationally. Surveillance efforts also extend to international wire transactions and other financial institutions, such as casinos and racetracks. The network depends on financial reporting agents working in the private financial sector, making the transnational policing regime a public-private partnership for surveillance of the global money system.

Then came the 11 September 2001 attacks. Before then, the game was about 'dirty money' becoming 'clean money'. The new concern was that sometimes 'clean money' could be used for nefarious purposes. What followed was the monumental task of engineering total financial system surveillance via the global system of FIUs, a task undertaken by a mixture of police, treasury and banking officials operating in the transnational policy space between sovereign jurisdictions, just as was the original FATF toolkit. The global banking debacle of 2008 exposed

Evolution of International Measures to Counter Money Laundering and the Financing of Terrorism (Council of Europe Publishing, 4th edn 2011); James Sheptycki, 'Policing the Virtual Launderette' in James Sheptycki (ed), *Issues in Transnational Policing* (Routledge, 2000) 147; Valsamis Mitsilegas, *Money Laundering Counter-Measures in the European Union: A New Paradigm of Security Governance versus Fundamental Legal Principles* (Kluwer, 2003).

[79] See Bowling and Sheptycki (n 4) 60–61.

the money system to a new kind of scrutiny and a new popular vocabulary came to prominence, one which concerned 'banksters', white-collar crime, elite crime, economic and financial crime and corruption generally.[80] The effects of this new popular discourse concerning the financial improprieties of economic elites are ongoing, raising the prospect that new legal tools might be fashioned for use in this regard.[81] What needs to be emphasised here is that efforts to govern the global financial system run up against powerful institutional interests.

Leaving aside the obvious point that technical limitations make it impossible to achieve total financial system surveillance, the practice of governing the global money system reveals transnational rule with law to be both two-faced and blind in one eye. While the financial and economic crimes of the powerful are under-policed, there are few limitations placed upon the use of legal power tools against what Peter Gill calls 'the usual suspects'.[82] This seeming reluctance to deploy legal tools against members of the economic elite and the exuberance with which they are used on the economically weak confirms Jeffrey Reiman's point that 'the rich get richer and the poor get prison',[83] but this time in the transnational domain and not merely the domestic one. Critical assessment of transnational rule with law suggests that some types of harmful financial activity become objects of control while other (perhaps equally harmful) financial practices do not. Be that as it may, the money system is obviously central to the global system, so it should be no surprise to find that it is policed – that *is* where the money is. Regardless of the limitations of this policing effort (or perhaps because of them), this brief perusal of the relevant literature shows clearly that this involves transnational rule with law and that policing global money system not only configures important aspects of the architecture of global policing, it affects the global system more broadly.

Example two: governing transnational mobility

Policing the mobility of people and things is another example of rule with law under transnational conditions. There is a growing literature on the policing of mobility that reveals some obvious and basic distinctions.[84] In airport transit

[80]Michael Levi, 'The Media Construction of Financial White-Collar Crimes' (2006) 46(6) *British Journal of Criminology* 1037; Michael Levi, 'Suite Revenge? The Shaping of Folk Devils and Moral Panics about White-Collar Crimes' (2009) 49(1) *British Journal of Criminology* 48; Michael Levi, 'Hitting the Suite Spot: Sentencing Frauds' (2010) 17(1) *Journal of Financial Crime* 116; see Bowling and Sheptycki (n 4) 121–3.
[81]Michael Lewis, *The Big Short: Inside the Doomsday Machine* (WW Norton, 2010).
[82]P Gill, *Rounding Up the Usual Suspects* (Ashgate, 2000).
[83]J Reiman, *The Rich Get Richer and the Poor Get Prison* (Allyn and Bacon, 6th edn 2000).
[84]KF Aas, '"Crimmigrant Bodies" and Bona Fide Travellers: Surveillance, Citizenship and Global Governance' (2011) 15(3) *Theoretical Criminology* 331; KF Aas and M Bosworth, *The Borders of Punishment: Migration, Citizenship and Social Exclusion* (Oxford University Press, 2013); M Bosworth, 'Border Control and the Limits of the Sovereign State' (2008) 17(2) *Social and Legal Studies* 199; see Bowling and Sheptycki (n 7) 57.

lounges, train stations and ports, several categories of global traveller stand out. The tourist, travelling for short periods, is an object of envy, humour or derision. The clandestine migrant, travelling for long periods over circuitous routes by uncertain means, is variously an object of sympathy, aversion or revulsion. Both the tourist and the vagabond are entangled in a web of police surveillance intended to govern populations and secure their relationship to territory. The practices of transnational rule with law reveal dualities. While the international tourist is enveloped in a bubble of governance conducive to the transnational order of consumption, one of the cruellest manifestations of global rule with law has to do with the hybridisation of immigration and criminal law. Crimmigration, the fusing of immigration and criminal law under transnational conditions, is a way of using law to control suspect populations who are sociologically defined by their economic and social precariousness.[85]

Crimmigration laws are set up to 'select, eject and immobilize'.[86] The bifurcation established by the tourist visa and citizenship laws on the one side and crimmigration laws on the other creates an ever-expanding population of the excluded and alienated as distinct from bona fide travellers and citizens.[87] Importantly, there is another dual effect: with human trafficking, very often both subjects of the discourse (the traffickers and the trafficked) are treated as problematic by the policing agencies and governmental bodies responding to the issue. The result is that victims of human trafficking are often subjected to secondary victimisation at the hands of authorities as they are transported back to their country of origin.[88] The way mobility governance currently creates differing categories of experience for the tourist and the crimmigrant, the alien and the citizen, the trafficker and the trafficking victim reveals the two-faced nature of existing transnational rule with law.

This can be described as the *negative* aspect of the governance of mobility, because it is the result of enforcement practices intended to deter and control through negative inducements. There is also a *positive* aspect since some legal tools are intended to foster certain categories of labour mobility.[89] Socio-legal discourse concerning transnational mobility control has often been focused through a

[85]J Stumpf, 'The Crimmigration Crisis: Immigrants, Crime and Sovereign Power' (2006) 56(2) *American Studies Law Review* 367.
[86]Leanne Weber and Ben Bowling, 'Policing Migration: A Framework for Investigating the Regulation of Global Mobility' (2004) 14(3) *Policing and Society* 195; Leanne Weber and Ben Bowling, 'Valiant Beggars and Global Vagabonds: Select, Eject, Immobilize' (2008) 12(3) *Theoretical Criminology* 355.
[87]Ben Bowling, 'Epilogue: The Borders of Punishment – Towards a Criminology of Mobility' in KF Aas and Mary Bosworth (eds), *The Borders of Punishment* (Oxford University Press, 2013) 291; Ben Bowling, Coretta Phillips and James Sheptycki, 'Race, Political Economy and the Coercive State' in Jill Peay and Tim Newburn (eds), *Policing, Politics and Control* (Hart Publishing, 2012).
[88]J Goodie, 'Migration, Crime and Victimhood' (2003) 5(4) *Punishment and Society* 415.
[89]See Bowling and Sheptycki (n 4) 102–4, 111–13.

criminological lens and much discussion has been about so-called international sex trafficking. While criminologists observe that current legal language creates sex-trafficking victims who are subject to transnational crimmigration law, it is interesting to see that the sex industry has also fostered policing in the positive sense of facilitating labour mobility.[90] For example, for a time the Canadian government issued temporary work visas to 'exotic dancers'. In response to public criticism suggesting that the government was part of a system facilitating the transnational trafficking of women for the purposes of sexual exploitation, in 2003 Citizenship and Immigration Canada made changes to the temporary work visa program, retaining provisions for workers in the sex industry *de jure* but reportedly eliminating it *de facto*. It was not until 2012 that the Canadian government announced that it had stopped issuing temporary work visas to women in this industry. At the time, it was reported that 496 had been issued since 2006.[91] These changes shifted policy from governing this category of worker with law in its 'positive' sense – visas and labour law – to governing with law in its 'negative sense' – criminal and crimmigration law.

People in the sex industry are employed in what sociologists call a tainted occupation and are therefore highly vulnerable to human rights abuse whether subject to positive or negative strategies of mobility governance. It is interesting to note that the temporary work visa programme in Canada has been used to expedite similar arrangements in other, less tainted occupations. For example, the Canadian Live-In Caregiver programme, which blends immigration law, social legislation, labour and contract law, facilitates work-related travel to Canada for (mostly Filipino) nurses for a stipulated period of two years. These individuals provide live-in care for elderly persons, providing a relatively low-cost alternative to other forms of assisted living because they are paid less than Canadian qualified nurses. The inequities of the Live-In Caregiver programme have led some scholars to suggest that the Canadian government contributes to the exploitation and trafficking of immigrant women.[92] The positive and facilitative policing of labour mobility has been characterised as supportive of 'transient servitude' and citizenship law has been characterised as productive of social and economic apartheid.[93] These patterns can be observed in North America, Europe, Australia and New

[90]A Macklin, 'Dancing Across Borders: "Exotic Dancers", Trafficking and Canadian Immigration Policy' (2003) 37(2) *International Migration Review* 464; L McDonald and N Timoshkina, 'The Trafficked Sex Workers from the Former Eastern Bloc: The Canadian Dimension' (2007) 31(2) *International Journal of Comparative and Applied Criminal Justice* 211.

[91]B Curry, 'Ottawa Brings Down Curtain on Foreign Strippers' *Globe and Mail*, 4 July 2012.

[92]L Langevin, 'Trafficking in Women in Canada: A Critical Analysis of the Legal Framework Governing Immigrant Live-In Caregivers' (2007) 31(2) *International Journal of Comparative and Applied Criminal Justice* 191.

[93]Harsha Walia, 'Transient Servitude: Migrant Labour in Canada and the Apartheid of Citizenship' (2010) 52(1) *Race and Class* 71.

Zealand and have had considerable effects on the policy and language surrounding 'multiculturalism'.[94]

A new issue has arisen in public discourse surrounding the observable patterns found in the facilitation of transnational labour mobility. Public concerns reflect the formalisation of a new hybrid labour-migration law facilitating transnational mobility for low-paid jobs picking fruit and harvesting other agricultural products, or working in mines and abattoirs or the construction industry.[95] For example, in late 2012 a furore erupted in Canada over a scheme to bring in some 2,000 Chinese migrants to work in coalmines in northern British Columbia at salaries reportedly far lower than the industry average for Canadian miners.[96] There were concomitant criticisms that health and safety regulations were being poorly enforced in the mines and that temporary guest workers had unequal access to health care compared to Canadian citizens. On the other hand, for highly skilled, highly salaried and/or high net-worth individuals the transnational regime governing mobility also serves to facilitate movement. Global patterns emerging out of the engineering of legal tools for managing transnational mobility are etched into the urban spaces of the so-called 'global city' that hold both the 'Global South' and the 'Global North' in its fold.[97] For example, in February 2014 CIBC Deputy Chief Economist Benjamin Tal let slip that changes to Canadian immigration law concerning high net-worth individuals would negatively impact the Vancouver and Toronto housing markets.[98]

Consideration of the dualities and distinctions produced when legal tools are used to govern transnational mobility is revealing of transnational rule with law. We can see patterns between positive and negative mobility governance and in the treatment of the tourist and the crimmigrant, and in the facilitation of transnational mobility based on differentiated categories of labour and wealth. These patterns show how political elites acting within a global polycentric power system use law symbolically to seemingly illogical and contradictory ends. On one hand, mobility governance works to facilitate global neo-liberal ends through upholding the transnational culture of consumption and the transnational economy of production. Amongst other things, this immiserates working class communities even as it profits transnational corporate capitalism whose logic is based on calculating labour power cost efficiencies. On the other hand, the instrumentality of negative mobility

[94]Christian Joppke, 'The Retreat of Multiculturalism in the Liberal State: Theory and Practice' (2010) 55(2) *British Journal of Sociology* 237; Christian Joppke, 'Exclusion in the Liberal State: The Case of Immigration and Citizenship Policy' (2005) 8(1) *European Journal of Social Theory* 43.

[95]Julia Lopez, 'Beyond the National Case: The Role of Transnational Labor Law in Shaping Domestic Regulation' (2007) 28(3) *Comparative Labor Law & Policy Journal* 547.

[96]T Walkom, 'BC's Low-Wage Migrant Coal Mining Jobs Send Us Back to the Future' *Toronto Star*, 12 October 2012.

[97]S Sassen, 'The Repositioning of Citizenship and Alienage: Emergent Subjects and Spaces for Politics' (2005) 2(1) *Globalizations* 79.

[98]Gary Marr, 'How Canada's New Immigration Rules Could Slow High End Real Estate Sales' *Financial Post*, 12 February 2014, Mortgages and Real Estate 1.

governance is evident in its emotional content. Part of the effect of these legal tools is to dramatically highlight certain categories for special treatment in the regime of mobility governance – the 'illegal alien', the crimmigrant and the sex worker – while leaving other effects of transnational mobility governance in the shadows.

Example three: global governance and intellectual property

Current global efforts at policing intellectual property interests are an important new frontier in transnational rule with law. Private intellectual property is a new legal tool and institutional connections are forged to uphold it, and currently these are being transnationalised. Historically speaking, there are three principal types of intellectual property (IP): copyright, trademark and patent.[99] IP entails property rights for such things as musical, literary and artistic works (copyright); words, phrases, symbols and designs (trademark); and discoveries and inventions (patent). The history of the term 'intellectual property' is revealing. Its substantive origins lie in the nineteenth century with the establishment of the United International Bureaux for the Protection of Intellectual Property, headquartered in Berne, but the term did not enter into widespread usage until later. According to economic historians, these legal tools have been cognisable in Western societies for centuries and have been adapted over time in different societies to fit the needs of interested parties. Currently, the effort to develop a transnational regime for policing intellectual property rights has caused conflict and controversy. When a property right is policed in the interests of the owner, there is always someone being policed against.

The establishment of the World Intellectual Property Organization (WIPO) as an agency of the United Nations in 1967 added a new dimension to the architecture of global policing, but its effects were slow in coming. In fact, it was probably domestic legislation passed in the United States in 1980, namely the Patent and Trademark Law Amendments Act (the Bayh-Dole Act), that accentuated transnational developments. Prior to this legislation, technical inventions made with the benefit of US federal government funds resided with the federal government. Bayh-Dole made it possible for universities and small business 'spin-offs' to hold patent rights. Because this allowed private interests to reap the rewards of publicly funded research where once there were only a few hundred patent applications stemming from university research annually in the United States, the newly fashioned legal tool made for thousands. At the end of the twentieth century this trend went global and the WIPO promoted intellectual property as a principal 'power tool for economic growth'.[100] Whose hands hold the tools and what have the tools been fashioned to do? The policing of intellectual property is replete with examples that give a sensible

[99]Robin A Schoen, Mary E Mogee and Mitchel B Wallerstein (eds), *Global Dimensions of Intellectual Property Rights in Science and Technology* (National Academies Press, 1993).
[100]Kamil Idris, *Intellectual Property; A Power Tool for Economic Growth* (World Intellectual Property Organization, 2003).

answer to that question. An early one stems from the 1980 decision of the United States Supreme Court in *Diamond v Chakrabarty*, in which it was held that 'anything under the sun that is made by man', including genetically altered microorganisms, could be patentable.[101] Historically, patents were only granted to things that were useful, novel, non-obvious and that could *not* be found in nature. This new legal tool conveyed the ability to patent genes and turn them into private property, which in principle could be stolen. Thus emerged a new type of crime: 'seed piracy'.

To preserve the value of patented seeds, corporate agribusiness concerns that own the patents have moved to forbid the practice of seed-saving. Seed-saving – when a farmer keeps a portion of the harvest for next year's planting – is as old as settled agriculture but the existence of legally patented seeds has transformed this practice into 'seed piracy'.[102] This has had transnational consequences. For example, Vandana Shiva has documented the policing of seed piracy in India, where private detectives gather information, intelligence and evidence while lawyers undertake prosecutions and also monitor farmers' fields once they have been convicted in the courts.[103] In India, a hybrid of both public and private forms of policing controls the activities of farmers and enforces the privatisation of nature. This has had untold consequences:

> … To secure patents on life forms and living resources corporations must claim seeds and plants to be their 'inventions' and hence their property. Thus corporations like Cargill and Monsanto see nature's web of life and cycles of renewal as 'theft' of their property. During the debate about the entry of Cargill into India in 1992, the Cargill chief executive stated 'We bring Indian farmers smart technologies, which prevent bees from usurping the pollen' … [but, it is really] genetically engineered crops manufactured by corporations [that] pose the risks. Crops such as Monsanto's Roundup Ready soybeans, designed to be resistant to herbicides, lead to the destruction of biodiversity and increased use of agrochemicals. They can also create highly invasive 'superweeds' by transferring the genes for herbicide resistance to weeds. Crops designed to be pesticide factories, genetically engineered to produce toxins and venom with genes from bacteria, scorpions, snakes and wasps, can threaten non-pest species [e.g. bees] and can contribute to the emergence of resistance in pests and hence the creation of 'superpests'. In every application of genetic engineering food is being stolen from other species for the maximization of corporate profit.[104]

Nor are these consequences confined to India. Marie-Monique Robin has documented how the 'gene police' have operated in North America – documenting

[101] *Diamond v Chakrabarty*, 447 US 303 (1980), cited in Keith Aoki, 'The Stakes of Intellectual Property Law' in D Kennedy (ed), *The Politics of Law: A Progressive Critique* (Basic Books, 1998) 259.

[102] M Laffey and J Weldes, 'Policing and Global Governance' in M Barnett and R Duvall (eds), *Power in Global Governance* (Cambridge University Press, 2005) 59.

[103] Vandana Shiva, *Stolen Harvest; The Hijacking of the Global Food Supply* (Zed Books, 2000).

[104] *Ibid*, 16.

the activities corporate private police, chiefly Pinkerton in the United States and Robinson in Canada.[105] Early in this century, Robin shows, Monsanto employed 75 full-time staff, with an annual budget of approximately US $10 million, as in-house police investigating seed piracy allegations in North America. Observing the strength of agribusiness corporations to police their intellectual property rights in the form of patented seeds, she argued that 'this situation is truly David versus Goliath, but this time Goliath is holding all the stones'.[106]

The idea of 'gene police' is perhaps rather far from the popular imagination. There are other manifestations of the power effects of the legal tools concerning intellectual property rights (IPRs) that are more resonant for mass urban consumers. For example, the capacity afforded to individuals to share digitally recorded music, video and other forms of cultural production over the internet (affecting IP copyrights) is a matter of considerable discussion.[107] The notions of 'music piracy' and 'informational piracy' are of primary concern.[108] These terms reflect the interests of IP owners who have a stake in images, trademarks, copyrighted materials and other markers for 'general character merchandising' (e.g. popstars) and the way that rule with law allows the use of legal tools from both criminal and civil law to give actors in the public-private policing nexus that governs these property relations a powerful double punch.[109] Copyright protects book authors and recording musicians and ensures them a livelihood should their works attain market success. Purchasers were once free to lend, give away or sell the books and records they bought. Purchasers who buy electronic copies of books or music are not so free. The changing socio-legal patterns stemming from the policing of these property rights reveal new power relations among publishers, users and creators.[110] For example, in 2012, Hollywood actor Bruce Willis began considering legal moves to ensure the inheritability of his extensive digital music collection – his lawyer was considering creating a family trust to act as the legal owner of the downloaded music and Willis was preparing to take legal action. Willis's lawyer stated, '… lots of people will be surprised on learning

[105]Marie-Monique Robin, *The World According to Monsanto: Pollution, Corruption and the Control of the World's Food Supply* (The New Press, 2013) 206–8.

[106]Stephanie M Bernhardt, 'High Plains Drifting: Wind-Blown Seeds and the Intellectual Property Implications of the GMO Revolution' (2005) 4(1) *Northwestern Journal of Technology and Intellectual* Property 1, 13.

[107]D Matthew, *Peer to Peer and the Music Industry: The Criminalization of Sharing* (Sage, 2009); M Yar, 'The Global "Epidemic" of Movie "Piracy": Crime-Wave or Social Construction?' (2005) 27(5) *Media, Culture and Society* 677.

[108]James Sheptycki, 'Technocrime, Criminology and Marshall McLuhan' in Stephane Lemain-Langlois (ed), *Technocrime: Policing and Surveillance* (Taylor & Francis, 2012) 133.

[109]D Wall, *Cybercrime in the Information Age* (Polity Press, 2007) 97.

[110]C Lynch, 'The Battle to Define the Future of the Book in the Digital World' (2001) 6(4) *First Monday*.

all those tracks and books they have bought over the years don't actually belong to them'.[111] This popular case is revealing of the conflicts shaped by the new legal tools pertinent to upholding IPRs in the digital age.

The tools for fencing IP were first developed at the height of the modern period in the late nineteenth and early twentieth centuries. By the beginning of the twenty-first century, defending the boundaries of IPRs had become a global enterprise involving hybrid governance structures that intertwined public and private actors in a struggle to establish ownership in a global knowledge economy.[112] These hybrid forms of policing and regulation are transnational in scope but have local effects. The legal power tools available extend well beyond those found in criminal law, although these also remain notable in their use. This is illustrated by the case of Kim Dotcom, a technological *cause célèbre* wanted in the United States for information property theft.[113] In January 2012, indictments filed in Virginia for online piracy, racketeering, conspiring to commit copyright infringement and money laundering led to the search and seizure of property and the arrest of Dotcom in Auckland, New Zealand that same month. In all, $17 million worth of assets were seized. Additionally, 64 bank accounts were frozen worldwide, denying the 'internet pirate' access to an estimated US $175 million. Such *causes célèbre* represent distortions of their own, because they are famous, but nevertheless provide interesting clues concerning the patterning of social order worldwide. As Palmer and Warren argue, the Dotcom case shows how law becomes a resource for extraterritorial policing activities and so it provides another good example of the operation of rule with law.[114]

Rule with law is predicated on the existence of legal tools available to those with the power to handle them, and it serves particular interests first and general interests second, if at all. Globally speaking, the policing of IP amply illustrates the point that rule with law configures institutions in complex networks of transnational interdependency and these include both state-based agents and non-state actors. When it comes to IP, legal tools have been engineered by corporate interests, which then affect social patterns as they are policed by a complex inter-institutional matrix of rule with law. The policing of IPRs is another example of legal instruments being deployed at the behest and in the interests of powerful corporate actors who thereby shape the practice of global governance.

---

[111] B Child, 'Bruce Willis to Fight Apple over the Right to Leave iTunes Library in Will' *The Guardian*, 3 September 2012.

[112] Peter Drahos and John Braithwaite, *Information Feudalism: Who Owns the Knowledge Economy* (Oxford University Press, 2002); S Burris, P Drahos and C Shearing, 'Nodal Governance' (2005) 30 *Australian Journal of Legal Philosophy* 30.

[113] D Palmer and IJ Warren, 'Global Policing and the Case of Kim Dotcom' (2013) 2(3) *International Journal for Crime, Justice and Social Democracy* 105.

[114] *Ibid*, 115.

Example four: high policing under transnational conditions

The concept of 'high policing' entered the academic lexicon of criminology in the 1980s. Referring to historical French usage, Jean-Paul Brodeur introduced the distinction between 'high' and 'low' policing. The latter term points to the everyday policing that most citizens in urban, suburban and rural communities experience, having to do with traffic tickets, public safety and general social order maintenance. High policing is a different matter. Brodeur's genius was to give social scientists a vocabulary for talking about political policing. He argued that such policing 'permeates the whole structure of police action' and the idea that it is somehow rare, deviant, and the product of a few bad apples, rogue agents or lone actors is 'the product of a deliberate illusion'. According to Brodeur, policing agents, political actors and various media collude in a 'secrecy corporation' and those who study policing ought to give these practices a more prominent place in theories of policing and social order.[115]

In Brodeur's classic formulation, high policing has four main elements. First, high policing casts a wide and absorbent surveillance net and street corner policing is thereby connected to agencies more recognisably involved in the business of political policing. Second, such policing mixes legislative, judicial and executive powers of government, collapsing the doctrine of the 'separation of powers' in the perceived functional need to preserve the integrity of the principal organs of social order – that is, the institutions of state. Third, high policing is concerned with maintaining of the existing social and political order. Fourth, since high policing is firstly concerned with the acquisition of 'intelligence' and 'information' (but not evidence), its functional logic is to expand the basis of its knowledge, in principle aiming for total information awareness (or as near to that as possible). High policing involves secrecy and deceit and, since high policing involves practices that would be considered improper in a democratic society, in states that are formally democratic, high policing entails the use of 'law against law'.[116] By using law against law, policing power is expanded in ways that contradict the spirit of constitutional government. As such, high policing is ungovernable by conventional means (e.g. police boards or criminal procedure).[117]

The problems associated with high policing under transnational conditions have become more acute because the transnational social order has 'overflowed' the sovereign containers that are the building blocks of the old international state system and new issue areas emerge in the global context. High policing

[115]Jean-Paul Brodeur, 'High Policing and Low Policing: Remarks about the Policing of Political Activities' (1983) 30(5) *Social Problems* 507.
[116]See Ericson (n 36).
[117]Jean-Paul Brodeur and Stephane Leman-Langlois, 'Surveillance Fiction or Higher Policing?' in Kevin Haggerty and Richard V Ericson (eds), *The New Politics of Visibility and Surveillance* (University of Toronto Press, 2006) 171; James Sheptycki, *Accountability Across the Policing Field: Towards a General Cartography of Accountability for Post-Modern Policing*, Centre for the Democratic Control of Armed Forces, DCAF Working Paper No 35, 2002.

practices are supplemented through the activities of private actors and, although they may still 'tilt towards the state', the social order to be preserved is a transnational one that includes corporate interests, state interests and interests of political and economic elites.[118] Global high policing responses have been imagined and calculated in secret by an elite of transnational technocrats and legal engineers based in corporate institutions and a wide variety of governmental bureaucracies nested within states and in supranational institutions above states.[119] Since the millennium, high policing and political resistance to it have manifested in several ways. For example, in Canada, 'ecological extremism' was considered a national security threat due to protests over the building of pipelines to transport tar-sands oil to international markets. Similarly, in Australia, 'international eco-terrorism' has featured as a security concern, resulting in the perceived need to develop new legal tools.[120]

High policing has been linked with the pursuit of 'economic intelligence' – in other words industrial espionage.[121] This came to light in Canada when the Snowden revelations disclosed that Canada's signals intelligence agency, the Communications Security Establishment Canada (CSEC), had passed confidential information from the Brazilian Ministry of Mining and Energy, gained via NSA surveillance, to individuals in the Canadian mining industry.[122] In the United States, during the height of the 'Occupy Movement' in 2011–12, a highly coordinated surveillance and disruption effort aimed to undermine the protests. This involved the Federal Bureau of Investigation, the Department of Homeland Security and other agencies, together with the 'in-house' security of several major

---

[118]Jean-Paul Brodeur, *The Policing Web* (Oxford University Press, 2007) 31; Darren Palmer and Chad Whelan, 'Counter-Terrorism Across the Policing Continuum' (2006) 4(5) *Police Practice and Research* 449; Conor O'Reilly and Graham Ellison, 'Eye Spy Private High: Re-Conceptualizing High Policing Theory' (2006) 46 *British Journal of Criminology* 641.

[119]Conor O'Reilly, 'The Transnational Security Consultancy Industry: A Case of State-Corporate Symbiosis' (2010) 14(2) *Theoretical Criminology* 183; Nicholas Dorn and Michael Levi, 'European Private Security, Corporate Investigation and Military Services: Collective Security, Market Regulation and Structuring the Public Sphere' (2007) 17(3) *Policing and Society* 213; Peter Gill and Mark Phythian, *Intelligence in an Insecure World* (Polity Press, 2006); James Sheptycki, 'Policing, Intelligence Theory and the New Human Security Paradigm' in Peter Gill, Stephen Marrin and Mark Phythian (eds), *Intelligence Theory: Key Questions and Debates* (Routledge, 2009) 166; James Sheptycki, 'Policing Theory and Research: What's in a Metaphor?' (2012) 25 *Cahiers Poltitiestudies* 55.

[120]Shawn McCarthy, 'Ottawa's New Anti-Terrorism Strategy Lists Eco-Extremists as Threats' *Globe and Mail*, 10 February 2012; Sarah Sharples, 'Tough New Laws Sought for Eco-Terrorists' *Lawyers Weekly*, 16 June 2009.

[121]Frédéric Ocqueteau, 'The "High Policing" Privatization Hypothesis and How to Explore It', François-Xavier Priour (trans) (2012) 9 *Champ Pénal*, http://champpenal.revues.org/8313.

[122]Isabel Teotonio, 'Brazil Demands Explanation over Reports Canada Spied on Mine Ministry' *Toronto Star*, 7 October 2013; Joe Castaldo, 'Is Industrial Espionage Putting a Chill on Foreign Investment in Canada?' *Canadian Business*, 6 November 2013.

banks. This suggested that private financial records and income streams could be used to choke off civil disobedience.[123] Also in the United States, a mid-2014 report by Human Rights Watch revealed that undercover police 'sting operations' had used enabling legal instruments embedded in the 2001 Patriot Act and the Foreign Intelligence Surveillance Act in a series of cases characterised as 'entrapment'.[124] All of these instances provoked protest about the legality and ethics of the practices in question, but these examples also show how broadly defined legislation and administrative rules had provided the necessary legal tools for high policing.

Understanding how high policing shapes and deploys legal tools provides many insights, but there is relatively little scholarship concerning this type of practice. One of the most powerfully suggestive manifestations of high policing as rule with law under global conditions is the development of 'lawfare'. Lawfare is a portmanteau of law and warfare, meaning generally the use of law as tool in the context of war, and it has both positive and negative senses.[125] In its positive sense it is used to describe attempts to develop legal language and legal justification for pursuing war. For example, in the context of the global war on terror, John Yoo (US Deputy Assistant Attorney General 2001–3) authored the 'torture memos' that caused much opprobrium and led to a charge of *illegal* brutality authorised by high-level officials.[126] It would be more accurate to say that they legalised brutality. In a paper entitled 'Courts at War', Yoo argued precisely for due process in a worldwide war on terror.[127] As José Alvarez has shown, the Bush White House relied extensively on international law and the United Nations, and lawyers, including Yoo, working for the administration 'repeatedly turned to the U.N. Security Council and its Chapter VII enforcement powers with

[123]Naomi Wolf, 'New Documents Prove What Was Once Dismissed as Paranoid Fantasy: Totally Integrated Corporate-State Repression' *The Guardian*, 29 December 2012; Partnership for Civil Justice Fund, 'FBI Documents Reveal Secret Nationwide Occupy Monitoring' (21 December 2012), www.justiceonline.org/fbi_files_ows.

[124]Spencer Akerman, 'Human Rights Watch Documents "Sting" Operations' *The Guardian*, 21 July 2014; Human Rights Institute at Columbia Law School and Human Rights Watch, *Illusion of Justice: Human Rights Abuses in US Terrorism Prosecutions* (report), July 2014.

[125]C Dunlap, 'Law and Military Interventions: Preserving Humanitarian Values in 21st Century Conflicts', paper delivered at the conference on Humanitarian Challenges in Military Intervention, Carr Center for Human Rights Policy, Kennedy School of Government, Harvard University, November 2001.

[126]David Cole, 'The Idea of Humanity: Human Rights and Immigrants' Rights' (2006) 37 (3) *Columbia Human Rights Law Review* 627; David Cole, 'The Man Behind Torture' reviewing Jack Goldsmith's *The Terror Presidency: Law and Judgment Inside the Bush Administration* (2007) 54(19) *New York Review of Books* 38; David Cole, 'The Torture Memos: The Case Against Lawyers' (2009) 56(15) *New York Review of Books* 14; David Cole, 'Rewarding Impunity; Why is Obama's Attorney General Handing Out Prizes for Sweeping Torture under the Rug?' *Foreign Policy*, 12 October 2012.

[127]J Yoo, 'Courts at War' (2005) 91 *Cornell Law Review* 573.

respect to issues regarding the international law of self-defense, counter-terrorism and weapons of mass destruction, and the occupation of Iraq'.[128] According to Alvarez, they 'used international law to justify, and to modify, the rules permitting force', and he lists many examples of how legal tools were deployed to further Bush's foreign policy aims.[129]

International human rights treaties – and many constitutions – permit concessions to the inevitability of exceptional state measures in times of emergency and so, even in democracies, it is perfectly legal for political leaders to suspend the protection of basic legal rights.[130] Richard Ericson named it 'counter law' – the technique of using law against law.[131] Understanding how legal tools can be used to manipulate or nullify the effects of other legal instruments helps us to comprehend the establishment of legal categories such as 'enemy combatant', the legal language allowing for the practice of 'enhanced interrogation'. Far from being law*less*, the Bush White House's use of legal tools to further its high policing aims were law*ful* – that is, 'full of law'.[132] That is, these undertakings used legal instruments (even if the probity of the tools has been contested) and sometimes law has been used against law to neutralise the intended effects of human rights norms.[133]

There are many examples of high policing and cycles of insecurity visible in the contemporary global scene. The actions of Edward Snowden, Chelsea (née Bradley) Manning and Julian Assange have divided opinion, but there can be no doubt that they made the transnational realities of high policing more transparent than they would otherwise have been. The catalogues of their revelations are too numerous to recount here and probably too new to be adequately theorised, but one feature deserves emphasis here: transnational high policing involves hybrid institutional forms that include both state-based and corporate-based actors. In our previously mentioned example from the Snowden revelations – Canadian mining executives receiving intelligence about the activities of Brazilian mining – this amounted to state collusion in industrial espionage.[134] What makes such secret activity possible in countries with freedom of information legislation is that legal tools have been used to modify those legal instruments intended to create governmental transparency – high policing routinely uses law against law,

[128]José E Alvarez, 'Contemporary International Law: An "Empire of Law" or the "Law of Empire"' (2009) 24(5) *American University International Law Review* 811, 816.
[129]*Ibid*, 817.
[130]See, for example, International Covenant on Civil and Political Rights (in force 1976), Art 4; European Convention on Human Rights (in force 1950), Art 15; American Convention on Human Rights (in force 1978), Art 27.
[131]See Ericson (n 36).
[132]Cf. Philippe Sands, *Lawless World; America and the Making and Breaking of Global Rules* (Allen Lane, 2005).
[133]See also David Fraser, 'Evil Law, Evil Lawyer? From the Justice Case to the Torture Memos' (2012) 3(2) *Jurisprudence* 391.
[134]'Canadian Spies Targeted Brazil's Mines Ministry' CBC News, Associated Press, 7 October 2013.

clouding the distinction between lawful and unlawful.[135] In this way, considerable ambiguity is generated concerning the nature of law under transnational conditions.

Discussion

The idea of international law is quite old, starting with the work of Hugo Grotius in the seventeenth century.[136] Despite its antiquity, the idea had limited application until after the Second World War. According to Philippe Sands, the Atlantic Charter, adopted in 1941, established the basis for the burgeoning place of law on the global stage. This became the foundation of the United Nations Charter which was signed in June 1945 and entered into force in October of the same year. Three essential principles underlay these agreements. Foremost was the goal of global economic relations through fostering free trade and related international obligations in the fields of foreign investment and intellectual property. To achieve this economic vision it was understood that states' use of force had to be restrained and held to strict conditions of 'self-defence' or be authorised by the international community acting through the UN Security Council. These were held in place by the capstone principle of the UN Charter, universal human rights. Ten years later, in 1955, Philip Jessup delivered the Storrs Lectures at Yale Law School and introduced the concept of transnational law to the legal lexicon. The term gained currency in 1989 with the end of the Cold War.

The idea of transnational law is essentially contested and there are competing terms for thinking about law in a global context, primarily revolving around the distinction between international and transnational law.[137] The former is understood to involve the set of rules regarded as binding in relations between states. The latter term refers to all law that pertains to actions or events that transcend state boundaries, including both public and private international law and other (supranational) rules that do not fit into standard categories. Globalisation fundamentally changes the nature of culture, economy and society, with important effects both on the law within states and in the transnational space between them, calling into question the appropriateness of conventional legal paradigms, methods and analogies. The distinction between transnational and international law in only one of a confusing array of dichotomies that have been used to frame discussions about the nature of law under conditions of globalisation. For

[135]Robert Hazell and Ben Worthy, 'Assessing the Performance of Freedom of Information' (2010) 27 *Government Information Quarterly* 353; Bryce Clayton Newell, 'The Massive Metadata Machine: Liberty, Power and Mass Surveillance in the US and Europe' (2014) 10(2) *I/S Journal of Law and Policy of the Information Society* 481; John Yoo, 'The Legality of the National Security Agency's Bulk Data Surveillance' (2014) 10(1) *I/S Journal of Law and Policy of the Information Society* 301.
[136]Steven Neff, *Hugo Grotius, On the Law of War and Peace: Student Edition* (Cambridge University Press, 2012).
[137]See Zumbansen (n 27).

example, realism, pragmatism, unilateralism, sovereignty, legal nationalism and legal pluralism have been variously counterpoised against idealism, utopianism, multilateralism, pluralism and legal internationalism.[138] Even accounting for the disaggregation of the state under transnational conditions, Anne Marie Slaughter envisages the global system as a new kind of legal order.[139] Looking out on the same world order, Philippe Sands sees a system that is increasingly lawless.[140] Transnational rule with law presents disturbing ambiguities, but, arguably, observing the way that legal tools are picked up and used by various kinds of policing agent helps to crystallise an overall understanding.

The rise in prominence of the concept of transnational law coincided with the end of the Cold War and the collapse of the bipolar world order into a multi-polar transnational state system. Interestingly, Sands identifies an important historical signpost in this development: the Pinochet moment – a legal case that made evident in a dramatic fashion how law works under transnational conditions. On 16 October 1998 Augusto Pinochet, the former president of Chile, was arrested in the UK of the basis of an extradition warrant issued in Spain for crimes associated with the 1973 coup d'état in Chile. It was an effort to advance universal human rights in the face of the *realpolitik* of rule with law. This landmark event in legal history was never fully played out because the then Home Secretary, Jack Straw, overruled on medical grounds the House of Lords' decision to extradite. Pinochet was released and died in Chile in December 2006 without ever being formally held to account for any of the crimes of which he was accused.

The ambiguities of transnational rule with law become sufficiently complex and nuanced that the 'Pinochet moment' might have provided opportunities to use law as a tool of resistance against the power elites that foster it. Despite the ultimate failure, the 'Pinochet moment' was emblematic of how legal tools can be used as instruments of political resistance. This reflects some of the concerns of lawfare practitioners who worry that legal tools might be fashioned and used to limit their freedom of action.[141] Even the remote possibility that legal tools might be used with respect to famous players in the field of international power politics – Henry Kissinger and Donald Rumsfeld might be examples – is indicative of ambiguities that the lawfare concept admits.[142] Activities of high policing make use of legal tools, sometimes

[138]Peer Zumbansen, 'Transnational Legal Pluralism' (2001) 1(2) *Transnational Legal Theory* 141; Guglielmo Verdirame, '"The Divided West": International Lawyers in Europe and America' (2007) 18(3) *European Journal of International Law* 553; Alvarez (n 128).

[139]Anne-Marie Slaughter, *A New World Order* (Princeton University Press, 2004) 13–14.

[140]See Sands (n 132).

[141]C Dunlap, 'Lawfare Today: A Perspective' (Winter 2008) 24 *Yale Journal of International Affairs* 146.

[142]AL Morgan, 'US Officials' Vulnerability to "Global Justice": Will Universal Jurisdiction over War Crimes Make Traveling for Pleasure Less Pleasurable?' (2005) 57(2) *Hastings Law Journal* 423.

as instruments to nullify other legal rules, but 'counter law' also contains within it a recognition of 'law's outside' – the politics of conflict inherent in culture, economy and society.[143] Understanding the way that legal power tools are used by a variety of policing agents provides a useful way to understand the trasnationalisation of law, even if it does not establish the ontological status of transnational law. We argue that this is a step forward in understanding the actuality of law under transnational conditions.

Conclusion

Scholarly research on transnational law and transnational policing are united by an interest in understanding the order of transnational phenomena. But while many legal scholars confine their research to the law in books, the policing scholar is concerned with understanding the law in action. A challenge for legal and socio-legal scholars is to develop a multidisciplinary approach to comprehend transnational law as a form of 'living law' in practice. Our brief survey of examples – policing the global money system, controlling transnational population flows, policing intellectual property rights and transnational high policing – provides evidence to advance three arguments.

First, transnational *rule with law* is a practical feature of contemporary global governance. Global policing is a synecdoche of the global system; it exemplifies global governance and is constituent of it. Drawing on socio-legal concepts, we have shown that technocratic legal engineers use legal power tools to achieve specified ends that are usually ones that uphold an existing global system dominated by seigneurial states and powerful private corporations. Police agents and other legal engineers also *create law* through its enactment. Law in action is always predicated on the discretion to invoke the law; this is why, to a cop on the global beat, the only real law is 'blue letter law'. Socio-legal studies of policing reveal law as a device to ratify police action after the fact. Seen this way, the *transnational culture* of policing and the *culture of transnational policing* embody rule with law in the global system. The situation is one of considerable nuance and ambiguity concerning the nature of law under transnational conditions. In this context, Justice appears Janus-faced and blind in one eye.

Second, we argue that the gap between 'law in the books' and the 'living law' suggests that the laudable attempts to codify transnational (criminal) law and procedure and to develop a 'rule of law' doctrine for transnational criminal law is unlikely succeed in constraining transnational police power. Rather than a constraint, law is a tool that *enables* the use of surveillant, coercive and other powers. Legal scholars are certainly right to inquire into the extent to which, and the ways in which, the ancient dictum 'law should govern' plays out in the global system. However, our observations of global policing in practice confirm

[143] See Ericson (n 53).

that for now, and for the foreseeable future, global governance can be described as *law without justice*.

Third, we argue that socio-legal enquiries regarding transnational policing show that it is not only *criminal* law instruments that apply; the legal toolbox contains every manner of legal instrument. Transnational policing is achieved using a variety of public and private law tools, only a minority of which result in criminal prosecution. Moreover, the range of problems that global policing seeks to solve is as broad as the 'omnibus mandate' of domestic policing and deploys power tools from many different spheres of law. All of which underlines the point that the currently existing global system is better characterised as rule *with* law rather than rule *of* law. In our view, the socio-legal study of the transnational practices of policing agents and institutions reveals the ways in which law is used in the governance of the global system and best informs an understanding of actually existing transnational law. Policing is central to the reproduction of the global order and is its most general characteristic. Understanding the empirical manifestations of global policing as transnational rule with law is a necessary first step in the search for global justice.

Acknowledgements

The authors would like to thank Anthony Amatrudo, Neil Boister, Simon Bronnitt, Philip Stenning, Andrew Goldsmith, John Phillips, Chris Townley, Peer Zumbansen and the anonymous peer reviewers of this journal for their comments on successive drafts. We would also like to thank, posthumously, Richard V. Ericson and D. N. MacCormick for their inspiration and ideas.

International criminal law's incongruity in Colombia: why core crime prosecution in national jurisdictions should be included in analyses of transnational criminal law

Michael Reed-Hurtado*

Senior Lecturer, Yale University, New Haven, USA

Using Colombia as a case study, this article tests the merits of the proposed delineation between transnational criminal law and international criminal law. The demarcation is based in part on the existence of the International Criminal Court to repress international core crimes as a direct enforcement scheme. However, most judicial activity relative to this type of criminal conduct takes place in national jurisdictions, subject to immense diversity in practice, and not in the International Criminal Court. The critical use of the transnational lens to monitor and evaluate this activity complements the current focus on international criminal law and provides a methodology that allows consideration of legal and cultural pluralism that is at play in the national repression of core crimes. National practice involves the indirect application of international law, and results in an amalgamation of international criminal law and national criminal law, which, in the end, can impact the content and the form that international law and systems adopt.

To demarcate the boundaries of transnational criminal law (TCL), Neil Boister has distinguished it from international criminal law (ICL) *stricto sensu*, arguing that core offences – namely war crimes, crimes against humanity and genocide – 'are now (since the adoption of the Rome Statute of the International Criminal Court [ICC]) subject to a direct enforcement scheme where the individual *may* be prosecuted before a permanent international criminal court'.[1] Hence, he argues: 'TCL is concerned with the treaty crimes *excluded* from the jurisdiction of the ICC.'[2]

*All websites accessed April 2015.

[1]Neil Boister, '"Transnational Criminal Law"?' (2003) 14(5) *European Journal of International Law* 953, 962. The same conception is sustained in Neil Boister, 'Further reflections on the concept of transnational criminal law', this volume.

[2]*Ibid.*

Using Colombia as a case study, I test the merits of the proposed delineation between TCL and ICL. Other case studies can be produced relative to national jurisdictions that have used ICL in different ways to address a legacy of atrocity, including Peru, Guatemala, Argentina, Uruguay and Chile. In this paper, I put forward evidence relative to Colombia to show that the direct enforcement scheme of ICL – the ICC – seldom operates and that it favours the operation of national criminal justice systems in its stead. As is well known, one of the central tenets of the Rome Statute[3] is the principle of complementarity (set forth in paragraph 10 of the Preamble, and Articles 17, 18, 19, 20 and 53), unfolding the ICC as an *ultima ratio* jurisdiction. Consequently, the prosecution, adjudication and sentencing of core crimes takes place in national jurisdictions much more than in The Hague. The complementarity regime, which promotes a 'system of international criminal justice', fits squarely into Boister's more recent definition of TCL and suggests that so-called 'core crimes' should not be eliminated from the still emerging map of TCL. The application and enforcement of ICL at the national level include 'the indirect suppression by international law through domestic penal law of criminal activities that have … transboundary moral impacts'.[4] This argument further supports the softening of formerly strict demarcations between ICL and TCL that can be detected in Boister's most recent paper, which he contributes to this symposium.

The Colombian case study offers some insight into the way national authorities 'domesticate' ICL, and internationalists could use the TCL lens to better comprehend the way international law interacts with national regimes. Colombia's legal system has been praised for incorporating ICL standards, as if diffusion was an end in and of itself. Representatives of all branches of power flaunt policies, norms and case law that employ ICL logic and terminology as a show of good faith in relation to the international criminal justice system. Internationalists who promote ICL, sponsor the direct application of the Rome Statute in national jurisdictions and advocate for the sprouting of ICC-like chambers in various national jurisdictions[5] applaud Colombia's efforts. However, internationalists rarely delve into the complexities of national legal systems and the failure of domestic courts to appropriately apply ICL.

Mark A. Drumbl has sharply dubbed the practice of transplanting ICL to the local level 'legal mimicry' and has presaged its negative effects.[6] He contends that 'internationalists ought to pause before concluding that the replacement of

---

[3]Document A/CONF.183/9 of 17 July 1998 and corrected by procès-verbaux of 10 November 1998, 12 July 1999, 30 November 1999, 8 May 2000, 17 January 2001 and 16 January 2002. The Statute entered into force on 1 July 2002.

[4]Boister, this volume.

[5]For example Uganda, Kenya and the Democratic Republic of Congo, to name just a few countries that have adopted or discussed the adoption of such bodies.

[6]Mark A Drumbl, *Atrocity, Punishment, and International Law* (Cambridge University Press, 2007) 1–22, and 123–48.

the "other" by that which is familiar to them, namely "international", is axiomatically beneficial'.[7] The transplantation process presents human rights concerns, including compliance with basic notions of due process such as the principle of legality and the non-retroactivity of criminal law. It also generates questions regarding power schemes and the selectiveness of justice.[8] Additionally, those who profess their faith in the ICC's complementarity regime have failed to adequately observe the critique that, in the face of mass atrocity, justice is not served by having the ICC assert its jurisdiction in one, two or any given number of (always limited) cases. Rather, justice is done on the ground, where mass atrocities are perpetrated, through the use of national criminal law – with all of its quirks and flaws. If ICL's integrity is to be maintained, internationalists should be more mindful of the processes at work in the national jurisdictions to apply and enforce ICL.

I will demonstrate how the transnational lens can complement the current focus on ICL and provide some of the missing pieces in the common goal of adjudicating crimes of international concern by examining local processes and demanding cultural fluency in the process of national application of international law. The national prosecution of conduct amounting to core crimes should be examined through the transnational legal lens, as it involves the indirect application of international law in national jurisdictions, and the amalgamation of ICL and national criminal law, which, in the end, can impact the content and the form that international law and systems adopt.[9] The domestication of ICL is a prescription used to describe different processes through which international law is incorporated on the national playing field. In the various national jurisdictions in which core crimes have been committed,[10] criminal justice is imparted according to diverse procedural and substantive frameworks. Furthermore, the administration of justice is also conditioned by practices that do not stem from the legal framework; these maybe especially relevant in cases dealing with complex crime and active power structures. This article illustrates some of those factors relative to Colombia; of course, every country offers a rich and complex blend of elements that should be examined. The TCL lens can assist in deepening understanding of the global governance structure that the ICC model pledges to put in place. Its contribution is especially pertinent as those limiting their study to ICL *stricto sensu* do not give proper consideration

[7]*Ibid*, 125. To be fair, in addition, to the word of caution against the veneration of the international, he also warns that local justice should not be sentimentalised. *Ibid*, 148.
[8]*Ibid.*
[9]This approach to TCL is probably closer to that proposed in Peer Zumbansen, 'Defining the Space of Transnational Law: Legal Theory, Global Governance and Legal Pluralism' (2012) 21 *Transnational Law & Contemporary Problems* 305, 307–8.
[10]For example, in addition to Colombia, consider the national legal and judicial responses in Uganda, Kenya, Chile, Argentina, Guatemala or Peru.

to the legal (and cultural) pluralism at play in the national repression of core crimes.[11]

Following this orientation, the first three sections of this paper illustrate Colombian legal culture and the national situation, which have motivated the use (and abuse) of ICL as a source of law in the national jurisdiction. These sections provide a synthetic exploration of social, political and normative forces that are at play in the application of ICL at the national level in Colombia. They aim to provide a sketch of the concrete environment in which the legal and political debates occur and the way the law is practised. The first section addresses how the struggle against impunity of core crimes has taken shape in Colombia. The second explores the momentum that criminal law (including ICL) has gained around the world and in Colombia, and the effects of its ascension in national affairs. The third section presents a simple characterisation of Colombian legal culture that contributes to explaining the ways in which the reception and incorporation of ICL have taken place.

The fourth section sets out concrete examples of the use and abuse of ICL in the administration of criminal justice in Colombia. Whereas the first three sections concentrate on cultural and political factors, the fourth centres on the judicial activities of Colombian authorities in the legal interpretation and application of ICL. Finally, a conclusive word is offered to iterate the pernicious effect that the uncontrolled diffusion of ICL can have on the value of justice and the struggle against impunity of atrocities in national jurisdictions such as Colombia. This closing section stresses the benefits of an examination under the 'methodological lens through which we can study the particular transformation of legal institutions in the context of an evolving complex society'.[12]

1. Atrocity everywhere, impunity scrambled

Countless atrocities have been committed in Colombia in the context of state repression and the internal armed conflict over the past 60 years.[13] Although numeric approximations to politically motivated crimes are based on partial registries, and reliable statistical exercises revealing the patterns and the magnitude of atrocities are not available, a recent government-sponsored study illustrates, to some extent, the dimensions of the challenges faced by the Colombian justice system. The study specified that 220,000 people were killed between 1958 and

[11] Again, consider the arguments presented by Zumbansen (n 9), particularly those related to 'the evolving nature of the transnational governance'.
[12] Zumbansen (n 9) 307.
[13] In fact, the time frame should probably refer to a greater past, covering the horrifying historical period known as *La Violencia* (1948–58). See generally Orlando Fals Borda, Germán Guzmán and Eduardo Umaña Luna, *La Violencia en Colombia, Tomos I y II* (Taurus, 2005) – originally published in 1962 (vol 1) and 1964 (vol 2).

2012 in relation to the armed conflict.[14] It also reports that 25,000 persons forcibly disappeared, over 27,000 persons were kidnapped and nearly five million persons were internally displaced in the same period as a consequence of the war.[15]

While some of the conduct resulting from the armed conflict falls within the temporal and subject-matter jurisdiction of the ICC, many atrocities amounting to international crimes in Colombia fall outside of the temporal scope of the Rome Statute, which accounts for some conduct from 2002 onwards. This temporal exclusion demonstrates the need to avoid a facile demarcation between TCL and ICL *stricto sensu*, given the unavailability of a direct enforcement mechanism for international crimes committed prior to 2002. Consequently, many core crimes continue to be the sole subject of national jurisdiction.

Unlike other states in which protracted conflict led to the collapse of state institutions, Colombia's legal system and government are recognised as being reasonably strong.[16] Notwithstanding this formal recognition, Colombian state institutions and official activities are tainted by the armed conflict and by illegality.[17] Private interests have seized institutions to varying degrees.[18] Additionally, frameworks of extreme privilege and prejudice are sharply observed in the operation of the law and other manifestations of state power.[19] The justice system's response to crime is not even-handed.[20] In relation to atrocities, it acts judiciously

[14]Gobierno de Colombia, Centro Nacional de Memoria Histórica, *¡Basta ya! Colombia: memorias y dignidad, Informe general Grupo de Memoria Histórica* (Imprenta Nacional, 2013) 31.

[15]*Ibid*, 33.

[16]Paradoxically, Colombia is recognised as a stable formal democracy with functioning institutions, including the justice system, whilst facing war, other ravaging manifestations of social and political violence, and organised crime. This paradox has been captured by Colombian historian Marco Palacios in *Entre la legitimidad y la violencia: Colombia 1875–1994* (Editorial Norma, 2nd edn 2003).

[17]For example, after the 2006 congressional election the paramilitary co-optation of dozens of elected senators and representatives was proven as a result of both confessions and criminal investigations, ending in convictions of several elected politicians for electoral crimes. The scandal is widely known in Colombia as *parapolítica*.

[18]For example, consider the situation of the health service providers in the northern department of La Guajira that were seized entirely by paramilitaries; or consider public works contracting in any major city of Colombia.

[19]As a simple illustration, consider all the discriminatory patterns that affect afro-Colombians living in the western departments along the Pacific coast, as manifested by racial slander, extreme poverty and festering public services.

[20]Demonstrating its ability to respond sharply to abhorrent crime, such as kidnapping, when perpetrated by the guerrillas, the Colombian justice system not only prosecutes principals engaged directly in the commission of criminal conduct, but also pursues the leaders of the criminal groups for their indirect involvement. See e.g. Corte Suprema de Justicia, Sala de Casación Penal, Proceso No 25974, 8 August 2007, a criminal cassation decision that confirms the possibility of bringing charges against the leaders of a guerrilla group (Fuerzas Armadas Revolucionarias de Colombia – Ejército Popular, FARC-EP) for the *attempted* kidnapping of a well-known journalist (Yamid Amat), using a co-perpetration

against enemies of the state that perpetrate abhorrent crime,[21] whilst turning a blind eye to state-sponsored killers.[22] It opts to prosecute individual stooges in the bureaucratic chain of the state but never addresses the organisational dimension of state-sanctioned atrocity.[23] In response, human rights defenders courageously promote legal and policy campaigns to confront impunity of state crime, and have demonstrated that the administration of the criminal justice system operates as a shield in favour of state agents and state-sponsored parties to criminal activity.

Compounding the situation of the repression of conduct amounting to core crimes, backlogs and impunity are overwhelming. The complexity of ongoing daily offences configures an unmanageable caseload of old cases and generates a perpetual sense of crisis. The impact of other violent crime in Colombia – known as 'common or ordinary' crime – should not be underestimated in an assessment of the Colombian criminal justice system. The incidence of common crime is very high and it is not as 'ordinary' as thought; it encompasses extreme use of violence and involves complex criminal networks coexisting or intermingled with the conflict.[24] The existence of this ever-growing caseload is yet another obstacle to reaching the human rights-related cases or those that would amount to core crimes.

Pressed by a complex crime scenario, the bureaucrats of the justice system (including the police, prosecutors, judges and prison guards) operate under constant strain and conform not to law but to pragmatism by simply doing what they can. They know that they are far from doing what justice demands and they adjust, conditioned by limited resources. Thus justice becomes polluted by pressure and a habitual sense of crisis. It also falls prey to constant and irrational

doctrinal development that allows the establishment of responsibility of individuals that are detached from the material crime scene. The same theory of liability has been used to convict *in absentia* the leadership of another guerrilla group (Ejército de Liberación Nacional, ELN) for other heinous crimes. See e.g. Corte Suprema de Justicia, Sala de Casación Penal, Proceso No 23825, 7 March 2007, Justice Javier Zapata Ortíz.

[21]The current High Commissioner for Peace, one of the highest-ranking members of the executive line-up, recently affirmed: 'the Colombian justice system has been implacable with the FARC and the ELN (the guerrillas).' Sergio Jaramillo, 'Transición en Colombia ante el proceso de paz y la justicia' *El Tiempo*, 13 May 2013, www.eltiempo.com/justicia/articulo-web-new_nota_interior-12796874.html (accessed April 2015).

[22]For a study illustrating the deficiencies of the Colombian justice system in relation to the effective investigation, prosecution and trial of state crimes, see Avocats sans Frontières (ASF) – Canada, *The Principle of Complementarity in the Rome Statute and the Colombian Situation: A Case that Demands More than a 'Positive' Approach* (ASF, 2012) 24–42, www.asfcanada.ca/documents/file/asf_rapport-anglais-v3-lq.pdf.

[23]See *ibid*, 24–42.

[24]Consider the reported offending rate, according to the National Police, at the end of the 1990s: over 230,000 reported criminal offences per year, including an average of 25,000 homicides per year. Imagine the resources required to close each one of these cases in a reasonable timeframe.

changes in criminal policy, which responds to the sense that 'nothing works' by deepening the punitive response.[25]

As the Colombian criminal justice system has not produced a meaningful response to atrocities, victim-based proclamations and rights-based claims constantly demand a robust response – particularly to state crimes. A very strident cacophony of voices demand '*justicia, justicia, justicia …*' in the form of criminal punishment.[26]

Some of the most noteworthy efforts against impunity for gross human rights violations committed by state agents or individuals acting with the acquiescence of the state have been litigated before the Inter-American Court of Human Rights.[27] Based on international human rights law, these cases are illustrative of dual responsibility triggered by the perpetration of crimes against humanity[28] – individual liability (attaching to persons) and state responsibility (derived from the use of state power to either plan, execute or cover up the crimes in question).[29] The influence of the Inter-American Court of Human Rights and international human rights law in the struggle against impunity and the effective prosecution of core crimes domestically should not be overlooked.

International humanitarian law (IHL) and human rights law shaped domestic penal law in Colombia that criminalised conduct of international concern prior to the creation of the ICC. The criminalisation of conduct that could amount to war crimes and crimes against humanity resulted from longstanding pressure from

[25]In the Latin American context, Zaffaroni has referred to the state of constant emergency of the criminal justice system as an ideological resource that assists in implanting and stabilising punitive structures within the state, regardless of whether policy goals are met. Raul Zaffaroni, 'Naturaleza y necesidad de los consejos de política criminal' in *Justicia penal y sobrepoblación penitenciaria: respuestas posibles*, ed Elías Carranza (Siglo XXI Editores, 2001) 86–88. The perpetual sense of crisis has also been described in David Garland, *The Culture of Control: Crime and Social Order in Contemporary Society* (University of Chicago Press, 2011) 19–20.

[26]For example, a recent national survey (promoted by the government) confirmed the national tendency to favour criminal punishment as the preferred response to atrocity. See Centro de Memoria Histórica y otros, *Encuesta Nacional, ¿Qué piensan los colombianos después de siete años de Justicia y Paz?* (Publicaciones Semana, 2012) 61–66.

[27]See: Inter-American Court of Human Rights (IACtHR), *Caso de la Masacre de Mapiripán c. Colombia*, Sentence, 15 September 2005, Series C No 134; IACtHR, *Caso Pueblo Bello c. Colombia*, Sentence, 31 January 2006, Series C No 140; IACtHR, *Caso de Ituango c. Colombia*, Sentence, 1 July 2006, Series C No 148.

[28]For a detailed study of the centrality of state policy in the demarcation of crimes against humanity versus heinous and atrocious crimes, see M Cherif Bassiouni, *Crimes against Humanity: Historical Evolution and Contemporary Application* (Cambridge University Press, 2011) 1–85.

[29]See e.g. IACtHR, *Caso Manuel Cepeda Vargas v Colombia* (Excepciones Preliminares, Fondo, Reparaciones y Costas), Sentence, 26 May 2010, para 117, citing various cases and restating the case law that addresses standards applicable to criminal investigations involving state offending. This particular case relates to the 1994 assassination of a communist senator by a military-paramilitary commando.

national and international humanitarian and human rights organisations. For example, in response to a campaign led principally by the International Committee of the Red Cross, the Colombian Congress included a special title in the 2000 Criminal Code codifying 29 crimes that correspond to serious international humanitarian law violations.[30] The preparatory works, presented in August 1998 by the then Prosecutor General of Colombia, reveal that the interest in including these offences derived from wanting to comply with international humanitarian law. In addition, further national codification of crimes related to international core crimes – namely genocide, torture, enforced disappearance and forced displacement[31] – took place in the Colombian Congress in 2000. Again, these laws were based not on ICL but on international human rights law, and the main advocates of this autonomous legislative initiative were human rights NGOs supporting family members of the disappeared.[32] These examples illustrate that human rights and IHL treaties have influenced national criminal law and therefore these bodies of law should not be ignored in examining the configuration of the justice system at the national level. The interplay of various branches of international law in the process of criminalisation supports the suggested departure from the sharp demarcation between ICL *stricto sensu* and TCL proposed by Boister.[33]

This section has presented broad strokes relative to the operation of the administration of justice and the complexity of ending impunity in Colombia – all important antecedents to the consideration of the reception of ICL, which will be addressed in the following sections.

2. The rise of criminal law

The turn towards criminal law as the preferred and, often, only response to atrocity is due, in part, to the rise of criminal law in the public realm, particularly at the end of the 1990s in Colombia. Sectors that had previously left the criminal law to criminal lawyers became eagerly engaged in heated debates regarding the efficacy of certain theories of liability over others or the probative value of certain types of evidence.[34] The popularisation of criminal law is the product

[30]After the adoption of the Rome Statute, Colombia incorporated war crimes into its Criminal Code in 2000: Law 599 of 2000, Arts 135–64.

[31]See Law 589 of 2000, incorporated a few weeks later into Law 599 of 2000, Arts 165 and 178.

[32]This legislative initiative had been in the works since the 1994 adoption of the Inter-American Convention on Forced Disappearance of Persons.

[33]Boister, this volume.

[34]In the first decade of the 2000s, traditional human rights organisations that had not engaged in criminal litigation garnered specialised teams to take on legal representations in criminal matters; women's rights organisations demanded a strong criminal response to cases of sexual violence; and seminars on criminal law and procedure were organised across the nation. In response to the hype, the international community approved funds

of multi-layered and multi-causal processes that respond to cultural, political and legal factors.[35]

The first two factors that contribute to explaining the rise of criminal law are global in nature and the subsequent three are local phenomena that impact the way atrocities are addressed. Though TCL is not concerned with parochial substantive and procedural issues, the TCL scholar does need to immerse herself in the subtleties of the national systems in order to detect the amalgam of new law being formed through the indirect application of ICL and apply the TCL 'lens to reveal the relationships between seemingly unrelated national criminal laws'.[36] The following subsections provide contextual elements to assist in this goal.

Crime as a form of government

The first trend affecting Colombia's criminal justice system is global in nature and relates to governments that use crime and the fear of criminals as a device to achieve its goals.[37] The use of 'crime as a form of government' was first documented in the US and European nations.[38] This phenomenon also exists in Latin America.[39] The trend of governing through crime, already evident in the 1990s, was exacerbated by the anti-terrorist paradigm that took over the security and

to support these activities. See e.g. European Union, 'Colombia: La Comisión Europea libera 1,5 millones de euros en apoyo de la paz y de la reconciliación en Colombia', IP/05/1699, Brussels, 22 December 2005, http://europa.eu/rapid/press-release_IP-05-1699_es.htm. Similarly, an ample body of victims, beyond victims of the state, started mobilising and demanding harsher criminal penalties; and journalists heightened their coverage of criminal cases and the inner workings of the administration of justice system. Moved by heinous crimes such as kidnapping, congressional debates have exploited the pain and suffering of victims to harshen criminal penalties. See 'El pueblo pide al Congreso terminar con el secuestro' *El Tiempo*, 27 August 1992, www.eltiempo.com/archivo/documento/MAM-187779. The exploitation of victim suffering was most evident in the adoption of Law 890 of 2004, which raised the maximum prison sentence to 60 years.

[35]Two Argentinean lawyers – a criminal lawyer, and a human rights activist and academic – sustained an exemplary discussion (in Spanish) of these issues. Arguments and counterarguments on the popularisation and the effects of the expansion of criminal legal agenda within the human rights movement in Latin America can be examined in Daniel R Pastor, 'La deriva neopunitivista de organismos y activistas como causa del desprestigio actual de los derechos humanos' in *Nueva Doctrina Penal, 2005A* (Editores del Puerto, 2005) 73–114; Leonardo Filippini, 'El prestigio de los derechos humanos: respuesta a Daniel Pastor' in *Nueva Doctrina Penal, 2005B* (Editores del Puerto, 2005) 727–54.

[36]Boister, this volume.

[37]One of the most systematic analyses is offered by Jonathan Simon, *Governing through Crime: How the War on Crime Transformed American Democracy and Created a Culture of Fear* (Oxford University Press, 2007).

[38]David Garland, *The Culture of Control: Crime and Social Order in Contemporary Society* (University of Chicago Press, 2011).

[39]See, for example, the public image campaign conducted in the Tony Saca government in El Salvador in relation to the *Mara Salvatrucha* and the *Pandilla Barrio 18*, leading to the

justice sectors in the US and internationally after the 11 September 2001 attacks.[40] The war on terror expanded the use of amorphous struggles against social threats, playing harder on the fears of individuals to achieve greater state powers through reforms that went against treasured, and now seemingly unnecessary, due process guarantees.[41]

A side effect of the 'war on crime', especially in societies with a high crime indexes like Colombia, is that governments take advantage of the situation and play on the volatile emotions of citizens to justify and augment the state's punitive powers and adopt measures that, under normal circumstances, would not be accepted by citizens. Succinctly expressing the mechanisms used to aggrandise states' penal power, Zimring and Hawkins note: 'The importance of public feelings of vulnerability about crime to support the expansion of punitive power explains not only the incentive of ambitious governments to scare their citizens but also the cyclicality of the public sense of emergency about particular crime problems.'[42] In the recent past, new criminal statutes have proliferated in Colombia, together with the steepening of criminal sentences.[43] Laws are not necessarily applied, but they are paraded as political capital and widely discussed in the media. Bombarded with images of heinous crimes and criminals – some real and others tainted – the Colombian public easily gave in to the spiralling punitive sentiment.

Colombian governments have used criminal law as a repressive tool to fight a hazy internal enemy – whether drug-traffickers, guerrillas, terrorists or 'narco-bandoleers'. Fundamental due process rights become uncertain. As an unconditional US ally, Colombia has been hit hard by the implications of the global war on terror. Playing on 1980s practices,[44] the new wave of alarm has sought, amongst other

---

adoption of hardline and wide-reaching security and justice policies, known as *Mano Dura* and its recharged sequel, *Super Mano Dura*.

[40]Simon (n 37) 259–83, underscoring that three decades prior to the 2001 attacks, the fear of crime had already reshaped the form of government and US society.

[41]*Ibid*, 261.

[42]Franklin E Zimring and Gordon Hawkins, 'Democracy and the Limits of Punishment: A Preface to Prisoners' Rights' in Michael Tonry (ed), *The Future of Imprisonment* (Oxford University Press, 2004 edn) 157, 162.

[43]Starting in 2004, with the adoption of Law 890 of 2004, which augmented the maximum prison term to 60 years, the Colombian legal regime has experienced at least 35 major modifications, always under the pretence of having to respond to a new wave of social panic. See M Reed Hurtado, *El camino irreflexivo de la cárcel en Colombia: un cuento de delirios y despelotes* (Woodrow Wilson Center, 2012), www.wilsoncenter.org/sites/default/files/Michael%20Reed%20Hurtado_0.pdf.

[44]For example, in the late 1980s, the executive established a special Public Order Jurisdiction, vested with exceptional powers, which arbitrarily assumed jurisdiction over persons and crimes without any respect for due process. Acting under powers granted by the state of siege declared by Decree 1038 of 1984, the then President Virgilio Barco adopted Decree 1631 of 1987, creating the first public order courts. The jurisdiction was known as faceless justice (*justicia sin rostro*), given that the identity of judges was withheld. Using exceptional powers, the executive modified the criminal code, including the

things, to depoliticise social conflicts in Colombia and criminalise many expressions of social protest,[45] to augment the reach of criminal law to younger Colombians,[46] and to lower thresholds for the official use of lethal violence by reinterpreting IHL in light of new US-sanctioned practices against so-called 'enemy combatants'.[47] These tendencies continue with vigour today.

This global trend, with clear implications in Colombia, is particularly important to our understanding of why due process considerations have less weight today and why judges are willing to stray from previously cherished procedural protection in order to achieve justice.

The ICC enters the international playing field

A second global process that contributed to the prominence of criminal law in Colombia started with the 1998 adoption of the Rome Statute and its entry into force in 2002. States were motivated to adopt or modify national legislation in order to comply with international obligations and align themselves with the emerging global justice model. Colombia was committed to this move, except for the fact that when it became a party to the Rome Statue, in November 2002,[48] it made use of the declaration under Article 124, suspending the ICC's jurisdiction over war crimes for seven years.

---

adoption of an ambiguous and far-reaching definition of the crime of terrorism. Código Penal de Colombia, Decreto Ley 100 de 1980, Art 187, modified by exceptional Decree 180 of 1988, Art 1.

[45]Recent legislative initiatives have sought to harshly punish conduct, such as the obstruction of roadways, as a means of criminalising activities that are inherent in striking and protesting. For example an ambitious legislative initiative was recently promoted by the Ministry of Defence to modify the criminal code, purportedly taking measures against terrorism. See Cámara de Representantes, Proyecto de Ley No 091 de 2013, 11 September 2013.

[46]A reform to the juvenile justice system extended the reach of the criminal legal system to Colombian minors. See Ley 1098 of 2006, 8 November 2006. Additionally, a wide-ranging criminal reform was adopted recently, deviating from due process standards, imposing harsher penalties and extending prison terms on minors beyond the 18-years age limit. See Ley 1453 de 2011, Diario Oficial No 48.110, 24 June 2011.

[47]Responding to the initiative of the Executive, the Colombian Congress adopted a constitutional reform in 2012 that called for a new IHL lens to interpret military actions against enemy combatants. See Acto Legislativo 02 de 2012. This reform was then subject to regulation through a statutory law 'developing Articles 116 and 221 of the Political Constitution of Colombia and enacting other provisions'. The version of IHL that inspired the legislative framework strays from the international protection scheme contained in Art 3 Common and Protocol II to the Geneva Conventions, and rather supports an expansive use of force that justifies killing and collateral damage.

[48]The Colombian Congress approved the Rome Statute in June 2002, through national Law 742 of 7 June 2002. According to the national framework, it was then subject to constitutional review in July 2002 by the Colombian Constitutional Court. Constitutional Court, Judgment C-578/02, 30 July 2002, Justice Manuel José Cepeda Espinosa.

With its track record of atrocities, Colombia could not escape examination by the Office of the Prosecutor of the ICC (OTP-ICC). In 2006, the OTP-ICC acknowledged that Colombia was under preliminary examination but it did not communicate its findings until December 2011.[49] At this late stage, it reported that it found that crimes under its jurisdiction had been perpetrated in Colombia.[50] However, it also conveyed that 'there is no basis at this stage to conclude that the existing proceedings are not genuine'.[51] Eight years after initiating its monitoring exercise, the prosecutorial authority of the direct enforcement scheme continued to gather information. Now, over 12 years after beginning its activities, the ICC-OTP continues to gather information on the Colombian situation.

The opacity of the preliminary examination has produced positive and negative effects. Positively, it instilled an air of mystery around the actions of the ICC, which contributes to the mobilisation of resources to achieve results in some national token criminal cases. OTP-ICC is an important source of pressure to administer justice nationally in relation to core crimes. The OTP-ICC has exerted pressure on Colombian authorities to investigate, prosecute and adjudicate cases nationally, though it has offered little guidance on how to accomplish these goals. Generally, however, the potential for ICC intervention is perceived, encouragingly or menacingly, as a type of boogieman – *el coco* in Colombian Spanish; that is, in hiding, but waiting to come out.[52] The Colombian justice system therefore prosecutes a few cases in order to avoid prosecution by the ICC. The uncertainty of the ICC's reach continues to perplex the Colombian authorities. In the name of 'complying with the Rome Statute', all kinds of strange initiatives have been approved. For example, the Colombian Congress embraces senseless initiatives such as incorporating into national law the Rules of Procedure and Evidence adopted by the Assembly of States Parties in September 2002.[53] Congressional intent or purpose in adopting such an instrument remains unclear. The pressure generated by the ICC has lacked strategic value and consistency, and thus the results are mixed.

In turn, the Colombian executive aggrandises the ICC any time it gets a chance. It promotes preposterous agreements to show its 'good faith' as a state party, such as offering its prisons for the execution of sentences of convicted international criminals even though Colombia's prisons are imploding as a result of

---

[49]International Criminal Court (ICC), Office of the Prosecutor, *Report on Preliminary Examination Activities* (13 December 2011).
[50]*Ibid*, para 72.
[51]*Ibid*, para 87.
[52]For example, examine different news stories equating the ICC to the boogieman: in 2009, 'La Corte Penal Internacional se volvió "el Coco" de los politicos' *Caracol*, 8 September 2009, www.caracol.com.co/noticias/actualidad/la-corte-penal-internacional-se-volvio-el-coco-de-los-politicos/20090908/nota/875198.aspx; Raul Eduardo Sanchez, 'La Corte Penal Internacional y el proceso de paz con las FARC' *Semana*, 12 September 2013, www.semana.com/opinion/articulo/corte-penal-internacional-proceso-de-paz/357379-3.
[53]See Law 1268 of 2008.

extreme overcrowding, violence and corruption.[54] A couple of months after reaching this agreement, a representative of the current Santos administration stated that 'the [Colombian] prison situation is not critical, it is extremely critical; it is *Macondo*-like'.[55] Nevertheless, the Colombian government still offered holding facilities to the ICC.

This odd game of mutual encouragement amongst Member States and the ICC is the result of a poor understanding and application of the 'positive complementarity' regime.[56] The dynamic can be presented as follows: so long as Colombia plays nice, so will the ICC. In an exemplary statement, a Colombian diplomat embraced the 'positive' contribution of the ICC, as it means no material reproach to its justice system: 'the cooperation provided by the [International Criminal] Court is highly beneficial for the purpose of eradicating impunity.'[57] This congenial proclamation belies the instrumental use of the notion of complementarity by the Colombian diplomat.

The judiciary's action has been no less vexing than that of the legislative and executive branches in relation to the ICC. Photo opportunities to demonstrate the close relationship between the national prosecuting authority and the OTP-ICC are seized and disseminated in the national press.[58] The Colombian prosecuting authority produced embellished reports to show that thousands of crimes are being investigated, and the OTP-ICC mirrors the numbers in its official reports.[59] These statistics might be impressive, but if complementarity is to work, official national reporting needs to be subject to careful and technical scrutiny by the OTP-ICC, including examination of the bona fide nature of the proceedings and the degree of diligence with which criminal investigations are undertaken.[60]

The Colombian judiciary also demonstrates compliance with the Rome Statute through its decisions, as evidenced in a 2009 decision of the Colombian Supreme

[54]*Acuerdo entre la República de Colombia y la Corte Penal Internacional sobre la ejecución de penas impuestas por la Corte Penal Internacional*, May 2011. The Colombian Congress recently adopted this agreement through Law 1662 of 16 July 2013.

[55]Vice Minster of Justice Luis Felipe Robledo, Statement at a Congressional Hearing on prison conditions, 30 August 2011.

[56]OTP-ICC, *Prosecutorial Strategy 2009–2012* (The Hague: February 2010), paras 16–17. The 'positive approach to complementarity' has been at the centre of all policy documents produced by the OTP-ICC from its outset.

[57]Assembly of States Parties of the Rome Statute, Declaration (under item 7) by Colombian Ambassador Alvaro Sandoval Bernal, Ministry of Foreign Affairs, *Director de Asuntos Jurídicos Internacionales*, 14 December 2011, www.colombiaun.org/Asamblea%20General/Eventos%20Especiales/Articulos_Eventos/14_diciembre_11_eventos.html.

[58]See "Paras' extraditados deberían ser repatriados hasta que digan la verdad: Baltazar Garzón' *Semana*, 26 August 2008, www.semana.com/on-line/articulo/paras-extraditados-deberian-repatriados-hasta-digan-verdad-baltazar-garzon/94811-3.

[59]ICC (n 49) paras 76–78.

[60]ASF (n 22) 10 ff, analysing the standards applicable to preliminary examinations and the Decision to Open an Investigation according to the Rome Statute and as should be applied in the Colombian case.

Court in which it ordered that its decision be remitted to the ICC.[61] The case involved a governor who conspired with paramilitaries and was found guilty of the murder of a former mayor who belonged to an opposition party. The conviction is undoubtedly an important contribution to the struggle against impunity. Nonetheless, the decision itself is at best sloppy. The law is applied dogmatically without providing robust reasons for findings of criminal liability,[62] and scattered references to ICL fail to apply it meaningfully in a national setting.[63]

The operation of the ICC has undeniably spurred a global trend that hypes ICL. What has been missed by those studying ICL is that in addition to consolidating the ICC as a jurisdictional body, its impact at the local level has also generated effects, both desired and undesired. I argue that relative to Colombia, many of the effects are undesired and are changing the way ICL is conceived and applied, through the process of 'domestication'. This process will be subject to deeper analysis in the sections to come. At this stage, the emphasis is on how the operation of the ICC has placed criminal law at the national level in the vortex of public attention.

As stated in the outline of this section, the remaining elements are local in nature and will be described summarily. Together they play a crucial role in heightening the social importance of criminal law, and thus ICL, in the national agenda.

Criminal law goes public

A criminal procedure reform was introduced in 2004 in Colombia that made criminal courts more accessible, as they moved from a written inquisitorial-based model to an oral accusatory model.[64] In the old procedural model the criminal justice process was equally ceremonial but limited almost entirely to concealed written exchanges. The new model introduced greater publicity into criminal proceedings and made the Colombian courtroom a place more accepting of the theatrics of judging criminals, where evil is put on trial. 'Doing justice' has become a public affair. Society generally also assimilates this new form of criminal justice to their routine dramatised TV experience of the US courtroom, which has been disseminated in the region and globally.[65] The reform was gradual and the change, in

[61] Corte Suprema de Justicia, Sala de Casación Penal, Proceso No 32672, 3 December 2009, Sentence convicting Salvador Arana Sus, the ex-Governor of the department of Sucre, '11.3. Intervención de la Corte Penal Internacional'.

[62] An overplayed and ideologically driven debate generally represented by opposing conceptions of criminal law offered by Günter Jakobs and Claus Roxin. See *ibid*, fnn 99 and 104.

[63] *Ibid*, '2.2. El concierto para delinquir con fines de paramilitarismo se tiene como delito de lesa humanidad'.

[64] Código de procedimiento penal, Ley 906 de 2004.

[65] Latin Americans 'experience' criminal justice through dubbed US police and courtroom TV dramas, such as *LA Law* in the 1980s and ongoing shows such as *Law & Order* and *CSI*, much more than through any real-life experience.

practice, was not as radical as promised.[66] Nonetheless, the new criminal procedure did bolster Colombians' interest in criminal law as it allowed, amongst other things, the public display of trials on the evening news.

Perpetrator depositions captivate the public's attention

A special criminal procedure was set up in 2005 to give reduced sentences to demobilised paramilitaries in exchange for confessions. A bill known as the Justice and Peace Law blended mechanisms to satisfy victims' rights with criminal benefits for confessed killers.[67] Human rights and victims' rights advocates greeted this instrument with particular mistrust. The system was opposed chiefly because it allowed confessed perpetrators 'off easy', with a minimum of a five-year prison sentence and a maximum eight-year sentence. However, while the Justice and Peace proceedings offered a stage for partial and controlled truths about paramilitary activities in Colombia, it did give some victims closure with respect to the fate of their loved ones. Additionally, given that denial of paramilitarism is so extreme in Colombia, the testimony of these individuals activated other truth-seeking initiatives and prompted some independent criminal proceedings.[68]

These proceedings ignited discussions surrounding theories of liability and charging strategies. ICL also became entrenched in the Justice and Peace proceedings, mainly due to the involvement of bilateral and multilateral agencies in the implementation the Justice and Peace Law.[69] These agencies turned to ICL

[66]The reform was gradually implemented; the new procedural model was applied progressively in the national territory according to a regional implementation scheme that started in 2005. Cases dealing with crimes committed previous to the entry into force of the new procedural law continue to be addressed through the previous code of procedure (contained in Law 600 of 2000), which prescribes a predominantly written system.
[67]Law 975 of 2005. The Justice and Peace Law was applied to a small number of demobilised paramilitaries who were, ultimately, selected by the executive power. This special criminal process is wrought with problems; it was the by-product of 'a secret process of transactions between the (Colombian) executive branch and the paramilitary groups'. See Michael Reed-Hurtado, 'Transitional Justice under Fire: Five Reflections on the Colombian Case' in Amanda Lyons and Michael Reed-Hurtado (eds), Contested Transitions: Dilemmas of Transitional Justice in Colombia and Comparative Experience (ICTJ, 2010) 87–114.
[68]Some of the non-official truth-seeking initiatives backed by victims are portrayed in Marcela Briceño Donn et al (eds), Recordar en conflicto: iniciativas no oficiales de memoria en Colombia (ICTJ, 2010).
[69]Immersion of international cooperation bodies was not minimal; by 2008, prosecutors were complaining of saturation. Events sponsored by USAID, the European Union, the Swedish International Development Cooperation Agency (SIDA), Deutsche Gesellschaft für Internationale Zusammenarbeit (GIZ), the Spanish cooperation agency (AECI), and various UN agencies and specialised NGOs regularly targeted prosecutors, generating tensions with growing caseloads. One of them candidly told me: 'This week I have three training seminars in international law to chose from … I do not know who is going to do the

experts because they were not familiar with national criminal law and faced conduct such as rapes, tortures, executions, disappearances and forced displacements that fell under the subject matter of similar international or hybrid tribunals.[70] These specialists were mostly academics, and few had hands-on experience in real life cases. Therefore, they could not share practical knowledge or experience related to case management, evidence gathering and evaluation strategies, and instead focused the training of justice officials and legal representatives of victims on normative accounts of ICL. The lecturers' interpretations of ICL varied depending on their respect for the sources of international law, the perceived import of the Rome Statute and ideological preferences. The result was the transmission of an ICL-inspired jumble that left prosecutors and judges dazed and confused. Although Colombian prosecutors and judges have a sense that ICL is important to the international community and retain some knowledge of ICL, they do not know how to purposefully and coherently integrate it in their legal practice.[71] Therefore, a poorly interpreted and applied form of ICL pervades Justice and Peace proceedings.

It is quite difficult to evaluate ICL's contribution to Justice and Peace proceedings given that the flawed design and management of these proceedings have rendered the special mechanism hopeless.[72] At the end of 2013, more than eight years after its adoption, out of thousands of confessed paramilitaries subject to the special proceedings only 14 men had been convicted.[73] Recently, a Vice Minister of Justice expressed that the intent of the law appears to have achieved, from the outset, '*de facto* impunity' for paramilitary groups. He stated that the 'law cloaked the most rampant impunity that the country has ever seen in a process that, in the end, did not imply justice nor peace'.[74] Once heralded as groundbreaking, Justice

---

work on my cases.' A European donor agent expressed another telling concern in 2010: 'We are promoting ICL, but prosecutors do not know what to do with it!'

[70]For example, the Office in Colombia of the UN High Commissioner for Human Rights organised several training seminars with prosecutors from the ICTY, ICTR and hybrid tribunals. Similarly, bilateral cooperation programs, such as ProFis supported by GIZ, promoted the positions of several international scholars, such as Kai Ambos, in order to 'solve the problems' of the Justice and Peace Law.

[71]There are some better-informed practices, though not without flaws, such as: Tribunal Superior de Bogotá, Sala de Justicia y Paz, rads 110016000253200883194; 110016000253200783070, 1 December 2011, criminal case against members of the Bloque Vencedores de Arauca for various offences including rape, analysed as crimes against humanity and war crimes, paras 71 ff.

[72]The Colombian government and international human rights monitoring bodies recognise that the system was poorly designed and managed, and that the results are dismal. See e.g. United Nations, *Annual Report of the United Nations High Commissioner for Human Rights*, Addendum, *Report of the UNHCHR on the Situation of Human Rights in Colombia*, 7 January 2013, UN Doc A/HRC/22/17/Add.3, para 60.

[73]Comité Interinstitucional de Justicia y Paz, Matriz, 31 December 2013.

[74]Declaration by Miguel Samper, 'Cuestionan falta de condiciones cuando se extraditó al "Tuso" Sierra' El Espectador, 13 May 2014, www.elespectador.com/noticias/judicial/cuestionan-falta-de-condiciones-cuando-se-extradito-al-articulo-492110.

and Peace proceedings are central in explaining how ICL became enmeshed in the arsenal of Colombian criminal law.

Criminal law takes a small bite out of crime in the national congress

The final occurrence that contributes to explaining the popularity of criminal law in Colombia is related to a series of high-profile criminal cases against politicians who colluded with paramilitary groups, known commonly as *parapolítica*. The alliances were denounced and debated, starting in 2005, by the press and a few members of Congress. In September 2009, after overcoming several impasses, the Criminal Cassation Chamber of the Supreme Court decided to reclaim jurisdiction over many of the cases and gave renewed support to a special investigatory commission.[75] The cases linking congresspersons to paramilitary forces required the development of law to address 'new forms of criminality', as was explained by the 2010 president of the Chamber of Criminal Cassation.[76] Criminal law was again in the news and the subject of heated academic and political debates.

The majority of cases are limited to electoral crimes; only a handful have explored the perpetration of violent crime as a result of the links.[77] Nevertheless, the cases received wide national and international attention, given the standoff between the judiciary and then President Alvaro Uribe Velez. At the peak of the Supreme Court's prosecutorial initiative, most of the 120 active cases were against Uribe's allies in Congress, including his cousin and political cohort, Mario Uribe.[78] The justices, their clerks and investigators came under fire. As

[75]Corte Suprema de Justicia, Sala de Casación Penal, Proceso No 31653, 1 September 2009, leading to the criminal investigation of former House of Representatives member Edgar Eulises Torres Murillo.

[76]María del Rosario González, 'Presentación' in *Procesos contra aforados constitucionales: parapolítica. Compilación de autos y sentencias de la Sala de Casación Penal de la Corte Suprema de Justicia. Diciembre de 2007 a septiembre de 2010* (ICTJ, 2010).

[77]Convictions deriving from this special prosecutorial initiative have centred on conspiracy and crimes against the electoral regime and voter rights. The few exceptions include: Corte Suprema de Justicia, Sala de Casación Penal, Aprobado acta No 56, 23 February 2010, criminal conviction of ex-Senator Álvaro García Romero (convicted of homicide in collusion with paramilitary groups) and two other locally elected officials; Corte Suprema de Justicia, Sala de Casación Penal, aprobado acta No 374, 3 December 2009, criminal conviction of ex-Governor of Sucre (convicted of the crime of forced disappearance and murder of a local mayor); Corte Suprema de Justicia, Sala de Casación Penal, aprobado acta No 148, 15 May 2013, criminal conviction of Cesar Perez García (a local parliamentary member convicted of a series of murders committed in the late 1980s).

[78]Corte Suprema de Justicia, Sala de Casación Penal, Proceso No 27918, 21 February 2011, sentence convicting Mario de Jesús Uribe Escobar. Based on evidence stacked against them and evident collusion with paramilitary groups, many of Uribe's political allies accepted the criminal charges, including Dieb Maloof, Miguel de la Espriella, Alfonso Campo Escobar, Carlos Arturo Clavijo, Muriel Benito Rebollo, Rocío Arias, Eleonara Pineda, Jorge Luis Caballero, Enrique Emilio Ángel Barco, Jorge Ramírez Urbina and Salomón Saade.

international attention and solidarity were heightened in favour of the Supreme Court, their rhetoric and some legal developments also turned to international law – particularly ICL. The *parapolítica* phenomenon marked national life and changed the way the very traditional and insulated Supreme Court was perceived by Colombian society.[79] The role played by the Criminal Cassation Chamber brought with it an amplification of the perception that criminal law could be used effectively to quash powerful criminals. This outcome does not take into consideration whether the *parapolítica* cases were effective in addressing the criminal infiltration of the Colombian Congress, or whether the effort was adequately managed from beginning to end. It simply acknowledges that criminal law regained symbolic expression in popular opinion.

While these five elements do not offer a total explanation, when taken together they represent the most salient reasons for the sharp increase in the popularity of criminal law in Colombia as the preferred tool to address atrocity.

3. Colombian law, lawyers and legal culture explained

Another account of how international law is transformed at the national level is based on the cultural elements of Colombia's legal community. Colombian legal culture is not monolithic. Fortunately, alternative and critical takes on the law exist. The way in which law is conceived, adopted, applied, experienced and circumvented is determined by manifestations of culture and power. Therefore, the way in which ICL is conceived, adopted, applied, experienced and circumvented in various national jurisdictions will also be impacted by culture and power. The expressions of culture and power should be considered alongside the transnational legal inquiry when assessing the application of international law in national contexts. Cultural 'fluency' is a necessary filter to examine local processes of emulation, transplantation and indirect application of ICL. '[T]he domestic experiences with law are crucial points of orientation'[80] to guide any analysis of how international law is conceived and used.

Below, I characterise Colombian legal culture as part of the backdrop that qualifies the transplantation of ICL. This brief overview contributes to explaining why international law has taken the shape that it has in Colombia.

[79]Throughout 2009, 2010 and 2011, the *parapolítica* prosecution initiative dominated national headlines. See e.g. 'Cómo está la paropolítica en Colombia?' *Semana*, 4 June 2009, www.semana.com/nacion/justicia/articulo/como-esta-parapolitica-colombia/103801-3; 'La foto de la parapolítica de 2010 a 2014' *La Silla Vacía*, 13 March 2014, lasillavacia.com/historia/la-foto-de-la-parapolitica-de-2010-2014-46856. The lead investigator in the *parapolítica* cases was named person of the year by leading news media: see e.g. 'Iván Velásquez: El juzgador' *El Espectador*, 20 December 2007, www.elespectador.com/impreso/cuadernilloa/especiales/personajes-del-ano-2007/articuloimpreso-ivan-velasquez-el-juzgador.
[80]Zumbansen (n 9) 324.

First, the legal culture in Colombia is well developed as compared with other states in the Latin American region. The Colombian legal system is nominally liberal and is influenced by a wide array of Western-bound legal thought. Though embedded in the continental European tradition, some common law influence can be detected, particularly in matters relating to managerial efficiency, a growing tendency to study the 'law of judges' (value of legal precedent), the implementation of oral proceedings, and the adoption of a (tempered) accusatory model in the criminal process.

Second, the Colombian legal culture is characterised by the fact that the law in Colombia acts as the remedy for societal needs and law is employed in public policy responses to most issues. Colombian governments espouse a high dose of legalism.

Third, law is conceived as a static system. Rarely are dimensions beyond the black-letter law considered. The dynamic dimension of the law – that is, its application through routine and practice – is seldom considered, though this dimension wields a heavy hand in the way the law is experienced. Pernicious and covert activity clouds the entire justice system in Colombia, especially the administration of criminal justice. Though corruption in the administration of justice is not only a Colombian phenomenon, its incidence is quite striking. In cases addressing complex criminality, the existence of 'dirty hands' in the 'business' of doing justice is not a rare occurrence.

Finally, the law is applied in exceptional ways in Colombia but there is sense of normalcy. Though the government no longer appeals to the formal suspension or derogation of the law through the formal declaration of a 'state of exception', it does rule exceptionally through the Constitution, driven by self-proclaimed necessity.[81] Described by Giorgio Agamben, this form of bending (or breaking) the law makes the state of exception appear permanent.[82] Appealing to a state of necessity in public affairs, the government invokes the law.[83] This practice is omnipresent in Colombia, given the extreme social inequality, the extended use of violence to respond to social conflict, the effects of the protracted war, and the acts of organised criminality. In the face of extreme poverty and all-out war, law is generally present and offers a formal yet inoperative solution to a social problem, such as the forced displacement of persons.[84]

These four characteristics of Colombian lawyering taint the way ICL is received and then used in legal practice in the country. Some openness exists in

[81]Giorgio Agamben, *States of Exception* (University of Chicago Press, 2005) 26: 'The modern state of exception is … an attempt to include the exception itself within the juridical order by crating a zone of indistinction in which fact and law coincide.'

[82]'[I]n conformity with a continuing tendency in all Western democracies, the declaration of the state of exception has gradually been replaced by an unprecedented generalisation of the paradigm of security as the normal technique of government.' *Ibid*, 14.

[83]*Ibid*, 32–40.

[84]See, for example, the legal regime regulating the prevention of forced displacement: Law 387 of 1997.

relation to international law, however formalism and lack of training make its reception difficult. Through the following examples, based on decades of experience and research in Colombia, I illustrate the implications of legal education and culture for the reception, conception and application of ICL.

For example, consider that most Colombian lawyers did not study international public law as part of their legal education; more recent generations might be an exception, but the approach to the course is formal. Few know how to conduct research in the field and only a minute proportion will properly address all sources of international law. Colombian universities offer masters programmes and graduate level courses on international human rights law and humanitarian law. These programs elaborate on substantive developments, such as the jurisprudence of the Inter-American Court of Human Rights on indigenous rights or women's rights. Few of these programs cover the basics of public international law, such as sources and evidence in international law, the relationship between international law and municipal law, and the regime of state responsibility. Debates tend to favour the philosophical over the practical, and methods of research are rarely taught. If this holds true for the younger generations of Colombian lawyers, the effects are compounded in relation to more senior lawyers and those that are comfortably buried in the bureaucratic judicial apparatus.

The lack of access to primary sources and the limited diversity of commentators hinder the proper application of ICL. Most Colombians speak only Spanish, which becomes a very serious limitation in relation to the general approach to public international law and to ICL, given that most authoritative sources are produced in English and French. This problem is not so marked in relation to IHL or human rights law, as some material in those areas is produced in Spanish. The few ICL commentators who do write in Spanish are enthusiastically circulated and tend to cover the entire field.

Additionally, the nascent and still uncertain development of ICL globally creates many problems for its reception at the local level. Colombian lawyers relate to ICL as if it were an established and unambiguous area of law, ignoring the fact that it is a body of law that is relatively new, responds to hybrid formation (as it '*derives its origin from* and continuously draws upon' IHL, human rights law and national criminal law), and is subject to abrupt changes, responding to sporadic and inconsistent development.[85] Authorised interpreters of ICL and distinguished jurists have different interpretations of the law. The general reach of the decisions adopted by the two ad hoc international tribunals is questioned, and the ICC has signalled that it will make its own way based on the Rome Statute. If all these elements represent hurdles for international lawyers dedicated to the direct application of ICL, they can become barriers for national lawyers operating under a different logic and having to deal with the specificities of due process at

[85]Antonio Cassese, *International Criminal Law* (Oxford University Press, 2nd. ed. 2008) 4-10 (emphasis in original).

the local level. In the face of such obstacles, there are two simple alternatives for Colombian lawyers: one, steer clear of anything that resembles ICL, or two, turn to what resembles a national criminal code, the Rome Statute. This second option is the most prevalent in Colombia; it is also quite problematic.

Consider the implication of this option, that is, treating the Rome Statute as though it is a universal criminal code. This assumption is wrong, as it misinterprets the nature of the treaty and annuls the vast majority of the field of ICL, particularly its foundations which give it cogency and purpose. As is well known, state obligations regarding accountability for core crimes derive not only from the Rome Statute but also from multiple human rights and humanitarian law treaties, as well as from customary law. This use of the Rome Statute annuls much of the richness of ICL. Additionally, it has serious implications for due process, particularly when applied to crimes committed prior to the Rome Statute's entry into force, as we will see in the following section.

This commentary on the effect of Colombian lawyering on the use and abuse of ICL closes our consideration of cultural and political factors that are at play in the diffusion of ICL in the Colombian justice system. Those studying ICL *stricto sensu* do not concern themselves with such elements. Whether considered as context or essence, the elements presented in the first three sections of this paper have played a crucial role in the way international law – international human rights law, IHL and ICL – shapes Colombian legal practice and how the Colombian response is shaping international law and institutions. If conducted in other national jurisdictions, this type of analysis would yield points of convergence and divergence. These elements would help to explain how ICL acquires particular contours through indirect application by judicial authorities.

4. Colombian justice and the twisted take on ICL

This section points to a few pressing areas of misapplication of ICL that derive from the domestic criminal repression of conduct amounting to core crimes. Though many internationalists generally praise the use of ICL in domestic proceedings, much of its use in Colombia is problematic and incorporates distortions in the way law is conceived and used.

A reflection of the erratic results of the international pressure to have national courts apply ICL is evident in the following self-conscious reference made by the Supreme Court's Criminal Chamber when reviewing whether a prosecutor had proceeded correctly in precluding a criminal investigation against a general who had been charged with 'conspiracy to commit crimes' in collusion with paramilitary forces. The Court found that, since crimes against humanity had been alleged, its decision had to be oriented

> *at all costs*, to avoid impunity for the crimes allegedly committed and, thereby, *to demonstrate to the international community that intervention by the international criminal justice system is not necessary* since Colombia is capable of trying those

responsible for such crimes and imposing the criminal sanctions determined by national criminal law for such crimes.[86]

This statement serves as a testament to the well-intentioned efforts of some justices in the struggle against impunity; however, it also stands as evidence of misunderstood pressure that leads to distortions of the law. The bar to the prosecution against the General was lifted and the investigation was reinstated. The military officer in question, euphemistically known as 'The Pacifier of Urabá', was eventually convicted in 2012 for another crime – a 1997 murder of an Afro-Colombian social leader in the Urabá region, in the north of Colombia.[87] Putting the criminal guilt of the convicted General aside, the Supreme Court went down a slippery slope in reaching its decision: it cited the Rome Statute as one of its sources to demonstrate that the 'conspiracy to commit crimes' that took place in 1996 and 1997 could be equated to a crime against humanity. Though the Court was dealing with an inchoate offence that was outside the temporal jurisdiction of the Rome Statue, it referenced this treaty to reach its decision. Fortunately, the Supreme Court also cited other sources of international law that do not present the temporal validity problem, though the decision still illustrates the type of distortion that can be generated when trying to appease the international community 'at all costs'.

Under pressure, many prosecutors and judges conduct their business in order to avoid the intervention of the ICC. In the wake of overarching impunity, the pressure is appreciated; however, the 'at-all-costs' implication should be a source of growing concern. When the cost is a quirky decision that invokes international law for symbolic purposes, criticisms can be set aside. But when ICL is used in ways that distort the operation of a legal system and produce due process violations, its transplantation needs to be put in check.

ICL and the ICC pressure mechanism can surely contribute to effective domestic prosecution of conduct that could be subsumed under international crimes. However, their paramount potential lies in the practical and methodological dimensions of criminal prosecution rather than the black-letter law itself, as conveyed through effective prosecutorial strategies, appropriate case management practices, pioneering evidence gathering and processing techniques, and innovative communication and outreach programmes.[88] Unfortunately, the practical dimensions of ICL have not reached the Colombian criminal justice system. For now, it is

[86]Corte Suprema de Justicia, Sala de Casación Penal, Proceso No 30510, 11 March 2009, Justice Yesid Ramírez Bastidas (translated from Spanish original).
[87]Juzgado Octavo Penal del Circuito Especializado, Rad 2009-063, Sentencia por homicidio contra Rito Alejo del Río, 23 August 2012.
[88]Two simple and accessible publications that provide references to these types of practices are: UNHCHR, *Rule of Law Tools for Post Conflict States: Prosecution Initiatives* (OHCHR, 2006), UN Doc HR/PUB/06/4; and International Criminal Tribunal for the former Yugoslavia (ICTY), *ICTY Manual on Developed Practices* (ICTY and UNICRI, 2009).

inundated with the bombastic use of ICL with very little legal purpose, or its overtly warped application to achieve some procedural or political goal.

ICL-induced rhetoric has tainted a wide array of cases within the administration of the criminal justice system in Colombia. In this section, three trends of flagrant misapplication of ICL by Colombian judicial authorities are exposed: (1) the distortion of the concept of crimes against humanity to avoid the application of statutes of limitations; (2) the alteration of the category of crimes against humanity to make it extensive to a domestic inchoate offence; and (3) the transplantation of discretionary practices used by the prosecution in international tribunals into the national regime, so as to diminish national backlogs.

Many other instances of misapplication of ICL exist in Colombian legal practice, but the chosen areas are illustrative of at least two points. One is that the praise for the Colombian experience is often misinformed, and the second is that domestic processes encompassing international core crimes offer propitious ground for the exploration of TCL.

Proclaiming crimes against humanity to avoid statutes of limitations from tolling

The first area of concern is related to the abuse by Colombian judicial authorities of the international rule of non-applicability of statutory limitations to crimes against humanity.[89] As is well known, this procedural guarantee was conceived to combat impunity for offences committed in pursuance of state policy or practice, including through the operation of the justice system to cover up criminal conduct. The overarching interest of the international rule is to promote the effective punishment of crimes against humanity.[90]

In the past five years, the Colombian prosecuting authority (Fiscalía General de la Nación, FGN) made several announcements that purportedly demonstrated its commitment to the struggle against impunity for crimes that were subsumed under international core crimes. In 2009, the Prosecutor General at the time stated that 'impunity cannot exist in Colombia in cases of gross human rights violations and breaches of international humanitarian law'.[91] Based on this statement, the head of the FGN announced that a series of cases had been declared crimes against humanity, thus eliminating the application of the statute of limitations. On its face, the statement merits praise; however, it was applied to cases that do

---

[89]Convention on the Non-Applicability of Statutory Limitations to War Crimes and Crimes against Humanity, GA Res 2391 (XXIII), annex, UN Doc A/7218 (1968) (entered into force 11 November 1970).
[90]*Ibid*, Preamble.
[91]FGN, 'Fiscal General (e) dice: no puede haber impunidad por violación de Derechos Humanos y DIH', 26 November 2009, www.fiscalia.gov.co/colombia/noticias/fiscal-general-e-dice-no-puede-haber-impunidad-por-violacion-de-derechos-humanos-y-dih/ (translation by the author).

not satisfy the criteria necessary for classifying an offence as a crime against humanity. In the long term, this practice distorts the definition of the international crime and introduces inconsistency in the domestic procedural system, as it dishonestly circumvents the limitation period of a criminal case.

The Colombian national prosecuting authority boasted of the categorisation of the 1989 assassination of presidential candidate Luis Carlos Galan Sarmiento as a crime against humanity according to the Rome Statute.[92] Retroactive application of the Rome Statute is becoming commonplace in Colombia, as prosecutors and judges do not know how to deal with the absence of 'positive law' before 2002. They were thus exempt from the regular limitation period that applies to all criminal cases.[93] The authorities then added that this thesis could be applied autonomously to other cases, depending on each independent prosecutor.[94] The statement was interpreted as a clear invitation to use the formula to avoid the statute of limitations tolling in other cases gone cold.

The 'crime against humanity' designation is given legal effect through prosecutorial decisions, adopted in a legal document subject to review. Prosecutors should analyse the merits of the case and present their finding based on legal argumentation. Though some exceptions exist, most decisions appeal to the retroactive use of the Rome Statute in order to categorise notorious murders as crimes against humanity.[95] To illustrate the practice, another example can be found in the 1984 murder of Rodrigo Lara Bonilla, the Minister of Justice at the time who was killed by hit men from the Medellin drug cartel.[96] Though some variation exists amongst the different cases, this 2012 resolution adopted by the prosecutor of a

---

[92]FGN, 'Crimen de Galán es un delito de lesa humanidad, explica Fiscal', 20 August 2009, www.fiscalia.gov.co/colombia/noticias/crimen-de-galan-es-un-delito-de-lesa-humanidad-explica-fiscal/ (translation by the author).

[93]The FGN announced that the declaration had been made in several other cases, including: the 1989 bombing of a national aircraft by the criminal organisation led by Pablo Escobar; the 1989 bombing of the presidential intelligence agency (Departamento Administrativo de Seguridad, DAS); the 1998 kidnapping of former President Andrés Pastrana; the 1998 homicide of a former Procurator General, Carlos Mauro Hoyos; the 1989 killing of a governor of Antioquia; the 1990 kidnapping and death of Luz Marina Montoya; the 1989 bombing of the offices of a national newspaper (*El Espectador*); and the 1990 kidnapping of Maruja Pachón and Beatriz Villamizar. See FGN (n 92); FGN, 'Homicidios de Lara Bonilla y de Low Murtra declarados crímenes de lesa humanidad', 18 July 2011, www.fiscalia.gov.co/colombia/noticias/homicidios-de-lara-bonilla-y-de-low-murtra-declarados-crimenes-de-lesa-humanidad/; and FGN, 'Fiscal General (e) dice' (n 91).

[94]FGN, 'Homicidios de Lara Bonilla y de Low Murtra' (n 93).

[95]This proposition was applied in relation to the murders of three prominent political figures: a presidential candidate (Luis Carlos Galán, killed in 1989), and two Ministers of Justice (Enrique Low Murtra, killed in 1991, and Rodrigo Lara Bonilla, killed in 1984). FGN, 'Homicidios de Lara Bonilla y de Low Murtra' (n 93).

[96]FGN, Unidad Nacional de Derechos Humanos y Derecho Internacional Humanitario, Fiscalía Octava Especializada, Proceso No 4321, Decisión sobre la declaratoria de lesa humanidad del homicidio de Rodrigo Lara Bonilla, 23 July 2012.

specialised prosecutorial unit concentrating on human rights cases offers an adequate frame of reference to examine the practice.

The resolution, a tortuous 60-page text,[97] was adopted to determine 'whether the April 30, 1984 homicide that was committed *against the humanity* of the then-Minister of Justice *Doctor* Rodrigo Lara Bonilla rises to the category of a crime *against humanity*'.[98] This issue arose because the statute of limitations for the criminal action was about to expire. Domestic (procedural or substantive) law does not contemplate this type of legal declaration. Therefore, the prosecutor appealed to international law through its incorporation in the Colombian Constitution. She declared that the 1984 homicide perpetrated by members of the Medellin cartel (Pablo Escobar's organisation) was a crime against humanity, thus removing the application of the statute of limitations to that particular homicide investigation.

The structure and content of the decision can be summarised as follows. Given the absence of a relevant domestic norm, the prosecutor uses the constitutional mechanism that incorporates international law 'in order to allow our positioning within the international juridical language'.[99] After providing an appalling account of how international law has been constitutionalised in Colombia,[100] the decision scurries through a historical account of the 'concept of crimes against humanity', starting with references to the Martens Clause of the 1899 Hague Convention with respect to the Laws and Customs to the War on Land and moving through various garbled historical events. Not a single legal source is cited directly; all references made are to Spanish-language ICL books.[101] The decision does not concentrate on disentangling the content of the relevant law at the moment of the commission of the crime.

After providing a version of the creation of the UN ad hoc tribunals (the International Criminal Tribunal for the former Yugoslavia (ICTY) and the International Criminal Tribunal for Rwanda (ICTR)), the prosecutor refers to the 1996 ICTY *Erdemovic* decision, citing a Colombian Supreme Court decision that provides a passage underscoring the emblematic angle of crimes against humanity as acts that are inhumane and demand punishment.[102] Immediately following the quote, the prosecutor states that in 1984, 'crimes against humanity existed as a

[97]Other similar decisions are nearly 200 pages in length.

[98]FGN (n 96) 'IV. Consideraciones de la Fiscalía'. The Spanish use of the word *humanidad*, meaning human body or corpulence, is rare and awkward. The repetition of the qualifier 'against humanity' is forced.

[99]*Ibid*.

[100]*Ibid*, 'El bloque de constitucionalidad'.

[101]For example, Jaime Cordoba Triviño, *Derecho penal internacional* (Ediciones Jurídicas Gustavo Ibáñez, 2001); Alejandro Ramelli Artega *et al*, *Jurisprudencia penal internacional aplicable en Colombia* (GiZ and Uniandes, 2011); Hector Olasolo, *Corte Penal Internacional* (Tirant lo Blanch, 2003).

[102]The citation of the Court is imprecise. I assume it refers to ICTY, *The Prosecutor v Drazen Erdemovic*, Trial Chamber, Judgement, Case No IT-96-22-T, 29 November 1996.

criminal offence with sufficient foreseeability and accessibility, according to national or international law'. The source of this statement is unclear. Nowhere in the decision does she conduct an analysis that allows us to determine what the status of the law was in the1980s, nor what definition is being used to define crimes against humanity.

Lastly, the historical narration addresses the adoption of the Rome Statute, which is presented as a universal criminal code. An extended discussion on how the treaty was ratified by Colombia is provided. She concludes this section with a transcription of Article 7 of the Rome Statute. The prosecutor then moves to set out the elements of the crime, utilising a hodgepodge of ICTR, ICTY and ICC wordage with little analysis, concluding that the Rome Statute 'codifies all principles and categories of crimes' and is 'the most complete and modern instrument' of ICL.

Factually, the decision shows how Lara Bonilla's homicide is linked to a long chain of heinous events – murders, kidnappings and bombings – attributed to the Medellin cartel. Given the ICL mélange, it is never clear what sources of law back the prosecutor's findings. Though she affirms deep in the text that the Rome Statute is *not* applicable to the events of 1984,[103] the entire analysis of whether Lara Bonilla's homicide should be considered a crime against humanity is based on Article 7 of the Rome Statute. She concludes that the leaders of the Medellin cartel 'planned, coordinated and executed multiple conducts described in Article 7.1 of the Rome Statute to achieve their goals', including the Lara Bonilla homicide. She supports this finding based partially on the fact that other prosecutors and the Colombian Supreme Court have also found that other cases were crimes against humanity. The decision ends with a finding of a 'common criminal plan' and some sort of *mens rea* attributable to the drug cartel as a whole. She thus declares the homicide an international crime and finds that the limitations period is inapplicable.[104]

This description of the decision appears *caricaturesque*; nevertheless, it is a succinct depiction that reflects the decision's structure and content fairly. The decision demonstrates very poor use of international law generally, and of ICL specifically. It lacks method and technique, as the appeal to ICL is mostly rhetorical. A deluge of unconnected ICL snippets replaces proper legal analysis. It shows how the Rome Statute is assimilated as a universal criminal code and applied retroactively. The resolution also illustrates the limitations that come with access to only Spanish-language sources and the circular references to other national decisions that have also misapplied ICL.

At no point does the decision address the significant issue of whether the acts of a drug cartel are included in the definition of crimes against humanity applicable to the events of 1984. In the end, what appears to be at work is a

[103] *Ibid*, 'El concepto de imprescriptibilidad en los delitos de lesa humanidad'.
[104] *Ibid*, 'Resuelve'.

formula that equates crimes against humanity with heinous and egregious conduct committed over a period of time. This type of equivalence is morally charged, but not legally based. There is no doubt that the crimes committed by the Medellin cartel were horrendous, but the egregiousness of the crimes does not make them international crimes. The consequence of the prosecutorial decision is to allow the continuing investigation of a crime that has not been investigated in 30 years. The decision masks the ineffectiveness of the Colombian justice system and drags out a resolution of the case. The most worrisome traits are the manipulation of ICL to achieve the result and the diffusion of mistaken concepts of ICL into Colombian practice, including an obscure definition of crimes against humanity. Recall that this practice is observable in many more decisions in order to reach the same goal.[105] It too has permeated the Colombian judiciary.[106]

Stretching crimes against humanity to contain conspiracy charges

The Colombian Supreme Court has toyed with ICL in the last decade. Its initial consideration of international law was limited to human rights and IHL, rendering important decisions establishing the lack of subject matter jurisdiction of the military tribunals over egregious violations[107] or overcoming procedural obstacles in criminal cases that had been subject to international human rights protection orders.[108] As presented earlier, the Supreme Court gained notoriety, more or less in 2007, as a result of the *parapolítica* trials and its decisions, standing as a court of appeals, in the Justice and Peace proceedings. Prior to this moment, the Colombian Supreme Court was not in the public spotlight.

In this context, the Criminal Cassation Chamber began to develop a series of judgments that included the indirect application of ICL. Given the high standing of this Chamber in the judicial hierarchy, these decisions impact the way the judicial system is perceived and how it proceeds. The application of ICL by the Supreme Court has won the praise of the international community.[109] The justices have

[105]See notes 93 and 95, referring to other decisions applying a similar logic.

[106]As shown in a 2011 decision adopted by a criminal appeals court concerning a 1985 case. See Tribunal Superior del Distrito Judicial de Bogotá, Sala Penal, Rad 10010704002-1999-04119-01, aprobado Acta No 125/2010, 8 September 2010. The case refers to the violent siege of the Palace of Justice by a Colombian guerrilla group, M-19. Applying the Rome Statute retroactively to 1985, the Court of Appeals of Bogotá determined that the criminal conduct of M-19 could be considered to amount to crimes against humanity. *Ibid*, 16–18. The author of the decision went on to become a Supreme Court Justice.

[107]See Corte Suprema de Justicia, Sala de Casación Penal, Rad No 25630, Justice Sigifredo Espinosa, 11 April 2007.

[108]See e.g. Corte Suprema de Justicia, Sala de Casación Penal, Rad No 24841, Justice Javier Zapata Ortiz, 6 March 2008.

[109]For example, former ICC Prosecutor Luis Moreno Ocampo states that no country is more active and diligent than Colombia on matters relating to transitional justice and praises the

interpreted the acclaim as a success and have increased their reliance on ICL. Unfortunately, the application of ICL is not in its best form. In fact, the Supreme Court, which should lead by example, is producing outlandish decisions and morphing important notions of ICL.

One of the most concerning developments is related to the interpretation given to the domestic crime of conspiracy. "Conspiracy to commit a crime"[110] is an inchoate offence that criminalises preparatory acts; it has its roots in 1970s national security doctrine.[111] Since that time, prosecutors and judges have used this broadly and vaguely defined criminal offence as a wildcard charge. In the absence of evidence of specific criminal activity, members of armed groups or organised crime gangs are charged with this subordinate offence, raising many due process issues. Nonetheless, the Supreme Court decided to scale up its reproach of this offence in the context of cases addressing paramilitary activity and declared it a crime against humanity in April 2008.[112] Several complaints have been raised on this classification and the Supreme Court continues to espouse the original position, contained in a 2008 decision.[113]

That case reached the Supreme Court as an appeal against a decision to exclude a member of a paramilitary group, Manuel Enrique Torregrosa, from the Justice and Peace proceedings, following a request for extradition by the US government on drug charges. The high court denied Torregrosa's exclusion from the Justice and Peace Law because, on the merits of the case, the justices considered that the legal criteria had not been satisfied. The Court appealed (at length) to international human rights treaties and resolutions, and found that the justice system has to protect victims' rights to truth, justice and reparation.[114] The case could have been decided on these grounds alone; however, the Supreme Court opted to take ICL down a slippery slope.

In a brief but messy fashion, the Supreme Court used ICL to reach the conclusion that the domestic crime of conspiracy (*concierto para delinquir*) is a crime against humanity.[115] The court advanced the following reasoning:

---

role of the Supreme Court in the *parapolítica* cases. See 'Ningún país hace tanto en justicia transicional como Colombia' El Tiempo, 15 September 2013, www.eltiempo.com/archivo/documento/CMS-13064207.

[110]The crime is defined in the national criminal code in article 340. Código Penal, Ley 599 de 2000, Art 340: 'Concierto para delinquir.'

[111]See Decreto 1923 de 1978, Estatuto de Seguridad, Art 3, providing the initial definition of the national crime of conspiracy that was adopted under the cloak of the National Security doctrine.

[112]Corte Suprema de Justicia, Sala de Casación Penal, Proceso No 29472, Justice Yesid Ramírez Bastidas, 10 April 2008.

[113]Corte Suprema de Justicia, Sala de Casación Penal, Proceso No 39665, Justice Fernando Alberto Castro Caballero, 7 November 2012, concerning an appeal in a Justice and Peace case against José de Jesús Pérez Jiménez and others.

[114]Corte Suprema de Justicia, Sala de Casación Penal, Proceso No 29472, 31–44.

[115]*Ibid*, 23–29.

> Considering that the wrongdoings committed by the [Justice and Peace] nominees relate to enforced disappearances, forced displacement, torture and politically-motivated homicides, etc., and since those misdeeds are understood as being contained in the category of crimes against humanity, such a categorisation must be extended to the crime of *aggravated conspiracy*, given that the criminal plan is designed for the purpose of committing such crimes.[116]

The high court backed this holding by erroneously inferring that the Rome Statute criminalises acts preparatory to the commission of crimes against humanity. Its reasoning, which is faulty both in interpretation of the treaty as well as in the syllogistic process, runs along the following lines: the Rome Statute takes into account both the conduct of perpetrators of crimes against humanity and the criminal motives behind such action, 'therefore preparatory conduct leading to the commission of crimes, including both the agreement itself as well as activity oriented at its realisation must be equally punished'.[117] The Supreme Court improperly based this stance on an English-language book written by a distinguished scholar, as cited in an Argentinean decision.[118] The foreign court decision is fascinating in itself; however, the Colombian court only cited it to get to the textbook and did not analyse any of its content, authoritative value or relevancy.[119] Cherif Bassiouni's text on crimes against humanity, the indirectly cited source, is an authoritative monograph on the subject. However, unlike the Colombian Court, Bassiouni does not sustain that the crime of conspiracy can be likened to a crime against humanity. In its argumentation, the Colombian court jumbled forms of liability with substantive crimes.

The Colombian High Court also wrongly supported the notion of conspiracy as a crime against humanity, based on the ICTR *Alfred Musema* judgment.[120] It is unclear why the Colombian Supreme Court cited this decision,

---

[116]*Ibid*, 23.

[117]*Ibid*, 24.

[118]*Ibid*, citing Cherif Bassiouni, *Crimes against Humanity in International Law* (Kluwer, 1999) as cited in República Federal de Argentina, Corte Suprema de la Nación, Causa no 259, *Arancibia Clavel, Enrique Lautaro s/ homicidio calificado y asociación ilícita y otros*, 24 August 2004.

[119] *Arancibia Clavel, ibid*. The decision relates to Enrique Arancibia Clavel, an agent of the Chilean intelligence structure who served in the 1970s as a liaison with the Argentinean authorities. Clavel participated in several crimes committed pursuant to *Operación Condor* and other Dirty War crimes. It is a landmark decision in the ongoing struggle against impunity in that country. It provides pertinent considerations by the Argentinean justices regarding the crime of illicit association to commit crimes, in connection with egregious conduct. The Argentinean decision contains relevant considerations regarding the use of international law, the dogmatic structure of the crimes, and practical evidentiary issues in order to address crimes against humanity as crimes of state.

[120]UN International Criminal Tribunal for Rwanda (ICTR), Trial Chamber I, Judgement, *Prosecutor versus Alfred Musema*, ICTR-96-13-T, 27 January 2000.

particularly, since the ICTR Chamber held that Musema was not responsible for conspiracy to commit genocide. He was found guilty of committing genocide and crimes against humanity (extermination and rape), pursuant to the ICTR Statute.

The Supreme Court then proceeded to cite a series of human rights treaties that have been incorporated into the Colombian regime as further evidence that the domestic offence of conspiracy should be treated as a crime against humanity. It blended the international obligation to suppress genocide based on the Genocide Convention and the criminalisation of the conspiracy to commit crimes against humanity.[121] The Court then intermingled the substantive offence of conspiracy with various liability theories in which conspiring to commit a crime can lead to individual criminal responsibility. To back its proposition, it incorrectly cited the special human rights conventions relating to torture and disappearance that bind states to adopt criminal law to punish these acts.[122] The Court recalled that the 1984 UN Torture Convention establishes that 'Each State Party shall ensure that an attempt to commit torture and … an act by any person which constitutes complicity or participation in torture [is an offence under its criminal law]'.[123] The Court offered no analysis whatsoever; it referred to the treaties, quoted the respective articles and simply left the rest to the imagination. The Colombian Court's international mirage spread to the individual criminal liability regime of the Rome Statute, under Article 25,[124] to reaffirm its position that conspiracy is a crime against humanity.

Based on this improper use of international law, the Supreme Court determined that the domestic offence of conspiracy to commit crimes should be considered a crime against humanity, and thus all the procedural and substantive consequences were engaged.[125] The legal and political repercussions of this judgment are immense: consider, for example, an eventual peace process in which the ramifications of this judgment impede the concession of amnesties for anyone implicated in the abstract and ambiguous offence of conspiring to commit crimes as a result of their membership of an armed group that committed heinous crimes. To further underscore the gravity of these mistakes, remember that the highest court within the national criminal jurisdiction adopted the judgment and it influences most judges.

[121]Corte Suprema de Justicia, Sala de Casación Penal, Proceso No 29472, 26 citing Convention on the Prevention and Punishment of the Crime of Genocide, adopted by UNGA Resolution 260 (III) A, 9 December 1948, Art 3 adopted by Colombia pursuant to Law 28 of 1959.

[122]*Ibid*, 26–27.

[123]UN Convention against Torture and Other Cruel, Inhuman or Degrading Treatment or Punishment, A/RES/39/46, 10 December 1984.

[124]Corte Suprema de Justicia, Sala de Casación Penal, Proceso No 29472, 28–29.

[125]*Ibid*, 25.

Case selection and prioritisation: applying best practices or conducting dodgy mimicry?

The final example of mimicry by the Colombian judicial authorities relates to the recent national adoption of a selection and prioritisation regime that was initially designed and applied by international tribunals to select the cases over which they would exercise jurisdiction.[126] This practice transplants the colourful use of ICL language and allegedly seeks to apply the best practices of the struggle against impunity by promoting judicial efficiency. The problem with such a transplantation is that national justice systems and international tribunals do not operate under the same logic. This practice is of direct evidence of what Boister characterises as 'the structured diffusion of legal norms through socialisation processes marked by emulation and persuasion, and sometimes by manipulation and coercion'.[127]

The ICC and the two UN ad hoc tribunals were at liberty to pick and choose their cases, and the residual caseload was left to be dealt with by the various national systems. Picking and choosing cases is at the core of success strategies for international initiatives. However, handpicking cases is not an option in national jurisdictions. Ultimately, national prosecuting authorities need to deal with the entire panoply of serious crime under their jurisdiction.

Properly evaluating its caseload can help a national prosecuting authority organise and prioritise its efforts. Unwanted cases of serious crime cannot be passed on to a residual mechanism, and stagnant accumulated caseloads need to be addressed head on. The Colombian regime is based on the principle of legality, with specific exceptions allowed under a judicially controlled principle of prosecutorial discretion.[128] National authorities are thus under the obligation to investigate and prosecute serious crimes, especially when they impact basic human rights.

In what appears to be a commendable effort to inject dynamism into many languishing criminal investigations, the current head of the national prosecuting authority (FGN), Eduardo Montealegre, has promised to revamp the entire criminal justice system by introducing the international practice of selection and prioritisation. When launching this policy, he stated:

> The current model of investigation based on a case-by-case (approach) is not sustainable. The leap proposed requires us to stop examining cases in an isolated fashion and establish connections amongst various criminal acts, in order to get to those most responsible in the criminal chain.[129]

---

[126] See Drumbl (n 6) 123–48.

[127] Boister, this volume.

[128] Constitución Política de Colombia, Art 250, allowing prosecutors, based on specific legal regulations, to suspend prosecution in cases with minimal social impact or conditionally suspend criminal action based on a balancing test of multiple interests involved. The prosecutorial decisions are subject to judicial review.

[129] 'Así será la estrategia de la Fiscalía contra la impunidad' *El Tiempo*, 25 October 2012, www.eltiempo.com/archivo/documento/CMS-12333082 (my translation).

Former and current ICTY and ICC functionaries, and very competent Colombian constitutional and criminal lawyers, provided qualified advice.[130] However, as will be revealed, this perfect pitch does not amount to sound practice.

The selection and prioritisation policy was adopted in October 2012 through an FGN institutional directive.[131] The order is supported by a solid introduction on due diligence standards applicable to criminal investigations developed by the Inter-American human rights protection system.[132] It also includes wide reference to the practice of international criminal tribunals,[133] and provides examples of prioritisation (not selection) as reflected in comparative criminal legal practice.[134] Lastly, as part of its conceptual support, the policy paper includes a section on constitutional law that seemingly supports the selection and prioritisation of criminal cases in Colombia.[135] After setting out this frame of reference, the document enumerates subjective and objective criteria for the selection and prioritisation of criminal cases and lays out a new operational structure by which the criteria are to be applied.[136]

Unlike other administrative and judicial acts commented on in this article, this directive is technically informed and was carefully crafted to appear pristine. Who would not support an initiative aimed at introducing coherency into the administration of criminal justice or giving a jump-start to a stagnant apparatus? Most national and international observers have backed the process: to the internationalists, it is expressed in a key that is familiar; to those in Colombia, it sounds new, dynamic and promising. However, at least two flaws in the selection and prioritisation arrangement adopted by the FGN tend to indicate that instead of promoting greater diligence in criminal investigation, its implementation can conceal waning judicial activity.

The first problem arises from the dual reference to selection and prioritisation. Despite the fact that these two notions appear to go hand in hand, they are separate concepts and the judicial effect of their application is quite distinct. Prioritisation concentrates resources on particular cases to obtain results. Once the results are achieved, new priorities can be established based on strategic or operational considerations. Selection is a less desired institution in the administration of criminal justice. Cases that are not selected are left out and remain in the growing cold case

[130]See e.g. FGN, *La priorización: memorias de los talleres para la construcción de los criterios del nuevo sistema de investigación penal* (Imprenta Nacional de Colombia, 2013); FGN, Relatoría del Seminario internacional 'Importancia de la construcción de contextos en las investigaciones judiciales', 14–17 May 2013, www.fiscalia.gov.co/colombia/wp-content/uploads/Seminario-Internacional-Construcción-de-Contextos.pdf.
[131]FGN, Directiva No 01, 4 October 2012 '*por medio de la cual se adoptan unos criterios de priorización de situaciones y casos, y se crea un nuevo sistema de investigación penal y de gestión de aquellos en la Fiscalía General de la Nación*'.
[132]*Ibid*, 4–11.
[133]*Ibid*, 11–16.
[134]*Ibid*, 16–18.
[135]*Ibid*, 18–24.
[136]*Ibid*, 24–34.

docket. The policy has not addressed crucial questions that stem from the exclusion of specific cases in the very complex web of criminality that ravishes Colombia and the concrete political interests that make the system turn. With so many unrepresented victims of gross violations, the selection paradigm will mean exclusion for many – especially the most disenfranchised.

The second problem derives from the fact that the FGN policy was allegedly designed to be applied exceptionally under a political transition from war to peace, although in practice the policy has been put in place before the announced transition takes place and applies across the board to all criminal cases.[137] According to one of its proponents, the selection-prioritisation scheme allows the Colombian state to comply with its international obligations 'as long as it does not exonerate from total liability those persons with the highest responsibility in the most serious crimes, [thus] not impeding the design of a hybrid system of justice that implies some degree of impunity based on the genuine purpose of reconstructing a society'.[138] This statement is sparklingly frank: the system was designed in the context of an eventual peace deal, to produce impunity whilst passing muster on the international front.

The prosecutorial policy, though submerged in the rhetoric of transitional justice, was designed and put into practice without any temporal or material connection to a transitional moment.[139] Though the logic of the Colombian selection-prioritisation scheme is presented as a sort of exceptional/transitional justice mechanism that allows departure from a legality-driven system in order to attain a negotiated peace settlement, its application is extending to the entire system – including all subject matters and persons – before the peace process has materialised. This exceptional response for exceptional times is being applied in the *exceptional normality* of the Colombian reality throughout the criminal legal system. To put it another way, the prosecutorial authority is applying an *exceptional* mechanism that is justified under a *state of necessity*.[140]

A special prosecutorial initiative may prove useful in the near future in the context of an eventual peace deal, but for now the scheme adopted by the FGN is overtly manipulating ICL and is being used to circumvent standard procedure.

---

[137]Constitución Política de Colombia, Art transitorio 66, approved by Acto legislativo 01 de 2012. The reform provides the executive and Congress with special powers in the framework of an eventual peace deal to adopt transitional justice tools, including a special system of selection and prioritisation of criminal cases. Nonetheless, its provisions have not been regulated, and the current selection and prioritisation scheme adopted and implemented by the FGN is outside its remit.

[138]Sebastian Machado, 'La priorización: experiencias comparadas y límites en el derecho internacional' in FGN, Huellas, No 57, August 2012, 57–68, at 68.

[139]The Colombian government is engaged in peace talks with the guerrillas, but the prosecutorial policy is not linked to that initiative. Peace talks with the Fuerzas Armadas Revolucionarias de Colombia, Ejército del Pueblo (FARC-EP) were formalised in August 2012 and are ongoing. Peace talks with the ELN have been informal, until now.

[140]See Agamben (n 81).

This policy is a clear-cut example of overt manipulation of practices familiar to internationalists. Instead of maximising the value of justice, the strategy being put in place, dressed up in ICL apparel, is exploring a minimum-effort logic to get away with impunity.

This critique may be unpopular. Most judicial operators in Colombia do not understand the issues that are at stake. They see the use of ICL as a progressive tendency and one that should not be questioned as it assists in combating impunity. Nonetheless, this improper use of ICL, whether conscious or unwitting, translates over time into a loss of cogency and violation of the rights of victims. The transplantation of a practice and rhetoric that might make sense in international and hybrid tribunals to a national jurisdiction distorts standards of justice by deviously lowering the bar of due diligence at home. If the practice is not corrected, international law will have been used to whitewash the Colombian justice system. The fact that the ICTY and the ICTR proceeded by selecting cases did not extend such a privilege to the concerned national jurisdictions. Colombian authorities clearly need a prosecutorial strategy to address the complex caseload – establishing priorities and choosing cases to meet goals will be required. But selecting certain cases of disappearances, for example, and leaving others aside, as international tribunals have done, is not an option under a proper interpretation of international law. This type of 'mimicry', as labelled by Drumbl,[141] is counterproductive to the struggle against impunity.

The legal issues at stake in the previous three examples involve important national and international interests, particularly since they are being resolved by appealing to human rights and ICL rhetoric. The practices described demonstrate that the national prosecution and adjudication of conduct that would be subsumed internationally under core crimes are processes that are not regulated and ordained by ICL, but rather subject to twists and turns in the process of the indirect application of ICL through national law. Applied to various national jurisdictions, the TCL lens could contribute to understanding these processes and provide an insight into the relation between ICL and the national prosecution of core crimes.

5. The rising risks of unchecked domestication of ICL and the unexplored potential of the TCL lens

The internationally motivated struggle against impunity cannot remain impervious to the fact that administering justice is national more than international business – due to both frequency and the nature of the enterprise. The ICC-centred take on ICL endorses top-down solutions that are not achieving the promised end to impunity of gross crimes. Instead, national jurisdictions are asked to confront impunity domestically, developing the so-called system of international justice in a very disorganised and often incoherent fashion.

---

[141] See Drumbl (n 6).

If this proposition is accepted, academics and activists promoting the struggle against impunity at the international level need to become more cognisant of all the entangled processes taking place in the local sphere. Cultural and legal pluralism are at play in the repression of international core crimes. The ICC-centred recipe has demonstrated its limits as a direct enforcement scheme. The attainment of the grandiloquent goals that framed the adoption of the Rome Statute – such as not allowing serious crimes to go unpunished or putting an end to impunity for the perpetrators of these crimes[142] – requires a reorientation of international efforts (strategically and technically) to push states to address atrocity on the home front. The current use of ICL in many jurisdictions, including Colombia, responds more to fetishism than to the aim of satisfying ICL's goals. In the process, key concepts have been displaced, and national political interests have supplanted global justice interests.

Given that the Rome Statute is not a universal criminal code, its purpose as an instrument that can assist in coordinating national practice and sovereign positions needs to be recovered. However, this task requires that international attention shift from the vertical paradigm, in which the ICC stands above state parties, to a horizontal paradigm, in which states make or break the logic of the purported global governance scheme through the exercise of their national jurisdiction. Concentration on the horizontal dynamics requires cultural fluency in each national setting and demands that internationalists that want to contribute to the struggle against impunity become imbued with local conditions – a step that will require the limits of despised parochialism to be questioned. Moreover, another obstacle in the proposed shift is likely to rise out of the fact that the efforts of most internationalists are concentrated, understandably, on saving the ICC mother ship from sinking.

Undoubtedly, both positive and negative effects have resulted from the ICC model. However, along with the positive repercussions of bringing the struggle against impunity 'out of the closet', the ICC-motivated drive to put ICL on display – for show and tell purposes – in national jurisdictions such as Colombia is generating distortions that need to be addressed. My emphasis on the adverse effects is due primarily to an unjustifiably long honeymoon period with an ever-emerging global criminal justice system. Some margin of error was to be expected at the outset; however, after more than a decade of mulling it over, the complementarity regime should be standing on firmer ground by now.

The unquestioned application of ICL in national jurisdictions as an end in and of itself is debilitating ICL's bite in the struggle against impunity, and altering basic principles and guarantees of due process. Instead of celebrating the fact that a Supreme Court in one country or another uses international law to label a vicious crime as a crime against humanity, the purpose and the role of international law need to be explicitly recovered. Simple questions such as 'why do we need

[142] See Rome Statute (n 3), Preamble.

international law?' need to have clear answers before the ICL arsenal is mobilised. Some national legal regimes are perfectly fit to prosecute, adjudicate and sanction international core crimes without ever using the international lingo. Believe it or not: criminal justice for atrocious crimes can be achieved without being doused in ICL!

The projection of ICL in national jurisdictions is due in part to pressure placed by various (arguably well-intentioned) international players hungry to see ICL do its magic. The process has played out dismally in Colombia. ICL embellishes political discourse, victims' claims, laws, regulations and case law, amongst other things. ICL flabbergasts with its presence in the legal and political arenas. For now, however, beyond a large dose of rhetorical punch it does not add much to the justice equation. The result is an almighty incongruous labyrinth submerged in resident legal inventiveness with undesired effects for accountability of atrocities and respect for due process guarantees. It is almost as if the means (of using ICL) has trumped the purpose (of combating impunity). Internationalists that promote ICL appear to have got their fix in Colombia; the Colombian legal system has not.

I contend that the TCL lens can help pull ICL out of the shadows of domestication and parochialism. In closing, I underscore some of the possible routes of action.

The TCL inquiry can be complementary to the study of ICL *stricto sensu* and comparative criminal law by concentrating on two angles. First, how do states indirectly apply ICL when responding to (international) crime in their national jurisdictions, and secondly, how does national practice underwrite the global system of international criminal justice predicated on the Rome Statute?

The first line of inquiry becomes intermingled with comparative criminal law, as it concentrates on the 'vertical component in TCL' – the 'national laws (that) constitute the legal normative goal of the system because they enable the suppression of criminal activities domestically'.[143] Comparative criminal law analyses juxtapose jurisdictions to understand ways in which various states respond to crime. This type of study is rich in the Latin American region, given that the various national jurisdictions share languages, traditions, influences and trends. The transnational lens could add a useful and novel dimension to cross-jurisdictional studies of core crime prosecution by examining the 'agency of international law' in the process of suppressing and prosecuting these crimes of international concern.

The second line of inquiry should concentrate on the purported global governance regime that was set in motion by the Rome Statute, 12 years after its entry into force. TCL can contribute to transcending the simplistic conception of the Rome Statute as a universal criminal code. Given TCL's scope, it can promote reflection on the use of the Rome Statute as an instrument that assists in

[143]Boister, this volume.

'coordinating sovereign positions'[144] on the prosecution and adjudication of crimes of international concern. Originally, the ICC system of complementarity was supposed to introduce a paradigm shift in international politics and law. However, its reach at the national level is precarious. Similarly, the ICC system theoretically transformed the way states and other actors, including individuals, conceived of security and justice both nationally and internationally. The effects of that transformation are unclear. Most of those studying ICL limit themselves to the ICC developments and do not concentrate on the 'horizontal component' of international law[145] according to which states continue to bear the primary duty to criminalise and adjudicate cases that could be subsumed under international core crimes.

As shown by the Colombian case, the TCL inquiry should be directed at the agents and the forces at play in both directions, as they influence the global system and as the global system influences them. States have a wide margin of appreciation regarding how to achieve international obligations related to core crimes and other discrete international crimes, such as torture or forced disappearances. Moreover, states meld their overall obligations under the Rome Statute with human rights treaties that contain criminalisation provisions.

Those concerned with TCL should examine the ways in which the promotion of the 'system of international criminal justice,' based on the ICC model of complementarity, is impacting national jurisdictions that stem from very different traditions and values. Concurrently, TCL scholars should also be concerned with the way national practice is contributing to shape this alleged system of global governance.

Some solutions to the problems can be sought at the national level, but others transcend the national scope and need to curb the ways in which the global system of criminal justice is being promoted, seemingly without governance. The TCL lens is particularly suited to examining both directions. It has been my contention throughout this case study that the transnational lens can assist in unmasking the de-territorialised scope and hybrid nature of the practice of law that is materialising through the uncontrolled diffusion of ICL and its domestication, in terms of its taming and subjugation, when applied to national jurisdictions wrestling with core crimes.

---

[144] *Ibid.*
[145] *Ibid.*

Governing the ungovernable: international relations, transnational cybercrime law, and the post-Westphalian regulatory state

Nicola Dalla Guarda*

Osgoode Hall Law School, York University, Toronto, Canada

In order to better understand the challenges facing transnational criminal law, the paper considers six regional anti-cybercrime regimes and traces their development and content. Insights from international relations theory and practical issues inherent in their implementation are then expounded and broader trends are discerned. These observations are linked to illustrate the ways in which modern nation states have shifted their traditional functions of 'security provider' or 'sovereignty generator' onto the transnational realm. Thereafter, the paper makes some tentative predictions regarding future attempts at transnational regulation. A number of conclusions are drawn. While a global tapestry of 'transnational cybercrime law' has been created, the differences and similarities between regimes can be attributed to the various legal and political arrangements amongst their signatories. Moreover, the regulatory challenges faced by these regimes demonstrate how Westphalian-based sovereign states are redeploying traditional legal and political paradigms to address novel transnational threats to a global man-made ecosystem. Finally, these trends suggest a continuation of current patterns of transnational regulation, despite the author's call for a change in approach to transnational cybercrime law.

1. Introduction

A. *Transnational criminal law*

The South African legal scholar Neil Boister first popularised the term 'transnational criminal law' in the early 2000s, in an attempt to capture various and increasingly frequent international agreements. These agreements relied on the criminal law apparatuses of nation states to suppress 'criminal activities that have actual or potential trans-boundary effects'.[1] Boister's original definition

---

*The views expressed in this paper are those of the author alone. All websites accessed April 2015.

[1]Neil Boister, '"Transnational Criminal Law"?' (2003) 14(5) *European Journal of International Law* 953, 955.

sought to unify the pre-existing criminological and legal concepts of crime with direct or indirect transnational effect and law regulating transnational activity, respectively.[2] Around a decade later, and against the background of a lively global discourse amongst criminal legal scholars, practitioners, judges and policy-makers,[3] Boister outlines a revised concept of transnational criminal law in his contribution to this symposium. These recent revisions retain much from his original inclination towards capturing the development of border-crossing criminal law at its international, rather than *trans*national, basis.

However, Boister now emphasises the growing scope in the promulgation of transnational criminal offences. He notes that the development of procedural mechanisms in the criminal codes of states addresses border-crossing criminal activity more adequately.[4] It will be argued in this paper that the distinction between inter- and transnational law remains important not only in navigating the different institutional, procedural and substantive layers of criminal law creation, but also with regard to the political and regulatory context in which criminal law norms are currently emerging. As we place the more recent development of criminal law – domestically, internationally and transnationally – in the larger context of recent and wide-ranging regulatory reforms and initiatives, the task of studying criminal law's globalisation becomes one of scrutinising its interplay with intricate and far-reaching dynamics of regulatory reform.[5]

In navigating this increasingly complex landscape of public, private and hybrid regulatory and institutional activity, the working distinction between transnational and international criminal law will continue to prove helpful. Boister explains that *inter*national criminal law has ostensibly been created by a community of states, which has introduced new legal concepts and procedures for the universal and unconditional condemnation of certain acts. He then clarifies that *trans*national criminal law 'is the product of an orthodox nineteenth century non-hierarchical order of formally equal centres of legal authority based on reciprocity, equality and sovereign consent'.[6] But, as alluded to above, transnational criminal law can be distinguished as it is highly influenced by non-state actors and intergovernmental organisations both in its formulation

[2] *Ibid*, 954; Neil Boister, 'Further reflections on the concept of transnational criminal law', this volume.

[3] See, for instance, the work by researchers and students at TransCrime (www.transcrime.it/en) and TraCCC (http://traccc.gmu.edu/), or scholars of international criminal law like Robert Cryer (www.birmingham.ac.uk/schools/law/staff/profile.aspx?ReferenceId=3796) or Clauss Kress (www.uni-koeln.de/jur-fak/kress/index_leh.html).

[4] Boister, this volume.

[5] See, for example, Ben Bowling and James Sheptycki, *Global Policing* (Sage, 2012); Ben Bowling and James Sheptycki, 'Global policing and transnational rule with law', this volume.

[6] Boister, this volume.

and implementation. These actors utilise 'soft law' or non-criminal sanctions, such as the Financial Action Task Force's anti-money laundering 'Recommendations', in order to further transnational criminal regulatory ends.[7] In this context, criminal law is placed in the midst of the complex and seemingly impenetrable web of norms and regulations that contribute to the modern 'law of global norm enforcement'. This shift in the role of criminal law prompts important questions regarding the implications of such regulatory amalgamation for the rule of law.[8]

With a sharp eye to the real-world operation of institutional competences, Boister maintains that the rise of transnational criminal law does not directly translate into a decline in state power. Since states retain the power to create, modify or implement transnational criminal law, it increases the scope and depth of their law making authority.[9] Rather than presenting us with a choice between international and national criminal law, Boister invites us to take a much closer look at the interaction between different states and non-state actors, international organisations and private security apparatuses that shape criminal law on a global scale. Predictably, the surge in scholars' and practitioners' interest in penetrating and illuminating these spatial regulatory dynamics has begun to leave direct traces in classroom instruction. Increasingly, criminal and administrative lawyers, criminologists, and law & development experts seek to expose their students to these developments at an early stage.[10]

Any legal analysis seeking to understand the formation of a new subfield of transnational law cannot overlook the political and economic context behind the formation and implementation of transnational criminal law. In light of the myriad and fast developing strands of transnational law enforcement, it is advisable to focus on one part of this dynamic field in order to scrutinise the different layers of institutional and normative ordering in greater detail. Transnational cybercrime law provides an excellent starting point, as it is a nascent and evolving area, embodied in various regional suppression conventions created in the past 15 or so years.[11]

[7]*Ibid*, at 11.
[8]Peer Zumbansen, *Transnational Legal Pluralism: Legal Theory and Global Governance* (Cambridge University Press, forthcoming 2015) ch 1.
[9]Boister, this volume.
[10]See, for example, the 2014–15 curriculum of the inaugural 'Transnational Law LLM' pathway at King's College London, which includes courses in 'Transnational and International Criminal Law', 'Transnational Law Enforcement' and a compulsory 'Transnational Law' course focusing on the actors, norms and processes that make up the institutional and normative 'DNA' of transnational regulatory governance: www.kcl.ac.uk/law/newsevents/newsrecords/2013-14/transnational-llm.aspx.
[11]The first such convention was developed by the Council of Europe, as will be elaborated upon below.

B. *Cybercrime: a case in point in 'transnational criminal regulatory governance'*[12]

Cybercrime refers to criminal activities facilitated by information communication technologies such as the internet. Cybercrime has come to encompass a multitude of activities, ranging from credit card fraud to whistleblowing on secret service agencies and even to international espionage.[13] While some estimates might put its financial impact roughly on a par with global narcotics trafficking,[14] there is a general expectation that its rate will increase as global access to the internet is enhanced.[15] Finally, cybercrime is a powerful illustration of an intricate merging of public and private regulatory activities. Private entities are almost uniformly in control of the infrastructure comprising the internet, with state agencies assuming regulatory and coordinating roles. States and businesses now sponsor private entities worldwide to conduct covert cyber-attacks on public or private targets deemed crucial to their national[16] or financial[17] interests. Meanwhile, major companies are joining together to resist government demands that they become complacent partners in mass surveillance.[18] Indeed, due to the differences between material and digital locations, debates over how to frame and address the problem revolve around whether to apply traditional notions of territorial jurisdiction or some new form of *sui generis* jurisdictional paradigm.[19]

This paper argues that the latter perspective is more useful for understanding and addressing the nature of the problem. Cybercrime poses a novel threat to public and private entities, which shatters the distinctions between borders, identities, roles, legal systems and nationalities. Thus far, the institutional mechanisms

---

[12]Zumbansen (n 8)

[13]Misha Glenny, *Darkmarket: CyberThieves, Cybercops and You* (Anansi Press, 2011) 88–95; *The Guardian*, 'Edward Snowden', www.theguardian.com/world/edward-snowden; Infowar Monitor, 'Shadows in the Cloud: Investigating Cyber Espionage 2.0′ (5 April 2010), www.infowar-monitor.net/2010/04/shadows-in-the-cloud-an-investigation-into-cyber-espionage-2-0.

[14]McAfee and the Centre for Strategic and International Studies, *The Economic Impact of Cybercrime and Cyber Espionage* (July 2013), https://csis.org/files/publication/60396rpt_cybercrime-cost_0713_ph4.pdf.

[15]Ronald Deibert, *Black Code: Inside the Battle for Cyberspace* (Signal, 2013).

[16]UK House of Commons – Intelligence and Security Committee of Parliament, *Annual Report 2012–2013* (2013) section 5, para 42, https://www.gov.uk/government/uploads/system/uploads/attachment_data/file/211553/31176_HC_547_ISC.PDF.

[17]Tom Harper, 'The Other Hacking Scandal: Suppressed Report Reveals that Law Firms, Telecoms Giants and Insurance Companies Routinely Hire Criminals to Steal Rivals' Information' *The Independent* (22 June 2013), www.independent.co.uk/news/uk/crime/the-other-hacking-scandal-suppressed-report-reveals-that-law-firms-telecoms-giants-and-insurance-companies-routinely-hire-criminals-to-steal-rivals-information-8669148.html.

[18]Reform Government Surveillance, *Letter to the Senate*, http://reformgovernmentsurveillance.com; The Day We Fight Back against Mass Surveillance, https://thedaywefightback.org.

[19]Robert Currie and Joseph Rikhof, *International and Transnational Criminal Law* (Irwin Law, 2nd edn 2014) 94.

developed to address this issue have been inadequate and ineffective. This is precisely because they rely on a Westphalian state system, predicated on distinct borders and legal/political systems. This paper aims to elaborate on this point by addressing the nature of the problem and explaining why existing transnational mechanisms are ineffective.

Accordingly, section 2 will first describe the regimes in question, conducting an analysis according to the 'actors/norms/processes' approach. Section 3 will apply international relations theory insights to the regimes to understand their formation (3.A). The paper will then consider the practical issues inherent in transnational regulatory processes and show how powerful state interests are reflected in the substantive rules (3.B). Section 4 examines broader trends in the regional and global legal implications of transnational cybercrime law (4.A). In this section there is a call for analysis of the evolution of a 'post-Westphalian' nation state more broadly, particularly in terms of the fundamental shift in its dual role to preserve sovereignty and provide security onto the transnational plane through recourse to the transnational cybercrime regimes in question (4.B). Thereafter, some tentative predictions will be made regarding future attempts at transnational regulation (4.C).

At this juncture, it is useful to lay out the four conclusions of this analysis, so as to preface the remainder of the paper. First, each of these cybercrime regimes exerts different degrees of influence on the domestic and transnational regulatory arrangements of its respective signatories, primarily in the fields of national security and criminal justice. Thus, regional spheres of harmonised cybercrime law have been formed, and a tapestry with a near-global reach can be made out where those regional regimes overlap with each other in their substantive and procedural content. This development has created a new and distinct branch of transnational criminal law, which will be termed 'transnational cybercrime law'.

Second, the analysis demonstrates that the differences and similarities between the regimes, as well as their differing degrees of integration, can be attributed to the various legal arrangements and political preferences amongst the signatories to each transnational cybercrime regime, as well as within certain key member states in particular.

Third, the content, context and regulatory challenges faced by transnational cybercrime regimes, considered either individually or collectively, serve as examples of how Westphalian-based sovereign states are using traditional legal paradigms and political tools to address new asymmetric non-state transnational threats to a global man-made ecosystem. Finally, the jurisdictional and institutional challenges faced by states seeking to implement transnational cybercrime law are, at bottom, connected to the attempt by sovereign states to govern an increasingly complex threat environment. This is accomplished by simply coordinating the core state function of 'security provision' on the transnational stage, be it through criminal or national security law. If this is any indication of present or future attempts at transnational regulation by states, regional cybercrime law can lend insight into the future of other branches of transnational criminal law, as well as the present transformation of the nation state displayed by transnational law more broadly.

2. Regional cybercrime regimes: actors, norms and processes

The six regional cybercrime regimes were chosen for the study since they were listed as binding international legal instruments in a recent UN Office on Drugs and Crime (UNODC) study on cybercrime.[20] While similar regimes exist under the guise of other regional organisations, such as the Commonwealth's Model Law on Computer and Computer-Related Crime, they are neither binding nor as influential as the following six.[21] Moreover, the regulatory regimes cover almost the entire globe, and, when considered alongside one another, they reveal an intricate mix of domestic and regional state and non-state actors. The stakeholders simultaneously follow different bilateral, multilateral and geopolitical dynamics, and thereby produce a variety of binding and non-binding legal and institutional arrangements.

This section analyses each regime using the 'actors/norms/processes' approach, advocated for by Peer Zumbansen for a more complete analysis of transnational regulatory regimes. 'Actors' encompasses the governmental, intergovernmental or non-state actors involved in each regime, while 'processes' refers to the 'dynamics of institutional evolution' and interrelationship between the actors. Finally, 'norms' include both the binding and non-binding rules that in turn reproduce and influence those same actor–process dynamics.[22] The following sub-sections, accordingly, will draw out the interplay between these three variables.

The rest of this section serves to delineate the evidentiary groundwork for the remainder of the paper. Each sub-section canvasses the actors, norms and processes involved in the formation and implementation of each respective regime. Travelling from West to East, only parts of Asia and South America are not covered. Even in those cases, the regimes in question may be informally adopted as best practices or as clubs to which certain countries, like India, aspire to obtain membership.

Through this short and non-exhaustive survey, a number of points relevant to the remainder of the paper come to the fore. On the one hand, differences between the regimes and the regional organisation that promulgated them become evident. These differences, again, are attributable to the clusters of legal and political systems that make up the regional organisations to begin with. On the other hand, there are patterns and similarities that can be seen among all six regimes. Despite stark differences in the forms of government amongst the signatories,

[20]United Nations Office on Drugs and Crime, *Comprehensive Study on Cybercrime* (United Nations, 2013) 64. 'Binding', as defined by the UNODC, in the sense that the instrument is binding while its content may be largely hortatory.

[21]Commonwealth of Nations, 'Commonwealth Model Law on Computer and Computer-Related Crime', https://www.commonwealthcybercrimeinitiative.org/resources.

[22]Peer Zumbansen, '*Lochner* Disembedded: The Anxieties of Law in a Global Context' (2013) 20(1) *Indiana Journal of Legal Studies* 28–29. See also Peer Zumbansen, 'Defining the Space of Transnational Law: Legal Theory, Global Governance, and Legal Pluralism' in Günther Handl, Joachim Zekoll and Peer Zumbansen (eds), *Beyond Territoriality: Transnational Legal Authority in an Age of Globalization* (Brill, 2013) 53–86.

none of them have even begun to consider the limitations inherent in attempting to address non-state threats with state-centric enforcement regimes. Moreover, the regimes have similar approaches to cybercrime: moulding existing forms of transnational state-to-state cooperation mechanisms onto the digital realm.

A. *Council of Europe (CoE)*

The CoE first took note of the international aspects related to computer crime in 1976, and gave it sustained attention starting in 1996.[23] After multiple meetings and revisions, the Convention was opened for signature in November 2001 to 30 states, including non-members that participated in its drafting.[24] At the time of writing, the CoE Convention on Cybercrime ('CoE Convention', also known as the Budapest Convention) has been ratified or acceded to by 45 states.[25]

There was limited opportunity for multi-stakeholder input during the CoE Convention's formation, although US representatives did receive some level of input from interested organisations, which apparently informed its position.[26] Today, the CoE Convention is generally considered to be a baseline legislative framework for nations seeking to address cybercrime. International organisations as varied as Interpol, the UN General Assembly, APEC (Asia-Pacific Economic Cooperation) and the OAS (Organization of American States) have emulated it when drafting their own cybercrime regimes.[27]

With regard to the norms created by the CoE Convention, it sets out seemingly modest goals of harmonising cybercrime laws, creating domestic procedural powers for investigation and prosecution, and providing a 'fast and effective regime of international co-operation'.[28] To that effect, Chapter I sets out relevant definitions designed broadly enough to adapt to changing technologies.[29] Chapter

[23]International Telecommunications Union (ICT Applications and Cybersecurity Division), *Understanding Cybercrime: A Guide for Developing Countries* (2nd edn, 2011) 197; Council of Europe, *Convention on Cybercrime: Explanatory Report* (ETS No 185), http://conventions.coe.int/Treaty/en/Reports/Html/185.htm, paras 8–10.
[24]International Telecommunications Union (n 23) 197.
[25]Council of Europe, *Convention on Cybercrime – Signatures and Ratifications* (21 May 2015), http://conventions.coe.int/Treaty/Commun/ChercheSig.asp?NT=185&CM=8&DF=&CL=ENG.
[26]Michael Vatis, 'The Council of Europe Convention on Cybercrime' in *Proceedings of a Workshop on Deterring CyberAttacks: Informing Strategies and Developing Options for US Policy* (National Academic Press, 2010) 207; 2003 WL 22702489 (White House); US Senate Executive Report, *Council of Europe Convention on Cybercrime*, S Treaty Doc No 108-11, www.gpo.gov/fdsys/pkg/CRPT-109erpt6/html/CRPT-109erpt6.htm; US Senate Executive Report.
[27]International Telecommunications Union (n 23) 198.
[28]*Convention on Cybercrime: Explanatory Report* (n 23) para 16.
[29]Currie and Rikhof (n 19) 427.

II, section 1 creates substantive offences, such as illegal access and data interference, computer-based fraud and child pornography,[30] and section 2 sets out procedural powers for computer offences, such as mandatory preservation and storage rules[31] and the 'real-time collection of computer data' by third parties acting on behalf of national authorities.[32] Article 15 requires signatories to 'provide for the adequate protection of human rights and liberties' according to international human rights instruments and the principles of proportionality and judicial oversight.[33] Finally, Article 22 requires that conflicts over concurrent jurisdiction be resolved through consultation.[34]

Chapter III provides for mutual assistance and extradition rules, and allows for the CoE Convention to be used as an extradition or legal assistance treaty, absent any pre-existing agreements between signatories.[35] It also provides for confidentiality arrangements,[36] expedited preservation and disclosure requests, the creation of 24/7 contact points,[37] and unfettered access to data which is either available publicly or can be provided to the party through 'the lawful and voluntary consent' of third parties (e.g. internet service providers).[38] The CoE Convention's final portion, Chapter IV, provides, *inter alia*, for mandatory periodic consultation to ensure its effective implementation and possible modification.[39]

Looked at as a whole, the CoE Convention can be seen as the face of transnational cybercrime regulation by 'Western' states. Its signatories are uniformly democratic nations with longstanding traditions of cooperation on matters related to transnational security, both of which are reflected in the regime's legal provisions. However, as will be elaborated upon in section 3.B, this also entails that the same institutional delays or gaps in rights and accountability that plague current transnational crime regimes are replicated in the CoE Convention.

B. *Economic Community of West African States (ECOWAS)*

The Draft Directive on Fighting Cybercrime within ECOWAS (the ECOWAS Draft Directive) was adopted in 2009 and explicitly builds on prior ECOWAS agreements regarding judicial cooperation, data protection and information and

---

[30] *Ibid*.
[31] Convention on Cybercrime, Council of Europe, ETS No 185 [23 November 2001], http://conventions.coe.int/Treaty/EN/Treaties/Html/185.htm, Art 16.
[32] *Ibid*, Arts 20–21.
[33] *Ibid*, Art 15.
[34] *Ibid*, Art 22.
[35] *Ibid*, Arts 24(3), 27(1).
[36] *Ibid*, Art 28.
[37] *Ibid*, Art 35.
[38] *Ibid*, Art 32.
[39] *Ibid*, Art 46.

communications technology (ICT) regulation.[40] Those prior agreements overlapped with international conferences that, since 2008, have involved both private sector actors and Western law enforcement bodies in seeking to address online fraud originating in the region and targeting European victims.[41]

Alongside such meetings, an intriguing coalition of interests, including both the World Bank and Microsoft Inc., have publicly urged the Nigerian parliament to pass cybercrime legislation in order to deal with the rise in online fraud.[42] Similarly, in 2012 the US Department of State co-hosted in Dakar (Senegal) the West African Cybersecurity and Cybercrime Workshop with the Government of Senegal, which it later publicised as having assisted in developing national strategies, fostering regional coordination, developing computer emergency response teams (CERTs), and 'signing the Budapest Cybercrime Convention'.[43] Superficially, such gatherings can be seen as an example of how self-interested actors attempt to pursue policy objectives wherever possible. However, these examples are included here as an illustration of the public/private processes at work behind the development of regional cybercrime regimes.

The ECOWAS Draft Directive is explicitly aimed at linking traditional criminal offences and procedures to specific offences committed via the internet, though it applies to all criminal offences 'whose detection shall require electronic evidence'.[44] While its definitions and substantive offences generally map onto those found in the CoE Convention, they are phrased more broadly.[45] Chapter V outlines procedural provisions, such as the ability of national authorities to search or access computer systems[46] and issue confidential data preservation orders for durations set by domestic legislation.[47] Furthermore, Articles 33 and 35 mandate cooperation, incorporation into domestic law and notification to the President of the ECOWAS Commission if there are any compliance issues.[48]

Although the ECOWAS Draft Directive resembles the CoE Convention, the notable level of influence from foreign state and non-state actors sets it apart. How the ECOWAS Draft Directive is implemented in practice, and to what

[40]ECOWAS Draft Directive, www.ecowas.int/publications/en/actes_add_telecoms/SIGNED-Cybercrime.pdf, Preamble.
[41]IT News Africa, 'Summit on Cybercrime Opens in Abuja' (30 November 2010), www.itnewsafrica.com/2010/11/summit-on-cybercrime-opens-in-abuja.
[42]Henry Osborne Quarshie and Alexander Martin-Odoom, 'Fighting Cybercrime in Africa' (2012) 2(6) *Computer Science and Engineering* 2.
[43]*Ibid.*
[44]Economic Community of West African States, 'Directive C/Dir. 1/08/11 on Fighting Cybercrime Within ECOWAS' (17–19 August 2011), www.ecowas.int/publications/en/actes_add_telecoms/SIGNED-Cybercrime.pdf, Preamble and Arts 2–3.
[45]*Ibid*, Art 12. This is the backbone of the offence of 'fraudulent manipulation of personal data'.
[46]*Ibid*, Art 30.
[47]*Ibid*, Art 31.
[48]*Ibid*, Arts 33, 35(1), 35(4).

extent it is accompanied by appropriate capacity-building measures, remains to be seen. Unfortunately, there is a dearth of research evaluating this and other transnational crime regimes on the African continent.

C. *African Union (AU)*

The AU's formal mandate in the field of cybercrime regulation began with the Oliver Tambo Declaration in 2009, which requested the AU Commission and the UN Economic Commission for Africa to draft a convention dealing with the regulation of cyberspace.[49] Although a final draft was scheduled to pass in January 2014, private sector actors and human rights NGOs raised concerns regarding the lack of transparency in its drafting and its consequences for free speech and privacy.[50] Nonetheless, in June 2014 the AU announced the adoption of the 'African Union Convention on Cyberspace Security and Protection of Personal Data' ('AU Convention').[51]

The AU Convention is intended to facilitate legislative and policy harmonisation for the AU in electronic transactions, personal data protection and cybersecurity.[52] With regard to international cooperation, states are required to modify their laws with a view to regional harmonisation, the establishment of dual criminality, the promotion and ratification of mutual legal assistance treaties (MLATs) and the formation of CERTs, as well as any other pre-existing means (e.g. public-private partnerships).[53] However, uniquely to the AU Convention, member states are specifically required to form public-private partnerships that 'engage industry, the civil society and academia' and promote information exchange between stakeholders.[54]

The substantive offences created by the AU Convention are defined broadly, effectively including any sort of unauthorised interference with a computer

[49]African Union, 'Oliver Tambo Declaration', Extra-Ordinary Conference of African Union Ministers in Charge of Communication and Information Technologies (2–5 November 2009), p 4, para 5.
[50]CCDCOE, 'African Union Adopts Convention on Cyber Security' (14 July 2014), https://ccdcoe.org/african-union-adopts-convention-cyber-security.html. Ephraim Percy Kenyanito, 'Africa moves towards a common cyber security legal framework' (2 June 2014), https://www.accessnow.org/blog/2014/06/02/africa-moves-towards-a-common-cyber-security-legal-framework.
[51]African Union, 'African Union Convention on Cyber Security and Personal Data Protection' (27 June 2014), http://pages.au.int/sites/default/files/en_AU%20Convention%20on%20CyberSecurity%20Pers%20Data%20Protec%20AUCyC%20adopted%20Malabo.pdf.
[52]*Ibid* Auguste Yankey, 'African Union Perspectives on Cybersecurity and Cybercrime Issues: The AU Draft Convention on Cybersecurity and Related Activities', Commonwealth Telecommunication Organization, Cybersecurity Forum 2013, www.cto.int/media/events/pst-ev/2013/Cybersecurity/Auguste%20Yankey.pdf, slide 12.
[53]African Union (n 51) Art 28.
[54]*Ibid*, Art 26(3).

system or digital communication, aside from specific content-related offences (e.g. dissemination of child pornography or xenophobic content).[55] However, the AU Convention is similar to the CoE Convention in that it requires signatories to implement its provisions while respecting the rights of citizens and the integrity of the 'African Charter on Human and Peoples' Rights'.[56]

Interestingly, the AU Convention remains the only regional cybercrime instrument that speaks to other fields of regulatory activity (e.g. personal data protection). However, given that it is a regional agreement that imposes obligations on member states to implement, oftentimes on other private actors, its practical application remains to be seen.

D. *League of Arab States (LAS)*

The LAS was established by a founding treaty in 1945, which in its Preamble explicitly aimed to further internal solidarity, use the LAS as an intermediary for solving disputes and encourage cooperation in various fields, while continuing to 'safeguard' the 'independence and sovereignty' of the individual states.[57] The organisation first entered the field of cybercrime regulation with a model law in 2004.[58] The first binding regional framework dealing with transnational cybercrime was formulated by the LAS in December 2010 with the release of the 'Arab Convention on Combatting Information Technology Offences' (the LAS Convention), which has since been signed by the vast majority of participating states.[59] With this background in mind, the LAS can clearly be categorised as an intergovernmental institution that lacks any significant supranational capabilities, since agreements like the LAS Convention itself are binding only on countries that voted in its favour.[60]

The LAS Convention states at the outset that it is applicable only to offences that have a transnational element, either in their preparation, commission or

---

[55] *Ibid*, Art 29.

[56] *Ibid*, Preamble.

[57] Pact of the League of Arab States, 22 March 1945, http://avalon.law.yale.edu/20th_century/arableag.asp. See also European Parliament – Directorate-General for External Policies, 'Policy Briefing: EU – League of Arab States Relations: Prospects for Closer Parliamentary Cooperation', www.europarl.europa.eu/RegData/etudes/briefing_note/join/2013/491494/EXPO-AFET_SP(2013)491494_EN.pdf; International Centre for Not-For-Profit Law, *NGO Law Monitor: League of Arab States* (6 June 2013), www.icnl.org/research/monitor/las.html#facts.

[58] See *Comprehensive Study on Cybercrime* (n 20). The UNODC Report provides one of the only mentions of the Model Law in the English literature.

[59] League of Arab States, 'Arab Convention on Combating Information Technology Offences' (2010), https://cms.unov.org/DocumentRepositoryIndexer/GetDocInOriginalFormat.drsx?DocID=3dbe778b-7b3a-4af0-95ce-a8bbd1ecd6dd.

[60] Arab League 24th Summit, 21–27 March 2013, http://arableaguesummit2013.qatarconferences.org/arab-league.html; International Democracy Watch, 'Arab League', www.internationaldemocracywatch.org/index.php/arab-league-.

consequences.[61] Furthermore, Article 4(2) explicitly protects the sovereignty of signatories by prohibiting the exercise in one state of 'jurisdiction or functions' which are the exclusive right of another state 'by virtue of its domestic law'.[62] Its substantive offences mirror those found in the CoE, ECOWAS and AU Conventions, as it requires their criminalisation according to domestic legislation.[63] Some offences unique to the LAS Convention include the criminalisation of the production or distribution of 'pornographic material',[64] the dissemination 'of the ideas and principles of terrorist groups', the facilitation of communication between terrorist organisations, and the diffusion of religious fanaticism or religious dissent.[65] However, the LAS Convention's search and seizure provisions are slightly more extensive and apply to all crimes committed using ICTs.

The closing portions of the LAS Convention address issues of cooperation and possible conflicts over jurisdiction. Article 30 provides for signatories to establish competence over offences (as well as competing extradition requests) if their execution impacts their territory or 'an overriding interest of the State'.[66] The LAS Convention is procedurally similar to the CoE Convention, however assistance can be refused if the offence is deemed political or where compliance would run contrary to the 'sovereignty, security, order or basic interests' of the requested state.[67] Finally, amendments that do not constitute a material departure from the LAS Convention are permitted, subject to unanimity.[68]

Taken together, the provisions in the LAS Convention seem to overtly reflect the social and political history of the region. However, on a more fundamental level it is worth noting the provisions specific to the preservation of sovereignty, such as how Article 4(2) curtails transboundary cybercrime suppression by the laws of the other state. In theory this would block cooperation as soon as any legislation stands in the way, allowing for the formation of legal jurisdictional safe havens.

E. *Commonwealth of Independent States (CIS)*

The CIS was originally formed in 1991 by the Alma-Ata Declaration[69] following the breakup of the Soviet Union. It was later revised with the CIS Charter[70] and

---

[61]League of Arab States (n 59) Art 3.
[62]*Ibid*, Art 4(2).
[63]*Ibid*, Art 5.
[64]*Ibid*, Art 12.
[65]*Ibid*, Art 15.
[66]*Ibid*, Arts 30, 30(3).
[67]*Ibid*, Art 35.
[68]*Ibid*, Ch V.
[69]Library of Congress, *The Alma-Ata Declaration*, http://lcweb2.loc.gov/frd/cs/belarus/by_appnc.html.
[70]Commonwealth of Independent States, *Charter* (1995) 34 ILM 5, 1279–97, www.jstor.org/stable/20698492.

currently includes Armenia, Azerbaijan, Belarus, Kazakhstan, Kyrgyzstan, Moldova, Russia, Tajikistan and Uzbekistan, while Turkmenistan remains an 'Associate Member'. The CIS is founded on the principle of sovereign equality and independence, and although it is intended to facilitate deeper regional cooperation the CIS itself explicitly eschews any supranational powers or role.[71] Cooperation amongst CIS states in matters of cybersecurity began in 1998, and in 2001 the CIS Council of Heads of State released its 'Agreement on Cooperation in Combatting Offences related to Computer Information' (the CIS Agreement), which entered into force in 2002.[72]

The CIS Agreement defines offences broadly, effectively criminalising any unauthorised interference with 'computer information'[73] or the violation of computer-related regulations resulting in 'significant damage', although what qualifies as meeting those harm thresholds is left to the signatories.[74] The remainder of the CIS Agreement deals with procedural matters, mandating cooperation[75] and compliance with assistance requests, or written reasons for non-compliance.[76] As the second oldest regional cybercrime regime covered in this paper, the CIS Agreement focuses less on substantive offences than it does on general principles of cooperation. In fact, the open-ended nature of the terms it employs and the formalised policy of having them defined by the parties employing them is likely crucial to its longevity and flexibility. How it operates in practice, and the extent to which it supplants or is supplanted by other regimes or sub-regional agreements, are questions ripe for analysis.[77]

F. *Shanghai Cooperation Organization (SCO)*

The SCO was initially founded in 2001 by the leaders of China, Kazakhstan, Kyrgyzstan, Russia and Tajikistan in order to assist in the demilitarisation of the border between China and the former Soviet Union.[78] While Uzbekistan joined

---

[71] *Ibid*, Section 1, Art 1.

[72] Avner Levin, 'Securing Cyberspace: A Comparative Review of Strategies Worldwide' (Ryerson University, Ted Rogers School of Management: Privacy and Cyber Crime Institute, 2013) 32.

[73] Commonwealth of Independent States, 'Agreement on Cooperation among the States members of the Commonwealth of Independent States in Combating Offences Relating to Computer Information', https://cms.unov.org/documentrepositoryindexer/GetDocInOriginalFormat.drsx?DocID=5b7de69a-730e-43ce-9623-9a103f5cabc0, Art 1 (a), 1(d).

[74] *Ibid*, Arts 3(1), 3(2).

[75] *Ibid*, Art 4.

[76] *Ibid*, Arts 6, 7(1), 8.

[77] *Ibid*, Art 13.

[78] Andrew Scheineson, Council on Foreign Relations: Backgrounder, 'The Shanghai Cooperation Organization' (24 March 2009), www.cfr.org/china/shanghai-cooperation-organization/p10883.

as an official member in 2001, India, Iran, Pakistan, Afghanistan and Mongolia have observer status, and Turkey, Belarus and Sri Lanka have Dialogue Partner status.[79] All of the SCO's goals are pursued, according to Article 2 of the 'Charter of the SCO', with 'mutual respect of sovereignty, independence, territorial integrity of States and inviolability of State borders'.[80]

Effective power in the SCO flows from the Heads of State Council, through the Heads of Government and Council of Foreign Ministers, and into the Council of National Coordinators, which coordinates member state cooperation with regard to SCO matters.[81] Looked at as a whole, the SCO can therefore be seen as an institution facilitating intergovernmental networking and cooperation, but with a strong leaning towards top-down control by the executive branches of member states.

Apart from its Secretariat, the SCO's Regional Counter-Terrorism Structure (RATS) was formed in 2004 and is currently based in Tashkent (Uzbekistan).[82] The RATS representative Council meets yearly to set its directions, and in 2012 it agreed on new measures to combat the use of the internet for 'terrorist, separatist and extremist ends'.[83] In general, however, RATS focuses on addressing all transnational security threats, and therefore works to coordinate information sharing and interoperability between the civilian or military security and law enforcement agencies of SCO members.[84] The SCO began dealing head-on with issues of cybersecurity in October 2006, with the founding meeting of the SCO Group of Governmental Experts on Cybersecurity.[85] This was followed by several declarations,[86] but throughout its evolution the SCO has never distinguished between

[79]SCO, 'Organization – Brief Introduction to the Shanghai Cooperation Organization', www.sectsco.org/EN123/brief.asp.
[80]SCO, 'Charter of the Shanghai Cooperation Organization', www.sectsco.org/EN123/show.asp?id=69.
[81]*Ibid.*
[82]*Ibid.*
[83]Dadan Upadhyay, 'SCO Members to Cooperate in War On Cyber Terrorism', *Russia and India Report*, http://indrus.in/world/2013/04/02/sco_members_to_cooperate_in_war_on_cyber_terrorism_23429.html.
[84]Regional Anti-Terrorist Structure of Shanghai Cooperation Organization (RATS SCO), 'Coordination Activities', http://ecrats.org/en/activity/coordination; Richard Weitz, 'Uzbekistan: A Peek Inside an SCO Anti-Terrorism Center', www.eurasianet.org/node/65960.
[85]Oleg Demidov, 'The Shanghai Cooperation Organization: Maintaining Cyber Security in the Central Asia and Beyond', www.pircenter.org/en/articles/536-the-shanghai-cooperation-organization-maintaining-cyber-security-in-the-central-asia-and-beyond/print/1, slide 10.
[86]SCO, 'Joint Communiqué of Meeting of the Council of the Heads of the Member States of the Shanghai Cooperation Organization' (28 August 2008), www.sectsco.org/EN123/show.asp?id=91; President of Russia: Official Web Portal, 'Yekaterinburg Declaration of the Heads of the Member States of the Shanghai Cooperation Organization', www.scosummit2013.org/en/documents/ekaterinburgskaya-deklaratsiya-glav-gosudarstv-chlenov-shanhayskoy-organizatsii-sotrudnichestva.

criminal and national security matters related to cybercrime or cybersecurity, as it considers its remit to include all matters of 'information security'.

The 'Agreement on Cooperation in the Field of International Information Security' ('SCO Agreement') came into effect in June 2011.[87] Since then, SCO and RATS statements have consistently promoted the importance of 'advancing common rules of conduct'[88] and cooperation.[89] However, since the SCO approaches 'information security' through the RATS counter-terrorism mandate, it eschews any open or multi-stakeholder approach involving non-state entities.[90]

The SCO Agreement begins by outlining the threats it is meant to address, such as 'information crime', including the militarisation of cyberspace, '[u]se of the dominant position in the information space to the detriment of the interests and security of other States', and the '[d]issemination of information harmful to social and political, social and economic systems, as well as spiritual, moral and cultural spheres of other States'.[91] Article 3 outlines the main areas for cooperation, which interestingly include securing stable 'global internet governance' and ICT infrastructure for signatories.[92] The main forms of cooperation provided by the SCO Agreement include a list of contact points, periodic consultations, and the ability to supplement the SCO Agreement with 'appropriate interagency treaties'.[93]

However, under Article 6, parties are not required to share information if they determine that 'the disclosure of such information might damage national interests'.[94] The SCO Agreement itself is deemed not to impinge upon any pre-existing international agreements of the signatories[95] and can be acceded to by any state that agrees to be bound by its terms,[96] though any unfulfilled obligations must be met, even if membership is terminated.[97] The provisions under Article 4 qualify cooperation by requiring parties to comply with principles of non-interference, respect the abilities of other signatories to control information within their borders,

[87]Demidov (n 85) slide 12.
[88]SCO (n 86).
[89]Demidov (n 85) slide 15.
[90]SCO, 'Astana Declaration of the 10th Anniversary of the Shanghai Cooperation Organization' (15 June 2011), http://webcache.googleusercontent.com/search?q=cache:Od9KNv5BQNAJ:www.sectsco.org/EN123/show.asp%3Fid%3D294+&cd=2&hl=en&ct=clnk&gl=ca; Demidov (n 85) slide 18.
[91]SCO, 'Agreement between the Governments of the Member States of the Shanghai Cooperation Organization on Cooperation in the Field of International Information Security', http://media.npr.org/assets/news/2010/09/23/cyber_treaty.pdf, Art 2.
[92]*Ibid*, Art 3(7)–(8).
[93]*Ibid*, Art 5(4).
[94]*Ibid*, Art 6(1).
[95]*Ibid*, Art 8.
[96]*Ibid*, Art 12(3).
[97]*Ibid*, Art 12(5).

and ensure the equal rights of signatories 'to protect the information resources and critical structures of their States from illicit use and unauthorized interference, including information attacks'.[98]

Annex 1 provides a number of broad and notable definitions. One such example is the definition of 'Information war', which is described as an interstate confrontation 'undermining political, economic and social systems, mass psychologic [*sic*] brainwashing to destabilize society and state, as well as to force the state to taking decisions in the interest of an opposing party'.[99] Another example is found in the concept of an 'information security threat', which includes 'factors which pose a threat to the individual, society, state and their interest in the information space'.[100] Annex 2 details cybersecurity threats, such as those posed by 'information crime', which includes any unauthorised interference with information systems,[101] or the '[u]se of dominant position in the information space to the detriment of the interests and security of other countries', which is a clear reference to the 'digital divide' between developed and developing nations.[102] Finally, '[d]issemination of information harmful to the socio-political and socio-economic systems, spiritual, moral and cultural environment of other States' includes threats emanating from any state or non-state actor using information infrastructure to distort the perception of, or pose a threat to, the social or political fabric of the state.[103]

The SCO Agreement is unique in its explicit blur of criminal and national security cyber threats, but follows the LAS Convention and CIS Agreement in its protection of the sovereignty of signatories. One can easily critique the regime for its authoritarian leanings and for supporting anti-democratic security practices. However, this overlooks how other cybercrime regimes, like the CoE Convention, frame asymmetric threats (e.g. Anonymous) in the same way.

G. *Summary*

While there is certainly value in having considered these six regimes in the abstract, it is worthwhile to note that little research exists which actually evaluates their operation in practice. The UNODC's Comprehensive Study on Cybercrime is a notable exception, but even that study draws its conclusions from voluntary responses provided to anonymous questionnaires. The lack of region-specific research is compounded by obvious legal, political and linguistic differences that are difficult to bridge. Nevertheless, some fruitful observations can be made even from this

---

[98] *Ibid*, Art 4(2)–4(3).
[99] *Ibid*, Annex 1.
[100] *Ibid*.
[101] *Ibid*, Annexes 2–3.
[102] *Ibid*, Annexes 2–4.
[103] *Ibid*, Annexes 2–5.

cursory analysis. The CoE Convention, for instance, reflects the shared democratic values of its signatories as well as shared levels of pre-existing transnational cooperation. The ECOWAS Draft Directive, by comparison, is so similar to the CoE Convention and was influenced by Western state and non-state interests that it exists as a veritable protégé of the CoE Convention. Conversely, while Western state actors also influenced the AU Convention, it is a markedly different regime, which is unique in its holistic approach to cybercrime regulation.

The LAS Convention, however, reflects the political and social values of its signatories while ensuring that sovereignty retains its prime importance. This latter aspect is also evident in the CIS Agreement, which serves more of a coordinating function. Finally, the SCO Agreement empowers its signatories with new offences and institutional capabilities related to cybercrime whilst enshrining sovereignty as a fundamental premise. In all, the regimes reflect the political, social and institutional histories of their signatories shared in each region. Why this is the case, how this plays out in practice, and what this means for transnational criminal law in general is the focus of the remainder of this paper.

3. Deconstructing transnational cybercrime law

In order to appreciate how the dynamics between and within the states and organisations involved in the creation of the foregoing cybercrime regimes influenced and continue to influence the implementation of those regimes, the analysis must take place against the backdrop of two main layers of theoretical and practical investigation.

First, international relations theory assists in situating transnational criminal law, and cybercrime in particular, within a wider debate on the role of the nation state, the status of the interstate system, and how both interact with regional organisations and formalised arrangements for cooperation. For its part, international relations theory has certainly influenced the study of transnational criminal law. Concepts of 'international comity', for instance, have found their way into more than one decision from Canadian courts tasked with interpreting domestic laws that address issues of transnational criminal concern.[104] Moreover, theories of state responsibility for creating and protecting the rights of their subjects, and their relation with interstate agreements on transnational criminal matters, are often the topic of academic debate.[105]

[104]See, for instance, *R v Karigar*, 2013 ONSC 5199, where Justice Hackland suggested that under the Corruption of Foreign Public Officials Act the prosecution was veritably mandated according to Canada's international obligations. See also Currie and Rikhof (n 19) 447–8.

[105]This issue is no exception, but see also the Special Issue of the *Utrecht Law Review* (Volume 9, Issue 4, September 2013) spearheaded by Sabine Gless and John AE Vervaele, entitled 'Law Should Govern: Aspiring General Principles for Transnational Criminal Justice'.

Three major schools of international relations theory – realism, institutionalism and liberalism – are therefore selected, and the foregoing regimes are each considered in turn. Realism illustrates how those arrangements can be seen as serving the interests of the most powerful participants. Institutionalism, however, lends insight into how states use regional organisations to produce transnational criminal laws characterised by flexible or non-binding arrangements. Finally, liberalism complements both approaches by highlighting how governmental and non-governmental networks actually implement the regional agreements themselves. Nevertheless, the three approaches collectively serve to illustrate how the nation state is transplanting its core function as 'security provider' onto the transnational stage, albeit in slightly different ways and with a variety of political and legal constructs.

Secondly, the actual application of these transnational cybercrime regimes brings to the fore an array of legal abnormalities, technical shortcomings and political issues that remain unaccounted for by the state and the interstate entities that created them. With both lines of analysis, it becomes clear that the common challenges faced by transnational cybercrime regimes are inextricably linked to their origin as products of a Westphalian state system that is using traditional regulatory tools to address a novel threat. Section 4, in turn, will explore how this link exposes issues at the heart of those same reigning legal and regulatory paradigms, and what this means for transnational criminal law and the future of transnational regulation.

A. *International relations*

(i) *Realism*

Despite the differences in their approaches, ranging from binding to hortatory obligations, the CoE, CIS and SCO regimes all display characteristics indicative of self-serving influence from the most powerful states involved. This is in line with basic precepts of realist international relations theory, which views such international institutions as predicated upon and thus reflecting the 'self-interested calculations of great powers', given how unitary states exist in a state of anarchy necessitating 'self-help'.[106] The substantive offences in the CoE, for instance, closely map pre-existing US criminal law. Given its influence in the CoE's formation, the US at least partially envisioned it as a convenient medium for promoting its own legal paradigms in the domestic laws of other states. Similar comments can be made regarding the involvement of the CoE (and some of its major European signatories), the US and various US federal agencies in the development and implementation of the ECOWAS Draft Directive.

[106]John J Mearsheimer, 'The False Promise of International Institutions' (1994/5) 19 *International Security* 7; Kenneth Abbott, 'International Relations Theory, International Law, and the Regime Governing Atrocities in International Conflicts' (1999) 93 *American Journal of International Law* 364.

The CIS and SCO regimes, conversely, adopted quite different approaches to cybercrime, yet both mimic the CoE Convention in the way they further the interests of their most powerful members, Russia and China. For instance, Article 4 of the SCO Agreement and Article 7 of the CIS Agreement seem to legalise a practice of compelled cooperation in cases where presumably public or private activities in one state threaten the 'information space' of another. This in turn provides the largest and most powerful players in both the SCO and CIS with ample legal footing for influencing co-signatories into regulating their domestic activities in a manner that furthers the interests of the most powerful players. This might explain why the US has not demonstrated the same levels of involvement with Russian[107] (until only recently[108]) and Chinese[109] cybercrime policy.

(ii) *Institutionalism*

The differences between 'Eastern' and 'Western' approaches to cybercrime regulation are certainly corroborated by ongoing international developments, as Russia and China have sought to promote sovereignty in transnational cybercrime regulation, which underpins both the SCO and CIS Agreements, at the UN. For instance, in 2010 during the Twelfth United Nations Congress on Crime Prevention and Criminal Justice, Russia, with support from other countries (including China), proposed the formation of a new international instrument regarding cybercrime.[110] However, the US, Canada, the UK and the EU – all leading parties to the CoE Convention – blocked this proposal, arguing that the negotiation of an international convention would derail the progress already achieved through the CoE Convention.[111] Several other nations correctly noted that significant disagreement persisted with regard to basic concepts of extraterritorial jurisdiction, sovereignty,

---

[107]John Markoff and Andrew E Kramer, 'U.S. and Russia Differ on a Treaty for Cyberspace' *New York Times*, www.nytimes.com/2009/06/28/world/28cyber.html?pagewanted=all&_r=0.

[108]Siobhan Gorman, 'US Backs Talks on Cyber Warfare' *Wall Street Journal* (4 June 2010), http://online.wsj.com/news/articles/SB10001424052748703340904575284964215965730; Duncan Hollis, 'Should There Be an International Treaty on Cyberwarfare' (13 June 2012), http://opiniojuris.org/2012/06/13/should-there-be-an-international-treaty-on-cyberwarfare; Adrian Croft, 'Russia Says Many States Arming for Cyber Warfare' *Reuters* (25 April 2012), www.reuters.com/article/2012/04/25/germany-cyber-idUSL6E8FP40M20120425.

[109]White House: Office of the Press Secretary, 'Briefing by Deputy National Security Advisor for Strategic Communications Ben Rhodes' (24 March 2014), www.whitehouse.gov/the-press-office/2014/03/24/briefing-deputy-national-security-advisor-strategic-communications-ben-r.

[110]United Nations, *Report of the Twelfth United Nations Congress on Crime Prevention and Criminal Justice*, A/CONF.213/18 (18 May 2010), para 202; Neil Boister, *An Introduction to Transnational Criminal Law* (Oxford University Press, 2012) 118.

[111]United Nations, *ibid*, para 203; Boister, *ibid*, 118.

human rights and the involvement of the private sector, and that they needed to be resolved before any global cybercrime regime could take shape.[112]

This divergence in approach between the strict preservation of sovereignty and hortatory transnational criminal law obligations (i.e. CIS and SCO) versus more substantive and binding legal harmonisation (i.e. CoE, AU and ECOWAS) surfaced again in a 2011 letter written by Russia, China, Tajikistan and Uzbekistan to the UN Secretary General and the General Assembly. The letter, entitled 'International code of conduct for information security', called for a voluntary code of conduct which would enshrine, *inter alia*, respect for territorial and political sovereignty, the refusal to use ICT to carry out hostile acts, and cooperation in combatting the illicit use of ICT, especially 'in curbing the dissemination of information that incites terrorism, secessionism or extremism or that undermines other countries' political, economic and social stability, as well as their spiritual and cultural environment'.[113] The most recent draft of the SCO's *International Code of Conduct for Information Security* suggests that this schism in models of internet governance has not substantively changed since 2011.[114]

Although one could interpret these statements as further evidence that regional cybercrime regimes are mere reflections of the interests of their most powerful signatories, the differences *between* regional approaches mask the similarities and increases in cooperation *within* those same regimes. If one considers those transnational cybercrime regimes, as well as the structures of intergovernmental cooperation that they create or facilitate, to be 'institutions', then the usefulness of the branch of international relations theory known as institutionalism is clear. Institutions, according to James March and Johan Olsen, can be defined as 'a relatively stable collection of practices and rules defining appropriate behaviour for specific groups of actors in specific situations'. Inevitably, these institutions coevolve with the histories of the parties involved and channel their future behaviour.[115] Over time, neo-functionalist cascades that begin as 'non-political' cooperation on minor technical issues foster mutual trust and shared interests.

[112]United Nations (n 110) para 204.

[113]United Nations, 'Letter dated 12 September 2011 from the Permanent Representatives of China, the Russian Federation, Tajikistan and Uzbekistan to the United Nations addressed to the Secretary-General' A/66/359 (14 September 2011), Annex – Code of Conduct – Arts (a)–(c).

[114]Kristen Eichensehr, *Just Security*, 'International Cyber Governance: Engagement Without Agreement?' (2 February 2015), http://justsecurity.org/19599/international-cyber-governance-engagement-agreement.

[115]James G March and Johan P Olsen, 'The Institutional Dynamics of International Political Orders' (1998) 52 *International Organization* 948, 958, 960. See also Robert O Keohane, 'International Relations and International Law: Two Optics' (1997) 38 *Harvard International Law Journal* 500. Keohane envisions the emergence of a sort of 'dependency cycle' between international regimes and international law, wherein '[i]nterests shape institutions, which affect beliefs, including reputations, which in turn affect interests'.

This, in turn, deepens into long-term patterns of participation and 'an expansion of the number of topics viewed as appropriate for discussion and the development of common definitions of problems and appropriate actions'.[116]

In practice, therefore, international organisations act as institutions that allow states to achieve their desired ends with greater efficiency and transparent information distribution.[117] It is no surprise, then, according to Kenneth Abbott and Duncan Snidal, that arrangements between states are increasingly 'legalized' using forms of 'soft law'. These non-binding agreements facilitate compromise and reduce uncertainty regarding commitments between states, making it easier to reach agreement on than 'hard law' addressing issues that strike at the core of state sovereignty, security or autonomy.[118] However, 'hard law' and 'soft law' are not mutually exclusive. Different levels of 'legalisation' will be preferred depending on both the 'sovereignty costs' and the levels of uncertainty surrounding state action that are associated with the issue being addressed.[119]

Applying these concepts, one would anticipate that cooperation levels would therefore be lowest in the CIS and SCO Agreements, given their emphasis on sovereignty and non-interference. Nonetheless, the CIS and SCO Agreements promote an overall culture of shared cybersecurity between state parties. This is evident through the framing of threats as both criminal and national security concerns requiring joint resolution and cooperation. In reality, the emphasis on 'soft' law obligations in both the CIS and SCO Agreements is deceptive. Both are part of a larger trend, which has become increasingly evident since the end of the Cold War, of forming regional security agreements between the states involved. Harmonising cybersecurity and cybercrime laws and procedures, therefore, is just another 'spillover' function that March and Olsen would attribute to the CIS and the SCO, regional organisations that have long since been evolving into or contributing to the formation of collective security structures.[120]

The CIS, for instance, has a Collective Security Treaty Organization (CSTO) that has acted as a military and security alliance between the parties since 1992,[121] despite significant internal fragmentation in favour of joining the EU-sponsored 'Eastern Partnership'.[122] It is in this light that joint military exercises quelling a

[116]James G March and Johan P Olsen, 'The Institutional Dynamics of International Political Orders' (1998) 52 *International Organization* 963–4.

[117]Kenneth Abbott and Duncan Snidal, 'Why States Act through Formal International Organizations' (1998) 42 *Journal of Conflict Resolution* 2, 4.

[118]Kenneth Abbott and Duncan Snidal, 'Hard and Soft Law in International Governance' (2000) 54 *International Organization* 423, 426, 435.

[119]*Ibid*, 425, 440–1.

[120]March and Olsen (n 116) 966.

[121]CSTO, 'Basic Facts', www.odkb.gov.ru/start/index_aengl.htm.

[122]European Commission, 'Eastern Partnership Implementation Well On Track – 1st Eastern Partnership Foreign Ministers Meeting', IP/09/1891, http://europa.eu/rapid/press-release_IP-09-1891_en.htm.

hypothetical 'Arab Spring'-like uprising,[123] the formation of a CIS Centre of Cybersecurity (a regional coordinating CERT)[124] and joint secret service activities in cyberspace, such as Operation Proxy,[125] should be seen.[126]

Turning to the SCO, which encompasses many of the nations involved in the CIS and CSTO, some have suggested that the partnership will be shallow and short lived, due specifically to the differences in Russian and Chinese foreign policy interests.[127] However, a recently signed cyber-security treaty between Russia and China suggests this is not the case, and that a distinct alternative approach to Western cybercrime regimes may be in the making.[128] As Abbott and Snidal predicted, resources, capabilities and information are efficiently pooled through international organisations and institutions in order to address common transnational threats.[129]

In practice, RATS has already openly begun to address the 'roles of the special services in providing security and their collaboration to fight against cyber-terrorism'. Furthermore, a 2012 agreement reached in Tashkent now authorises RATS to 'provide legal guidance and make recommendations to enforce transnational standards'.[130] How future developments begin to take shape, such as India's desire for an increased role in RATS[131] and the

123 James Kilner, 'Central Asian Armies Start Exercises to Counter Potential Arab Spring-Style Unrest' *The Telegraph* (20 September 2011), www.telegraph.co.uk/news/worldnews/asia/tajikistan/8777123/Central-Asian-armies-start-exercises-to-counter-potential-Arab-Spring-style-unrest.html.

124 Andrei Soldatov and Irina Borogan, 'In Ex-Soviet States, Russian Spy Tech Still Watches You' *Wired* (12 February 2012), www.wired.com/dangerroom/2012/12/russias-hand/all.

125 Russia Beyond the Headlines, 'CSTO Countries Hold Operations against Cyber Crimes', http://rbth.com/articles/2012/10/24/csto_countries_hold_operation_against_cyber_crimes_19409.html.

126 Soldatov and Borogan (n 124).

127 Andrew Scheineson, 'The Shanghai Cooperation Organization' (24 March 2009), www.cfr.org/china/shanghai-cooperation-organization/p10883. In fact, the SCO's 2012 exercise was its smallest since 2003.

128 Olga Razumovskaya, 'Russia and China Pledge Not to Hack Each Other' *Wall Street Journal* (8 May 2015), http://blogs.wsj.com/digits/2015/05/08/russia-china-pledge-to-not-hack-each-other/?mod=e2tw.

129 Abbott and Snidal (n 117) 2, 4, 11.

130 Regional Anti-Terrorist Structure of Shanghai Cooperation Organization (RATS SCO), 'On Participation of Zhang Xinfeng, Director of SCO RATS Executing Committee, in the 12th Meeting of the Heads of Special Services, Security Agencies and Law Enforcement Bodies of Foreign States', http://ecrats.org/en/cooperation/conferences/2784; Dadan Upadhyay, 'SCO Members to Cooperate in War on Cyber Terrorism' *Russia and India Report* (2 April 2013), http://indrus.in/world/2013/04/02/sco_members_to_cooperate_in_war_on_cyber_terrorism_23429.html.

131 'India Pitches for Larger Role in Shanghai Cooperation Organization' *Economic Times* (7 June 2012), http://articles.economictimes.indiatimes.com/2012-06-07/news/32101375_1_shanghai-cooperation-organisation-sco-security-grouping.

SCO,[132] or the possibility of a de-anonymised 'SCO information superhighway' (a regional internet),[133] will indicate the coming trajectory of cooperation in the organisation. Taken together, this is all further evidence of the trends that institutionalism would predict regarding the influence of international organisations on foreign policy, transnational law, and the very norms, practices and interests of the states that initially created them.[134]

(iii) *Liberalism*

Whilst institutionalism assists in gauging how hard and soft legal regimes and governmental organisations influence the surrounding transnational regulatory framework, the prominent role played by both state and non-state entities in the practical implementation of transnational cybercrime regulation suggests that liberal international relations theory could offer insight to the analysis.

According to Andrew Moravcsik, liberal theory is underpinned by the premise that 'the relationship between states and the surrounding domestic and transnational society in which they are embedded critically shapes state behavior by influencing the social purposes underlying state preferences'.[135] Correlated with this are basic assumptions which hold that private actors are fundamental to the analysis because states act as interest aggregators for a dominant subset of their given domestic society. Thus, state action is constrained by the international policy interdependences created by its own domestic policy externalities.[136] As such, there is general consensus among liberal theorists that traditional notions of separate domestic and international law are no longer sustainable, entailing that research should consider the influence of transnational networks of private individuals or government bodies.[137]

A leading example of such research can be found in Anne-Marie Slaughter's seminal 2004 book, *New World Order*. In this book she draws on liberal theory to explain how transgovernmental networks are formed between government institutions, civil society and the private sector, both amongst themselves horizontally and with international organisations vertically, in an effort to address transnational

[132] Alexander Korbalinov, 'Sujatha Singh Calls for Wider Indian Security Cooperation with SCO' *Russia and India Report* (27 February 2014), http://indrus.in/world/2014/02/27/sujatha_singh_calls_for_wider_indian_security_cooperation_with_sco_33361.html.
[133] SCO, 'Joint Communiqué of Meeting of the Council of the Heads of Government (Prime Ministers) of the SCO Member States' (14 October 2009), www.sectsco.org/EN123/show.asp?id=145.
[134] Abbott and Snidal (n 117) 28.
[135] Andrew Moravcsik, 'Taking Preferences Seriously: A Liberal Theory of International Politics' (1997) 51 *International Organization* 516.
[136] *Ibid*, 516–20.
[137] Kenneth Abbott, 'International Relations Theory, International Law, and the Regime Governing Atrocities in International Conflicts' (1999) 93 *American Journal of International Law* 367, 377.

issues.[138] Through such networks, according to Slaughter, governments can combine and use both hard and soft power to promote cooperation while also efficiently collecting and disseminating information, allowing for better-tailored regulation that responds to varying transnational issues that have domestic origins.[139] Rather than fear or resist their formation, states should actively seek to create networks.[140] Nevertheless, Slaughter cautions that such developments will necessitate corresponding norms or rights that rein in and channel the power of government networks. She maintains that some issues or functions, such as 'issues of high domestic political sensitivity', may not be amenable to these answers or may develop networked solutions with limits to inclusion or expansion.[141]

As the above review of the six regional cybercrime regimes demonstrates, transnational cybercrime law is certainly not an area free from transgovernmental network activity for reasons of political sensitivity. Nonetheless, there are provisions in all six regimes that allow for what Slaughter calls 'informed divergence', either by amendments, exceptions or provisions that safeguard sovereignty and non-interference.[142] Indeed, as cybercrime touches the very core of traditional Weberian notions of the function of the nation state and the preservation of sovereignty, a dearth of involvement from private actors is, as Boister predicts, to be anticipated.[143] Nevertheless, private industry actors such as Microsoft and Western Union VISA did play a crucial role in promoting cybercrime awareness in the ECOWAS region prior to the release of the Draft Directive, and civil society representatives had input, at least through the US delegation, into the CoE Convention. Moreover, it is clear that all six address the fact that signatories will need to interact with private sector infrastructure owners in order to implement many of the procedural requirements of each regime, such as in data retention. Taken together, however, the evidence suggests that private and civil society actors played the most substantial role in shaping regimes where arguably 'weaker' states were concerned, such as in Africa.

Despite the lack of private actors in transnational cybercrime regimes, liberal theory still serves to illuminate how transgovernmental networks have been formed to operate under the mandate of transnational cybercrime regimes. In all six regimes, specific domestic or regional institutions are largely excluded, suggesting that the aim is instead to facilitate interstate communication and cooperation, though their use is left entirely to the discretion of states, which might have more effective pre-existing bilateral relationships. This could be

[138] Anne-Marie Slaughter, *A New World Order* (Princeton University Press, 2004) 10, 163, 270–1.
[139] *Ibid*, 168–9; 170, 186–7, 194, 203–4.
[140] *Ibid*, 162, 164.
[141] *Ibid*, 144, 208, 215.
[142] *Ibid*, 144, 182–3, 208, 215.
[143] Moravcsik (n 135); Boister, this volume.

seen as an example of Slaughter's recommendation that states could facilitate network formation by adopting international commitments with domestic implications, but without explicitly prescribing how those commitments are to be fulfilled.[144]

The concept of the state as an aggregator of domestic interests offers one explanation for why the approach has been largely 'regional' in scope, and neither more nor less inclusive. As the UNODC contends, different forms and levels of legal harmonisation can be attributed to different legal traditions, 'prevailing socio-cultural and constitutional orders', and historical coincidences or differences in technical opinions during the drafting stage.[145] Liberalism, therefore, offers an explanation for the correlation between the domestic political orders of signatories and the overall constitution of each regime.

For instance, the unique substantive offences in the LAS Convention relating to pornography reflect the importance of Islam and Shari'a law shared by the signatory nations.[146] Conversely, in states like Russia and China, where the preservation of internal stability is paramount, it is to be expected that the transnational cybercrime law promulgated by the CIS and SCO facilitates cooperation without restricting the right of participating states to protect their own national interests when deemed necessary, even against non-signatory states in non-criminal law related fields. Similarly, liberalism explains why developed democratic nations opted for the deeper levels of procedural and substantive harmonisation in the CoE Convention: precisely because it would complement their pre-existing levels of bilateral cooperation and domestic procedural guarantees.

Perhaps most importantly, if the regional cybercrime regimes in question are as inextricably linked to the shared domestic political and legal conditions of their signatories, then the path to breaking down regional barriers and facilitating truly international cybercrime cooperation will require a measure of global political and cultural harmonisation which is difficult to foresee. In fact, all six regional cybercrime regimes share a common thread in their commitment to the preservation of Westphalian sovereignty. All six regimes focus on transnational investigative and prosecutorial cooperation and capacity building, and none delegate these functions to international parties or even explicitly mandate forms of joint operation in specific circumstances. Although the CoE Convention provides that disputes over its provisions can be settled by impartial third parties, such as the International Court of Justice or binding arbitration, even that is subject to the agreement of the parties concerned.[147]

---

[144]Slaughter (n 138) 162, 164.

[145]*Comprehensive Study on Cybercrime* (n 20) 57–58; Tim Büthe and Walter Mattli, *The New Global Rulers: The Privatization of Regulation in the World Economy* (Princeton University Press, 2012) 4.

[146]See League of Arab States (n 59) Preamble.

[147]*Convention on Cybercrime* (n 31) Art 45.

For realism, liberalism and institutionalism, it is entirely predictable, albeit in different ways, that the transnational cybercrime regimes under consideration do not encroach on basic concepts of sovereign authority regarding matters of internal security and governance. For this reason, the analysis must turn to an examination of the practical implications of this form of transnational regulation. Absent such analysis, one cannot appreciate the issues facing transnational cybercrime regulation and transnational criminal law as a whole.

B. *Transnational regulatory process: an interim assessment*

(i) *Legal/regulatory issues*

In practice, there is little difference between the six transnational cybercrime regimes outlined and traditional examples of transnational criminal law. It is expected, for instance, that transnational criminal cooperation agreements will contain 'escape clauses' for sensitive issues related to national security or internal politics, or that they will be intentionally drafted in an open-ended manner so as to facilitate later accession and ratification. However, this also leaves open the possibility of a host of legal or regulatory issues, such as the risk of inconsistent application at the domestic level.[148] The latter was explicitly recognised by the Department of Justice in the case of US accession to the CoE Convention. It was publicly noted that where the Convention materially departs from existing US law on cybercrime, its enactment would not modify existing laws.[149] In other countries this has resulted in procedural provisions being included in the CoE Convention that are not provided for in domestic law and institutions. These include the lack of uniform structures for providing real-time data collection by ICT infrastructure providers.[150]

Amalie Weber posits that this 'overreaching' by the drafters of the CoE Convention in an attempt to include all the offences parties sought to criminalise and thereafter allow for reservations, instead of just criminalising those offences upon which there was consensus, resulted in a failure to develop a coherent body of law.[151] This could have contributed, at least partially, to the CoE Convention's failure to gain signatories from other regions, despite being the first substantive and procedural transnational cybercrime regime ever enacted. As it stands, the only truly global regime touching on cybercrime remains the UN's 'Optional Protocol to the Convention on the Rights of the Child on the sale of children, child prostitution and child pornography'.[152]

---

[148] Amalie M Weber, 'The Council of Europe's Convention on Cybercrime' (2003) 18 *Berkeley Technology Law Journal* 436, 442–3.
[149] *Ibid*, 436.
[150] Currie and Rikhof (n 19) 433–5.
[151] Weber (n 148) 444.
[152] *Comprehensive Study on Cybercrime* (n 50) 67.

The result is what the UNODC describes as a 'clustering' of approaches, wherein regional cooperation is facilitated but inter-regional cooperation is unchanged.[153] Compounding this problem, the UNODC reports that many nations have harmonised their domestic laws according to what nations they perceive are important partners in suppressing cybercrime.[154] This produces discrepancies in jurisdiction, but, unlike those found in other fields of transnational criminal law, the particular difficulty associated with efficiently tracking or attributing given acts of cyber-criminality to any one jurisdiction make them all the more problematic. In practice, they have also resulted in some novel, and legally questionable, approaches to enforcing domestic criminal laws against citizens of nations with which authorities do not have any existing legal framework for extradition.[155]

However, and contrary to much of the literature already published on the topic, the extent of these gaps cannot be accurately estimated without taking into consideration the role played by pre-existing MLATs and other bilateral agreements between states. This is precisely because the cybercrime regimes outlined complement, rather than replace, pre-existing arrangements and traditional notions of territorial jurisdiction. Many countries, for instance, assert jurisdiction when only part of the offence took place within their territory.[156] Moreover, all six of the cybercrime regimes required states to exercise jurisdiction once their respective territorial requirements were met. Some went further to ensure that signatories exercise jurisdiction over their own citizens worldwide (the active nationality principle) or once key state interests are threatened (the protective principle).[157]

Although promising from an enforcement perspective, data forming the evidence or *actus reus* of a cybercrime can be automatically routed through or stored remotely in any number of jurisdictions. Coupling this with the open-ended nature of the substantive offences delineated raises broad concerns that the regimes violate basic notions of legality. Unless transnational cybercrime regimes are made uniform across regional jurisdictions and differences are controlled for with strict dual criminality requirements, conduct in one state can implicate an individual in another jurisdiction simply because inculpatory data traversed that jurisdiction.[158] This leaves open an overly broad 'zone of danger'

[153] *Ibid*, 28.
[154] *Ibid*, 56–59.
[155] Weber (n 148) 428. In one case, the FBI tricked a Russian hacker into visiting the US for a fictitious job interview, upon which he was arrested and prosecuted for computer offences the US was unable to secure an extradition for under Russian law (see *United States v Ivanov*, 175 F Supp 2d 36 (2001)).
[156] *Comprehensive Study on Cybercrime* (n 50) 191–2.
[157] *Ibid*, 191, 193–4.
[158] Sabine Gless and John AE Vervaele, 'Law Should Govern: Aspiring General Principles for Transnational Criminal Justice' (2013) 9 *Utrecht Law Review* 1, 3; Sabine Gless, 'Bird's-eye view and worm's-eye view: towards an individual-based approach in transnational criminal law', this volume.

where an individual's expectations of what is or is not prohibited conduct may be incorrectly derived from their nationality.[159]

(ii) *Enforcement issues*

These issues can be contrasted with the obvious difficulties in investigating transnational cybercrime. Gathering evidence of an offence, for instance, can be almost impossible when innovative offenders can cross jurisdictions on any continent at any given moment. This leaves law enforcement agencies mired in different data protection laws or delays caused by procedural and constitutional constraints on their counterparts in another nation.[160] These issues are compounded when jurisdictions lack the necessary resources to properly investigate cybercrime, which 75 per cent of authorities responding anonymously to a UNODC survey said they did.[161] Together, these problems of jurisdiction and lack of capacity have resulted in a number of highly problematic outcomes in practice.

First, the UNODC reports that investigators are increasingly resorting, albeit sometimes unwittingly, to extraterritorial searches conducted without appropriate legal authorisation.[162] As the use of remote (or 'cloud') computing increases, traditional notions of location and jurisdiction are becoming irrelevant. Therefore, investigators are increasingly addressing their transnational data requests to service and content providers, irrespective of where that data is actually located.[163] As a result, informal and unregulated partnerships often develop between law enforcement agencies and private sector businesses with varied success and compliance rates.[164] This builds on the provisions in many of the cybercrime regimes outlined, allowing for warrantless disclosure of data by private parties. Such parties include internet content and service providers, as they generally retain the right to voluntarily disclose user data upon request in their service agreements.[165]

Secondly, the same roadblocks of jurisdiction and investigation are prompting informal interstate cooperation. Although in over 70 per cent of cases evidence requests are made through formal MLATs, the vast majority are under bilateral, not multilateral, instruments.[166] Given that response times for formal cooperation generally entail months of delay, the current situation is derisory.[167]

[159]Marianne L Wade, 'General Principles of Transnationalised Criminal Justice? Exploratory Reflections' (2013) 9 *Utrecht Law Review* 165, 168.
[160]*Comprehensive Study on Cybercrime* (n 50) 23–24.
[161]*Ibid*, 152–56, 178–80.
[162]*Ibid*, 222.
[163]*Ibid*, 216, 221–3.
[164]*Ibid*, 144–52.
[165]*Ibid*, 218–19.
[166]*Ibid*, 197.
[167]*Ibid*, 205.

Even 10 years ago, large-scale internet-enabled credit card fraud could be planned and executed in a matter of days.[168] In response to this dilemma, informal cooperation is allowed for and even promoted, in one form or another, under the procedural provisions of all of the regional cybercrime regimes outlined. The formation of 24/7 contact points, CERTs and informal assistance requests in matters of urgency are just some examples. Though response times for informal practices are largely unknown,[169] the UNODC reports a growing trend among authorities of using transnational trust-based relationships to facilitate informal interagency coordination, prior to or in the furtherance of formal assistance requests.[170]

Thirdly, human rights and accountability concerns arise regarding the outsourcing of investigative and policing capabilities to other governments. Returning to the US, Caitlin Street notes that any evidence seized by foreign authorities contrary to domestic constitutional protections or international human rights law is admissible in court under the 'international silver platter doctrine', unless US authorities operated in a 'joint venture' with their counterparts abroad or acted in a manner which 'shocks the conscience' of the courts.[171]

A similar situation persists in Canada, as Supreme Court decisions subsequent to *R v Hape* (from 2007) suggest that the Charter of Rights and Freedoms does not apply, absent state consent, when Canadian authorities are operating overseas.[172]

Although in other fields of transnational criminal law courts have sought to develop fair trial protections against the use of unconstitutionally obtained foreign evidence in criminal prosecutions, there is little known judicial implementation of *lex fori* principles. This further undermines the legitimacy of domestic constitutional protections and transnational criminal provisions.[173] Although Sabine Gless argues that states should be seen to have a positive obligation to intervene given this rights deficit,[174] and Street lays out a number of ways in which this can be done by either the judicial or legislative branches of governments,[175] the reality is that in the field of transnational cybercrime law there is

[168]Glenny (n 13) 88–95.
[169]*Comprehensive Study on Cybercrime* (n 50) 214, 207–8.
[170]*Ibid*, 187.
[171]Caitlin T Street, 'Streamlining the International Silver Platter Doctrine: Coordinating Transnational Law Enforcement in the Age of Global Terrorism and Technology' (2010–11) 49 *Columbia Journal of Transnational Law* 411, 433. However, lower courts have interpreted the 'joint venture' exception in various ways (see *ibid*, 434–5).
[172]Currie and Rikhof (n 19) 567–74; *R v Hape* [2007] 2 SCR 292, 2007 SCC 26; Chanakya Sethi, *Does the Charter Follow the Flag? Revisiting Constitutional Extraterritoriality after R v Hape* (2010) 20 *Dalhousie Journal of Legal Studies* 71.
[173]Sabine Gless, 'Transnational Cooperation in Criminal Matters and the Guarantee of a Fair Trial: Approaches to a General Principle' (2013) 9 *Utrecht Law Review* 90, 95–96, 102.
[174]*Ibid*, 108.
[175]Street (n 171) 460–5.

little or no evidence that states are keeping up with such concerns. While piecemeal judicial solutions are certainly welcome, they are not a panacea for such profound gaps in regulation.[176]

(iii) *Political questions*

Looked at as a whole, transnational cybercrime law is implemented through a blend of formal and informal, as well as public and private, investigation and enforcement. While this might help to compensate for issues of jurisdiction or capacity, due to their lack of transparency or regulation, it is unknown how effective these practices are in tackling cybercrime, let alone conforming to applicable law.[177] Keohane rightly argues that since institutions create persistent patterns of specific kinds of interaction, governments should ensure that the principles and values they further reflect their own, while remaining flexible enough to change with the demands of international society.[178] Unfortunately, this is often not the case.

While transnational criminal law has certainly been accused of having a 'crime control' bias for some time,[179] it is noteworthy that out of the six transnational cybercrime regimes outlined, only the CoE and AU Conventions contain any explicit references to international human rights standards.[180] The four remaining regimes only make passing reference to them in their Preambles. Though it may certainly be easier for states to agree on criminalising provisions than on common rights protections,[181] Marianne Wade suggests that the lack of the latter both delegitimises much of transnational criminal justice and undermines the authority of sovereign democratic nations to govern.[182]

Taken together, these concerns of jurisdiction, capacity, efficacy, legality, transparency, accountability and legitimacy have been acknowledged by Slaughter as legitimate critiques of transnational government networks more generally.[183] According to Slaughter, these issues can and must be overcome, such as by imposing positive obligations on states to engage with regulatory partners, or by

---

[176]See, for instance, the dissent of Justice Karakatsanis (joined by Justices Abella and Cromwell) in *Wakeling v USA*, 2014 SCC 72 at para 105.
[177]*Comprehensive Study on Cybercrime* (n 50) 211.
[178]Robert O Keohane, 'International Relations and International Law: Two Optics' (1997) 38 *Harvard International Law Journal* 487, 502.
[179]Gless and Vervaele (n 158) 8–9.
[180]Convention on Cybercrime (ETS No 185), Art 15; African Union, 'Draft African Union Convention on the Establishment of a Legal Framework Conducive to Cyber Security in Africa or Draft African Union Convention on the Confidence and Security in Cyberspace', http://au.int/en/sites/default/files/AU%20Convention%20EN.%20%283-9-2012%29%20clean_0.pdf, Art III-4, III-6.
[181]Wade (n 159) 169.
[182]*Ibid*, 170, 178–82.
[183]Slaughter (n 138) 219–21.

accepting on a fundamental level that since transgovernmental networks are needed to address transnational issues, they must be proactively regulated.[184] Fundamental reconsiderations, according to Slaughter, must also be made by democratically accountable governments, such that national officials necessarily perform dual national and transnational functions, transparently involving subnational stakeholders wherever possible in the creation of a 'disaggregated state' where transgovernmental networks are embraced but the nation state remains the creator and enforcer of global rules.[185]

However, as the analysis of the regimes according to international relations theory reveals, transnational cybercrime law is uniform in its allegiance to the Westphalian state system, despite the fact that this very link is the cause of most of its shortcomings. As such, the success of such a tactic depends on both ending the 'clustering' of approaches to transnational cybercrime regulation and refining the transnational law enforcement capabilities of modern nation states, thereby enabling them to respond uniformly to denationalised threats operating in a borderless environment. Without such uniformity, the 'disaggregated state' will likely only succeed in mirroring the failings of the current interstate system of transnational regulation. What this 'interim assessment' of the current approach to transnational cybercrime regulation means for transnational law, as well as for the dynamics of global regulation more broadly, will be canvassed below.

4. Cybercrime, transnational criminal law and the post-Westphalian legal order

Having considered both the formation and the failings of the regional cybercrime regimes in question, the link between the two demands further consideration, and, as the following sub-sections illustrate, a number of important conclusions arise. First, the 'clustered' regional regimes, when considered alongside existing bilateral or multilateral instruments, can be seen to have global reach. Secondly, the dynamics at play suggest that the 'post-Westphalian' nation state is not undergoing as fundamental a transformation as many suggest. Rather, traditional state functions are being adapted and transferred onto the transnational plane, fundamental roles of protecting sovereignty and suppressing crime are not being delegated, and, just as Boister suggests, laws of coordination are the result.[186]

Thirdly, one can anticipate that this trajectory will ensure the perpetuation of the regulatory issues outlined above (see above, section 3.B.i). Therefore, suggestions from European scholars advocating new forms of law and regulation will be canvassed, leading to two insights. On the one hand, the work of Karl-Heinz

[184] *Ibid*, 231, 216–60.
[185] *Ibid*, 231, 216–60, 262–3.
[186] Boister, this volume.

Ladeur suggests that any attempt at regulating an environment like the internet must, at its outset, take into consideration its very architecture. On the other hand, the complexity of a regulatory environment like the internet suggests the usefulness of some form of 'reflexive' regulatory mechanism, drawn from the work of Gunther Teubner, which would adjust their regulatory goals based on the results of prior attempts at regulation.

A. *Global cybercrime law*

There is ample evidence to support the proposition that a new branch of transnational criminal law is emerging to address the threat posed by cybercrime, even if the prospect of full global harmonisation appears unlikely in the foreseeable future. Yet nothing prevents participants in different regimes from cooperating by combining offences in their regional suppression conventions (if not their national criminal codes) with other bilateral or multilateral agreements, such as under Article 3(1)(b) of the UN Convention against Transnational Organized Crime.[187]

Given this potential for a truly global reach, the implementation of transnational cybercrime law, either intra- or inter-regionally, brings to the fore pre-existing concerns in the field of transnational criminal law regarding the influence of unaccountable private and public actors. Both in this symposium issue and elsewhere, James Sheptycki has highlighted the autonomy, cooperation, competition, and law-making powers of many state and non-state actors involved in transnational policing.[188] In the 'war on drugs', Sheptycki notes how the autonomy of law enforcement agencies allowed them to test the boundaries of their authority, and thereby exert pressure on the judicial and legislative branches of government. This in turn resulted in legal interpretations and developments that were 'determined and conditioned' by law enforcement personnel in the wake of their activities.[189] In 2001 Jack Goldsmith expanded on such ideas, noting (prior to US ratification of the CoE Convention) that the need to suppress cybercrime in cases where inter-jurisdictional cooperation was lacking would have two possible outcomes. It would either require law enforcement agencies to conduct remote extraterritorial searches, in turn requiring a reinterpretation of existing prohibitions on extraterritorial enforcement jurisdiction, or states would still 'find ways to

[187]Convention against Transnational Organized Crime, 15 November 2000, 2225 UNTS 209. Art 3(1)(b) allows for the Convention to apply to facilitate investigation and prosecution between nations for any 'serious offence' (i.e. carrying a maximum penalty of four or more years of 'deprivation of liberty') which is 'transnational in nature'.

[188]James WE Sheptycki, 'Law Enforcement, Justice and Democracy in the Transnational Arena: Reflections on the War on Drugs' (1996) 24 *International Journal of the Sociology of Law* 61–62.

[189]*Ibid*, 70.

achieve *indirect* extraterritorial effect' by using local actors to target the perceived harm on their behalf.[190]

Both predictions proved to be quite accurate. For instance, private non-state actors were able to participate in the formation of more than one regime. Moreover, the UNODC recently stated that the growth in 'cloud computing' poses such challenges to transnational cybercrime suppression that achieving consensus and respecting fundamental rights 'will require' a reconsideration of both the usefulness of concepts like 'data location' as well as 'the development of common standards and safeguards' governing 'direct access to extraterritorial data'.[191] Apart from the insight this provides for the future of transnational cybercrime suppression, this conclusion exposes two additional points, expanded upon in the next two sub-sections, which remain applicable to both transnational law and the future of the Westphalian nation state more generally.

B. *The post-Westphalian state*

Constructivist scholarship suggests that social spaces must be 'made meaningful' prior to their control.[192] How those spaces are rendered 'meaningful' in turn depends on how identities, produced through interactions that result in 'internalizing new understandings of self and other', can shape interests, which then assist states in choosing between policy options and possible outcomes.[193] According to John Ruggie, this lack of emphasis placed on identities and social processes by neo-utilitarian international relations theories explains two additional constructivist concepts. First, social processes form 'constitutive rules' that collectively designate what practices do, and do not, qualify as a given activity.[194] Secondly, by understanding identities and interests as social constructs, we can end their perpetual reification (i.e. their treatment as variables independent of the social practices that produce and sustain them), and analyse them for what they really are.[195]

Given the uniform emphasis on the preservation of sovereignty in transnational cybercrime law, sovereignty itself can be seen as one such 'constitutive rule' animating traditional notions of the modern Westphalian nation state, and thus shaping the approaches they take to transnational

---

[190]Mireille Hildebrandt, 'Extraterritorial Jurisdiction to Enforce in Cyberspace?: Bodin, Schmitt, Grotius in Cyberspace' (2013) 63 *University of Toronto Law Journal*, 219–20.

[191]*Comprehensive Study on Cybercrime* (n 50) 223.

[192]Peter K Manning, 'Policing New Social Spaces' in James Sheptycki (eds), *Issues in Transnational Policing* (Routledge, 2000) 180 (emphasis added).

[193]John G Ruggie, 'What Makes the World Hang Together? Neo-Utilitarianism and the Social Constructivist Challenge' (1998) 52 *International Organization* 863–6; Alexander Wendt, 'Anarchy is what States Make of it: The Social Construction of Power Politics' (1992) 46 *International Organization* 396–7, 417.

[194]John G Ruggie, 'What Makes the World Hang Together? Neo-Utilitarianism and the Social Constructivist Challenge' (1998) 52 *International Organization* 871.

[195]Wendt (n 193) 410.

cybercrime.[196] Indeed, none of the regimes in any way advocates for an approach that challenges the concept of sovereignty; instead, they all serve various degrees of coordinating functions. As such, there can be no expectation that any transnational cybercrime regime, created by states, would do anything other than extend the effective reach of what Max Weber called the 'monopoly of the legitimate use of physical force within a given territory'.[197]

In the field of transnational cybercrime law, this is precisely what has occurred. Cybercrime, like other challenges posed to the Westphalian nation state by globalisation, has forced a change in how the state performs its traditional roles. According to Saskia Sassen, the state is not merely a 'victim of external globalizing forces', but rather acts as the very platform through which globalising processes take place.[198] As such, specific components of the modern nation state and its institutions are being 'denationalized' and reoriented towards global logics.[199] Traditional state functions, therefore, are assuming new roles and significance – a process Sassen defines as 'switching' – and are being shifted towards objectives that are different from those for which they were originally developed.[200] This, however, entails that old state capabilities are critical to the constitution of the globalised world, as they are repositioned in a new set of 'organizing logics'.[201]

In applying these concepts to the case of transnational cybercrime law, it becomes evident that sovereignty, security provision, policing and prosecution are all functions traditionally performed by the nation state. Such functions have now, through the regimes canvassed and without losing their connection to the state, been shifted onto the transnational plane. Through this lens, the conclusions of the UNODC relating to cybercrime and territorial sovereignty gain new meaning. The same can be said for the recent decision to shift the governance of ICAAN to the International Telecommunication Union (ITU), contingent on it remaining a multi-stakeholder system of governance open to control by and for states.[202] Most importantly, if, as Sassen suggests, former state capabilities are

---

[196] Ruggie (n 194) 872.

[197] Max Weber, 'Politics as Vocation' in Hans Gerth and C Wright Mills (eds), *From Max Weber: Essays in Sociology* (Oxford University Press, 1946) 78.

[198] Florian F Hoffmann and Peer Zumbansen, '*Territory, Authority, Rights: From Medieval to Global Assemblages* by Saskia Sassen' (2008) 46 *Osgoode Hall Law Journal* 667.

[199] Saskia Sassen, *Territory, Authority, Rights: From Medieval to Global Assemblages* (Princeton University Press, 2008) 2.

[200] *Ibid*, 6, 8–9, 419.

[201] *Ibid*, 8. Hoffmann and Zumbansen describe Sassen's 'organizing logics' as 'the prevailing organizational formations in which capabilities are played out and which initiate particular tipping points': Hoffmann and Zumbansen (n 198) 668.

[202] US Department of Commerce: National Telecommunications & Information Administration, 'NTIA Announces Intent to Transition Key Internet Domain Name Functions', www.ntia.doc.gov/press-release/2014/ntia-announces-intent-transition-key-internet-domain-name-functions.

foundational of subsequent orderings of governance, then it is difficult to see how such trends forebode anything other than an adaptation of traditional concepts of territorial sovereignty to the internet in a manner which serves the security-providing function of the Westphalian nation state.[203] Consider, for instance, how fundamentally similar all of the regimes really are: all seek to address cybercrime through the facilitation of traditional interstate cooperation mechanisms (e.g. MLATs, informal police cooperation, and institutional linkages between executive branches of governments), all enshrine the sovereignty of their signatories, and none have any robust supranational capabilities.

Nevertheless, the 'post-Westphalian' nation state that is emerging is not as 'profoundly changed' an entity as Sassen suggests.[204] Instead, states have accrued power and authority and have solidified pre-existing concepts of territorial sovereignty in a number of ways including, but not limited to, working through regional organisations, strategically deploying flexible 'soft law' arrangements, and consolidating new procedural powers.[205]

Since sovereignty and flexibility remain the base values orienting transnational cybercrime law, just as they do transnational criminal law, the issues raised in the 'Interim Assessment' regarding jurisdictional and institutional challenges will remain unaddressed.[206] More sinisterly, it remains to be seen how non-state actors that are deemed to be a threat to the national security of certain states will be treated under any given regime. Given that each regime purportedly embodies certain shared collective values on cybersecurity (i.e. shared concepts of what should and should not be criminalised), difficulties are to be expected if, or rather when, competing and highly charged political values are pitted against the arrangements made in a given regime in ways that evade the usual 'political question' clauses they all contain. This, however, leads to a final observation regarding transnational law and regulation in a 'post-Westphalian' global order.

C. *Network(ed) regulation and reflexive law*

As the above analysis suggests, unlike areas of private law regulated by transnational regimes, in transnational criminal law the state will remain the primary actor charged with creating and enforcing this body of law in the foreseeable future.[207] If so, then the aforementioned issues will remain unresolved, and one can expect a concomitant push for accountability or systems of organising norms to rein in this body of law.[208] Yet it is difficult to foresee where such norms or institutions will

[203] Sassen (n 199) 15–16.
[204] *Ibid*, 423.
[205] Boister (n 110) 276.
[206] Boister, this volume.
[207] Büthe and Mattli (n 145) 1–2, 5.
[208] Jeffrey L Dunoff and Joel P Trachtman, 'A Functional Approach to Global Constitutionalism', Harvard Law School: Harvard Public Law Working Paper No 08-57 (2009), 7, 19, 35.

originate or how they will maintain relevance in this regulatory arena. Any regulatory body would require complex systems of knowledge to be deployed when designing rules to tackle amorphous threats emanating from borderless political and non-political actors. In this respect, two bodies of transnational legal scholarship offer valuable insights into some possible solutions.

First, any attempt to regulate such a complex environment must take into consideration the architecture of that very ecosystem. Current proposals to expand traditional concepts of enforcement jurisdiction to cover cyber-criminality[209] or to transform the relationship between state and citizen under international law to create a new form of international legal jurisdiction[210] fall short. They either overestimate the ability of the state to practically regulate activity in cyberspace[211] or they underestimate perceived state interests in securitising cyberspace. More innovative approaches seek to reconceive of the Grotian concept of territory 'in a way that defies the original connection of the notion of territory to the land, to the earth', rendering it an inclusive and overlapping 'cyberspace *liberum*' rather than an exclusive and gapless *res nullius* awaiting occupation by sovereign power.[212] Though this is certainly a viable avenue for preserving cyberspace as a common good and for reconceiving of rights and legality as detached from territorial sovereignty, it downplays the amenability of cyberspace, more so than even the 'high seas', to occupation and control by a sovereign authority.[213] Think, for instance, of the political implications that come with drawing an analogy between an Internet Exchange Point and the Panama Canal.[214]

Indeed, the six regional cybercrime regimes in question have already begun endorsing traditional notions of sovereign authority in cyberspace. Consider, for instance, Article 4(2) of the LAS Convention, which limits actions taken by domestic authorities to suppress cybercrime to only those areas within their own national boundaries. As for the other regimes, from the baseline role they play as coordination regimes one can infer that they also reinforce the longstanding doctrine of non-interference in the domestic management of cyberspace.

Practically speaking, this means that any attempt at regulating cyberspace must first look to the architecture of the internet, and as such Ladeur's proposal of law

---

209 Georgios I Zekos, 'Cyber-Territory and Jurisdiction of Nations' (2012) 15 *Journal of Internet Law* 12, 16–17.

210 Matthias C Kettemann, *The Future of Individuals in International Law: Lessons from International Internet Law* (Eleven International, 2013) 166.

211 See Jeffrey Carr, *Inside Cyber Warfare: Mapping the Cyber Underworld* (O'Reilly, 2009) ch 8.

212 Hildebrandt (n 190).

213 *Ibid*, 223.

214 Neal Stephenson, 'Mother Earth Mother Board' (1996) 4 *Wired* 12; *Comprehensive Study on Cybercrime* (n 50) 4 (Figure 1.4); Ronald Deibert, John Palfrey, Rafal Rohozinski and Jonathan Zittrain (eds), *Access Controlled: The Shaping of Power, Rights, and Rule in Cyberspace* (MIT Press, 2010). 'Internet Exchange Points' (or IXPs) are locations where large amounts of data are shared between ISPs.

for a 'society of networks' may offer insight.[215] According to Ladeur, the society of networks has worked to fragment existing law and isolate institutions of knowledge generation, resulting in a body of transnational regulatory law that is democratically unaccountable and rife with vague legal principles and unenforceable individual rights.[216] Such tendencies are certainly visible in transnational cybercrime law as, for example, the limited scope of public-private partnerships and the lack of rights protections upon domestic implementation and enforcement suggest.

Nevertheless, this would entail a regulation of the internet that moves beyond seeing it as simply consisting of a 'number of linear relationships of exchange between individuals'.[217] Balances between state and individual rights would not be seen in absolutist terms as some sort of scale between rights and security.[218] Instead, institutions could be designed that provided different levels of freedom and privacy protection to different activities within networks like the internet.[219] Levels of investigation, for instance, could be designated and separated depending on the offence under investigation, providing deeper levels with more powerful investigative tools (e.g. the ability to de-anonymise suspects), subject to increasingly stringent judicial oversight.[220]

While network law might help us understand how to regulate complex environments like the internet, it is still susceptible to a broader critique of modern Westphalian law. That critique asks how such systems of law are to adapt to changes in their regulatory targets in order to maintain their relevance. In answer to this dilemma, and rejecting the Weberian concept of formally rational legal systems overburdened by the forces of globalisation, scholars such as Gunther Teubner developed the concept of 'reflexive' law and regulation.[221] In essence, Teubner envisions a role for law in which it becomes 'a system for the coordination of action within and between semi-autonomous social subsystems'.[222] This post-modern law would orient itself according to rationalities of purposiveness and participation, recognising the segmented, stratified and functionally differentiated aspects of social systems, and drawing from the 'social

[215]Karl-Heinz Ladeur, 'Toward a Network-Oriented Law of the Internet! The Necessity to Find a New Balance between Risk and Opportunity in Network Communication' (2009) 10 (9) *German Law Journal* 1201.

[216]Karl-Heinz Ladeur, 'Constitutionalism and the State of the "Society of Networks": The Design of a New "Control Project" for a Fragmented Legal System' (2011) 2(4) *Transnational Legal Theory* 469–73.

[217]Ladeur (n 215) 1206.

[218]*Ibid*, 1202; Mireille Hildebrandt, 'Balance or Trade-off? Online Security Technologies and Fundamental Rights' (2013) 26 *Philosophy & Technology* 372–4.

[219]Ladeur (n 215).

[220]*Ibid*, 1213.

[221]Gunther Teubner, 'Substantive and Reflexive Elements in Modern Law' (1983) 17 *Law & Society Review* 240.

[222]*Ibid*, 242.

organizational principles' that arise from processes of communicative interaction.[223]

Law, therefore, would be justified in intervening in social processes only to the extent necessary for creating and adjusting the interaction of self-regulating and self-sustaining, or autopoietic, social systems.[224] Within those social systems, therefore, law would work as a parameter setter so as to create discursive structures which democratise internal decision making processes, in turn optimising the legitimacy and efficacy of the output.[225] Between social systems, law would serve a coordinating function, regulating the interaction and coordination between systems so as to provide 'the structural premises for reflexive processes in other social subsystems'.[226] While this may work to impose substantive regulation on social systems that were previously free,[227] the promise that 'reflexive law' holds for transnational regulation is rather how the quality of such regulation would change if the object of regulation is indeed as diffuse and spatially (cf. jurisdictionally) oriented as the foregoing analysis of transnational cybercrime suggests.[228]

By changing transnational regulation into a results-oriented system able to formulate rules and decisions 'with reference to an internal legal representation of social reality',[229] the issues of jurisdiction and implementation in transnational cybercrime law would necessarily be addressed from a sub-state level. Furthermore, the ways in which cybercrime and cybersecurity are socially constructed in the different regional regimes would become exponentially more important, since those constructs define what the regulatory targets can and cannot be. Finally, it would force transnational criminal law to pay heed to the disaggregated, transnational and adaptive nature of the threats it addresses in a functionally differentiated and globalised society, while remaining perpetually ready to adjust its means once those targets change.[230]

However, any attempt to design such a regime would need to overcome the privileged position which the post-Westphalian nation state has retained, both in terms of its monopoly on the use of force and in the framing of threats requiring a deployment of that force. Both of these fundamental roadblocks, the above

---

[223] *Ibid*, 243–4. For a more detailed engagement with how far Teubner draws on the works of Philippe Nonet, Philip Selznick, Niklas Luhmann and Jürgen Habermas, see Peer Zumbansen, 'Lar after the Welfare State: Formalism, Functionalism, and the Ironic Turn of Reflexive Law' (2008) 56(3) *American Journal of Comparative Law* 768.
[224] Teubner (n 221) 255–7.
[225] *Ibid*, 273, 275.
[226] *Ibid*, 257, 275.
[227] Erhard Blankenburg, 'The Poverty of Evolutionism: A Critique of Teubner's Case for "Reflexive Law"' (1984) 18 *Law & Society Review* 273–4.
[228] Gunther Teubner, 'Autopoiesis in Law and Society: A Rejoinder to Blankenburg' (1984) 18 *Law & Society Review* 300.
[229] *Ibid*, 297; Teubner (n 221).
[230] John Braithwaite, 'The New Regulatory State and the Transformation of Criminology' (2000) 40 *British Journal of Criminology* 235.

analysis suggests, are currently enshrined in a growing body of transnational cybercrime law. Unfortunately, current approaches seem to leave no room for any sort of different approach to transnational cybercrime regulation, and thus the problematic outcomes identified above seem destined to repeat themselves.

5. Conclusion: governing the ungovernable

Transnational cybercrime is a complex threat that has stimulated a bloom in legal regulation in recent years. As a basic analysis of the regimes according to the international relations schools of realism, institutionalism and liberalism suggests, the differences and similarities between approaches can be attributed to the legal arrangements and political preferences of their signatories and key participating states. Furthermore, the transnational regulatory issues faced by these regimes can be seen, like other branches of transnational criminal law, as examples of how Westphalian states are using traditional legal and political tools to address novel threats.

However, the emergence of this new branch of transnational criminal law is evident not only in the regional approaches, but in the ways they overlap and form a body of law with potentially global reach. In turn, this nascent branch of transnational criminal law illustrates two issues shared with transnational law and regulation more broadly. First, transnational cybercrime law can be seen as a case study of how the modern nation state is shifting its traditional functions – in this case, that of security provision – onto the transnational plane. This does not suggest a fundamental break with the past, but rather a shift in how the post-Westphalian nation state performs its functions in a globalising and functionally differentiated world.

Secondly, since the issues that transnational cybercrime law faces with regard to jurisdiction and implementation are attributable to the very attempt at addressing denationalised threats with nation state-based tools, two issues inherent in current approaches to transnational regulation come to the fore. On the one hand, any attempt at regulation must take into consideration the architecture of its regulatory target which, in this case, suggests the appropriateness of a network-oriented approach to regulation. On the other hand, regulation in a constantly evolving and increasingly complex environment must consider the results of its regulation, factoring them into a constant struggle to perfect its regulatory framework. How this can happen in the field of transnational cybercrime law, given the evidence canvassed above regarding how the nation state is adapting to this new regulatory environment, is beyond the scope of this paper.

Acknowledgements

The author would like to thank Professor Peer Zumbansen, John David Lee, the anonymous peer reviewer of this piece, and the student team at *Transnational Legal Theory* for their invaluable assistance.

Index

For Product Safety Concerns and Information please contact our EU
representative GPSR@taylorandfrancis.com
Taylor & Francis Verlag GmbH, Kaufingerstraße 24, 80331 München, Germany

www.ingramcontent.com/pod-product-compliance
Ingram Content Group UK Ltd.
Pitfield, Milton Keynes, MK11 3LW, UK
UKHW020012200926
475702UK00014B/1844

* 9 7 8 0 3 6 7 0 2 9 8 5 2 *